CIRCULAR
BREATHING

CIRCULAR
BREATHING

THE CULTURAL POLITICS

OF JAZZ IN BRITAIN

George McKay

Duke University Press   DURHAM AND LONDON 2005

© 2005 Duke University Press

All rights reserved

Printed in the United States of America on acid-free paper ∞

Designed by Rebecca Giménez

Typeset in Garamond 3 by Tseng Information Systems, Inc.

Library of Congress Cataloging-in-Publication Data and illustration

credits appear at the end of this book.

In loving memory of FEDERICO ALICATA,

6 JULY 1986 – 25 AUGUST 2003

Caro, caro Freddie, re del mare!

CONTENTS

The fact that British working-class boys in Newcastle play . . .
[jazz] is at least as interesting as and rather more surprising
than the fact that it progressed through the frontier saloons of
the Mississippi valley.—FRANCIS NEWTON (pseud. of Eric
Hobsbawm), *The Jazz Scene* (1959, 1)

The more you shore up their conditioning, the more gigs you get.
—The improvising pianist STEVE BERESFORD, 1979
(quoted in Wickes 1999, 315)

PREFACE

This is not really (only) a book about music, about the history of the
sounds of jazz in Britain, but a study of the circulation and political
inscriptions in and usages of that music's form and history.[1] My aim is
to undertake two projects, with the argument that they are related to
rather than distinct from each other. First, I want to consider African
American jazz music as an export culture, as a case study in the operation of the process or problem of "Americanization." Doing so involves
exploring questions of cultural and economic power and desire, of empires even, and the limits and problems of these. I remain surprised
that jazz as a cultural form has been insufficiently considered as a prime
export culture, and I seek to balance that. Discourses of Americanization are always as much concerned with the import society as with the
export culture itself, and I do also want to look at the effort at finding
an indigenous (in this case, British) voice in an American form. Questions of imitation apply here, of course, but more importantly for the
specific attitudinal culture of jazz—predicated on the authentic, the
original—are questions of inauthenticity and unoriginality. As far back
as 1934, the English composer and critic Constant Lambert recognized
in his book *Music Ho!* one duality in jazz, that it "is internationally com-
prehensible, and yet provides a medium for national inflection" (158). I
want to explore the British experiences of jazz.[2] Note that the focus on
Britain should not imply a chauvinistic impulse on my part, nor is it in-

tended to reduce the inter- or outernationalism of the music. The book aims to be one of those that are awkwardly—I prefer energizingly—situated at a nodal cultural location, while acknowledging that "different nationalist paradigms for thinking about cultural history fail when confronted by . . . intercultural and transnational formation[s]" (Gilroy 1993, ix). It *is* designed to focus on a specific geographical and cultural cluster of dialogues, network of circulations, chart of activisms. Also, and to further problematize the chauvinistic gazes of the United States and the United Kingdom, I introduce the extraordinary global cultural mixing that has featured in British jazz practice, in part because of Britain's own (post-)imperial connections—Caribbean, English, Australian, Indian, Scottish, South African . . .

Second, I want to interrogate the political inscriptions or assumptions of jazz, both formally in the notions of freedom and expression claimed for the music as an improvisatory mode, and in the particular. Here I am referring to the detailed work that follows on the cultural politics of jazz in Britain, the ways the cultures of jazz have been used or understood by musicians, critics, and enthusiasts, as well as by its enemies, in British social and political realms. I deplore the lack of attention that has been paid to the ideological development and engagement of jazz in Britain—compared with what may well be the more temporary (or temporarily innovative) subcultural practices of (to pluck examples from my own previous writings) punk rock, festival culture, dance music in its "rave" moment. Did British jazz really have no politics? Then why on earth (from circum-Atlantic origins it became a global culture) choose a music forged in diaspora, struggle, and celebration? And for the British left, why the attraction of particularly American—read global capitalist and militarily oppressive for many—music? Also, I argue that the two projects are related: this may not always be apparent, and I would quite like it if the reader were able temporarily to lose sound or sight of some of the apparently wider and more important global issues of American power, the shift of imperial authority, in the minutiae and conflicts of largely leftist and liberatory politics, campaigns, experiments, hyperbole. For micropolitics matter, and are rarely as small as appearance suggests.[3] The period of music under consideration largely covers the years of the Second World War and later—the founding of George Webb's Dixielanders in 1943, which eventually triggered the traditional jazz boom of the 1950s, the impetus given by West Indian musicians of the Windrush generation of 1948 and earlier, the growth in British bebop in the early 1950s, the foundational Beaulieu Jazz Festivals of 1956–61—these form a cluster of energetic developments through which jazz in Britain may have begun to become British jazz. Where necessary, though, I offer a greater historical reference.

It is quite possible that this book originated in visits that I made as a youngster with my father, also George, a Scottish saxophonist, to local gigs in English pubs and jazz clubs, and I thank him for that. I would wonder about his short explanations of players: "in the Lester Young style," or "He plays like Parker." The English Pres really did hold his horn sideways; the Brit Bird—the one I saw—alas did too many bop triplets. Why, I wondered to myself, were these musicians pretending to be Americans, even down to trying to present their bodies in certain jazz ways? I wasn't contemptuous of these impersonators (though on other occasions I could be: "Failed Yanks!" was how I remember shouting at elderly teddy boys, grown men, chasing us young punks down the street for a beating and a laugh in the late 1970s). After all, they were gifting us some music, making it up there and then, sort of, and I admired and envied that deeply. But it stuck in my mind, as I arched my neck to see past the front line to what the bassist was doing.

ACKNOWLEDGMENTS

The research for this book was made possible by two grants from the Arts and Humanities Research Council: a small grant in the creative and performing arts in 2001 and a research leave grant in 2002. I am grateful for the council's support. The research leave grant extended a sabbatical from the Department of Cultural Studies, and I thank my departmental colleagues at the University of Central Lancashire for helping to make that time available to me.

Alan Rice really did give incisive and enthusiastic help above and beyond. Gwen Ansell, Bruce Johnson, Helen Taylor, Andrew Blake, Julie Dawn Smith, and Graham Taylor all kindly advised and supported. Val Wilmer, on whose pivotal work on black jazz music in Britain we have all relied, was an absolute star! In the AMATAS project, Jude Davies and Neil Campbell in particular tried to sharpen my theoretical understanding. My co-editors at *Social Movement Studies: Journal of Social, Cultural and Political Protest*, Tim Jordan and Anne Mische, kept me focused on the politics of culture. At UCLan, Eithne Quinn and Will Kaufman took me into different musics, while Daniel Lamont has always been supportive. At UCLan library, Aidan Turner-Bishop and Ian Sheridan were helpful. Thanks too to Derek Drummond for his technical assistance on digital image reproduction.

David Nathan at the National Jazz Archive was always friendly and informative; Andy Simons at the National Sound Archive of the British Library and Andrew Potter at the Royal Academy Library helped at critical points. I thank Mike Ferris in Norwich for an essential book—hope he thinks it's worth it—Nick Cooper for the loan of his collection of the *Wire*, Julia Smith and her old man for passing on to me his copies of *Jazz Journal International*, and Maran McKay Sr., Jim McKay, and Marigold Hall for passing conversations about jazz. My dad is in the preface, but when you have an alto sax blowing through your life it resonates, so the uncompromising soundtrack he gave me is here too.

Interviewees and correspondents: you are all listed at the back. Sincere thanks for your time and patience.

Thanks as well to: Chris Atton, Les Back, June Bastable, Eric Benner at the Campaign for Nuclear Disarmament, Chris Blackford (editor of *Rubberneck*), Ian Brownlie at Community Music East, Nick Couldry, Alan Dawson at the Centre for Digital Library Research at Strathclyde University, Pete Fordham at the Musicians' Union, Mike Fowler, Neil Foxlee, the late Kate Fullbrook, John Gill, Robert Greenwood, Will Guy, Stuart Hall, Eric Hobsbawm, Chris Hodgkins at Jazz Services, David Horn, Pete Martin, Helen Milner, Mike Parker at the Knitting Circle website, Alasdair Pettinger at the Scottish Music Information Service, John Powles at the Centre for Political Song, Alysoun Sanders at the Macmillan archive, Tony Whyton, and Bill Wood.

Sections were given as papers at research seminars and lecture programs at the Centre for Translation and Cultural Studies, University of Warwick (thanks to Ruth Cherrington for the invitation), the School of American and Canadian Studies, University of Nottingham (thanks to Pete Messent), the London College of Music and Media (a nice touch, to be introduced by Eddie Harvey), the Cultures of Performance series at UCLan (thanks to Stuart Hampton-Reeves and Dave Pearce).

At Duke University Press, Ken Wissoker, Fred Kameny, Courtney Berger, Christine Dahlin, Katie Courtland, Emily Young, and two anonymous readers were extremely helpful.

Sections of chapter 1 have appeared in different contexts, and I am grateful for permission to revisit them: "Just a Closer Walk with Thee: New Orleans–Style Jazz and the Campaign for Nuclear Disarmament in 1950s Britain," *Popular Music* 22, no. 3 (autumn 2003): 261–81; "'Unsafe Things like Youth and Jazz': Beaulieu Jazz Festivals (1956–61) and the Origins of Pop Festival Culture in Britain," *Remembering Woodstock*, ed. Andy Bennett (Ashgate, 2004).

Finally, thanks as always to Dora (still playing keyboard?), Ailsa (do the troke!), and Emma (life & love).

INTRODUCTION

Jazz, Europe, Americanization

And they dreamed dreams, above all of the United States,
the land of modernity, freedom, space, jazz, spontaneity. . . .
—MALCOLM BRADBURY (1982, 8), on young Britons in the 1950s

In Paul Gilroy's bold phrase, the "planetary force" (quoted in Hutnyk 2000, 215) of black music today has come about in part through the circulations of jazz.[1] In its international origins, jazz was always already a globalizing culture—consider only the familiar narrative of the "syncretic mixture of African and European influences that came together in the United States" (Shipton 2001, 830) through modern slavery. Jazz here is the musical culture or legacy of the triangulation, a music of modernity, the sonicity of the black Atlantic. James Campbell argues that "what sets black American music apart from other folk musics is the circumstances of its creation, which is what gives it its sense of urgency" (1995, 5). Does music have a privileged position as a cultural product of transatlanticism, more so than food (from the potato to gumbo), some literature (slave narratives, pirate and explorers' testimonies), some linguistic developments like Creole? I think of calypso, reggae, carnival, and most of all jazz and blues—formed from the experience of global circulation, and even being born before the development of mass media that would give later, newer musics a rapid international profile. Further, in its practice and development through the twentieth century jazz was characterized by a restless internationalism, and its sense of timing was as good as one would expect of that music: its early period of creativity coincided with, was aided by, developing transatlantic media and mass communications institutions and transport structures, for instance.[2] So in a very obvious way jazz has been a product of modernity: its multiple nature and influences (Africa, Europe, America) were only possible because of the developing global economy. It was the cultural product of diaspora, in origin *and* subsequent trajectory. The British jazz historian Alyn Shipton is sensitive to the globalism of jazz: "Today jazz is being shaped just as much by musicians from Norway and Brazil or from the South African townships and the bustling cities of Japan as it is by Americans" (2001, 358). Yet there is also something contradictory in the characteristic flexibility of the music, which fits best as an emblem of a modernity of flux and change rather than a monolithic modernity, even while jazz is undeniably a culture of the great hegemon of late modernity, the United States of America.

Even in the parochial narrative of early jazz in Britain there was an internationalism that moved beyond the obvious American origins of the music. For example, what David Boulton in *Jazz in Britain* describes as "the first jazz records of genuine worth to be made entirely by a British unit" (1958, 52) were made by the Quinquaginta Ramblers, led by the Spanish pianist, composer, and self-publicist Fred Elizalde in 1926. Phillippine-born, Elizalde had begun playing jazz in California in 1923. By 1928, in England, Elizalde "had managed to entice a galaxy of American stars to cross the Atlantic and work with him . . . The recordings made by Brunswick [record company] of this Anglo-American group were undoubtedly the finest made in England during that decade" (Boulton 1958, 53). The band included the exceptional Adrian Rollini on bass saxophone. Elizalde returned to Spain in 1930 to continue his music studies and fight for the Caudillo as an officer in Franco's army—"a strange role for the leader of a jazz band," as Jim Godbolt notes (1984, 70). The double bassist and critic Patrick "Spike" Hughes—though London-born, he was of Irish parentage, and educated in Europe—effectively took over from Elizalde as the leading local player and critic, in the same year, 1930. Spike Hughes and his Decca-dents made their first "hot" recordings then, and Hughes tirelessly wrote music and music criticism, and played bass, over the next few years before suddenly dropping his enthusiasm. Boulton describes his best recordings as "the first British jazz compositions of real intrinsic (as distinct from historical) value" (1958, 58). British jazz, if such a thing there was at that time, was thus from its beginnings a hybrid, transnational affair, as Godbolt elaborates in *A History of Jazz in Britain: 1919–50*: "It was a racially and socially mixed quartet that made such positive efforts to present jazz, live and recorded, to the British public in the late twenties and early thirties: a British-Jewish dance-band leader in the London-born Bert Firman, a wealthy Cambridge

University undergraduate from Manila in [Fred] Elizalde, an orchestral violinist from Wales in Philip Lewis, and an Anglo-Irish, Chelsea-born Cambridge undergraduate in Spike Hughes" (Godbolt 1984, 76–77).

That said, the attractions of jazz require elaboration, and must often be read in terms of the music's Americanicity. Indeed, what follows directly is a discussion of the appeal of jazz *as an export culture* in terms of issues and problems in Americanization, and it may be that jazz stands as a suitable synecdoche for America/Amerika—the "all-American jazz" beloved of American radio announcers in the 1940s and 1950s. Dick Hebdige almost makes this point when in discussing the British design establishment's critical pronouncements on cultural innovations between the wars, he observes that "the words 'jazz' and 'America' are virtually interchangeable in this kind of writing" (1988, 62).

THE APPEAL OF JAZZ[3]
(AS GLOBAL CULTURE)

It is important to consider European roles in jazz because Europe is part of the originary axis: jazz as a mixed culture from its beginnings, as triangulation between (West) Africa, (North) America, and Europe. The primary focus for me is a transatlantic one, between North America, the Caribbean, and Western Europe, with a timely dip to Africa at one point. So the story goes, in Storyville of course: the Mississippi port of New Orleans birthed jazz from its mix of French and Spanish influences, Creole, African American slaves and their descendants, and various Southern whites, in the mythic space of "a festive riot of music and dance"—music at the festival of Mardi Gras, dancing to the drums in Congo Square. In this legendary version of things, Shipton writes, "the city became a sort of musical hot-house that forced the cross-pollination of syncopation and blue notes, leading to the flowering of collective polyphonic improvisation" (2001, 75).[4] Jelly Roll Morton has captured the internationalist originary plot: "We had Spanish, we had colored, we had white, we had Frenchmens, we had Americans, we had them from all parts of the world" (Morton 1949, 17; see also Roberts 1999, ch. 1). Jazz spread "like wildfire" (Shipton 2001, 1) through the United States in the early years of the twentieth century. The export of jazz, newly formed, through live performances and the contemporaneous mass communications technology and industry can be seen as a secondary, a cultural diaspora, an identifiably American culture listened to and played across Europe, across much of the globe, including the Caribbean, West and South Africa, Japan, Southeast Asia, Australia, South America. The history of jazz is one of a broadly simultaneous development of styles alongside an international spread of enthusiasts, throughout the twentieth century.

The diasporic narratives and energies of jazz were intertwined, but as one original mix-music it already presents adjectival problems for critics. It is often called "syncretic" (as it is by Shipton above) or, more commonly, a "hybrid" form. Helen Taylor offers one apparently clear description, following Paul Gilroy, of the music's originary "routes rather than roots": "Jazz was always *hybrid*, played from the outset by mixed-race and white musicians, using European forms and often relying on extended visits to Europe. For many critics, the idea of appropriating jazz . . . for Afrocentrism is to distort and diminish it, since it is inextricably linked to European practice. Jazz in particular is today an 'international "language"'" (Taylor 2001, 23–24; my emphasis). But both terms are problematic. "Syncretism" originally means an *attempted* union of diverse or opposite beliefs or practices; it holds within it the possibility, even the assumption, of failure in that union. If a music is syncretic it is at best aiming toward a successful combination or mixing of divergent trends or influences, while at worst the term projects a doomed ending to combination. Because of the explosive racial mixings of jazz, "hybrid" is more problematic still, as John Hutnyk explains in *Critique of Exotica*: "The criticisms of hybridity can be collected into several categories: the heritage of hybridity's botanical roots; the sterility of the hybrid mule, and its extension to mulatto, mixed race, half-breed and other obscene racisms; the reclamation of the term reconfigured as creativity at the margins and as advent of vibrant intersections that cannot be otherwise incorporated; the hegemony of the pure that co-constitutes the hybrid; the inconsequence of hybridity in the recognition that everyone is hybrid, everyone is 'different'; the commercial co-option of multiplicities; and that if everyone is hybrid, then the old problems of race, class, gender, sex, money and power still apply" (Hutnyk 2000, 114–15).

Jazz will mostly be recognized here only as a creative, marginal, vibrant, "hybrid" culture: its overtly racist or fascist critics alone will see some of the other definitions as accurate. (I have in mind Joseph Goebbels's truly transatlantic hybrid description of this "Americano nigger kike jungle music": quoted in Zwerin 1985, 6.) But what Hutnyk calls "the hegemony of the pure," the trace of a pre-hybridized pure form or state, may be important in outlining one other area of the music's identity and struggle, which is why I quoted Helen Taylor's passing criticism of Afrocentrism above. For some, jazz has been defined by the political struggle of culture to express against the historic dominant (white) center of Europe. For Amiri Baraka, to emphasize the white contribution to jazz is to participate in the "Great Music Robbery," while even the neoclassicist Wynton Marsalis has argued that "the great innovators in jazz have been African American and . . . it is necessary to spotlight the top rung first before moving on to the lesser contributions of whites" (quoted in Atkins 2001, 27, 26). The African American novelist James Baldwin, for example, preferred to articulate the non-European aspect of jazz alongside its place from slavery: "the music began in captivity . . . on the auction-block. . . . That auction-block is the demolition, by Europe, of all human standards" (1979, 329–30). Baldwin continues: "This is exactly how the music called *jazz* began . . . to checkmate the European notion of the world. . . . There is a very great deal in the world which Europe does not, or cannot, see: in the very same way that the European musical scale cannot transcribe — cannot write down, does not understand — the notes, or the price, of this music" (326).

Syncretic, hybrid: if these words are to be used in the context of jazz it should at least be with knowledge of their limitations. Yet they are useful to us. Not only do "we need to formulate new ways of addressing such issues as influence, exchange, appropriation, 'hommage,' intertextual dialogue, 'signifying,' 'capping,' borrowing, theft, synergy and cross-fertilization" (Fishkin 1996, 275), but we must also carefully revisit those cultural arenas where such processes of dynamic exchange have historically happened. Jazz itself remains an intriguing if familiar case study of this; jazz as *export culture* is a provocative and neglected example. The white South African pianist and bandleader Chris McGregor's experience illustrates the energetic and liberatory potential of hybridity in global jazz. According to Denis-Constant Martin, what became McGregor's characteristic "musical code switching" (1995, iv) had its origins in his "early exposure to very differ-

1. Jazz tourism? The critics and historians (from left) Vron
Ware, Val Wilmer, and Paul Gilroy outside the Apollo Theater,
125th Street, New York City, 1982. © Val Wilmer Collection.

ent sorts of music — rural Xhosa, with cyclical motives and intricate
harmonies; urban South African, cyclical but relying on two or three
chords, underlined by a heavy accent on the beat; western classical and
contemporary, Bartók and Schoenberg included — [that] convinced
him of the possibility of combining elements borrowed from these different traditions. And jazz — discovered through American records but
also by playing with Cape Town dance bands — offered the experimental terrain he needed" (Martin 1995, ii).

On McGregor's arrival in Europe and through his subsequent immersion in free improvisation in Britain and France in the 1960s and
1970s, his music gained one further element in the mix, facilitating the
utopian sonic and rhythmic experiments of his various Brotherhood of
Breath big bands.

According to David Meltzer, a significant part of the appeal of jazz for its white enthusiasts in the United States and, after its secondary internationalization, in Europe was that it offered "a route of sensational tourism, going 'native,' allowing the inner savage escape into a world of dark strangers exuding carefree primitivism, a space to let one's 'hair down,' be uncivilized, revel in nightclub wonderlands of prelapsarian and essential being" (Meltzer ed. 1993, 39). Jazz, perhaps uniquely, offered a black screen on which were projected whites' images of exoticism. For its white consumers in Europe the exoticism of blackness was frequently sexualized as the object of female threat (captured in John B. Souter's painting *The Breakdown*, 1926) or male desire (Josephine Baker), criminalized (the music of the underworld), primitivized ("the charming savages to whom [jazz] owes its birth": Lambert 1934, 153), narcotized (from marijuana to heroin), animalized (Baker variously described in contemporary reviews in Paris as a "monkey," "snake," "kangaroo," and "giraffe": Borshuk 2001, 45). These were familiar tropes of fantasy for all manner of white masculinities, whether to be embraced, resisted, or, conveniently and pleasurably, both. Indeed, Andrew Blake extrapolates a tradition of British racism in the reception of American popular music: "Resistance [to American music] in general often took the form of specifically racialised discourses: hot jazz in the 1920s, swing in the 1930s, and rock 'n' roll in the 1950s were all resisted from within and without the British musical establishment on the grounds that these were black or black-derived forms and that black music was dangerous; that it would infect the white 'race' with its open eroticism and its association with illegal narcotic drugs . . . the common fear of 'miscegenation' around which many forms of racism have been organised" (1997, 85).

Yet in discussing the reasons for the spread of jazz across Europe in the early decades of the twentieth century, Eric Hobsbawm argues that "American Negro music benefited from being American. It was received not merely as the exotic, the primitive, the non-bourgeois, but as the modern. Jazz bands came from the same country as Henry Ford" (1998, 266–67). "Any color you want as long as it's black" seems to point toward a paradox in the white European reception of jazz. It is clear that for many black musicians from the United States, jazz is an important constituent of their culture's achievement. Archie Shepp makes this point in connection with his experience of the European situation: "I think many Europeans feel today that they have created a form of so-called jazz music which is equivalent to African-American jazz music. That's another danger in using the term 'jazz,' because if we call it 'African-American music' it localizes it, it fixes it, it's ours. So now they ask me when I go to Europe what I think of 'Polish jazz' which is like asking me what I think of Polish slavery. Because that music they call 'jazz,' grew out of slavery. It grew out of our suffering, it tells our story, but nobody wants to look at it like that because that's too political" (quoted in Menter 1981, 220).

For many white Europeans, on the other hand, the racial element of the music's origins, its dominant blackness from the United States, is to be lost in translation, or ignored, or considered secondary, while their own ethnic identity, as whites, is barely worth consideration at all. As we will see in greater depth later, this is true of white British jazz across the spectrum. The percussive and rhythmic aspects of jazz are identified as among its most evidently "African" features, so citing the views of two white British jazz drummers, from different fields of the music, will illustrate this point. From the traditional end of the spectrum, Colin Bowden, a drummer with the purist Ken Colyer in the 1950s, recalls of his experiences with the Omega Brass Band, probably Britain's first formal New Orleans parade outfit, "we never thought about ourselves being white. I do think that *when you get into black and white it's a dicey area for jazz*" (personal interview, 2002). In the field of free improvisation in its more experimental, non-swinging form, the drummer and educationalist Eddie Prévost told me: "Ethnic identity has been very important for black American jazz musicians. My own view is that the ethnic-colour stratification is a localised way of dealing with class struggle (there's an old-fashioned term for you!). National and/or ethnic identity is of no importance to me at all" (personal interview, 2002).

Sometimes described as a universal language or musical Esperanto, jazz has often been rosily received as a global culture, one that manages to evade the dangers of the globalization thesis commonly identified today, even as it is recognized as an exemplar of that process. I agree that it is (too) easy to draw attention to the coca-colonizing alternative reading in which the world sings together in perfect harmony, as suggested by the words of an American critic in Europe, Mike Zwerin: "Jazz unites people, it can help bring the world together" (1985, 53).

In this version, jazz played a key role in the production of what Atkins calls, with some critical intent of his own, "a postmodern utopia, where cultural globalization renders national identities, prejudice, and concomitant authenticities moot and anachronistic" (Atkins 2001, 276). The Norwegian saxophonist Jan Garbarek articulates the binary power of jazz as world music, as global culture, and begins to move toward a critique of it: " 'World music' to me has at least two meanings. First of all the regular meaning—a music composed of ethnic elements from various parts of the world. But on the other hand, American pop music is the real world music. It's everywhere in the world and *everybody listens to it whether they like it or not*" (quoted in Shipton 2001, 830; my emphasis).

We begin to note numerous dualities, some contradictions, within the music, and here is another. Its significant origins as an American form suggest jazz as an early soundtrack of the hegemon, and its global spread coincided with, contributed to, hegemonic authority throughout the twentieth century. Indeed, for Peter Taylor its status is as *founding* soundtrack: "America was to make its first major foray into dominating popular music through the international spread of jazz" (1999, 111). In the negative reading, jazz is a long-lasting sonic appareil blaring out in twitchy relentlessness the dismal influence of America to the unclosable ears of much of the rest of the world, doping and duping its "victims" (yeah, Adorno: 1967, 123). At the same time, the largely African American cultural achievement and invention that was jazz became rapidly understood, consumed, and valued as a music from the margins of the United States, played against the country's ideological and social dominant. Even when jazz was exported, Eric Hobsbawm could claim in 1959 that "the music lends itself to any kind of protest and rebelliousness much better than most other forms of the arts" (Newton 1959, 254). Thus jazz was read as hegemonic and counter-hegemonic at one and the same time. Doreen Massey argues from the contemporary British left that "surely we want a kind of globalisation? . . . an internationalism that respects local differences and the possibility of certain kinds of local action, yes; but emphatically not a localist future of hermetically sealed countries or cultures. . . . 'Globalisation' really just means global interconnectedness, and . . . we need to wrest back the term for ourselves and argue for and imagine not the local rather than the global, but an alternative form of globalisation" (Massey 2000).

Is it possible that jazz is already one historic form of such an alternative construction of globalization?[5] One whose trajectory moved through national popular to global popular, *and* maintained the option of localized reinscription? Homi Bhabha has urged us to "think beyond narratives of originary and initial subjectivities and to focus on those moments or processes that are produced in the articulation of cultural differences." In these "in-between spaces," "innovative sites of collaboration" may be initiated (Bhabha, quoted in Campbell, Davies, and McKay 2004, 23)—and this process may have happened twice in jazz: first in its diasporic transnational invention, and second in its exported and mediated outernational trajectory. One recent, largely European group of academics working on the reception of American popular culture in Europe has called for a move beyond simple questions of cultural imperialism in contemporary consumption. According to the NIAS group, " 'Global' mass-mediated culture does not by definition mean American culture. And the cultural imperialist model—nation versus nation—must be replaced by a postimperial model of (in principle) an infinite number of local experiences and responses to something globally shared" (NIAS 1993, 332). It seems to me that the parenthesized qualifier "(in principle)" here betrays a shift, from description to prescription, and my concern is that it actually also betrays some evasion of residual—no, fundamental—questions of (post-)imperial power. In theoretical debates on Americanization and globalization, there is this frequent dialectic that swings between the need to move beyond the national limits of Americanization and the reinsertion of a national frame of reference. In *Globalization and Culture*, for instance, John Tomlinson has argued for "alternative ways of thinking about globalized culture that do not keep us continually in the shadow cast by national cultures" (1999, 105). He offers the term "global capitalist monoculture" instead—but this is swiftly followed up by the observation that the producers of such GCM, the "capitalist firms . . . are regularly *American* ones" (1999, 81, 83, my emphasis; see also Campbell, Davies, and McKay 2004, 298). The English composer, bandleader, bassist, and jazz writer Graham Collier identified something important in this debate at a jazz conference in New Orleans in 2000, with his view that as "a European, and a confirmed cynic, here in America globalisation usually means invading somewhere" (Collier 2000). We would do well to keep in mind the wider point made by John Hutnyk in his work on musical export and reinvention, a more recent cultural manifestation of diaspora. While the context of global power relations may be quite different (jazz exported from the United States to Britain may be a reverse cultural power trip to bhangra exported from India to Britain), Hutnyk offers a sobering reminder of "that master trick of the capitalist system—pretending that all exchanges take place on an equal plane": "A 'cultural' exchange that assumes a level of equivalence—a terrain of multiculti creativity—... occludes the underlying structural inequalities of the contemporary field" (Hutnyk 2000, 125, 117).

But power does shift, and cultural innovation too. To periodize a little, Richard Pells argues that by the mid-1960s the apparent cultural hegemony of the United States was, if not attenuating, certainly being challenged across the entire range of cultural production: "The impact of European culture on the United States (in contrast to the opposite influence characteristic of the 1940s and 1950s) took on greater significance. Italian leather goods, German (and, of course, Japanese) cars, British raincoats and sweaters, Scandinavian furnishings and glassware, became staples of American consumption. American academics started looking again (as they had before World War II) to France and Germany for theories, methods, and terminologies. ... British rock groups replaced American jazz ensembles as the musicians of choice for the European (and American) young" (Pells 1993, 80).

To finesse this, it is also true that the growing free improvisation scene during this period in Britain was looking less to the United States than to, for example, musicians in Germany and Holland for collaborative opportunities to develop the idiom. "Swing," the rhythm of African American jazz, could now be heard by free improvising musicians in Europe, mostly white, as at best an obstacle, at worst a tyranny. While I am not remotely suggesting that their music became, like some British rock music, "a staple of American consumption," European free musicians were altogether more forceful in articulating the validity of their (non-American) praxis, as the English trombonist and communist Paul Rutherford outlined in 1973: "We Europeans have had a doff-the-hat attitude to Americans for a long time, but there's no need to any more; they're no longer the sole leaders, innovators, establishers of style. In fact the American avant-garde is static at the moment—they can't step far enough away from the jazz thing. In a way we can't either, come to that, but because jazz isn't our complete musical language, it's easier for us to make the break and do something new; but it's still related to what's gone before" (quoted in Wickes 1999, 249).

I do not wish to imply that non-American voices and styles were developed solely or primarily with the avant-garde outside the United States. Quite apart from the major achievement of the Quintet of the Hot Club of France in Europe, there was in something as apparently parochial as the trad boom of the late 1950s in Britain a nationalist imperative. Trad, with waistcoats and bowler hats, eccentric festivals and subcultures, bands with names like the Merseyssippi or the City Gents, was the beginning of one British version of jazz, in style if not musical content. The related skiffle explosion of the late 1950s was, David Boulton argues in the first book-length study of the subject, *Jazz in Britain*, "essentially a British product — British in that it is more or less confined to the British Isles. When Bill Haley was busy introducing rock 'n' roll to Britain, Lonnie Donegan was attempting to sell skiffle to the Americans" (1958, 126).

THE CHIC OF THE NEW

Let us remember that African-American music, from
the blues through jazz and all its evolving forms, is symbolic of
fundamental and provocative changes that society is experiencing.
—TED VINCENT (1995, 212)

There is a seductive and "remarkably persistent" (Taylor 2001, 13) grand narrative of the American sociocultural project as predicated on innovation — think of the poet Ezra Pound's famous call from *The Cantos*: "MAKE IT NEW" (Pound 1975, 157), or of the "New Negro" movement of the 1920s. This is not only a modernist impulse (though the heyday of modernism may have been one of its most intense periods): a rhetoric of newness can be readily identified in many of America's self-images, from de Crèvecoeur's "American, this new man" of the eighteenth century to the New Age(s) of Aquarius of the 1960s and 1990s. More critically, Toni Morrison has argued that "modern life begins with slavery. From a woman's point of view, in terms of confronting the problems of where the world is now, black women had to deal with 'postmodern' problems in the nineteenth century and earlier . . . certain kinds of dissolution, the loss of and the need to reconstruct certain kinds of stability" (quoted in Campbell, Davies, and McKay 2004, 12). For Peter Taylor, novum is a privilege of empire: "The meaning of a hegemonic place is more than the usual sovereign territory and national homeland; it is a special place which expresses the future today. . . . Representing hegemons as *special places of the future* gives them a massive cultural power" (Taylor 1999, 40; my emphasis).

Special places should require special music, and "America's only original art form, jazz" (Taylor 2001, 7), was also the first recognizable music of the modern city. (Its privileged urban position would not last: in the United States during the 1990s, according to Geoff Dyer, "jazz today is too sophisticated to articulate the lived experience of the ghetto; hip-hop does that better. While it used to be jazz that best expressed the syncopated rhythm of New York, now the city moves to the beat of house" (though intriguingly house music has no syncopation: Dyer 1991, 205). Atkins perhaps only slightly overstates the centrality of jazz in modernism: "No single art captured the fascination with primitivism, the flirtation with atonality, and the fast pace and repetitive rhythms of modern life better than jazz, a music that virtually all contemporary commentators (and subsequent historians) agreed expressed the very essence of modernism" (2001, 101).

As far back as ragtime, championed at the Chicago World's Fair in 1893, some instrumental syncopated African American sounds were catching the ear more widely. Jazzy forms were not alone in this diffusion—Hobsbawm cites as other examples the Buenos Aires tango and Cuban music (1998, 266). It is not coincidental that all three involved dancing: jazz combined corporeal and sonic novelty. In Australia, Bruce Johnson tells us, "it was meaningfully noted that 'syncopation' began with 'sin.' . . . Jazz was declared to be 'Joy, Animation, Zip, Zest' " (2000, 11, 12). The physical movement of audiences ranged from the Charleston or shim-sham of the 1920s to the jitterbug of the 1940s, or, within the single scene of the New Orleans jazz movement of the 1950s, from seated absolute stillness in the intensity of listening to the wild "anti-dancing" (George Melly's term) of the bohemian "leapniks" (personal interview, 2002). There were new sounds to hear from the bandstand as well as new moves to make on the dance floor. The relatively new instrument of the saxophone, only invented in the mid-nineteenth century, became and remains the icon of jazz. Orchestral instruments were extended in terms of their technique (the early emphasis on pizzicato on the double bass, the later use of the instrument's body for percussive purposes), or materially adapted (Dizzy Gillespie's bent trumpet). Freaky or trick sounds drew attention to technique and self-consciously foregrounded the physicality of playing, from exploring harmonics or circular breathing on reed instruments, to vocalizing or multiphonics through brass, to overblowing on the flute. Innovations in technology were swiftly exploited, such as improved capacity for recording kit drums in their entirety and new microphones for a more intimate singing delivery in live performance. The Japanese music writer Horiuchi Keizō wrote in 1929: "Around the world the desires of today's people are poured into jazz. Denying jazz music is tantamount to denying the present day" (quoted in Atkins 2001, 107). Over half a century after the World's Fair, Ornette Coleman was releasing albums of the latest innovation in the music, free jazz, with bravura titles like *Tomorrow Is the Question* and *The Shape of Jazz to Come*. Meanwhile in Britain round the same time, the 1950s, according to Christopher Booker in his aptly named study *The Neophiliacs*, an "image of cool modernity" was being projected by the social winners in the new Age of Affluence: "He who was with-it was 'with' the image of the age—jazz, speed, irreverence, new architecture, the whole progressive attitude—while he who was not with-it was against 'life' itself, dull, reactionary and old" (Booker 1969, 45). During that first half-century it really did seem that the *jazzeitgeist* was present; it was, in the concluding words of R. W. S. Mendl's first British study of jazz, "the spirit of the age written in the music of the people" (Mendl 1927, 187).

The generational appeal of jazz may not have endured (more frequently now it is an older man's—usually—pleasure), and it should be stressed that not all exported jazzes were read in terms of their modernity. For example, in Britain at least the traditionalist and revivalist movements from the 1940s to the 1960s understood their music as atavistic, which temporally it was—seeking to revive the New Orleans music of the teens and twenties.[6] Also, the record reviews of the poet and jazz critic Philip Larkin are indicative of a wider retro appeal for jazz in Britain. Throughout the 1960s Larkin wrote a monthly record review column for the *Daily Telegraph*, collected in *All What Jazz* (1985).

These writings appear to be consistently anti-modernist, and there are regular appeals to the school of what he terms the "Old Nostalgians."[7] Larkin's final ambivalence of touch with jazz is identified most powerfully by him himself. In the "footnote" prefacing the second edition he wonders whether his own writings type him "as a disliker rather than a liker" (1985, 31) of jazz, and in fact the (in)famous curmudgeonly introduction, written in 1968, does the reviews a disservice by overstating Larkin's own distaste for bop and post-bop jazzes. For each swipe at Parker or Davis or especially Coltrane (the *Telegraph* refused to publish Larkin's appalling, untimely rant after Coltrane's death: see 1985, 186–88), there are many knowledgeable and enthusiastic praises — from the poet who had declared in 1965, "I can live a week without poetry but not a day without jazz" (quoted in Palmer and White 1999, 4). There are some succinct observations on the development or pretensions of British jazz, as it attempted to progress beyond what Larkin termed "intelligent parody." In one review in 1961 which was later titled "Cool, Britannia" he writes: "Not so long ago, the unlikelihood of the Briton as jazzman would have been perfectly expressed by thinking of him in a bowler hat. . . . Yet today the bowler is worn with jolly unselfconsciousness by some of the country's most popular groups as part of their stand uniform. . . . British jazz has arrived, in Britain at any rate" (1985, 42).[8]

"New" also denotes the place of jazz, the new world itself (or one of the new worlds). From the outside, from Europe — the ones left behind, the ones who did not journey to constitute the immigrant society of the United States — European intellectuals looked to the United States through the prism of the twentieth century. Peter Taylor outlines some views: "While Antonio Gramsci, writing in 1929 and intrigued by the high wage regime of the USA, was wondering whether the 'new culture' and 'way of life' represented 'a new beacon of civilization' or merely 'a new coating' on European civilization, Jean-Paul Sartre had no such doubts: 'Skyscrapers were the architecture of the future, just as the cinema was the art and jazz the music of the future' " (Taylor 1999, 112–13).

For Jean Baudrillard toward the end of the century, the United States was "a world completely rotten with wealth, power, senility, indifference, puritanism and mental hygiene, poverty and waste, technological futility and aimless violence, and yet I cannot help but feel it has about it something of the dawning of the universe" (1986, 23). Even with Baudrillard's sharp European recognition of enervation and decadence, there remains the desire to locate the United States as new, to believe the story. Later, in the book *America*, Baudrillard writes that "America is the original version of modernity. We are the dubbed or subtitled version" (1986, 76). The imitative aspect, or secondary stage of jazz practice outside the United States, is an issue I will touch on again in considering cultural appropriation and reinscription. While the imitative imperative of much jazz rubs up uncomfortably against the valorized claim of the individual voice—leading it to continually flirt with what the improvising guitarist Derek Bailey has termed "the dangers of sequacity" (1992, 52)—theorizing unoriginality makes particular sense in a national framework, such as in British efforts to play that American music.

Writing in 1961, with a certain summative approach to the twentieth century's music to date, Henry Pleasants, American music critic and author of *Death of a Music? The Decline of the European Tradition and the Rise of Jazz*, explored the tensions and connections between American and European music practice, with a particular focus on the cultural establishment's valorization of classical or "serious" music at the expense of jazz, or what he called throughout "American indigenous music." In Pleasants's view, at least the European enthusiast recognized the threat: "To the music-lover brought up on European music, moreover this [jazz] was not only a new kind of music; it was *the music of a new kind of society* that was shaping itself—and its music—with a cheerful and careless disregard for the past and its heroes, conventions and traditions" (Pleasants 1961, 129; my emphasis).

When new societies and cultures form, existing ones can feel threatened, and can mobilize their cultural institutions, venerable but beginning to feel vulnerable, to resist. Jim Godbolt reminds us that not everyone wished to recognize in jazz an extraordinary pace of change and innovation through the twentieth century: "The first definition of jazz in the *Concise Oxford English Dictionary*, in 1929, was the same as it gave as late as 1969" (1984, 57). With his identification of jazz's disregard for the past, Pleasants also pinpoints the larger national issue of new, potentially *democratic* American cultures contrasting with a European élitist tradition.

American culture was self-consciously seeking a democratic alternative
to elitist [European] forms. Not literature for the few but Whitman's
"the word democratic, the word *en masse*." Not classical music, but
jazz. Not private palaces but palatial railway stations and movie
theatres — NIAS (1993, 324)

Cultural democracy, for outsiders, implied social democracy. There
is a compelling, indeed stereotypical American narrative of freedom
and opportunity — the so-called American Dream; the embodied material of the Statue of Liberty welcoming immigrants at the port ("Bring
me your tired, your poor, / Your huddled masses") that is in part ad-
dressed to European disembarkers; the metaphors of the melting pot
or rainbow nation, through which the migrant is Americanized; and so
on. These images, myths are promulgated by the United States as con-
stituents of its self-image, and at the same time they are and have been
maintained by a desire, a need from the Old World (or one of the old
worlds) for such a land of opportunity or plenty or equality. The European Rob Kroes elaborates on this point: "To the extent that America
holds up a phantasma, a dream world, to the extent that it conjures up
a land of freedom, without inhibitions and constraints, we are reading
a leaf from our own book. The European imagination had already invented a mythical West before America was discovered. . . . 'America'
is non-Europe, . . . it provides a counterpoint to our culture, a utopian
realm for our dreams of escape" (Kroes 1993, 313).

Counterpoint or polyrhythm? Either way, there is a "jazz/democracy
perspective," Robert G. O'Meally writes, through which "in the growing blueprint society that is the United States we are all improvisers,
making it up as we go along" (O'Meally ed. 1998, 118).[9] The historic
reception of jazz music outside the borders of the United States was
such that it confirmed "America" as a — *the* — zone of cultural liberation
and innovation throughout the twentieth century, interestingly even
when this the export culture included a criticism of American society
(black jazz in Paris championed by the French as an American culture
formed against American racism, for instance — jazz as "the sound of
black fire and fury and revolution," in O'Meally's alternative reading:
1998, 118). Jazz became for a while, in E. Taylor Atkins's words, "an in-

tegral element in a self-aggrandizing narrative of American ingenuity, dynamism, and creativity" (Atkins 2001, 11), and in a sense, as noted already, the historians of jazz reception outside the United States confirm this version of the music. Henry Pleasants effuses on the cultural politics inscribed within the form of jazz in the transatlantic framework: "it is probably correct to describe the difference between jazz and serious (between American and European) [music] as essentially rhythmic. . . . It is this quality of free swinging, with its invitation to free melodic variation, elaboration and invention, that has proved so attractive and has caused this American music to be loved and imitated all over the world. It is an uninhibited music in a world and particularly in a youth longing for freedom of expression and behaviour" (Pleasants 1961, 151, 158).

If jazz was, in Kroes's term about America, "non-Europe," it could also be un-British: when the Original Dixieland Jazz Band played in London in 1919, the entire audience was "shouting and clapping in a manner that was *peculiarly un-British*," according to H. O. Brunn in *The Story of the Original Dixieland Jazz Band* (Brunn 1961, 126; my emphasis). Such induced "un-British"-ness, an explosion of, in Pleasants's term, "uninhibited music" against the repressed social self, was part of the exhilarating attraction of jazz, first for audiences and then for local musicians. This characteristic was construed by British musicians and enthusiasts for generations as energetic, liberatory, democratic — directly counter to what they perceived as the daily bread of class-bound, past-oriented Britain. The English big band leader Ivy Benson, who led a succession of women-only ensembles for around forty years, has wonderfully crystallized the socially transformative possibilities of jazz: "I took a girl from a pie factory once, and made her a bass guitarist" (quoted in O'Brien 1995, 73). The composer and pianist Mike Westbrook traced for me the importance of the jazz tradition to his musical and political development: "I first became interested in jazz at school in the late '40s — began collecting '78' records — Louis Armstrong, Jelly Roll Morton, boogie woogie, Fats Waller, etc. It was much more exciting than any other music around. It was also subversive: jazz was banned at my school. Jazz was mostly American, but the New Orleans revival in Britain, in its purist days, was important. Part of a new, alternative proletarian culture that acknowledged black American music as its inspiration. Likewise blues and skiffle, before they meta-

2. The New Teao Brass Band at a socialist rally (Ken Colyer, trumpet, center), London, May Day 1962.

morphosed into pop. After school I began to hear more modern jazz. In this postwar period people went out dancing to big bands. This was a time when 'progressive' jazz seemed a part of building a new socialist Britain" (personal interview, 2003).

It happened again in the late 1950s and 1960s. The art critic, actor, New Orleans trumpeter, and cultural provocateur of the 1950s and 1960s Jeff Nuttall explained to me what he and many of his generation understood: "American culture was free of our snobbery, was against the British class system. You take some of the energy—whether it's [William] Faulkner, Krazy Kat, Lenny Bruce—because it really did seem to be enormously liberating at the time" (personal interview, 2001).

Nuttall touches on the *bricolage* openness of American culture. For Gilles Deleuze and Felix Guattari, the "flight" of American artists was part of the dynamic appeal: they know "how to leave, to scramble the codes, to cause flows to circulate. . . . They overcome a limit, they shatter a wall, the capitalist barrier. And of course they fail to complete the process, they never cease failing to do so" (quoted in Campbell, Davies, and McKay 2004, 7–8). Deterritorialization is combined with cultural fluidity. That apparently democratic blurring and subsequent merging of high and low culture which would challenge the hierarchy of cultural value was recognized quite early on by Constant Lambert as part of the appeal of jazz: "It is the first dance music to bridge the gap between highbrow and lowbrow successfully" (1934, 150). This high-lowness is often identified as a feature of American culture more generally, particularly when contrasted with European cultural practice, as Kroes reminds us: "the authenticity of American culture consists in its picaresque tradition of creolisation, its freedom from genteel control, its freedom to borrow, to cut up and hybridise. . . . European forms of music, such as marching music, European musical instruments, European standards on how to play them, underwent drastic creolisation in that American musical idiom *par excellence*: jazz music" (Kroes 1993, 310, 308).

The simplistic opposition constructed here is inadequate as a conclusion—we will see that the dialogic possibilities of jazz significantly problematize it. But in a way the opposition was also recognized, articulated by American musicians, on hearing Europe's pleading for approval. In his autobiography *Beneath the Underdog*, Charles Mingus characteristically slapped down, even as he conflated, Britain, Europe, and the Middle East. When approached between sets in a New York club by an "English critic" who asked, plaintively, "What about British jazz? Have we got the feeling?," Mingus replied: "If you're talking about technique, musicianship, I guess the British can be as good as anybody else. But what do they need to play jazz for? . . . You had your Shakespeare and Marx and Freud and Einstein and Jesus Christ and Guy Lombardo but we came up with *jazz*, don't forget it. . . . British cats listen to our records and copy them, why don't they develop something of their own?" (1971, 220; emphasis in original).

There is an important point here, identifiable also with other African American statements, such as those by Shepp, Baraka, and Wright elsewhere in this introduction, about the *ownership* of the cultural capital of jazz—specifically in relation to white appropriations or pleasures of the music.[10] The success of jazz outside the United States is not understood by African American musicians as part of the aggrandizing narrative of America the cultural hegemon, not even comfortably celebrated as recognition of a unique contribution to world culture. Sometimes it is viewed with suspicion, even resented, in anticipation or acknowledgment of a denigratory conclusion.

Atkins observes that as an export culture, "jazz music itself was not a mere byproduct but rather an *agent* of cultural transformation" (2001, 96; emphasis in original). For jazz has been as well, is indeed fundamentally characterized as, a *participatory* culture, containing a notable capacity to foster the creation of indigenous forms, to take its emphasis on improvisation and its aural innovations and recontextualize these within local musical and cultural practice. Its participatory impulse drew musicians in, even when the technical demands of the music may have been intended to exclude rather than include (as is frequently claimed with bebop). Its audiences, from the earliest, participated through the moving body: the sheer physical pleasure of dancing was a key anticipation, and notably a gendered one. Eric Hobsbawm posits that there were important social consequences for new jazzy dancing:[11] "Jazz made its way and triumphed . . . as a music for dancing, and specifically, for a transformed, revolutionized social dance of the British middle and upper classes, but also, and almost simultaneously, the British working-class dance. . . . Dance lost its formality and ordered succession. At the same time it became simpler, more easily learned" (1998, 267). American jazz, for many European musicians and fans through much of the twentieth century, was enthusiastically, even uncritically embraced as an affirmatory culture. It was received in the same way as Philip Larkin described his own experience of listening to Sidney Bechet in the title of one of his poems: "Like an enormous yes" (in Campbell 1995, 181).

Jazz has also been received historically or romantically as a music of struggle—and frequently translated into a product of rebellion for, or by, its new consumers in Europe. Historically, Ted Vincent charts musical and social links for African Americans in the 1920s and 1950s, connecting jazz innovations, civil rights, and an international consciousness of postcolonialism: "As the Jazz Age corresponded with the political militancy of the 'New Negro' and great expectations in the Black community for a better life a-coming, so too was there a movement and spirit of high expectation in the 1950s. It was pride in Martin Luther King Jr., and the victory over bus discrimination in Montgomery, Alabama. It was pride in the coming independence of Africa—Ghana in 1956 and Guinea in 1958, with Nigeria, Kenya and dozens of others to follow in the early 1960s" (Vincent 1995, 200).

For the mostly white European consumers of the music its identification as a culture of struggle—or struggle's less politically activist manifestation, "suffering"—could itself have been part of its romance, a reductive strategy effectively confirming the social hierarchy and black cultural practitioners' allotted place in it. Interestingly, the reception of jazz elsewhere in the world sought to recognize and identify directly with the blackness of the music (in its Afrocentric version), "promoting a nonwhite solidarity": "If Japanese, whom the eminent poet Terayama Shūji called 'yellow Negroes,' had a natural affinity and a shared history of humiliation and white oppression with other 'colored' peoples, then did it not stand to reason that 'yellow Negroes' had a deep emotive vocabulary analogous to African American blues, an artistic language of resistance to the subsuming and homogenizing forces of cultural imperialism?" (Atkins 2001, 252).

At the same time, there is little doubt that the liberatory inscriptions of jazz were felt at their most powerful in Western Europe after the First World War and during the Second World War, and in eastern Europe during the cold war (see my later discussion).[12] Variably, some of this desire for American cultures of liberation was prompted by the propagandist actions of the State Department. The politics of jazz here stand as an escape route, enabling the denial of Old World social crisis, mess. James Reese Europe's military band of African American musicians, the Hellfighters, swept through France in 1918, their "rough blend of brass band music and ragtime" cheered from town to town. Chris Goddard explains that "such music, which so boldly flouted tradition, fitted the mood of the time exactly. Europeans who had so recently escaped Armageddon were ready for anything. From now on everything was going to be different and that went for music too" (1979, 15). During the Second World War, "American soldiers arrived in Britain equipped with 'V-discs' of swing music given away free to the GIs by the US government" (Chambers 1986, 140). One of the leading New Orleans revivalist bands in Europe, the Dutch Swing College Band, was actually formed in the Netherlands *on* liberation day, 5 May 1945 (Dutch Swing College Band 2003). For some European enthusiasts, the memory of cultural struggle has produced a Golden Age of Jazz, a musical nostalgia intended to block heavier memories of fascism. So while the Nazis would label jazz as *entartete Musik*, one more degenerate culture, there were interstitial moments, gaps, gasps, in both jazz consumption and production—the Swing Youth subculture of jazz stylists, a constructed youth identity in direct opposition to the official Hitler Youth and other Nazi youth organizations (see Beck 1985; Kater 1992), the similar Zazous subculture of jazz fans in France and Swing Crazies in Denmark, jazz bands even in the concentration camps—the Kille Dillers, the Ghetto Swingers (Vogel 1961; Zwerin 1985, 24–27; Kater 1992, 177–201). In the Italian fascist press, jazz "was portrayed as music for effete intellectual snobs, as well as Jews, blacks and communists, inducing overexcitement *and* languor and thereby sapping the energy of Fascist youth," though it was only the declaration by Italy of war on the United States in 1942 that finally ended the broadcast of American music on Italian radio (Forgacs 1993, 161–62; my emphasis).

Aside from its pleasures and assumed freedoms already noted, jazz could sweep across Europe as it did also because it was an American and largely instrumental form. In export form, jazz was experienced as a lingua americana, not so much untranslatable as unnecessary to translate: many could understand its American. The more important observation is that jazz has been primarily an instrumental form, and its non-lyrical, non-textual characteristic (relatively rare in popular music —techno is one other example perhaps) facilitated rather than arrested its popularity. The accessibility of jazz then provides evidence contrary to Richard Pells's argument that in the postwar period, "America's cultural influence was . . . restrained by Europe's disparate languages" (1993, 82). In fact others have argued more generally that "the only culture the 320 million people of Europe have *in common* is American culture" (NIAS 1993, 329; emphasis in original). Yet did Britain, speaking English, somehow have a privileged position? Eric Hobsbawm certainly thinks so: "The reception of the music was far more broadly based in Britain than elsewhere [in Europe], since Britain already formed part of a linguistically and musically unified zone of popular culture with the USA. It therefore formed a bridge between the USA and the rest of Europe" (1998, 269). This seems to move toward the argument of Mel van Elteren (1994) about the process of what he calls "(Anglo-)American" popular culture reception in Europe—the transatlantic export of much contemporary American youth culture mediated through Britain, thence on to other European countries—though the experience of jazz may not be the most convincing illustration of this.[13] Think only of the Paris Jazz Festival of 1949, when British bop fans crowded the channel ferries to reach France for the opportunity to hear Charlie Parker live, a concert that would have been illegal in Britain at the time because of a ban on live performances both there and in the United States. In Alyn Shipton's view, "Because Britain shared a language with the United States, . . . it was natural that Britain should become a primary destination for Americans seeking work overseas, and this applied to both black and white performers" (2001, 360).

At the same time, there were compelling reasons why other European countries should play the leading role in the Americanizing impulse of jazz exported. France, for instance, was hugely significant, because of its recognized sympathetic ambience for African American and other black cultures. The first Pan-African Congress in nearly two decades was held in Paris, at the suggestion of W. E. B. Du Bois, in February 1919 (Stovall 1996, 34). The African American writer Langston Hughes and the Jamaican poet Claude McKay lived in Paris for periods during the 1920s (Stovall 1996, 59)—in McKay's case, after a year in the Soviet Union witnessing its socialism. Paris's enthusiasm for black America is best exemplified in the city's embrace of Josephine Baker and the show La Revue Nègre in 1925. From another perspective, the primitivist desires of the modernist movement in painting, seen already in Picasso's cubism as well as the Dadaist *soirées nègres* in Zurich in 1916 (Stovall 1996, 69), and its related fascination with traditional African art, were also strong in France. The influential *négritude* movement of French-speaking black intellectuals in the 1930s, to which there was some African American contribution, provides further evidence of the opportunity taken in Paris by transatlantic blacks. Some of this ambitious engagement with a black aesthetic or (post)colonial political theorizing was also visible in important gatherings and groups in Britain. At the same time in France, the gypsy tradition of improvising stringed instruments contributed to Django Reinhardt's startlingly unique stylistic achievements in jazz. Reinhardt, born in Belgium from a German gypsy background, founded the Quintet of the Hot Club of France, which is generally and rightly acknowledged as Europe's first absolutely original contribution to the American music of jazz. And historic French or Spanish links with Creole culture could be played up for an indigenous interest in New Orleans—musicians named Bechet, Bigard, Desvigne, Petit, and Picou betray at least some sort of lineage—although in musical terms the "Spanish tinge" introduced by Jelly Roll Morton in some late recordings is a more concrete Creole-Europe connection. Finally, the role of founding French jazz critics like

Hugues Panassié and Charles Delaunay also is significant, as Goddard, uncharacteristically sniffy, acknowledges: "though France may not have been a country where jazz history was made, it was certainly the place where it was first written about" (Goddard 1979, 139).

In Britain, while the early reception of black and white American jazz and related bands may have been promising and inspiring (among other reactions), from 1935 jazz began to stall. There had been impressively lengthy stays in Britain, for periods of years, by leading (or soon-to-be leading) African American musicians: Sidney Bechet (1919–22), Benny Carter (1936–38), and, for five years till the outbreak of war, Coleman Hawkins (1934–39). There is no doubting the importance of stays like these by accomplished musicians in the development of British jazz, and Shipton goes further in identifying for Carter and Hawkins "a reverse benefit, as neither saxophonist . . . would have been able to spend as much concentrated playing time as a small-group soloist as they managed in Europe, had they stayed in their respective American big bands" (Shipton 2001, 369). For slightly earlier African Americans relocating to Europe, Ted Vincent is more concerned with the negative impact that their absence would have for black cultural and political development back in the States (both Baker and Bechet were politically articulate: Vincent 1995, 107): "In 1925 Josephine Baker, Sidney Bechet, and what seemed like a boatload of other musical stars of Black America left for Europe, with a good number of these artists choosing to settle abroad and rarely, if ever, returning to perform professionally in the United States. . . . One wonders what might have been produced had they remained" (Vincent 1995, 174, 183).

PROBLEMS IN AMERICANIZATION AND
BRITISH CULTURAL POLITICS

Urgent questions of national identity and culture cannot be
formulated, let alone answered, within the discourse of
Americanisation. — DUNCAN WEBSTER (1989, 74)

Actually, they can at the very least be formulated, particularly in the *problematic* of Americanization that critics like Duncan Webster have successfully articulated in their efforts to chart the limits of the discourse. As Atkins points out in *Blue Nippon*, "Jazz provides an ideal and fascinating case study for the importation, assimilation, adaptation, and rejection of American popular culture and the identity anxieties such processes provoke" (2001, 10). More than that, jazz is a still overlooked arena in which dramas of anxiety or desire around American pop culture have been played out. We are beginning to see that there remain unexplored questions in jazz export about American cultural power, imitation, desire, and appropriation.

Viewing its reception from a British perspective, John Storey has explained that standardized mass culture "is not just an imposed and impoverished culture, it is in a clear identifiable sense an imported American culture." British political blocs alike criticized and sought to limit the appeal of American popular culture generally, of which jazz was at various times a key type: "there are political left and political right versions of the argument. What is under threat is either the traditional values of high culture, or the traditional way of life of a 'tempted' working class" (Storey 1993, 10–11). Other American pop culture imports that were variously condemned by protectors of versions of Britishness include, in rough chronology, Hollywood, streamlining (called "the jazz of the drawing board" by one opponent: quoted in Hebdige 1988, 65), pulp fiction, comics, juvenile delinquents, rock 'n' roll, pop art, video nasties, burgers, gangsta rap . . . and more, *much* more . . . all happily attriting away at British social consensus and cultural hierarchy through the century (Webster 1988, ch. 7; McKay 1997; Campbell, Davies, and McKay 2004). That writers on the British left—such as George Orwell in the late 1930s and Richard Hoggart in the late 1950s—should be preaching "cultural if not political conservatism" is viewed by Dick Hebdige as a "more complex and ambivalent resistance to cultural innovation"—and again, it is specifically in response to innovation from the United States (Hebdige 1988, 51). Writing of British cultural consensus from the 1930s to the 1960s, Hebdige continues: "A number of ideologically charged connotational codes could be invoked and set in motion by the mere mention of a word like 'America' or 'jazz' or 'streamlining.' Groups and individuals as apparently unrelated as the British Modern Design establishment, BBC staff members, *Picture Post* and music paper journalists, critical sociologists, 'independent' cultural critics like Orwell and Hoggart, a Frankfurt-trained Marxist like [Herbert] Marcuse, even an obsessive isolationist like Evelyn Waugh, all had access to these codes. Together they form a language of value which is historically particular. With the appearance of imported popular phenomena like 'streamlining' and 'jazz' this language . . . was thrown into crisis" (1988, 70–71).

The best-known jazz trumpeter of the late 1950s in Britain was not Miles Davis, then rejecting bop for the cool linearity of modal improvisation, nor Louis Armstrong, becoming a frequent visitor now that there was a lifting of the twenty-year ban by the Musicians' Union and the American Federation of Musicians on transatlantic music exchange—called an Anglo-American "cold war" by Larkin (1985, 39). It was not even, back from New Orleans, the stubborn traditionalist purist Ken Colyer. Jimmy Porter, angry young man of John Osborne's instant classic of a changing world, *Look Back in Anger* (1956), would blow solo jazz trumpet offstage while railing onstage that "it's pretty dreary living in the American Age." "Perhaps all our children will be Americans," he adds (Osborne 1957a, 17), ignorant of his wife's current pregnancy. (Alison loses the baby and cannot conceive again, so Osborne, I guess, does resolve that masculine nightmare of Jimmy's.) The radio music that Jimmy listens to is Vaughan Williams—"Something strong, something simple, something English" (17)—so it may be all the more surprising that he does not recognize the Americanness of his great enthusiasm, jazz. Dan Rebellato suggests that the play is "animated by a certain kind of imperial nostalgia," though he does not pick up the significance of jazz as a cultural symptom of this (2001, 87). Jimmy's loud, masculine, New Orleans trumpet, learned in a student band before he met Alison, is always solo—like Godot, his banjo-playing friend Webster never actually turns up to accompany him. As I explore in greater depth later, jazz functions here, as for the Movement more generally, in part as a compensatory white masculine culture, its praxis confirming the non-place of women. Lynne Segal describes it: "A stifling domesticity has killed the spirit and ripped out the guts of men, and who is there to blame but women? Who indeed, if, like Osborne and most of the other 'Angries,' you are a rebel without a cause and believe that class struggle is obsolete and Marx a fraud?" (1997, 15). In fact, in a way this mirrored the situation in the burgeoning New Left politics of the period—one female activist, Jean McCrindle, has spoken of "a pathological absence of women, silencing of women" in leftist politics of the time (quoted in Segal 1997, 2).

Jimmy's music complicates his relation with America, although his appreciation of the music is conventionally absolutist: "Anyone who doesn't like real jazz, hasn't any feeling either for music or people" (Osborne 1957a, 48). Jeff Nuttall recalls 1956 not only for its familiar conjunction of crisis and new cultural energies but also, more importantly perhaps, for Jimmy's jazz: "To me 1956 meant Suez, the film *The Blackboard Jungle*, Elvis—and of course *Look Back in Anger*. I identified myself very closely as a twenty-four-year-old with Jimmy Porter, I really did. Every time I played the horn then in fact I imagined myself as him, making those wonderful speeches" (personal interview, 2001). Osborne himself wrote elsewhere of the impossibility of refusing American cultural export: "we can't expect to put [up] some kind of tariff barrier when they start sending over their own particular anxieties and neuroses" (Osborne 1957b, 270), and one of the key cultural forms associated with the export of American neurosis has been jazz—from free jazz back to bebop back to the febrile energy of traditional and revivalist jazz. It is somehow ironic that just before Osborne wrote these words, such a barrier had in fact been lifted—the twenty-year-long ban on transatlantic exchanges that finally collapsed in 1955. But as Neil Nehring acutely observes of the English literary group known as the Movement, "jazz had long received an exemption from the Americanization thesis by English intellectuals" (Nehring 1993, 203; for the Movement and jazz see Sinfield 1989, 158–71).[14] Nehring explains that "this contradiction in the taste of the Leavisians is resolved by reading jazz as a more authentic 'folk' or at least intermediate 'popular' form (à la Hall and Whannel), [even] though its importation required essentially the same commercial processes, differing only in scale, as Hollywood film" (1993, 203). Eric Hobsbawm offers a more prosaic explanation: the likes of Kingsley Amis, Philip Larkin, and Osborne "advertised a taste" for jazz in the 1950s "because it was the badge of the provincial and the outsider" (1998, 270).

The mixed feelings toward jazz as an American export culture are seen in both Osborne and his protagonist, Jimmy Porter: they may articulate a critique of or resentment toward Americanization in some form, but jazz music is privileged in its exemption. The aporia is due not only to enthusiasts' uncertainty of critical position; it is also the result of the fluid form of the music—"the riddle is jazz itself" (Atkins 2001, 275). No one agrees in jazz; it is such a flexible form, so invitingly dialogic. The cultural and political starkness of fascism provides an altogether more dramatic example of this contradiction than the grey austerity years of postwar Britain. One German critic, Joachim Ernst Berendt, who had seen his own father marched off by the ss to his death in Dachau, and who was later drafted into the German army to fight at the eastern front (Kater 1992, 122, 196), hears jazz familiarly in contrast to "totalitarian music[, which] is martial, right on the beat; you march in step" (quoted in Zwerin 1985, 51). Another, Theodor Adorno, hears in jazz not an anti-fascist syncopation but, extraordinarily, its opposite. Michael Kater writes that "having hated jazz with a passion even at the end of the [Weimar] republic, early in the Nazi regime [Adorno] was enthused over the prospect of the Nazi authorities forbidding the music altogether—a strange position for a Jew who was to emigrate to England in 1934" (1992, 33). It was what he saw as the mass irrationalism engendered by the music that appalled Adorno. Later, writing in the United States of jazz fans ("short for fanatics," he reminds us: 1967, 123), Adorno claims: "Rebelling feebly, they are always ready to duck, following the lead of jazz, which integrates stumbling and coming-too-soon into the collective march-step. . . . While the leaders in the European dictatorships of both shades raged against the decadence of jazz, the youth of the other countries has long since allowed itself to be electrified, as with marches, by the syncopated dance-steps, with bands which do not by accident stem from military music" (1967, 127–29).

While Geoff Dyer observes that this notorious essay, "incidentally, is a very silly piece of work indeed" (1991, 221), Adorno when most stridently opposed to mass culture is still worth reading, for he can still surprise us with a piercing observation to undercut our assumptions—such as the final one here. After all, we will see white British *marching* jazz brass bands shortly, marching, ironically, for peace, while bebop drummers, good patriotic Americans, liked to "drop bombs." Adorno views jazz here and in the brilliant essay "On Popular Music" as schematic and standardizing, entirely reliant on "well-defined tricks, formulas and clichés" (1967, 123), dependent on the mass media institutions of record industry and radio for its success. Its innovations in rhythm and improvisation are negated: "the ostensibly disruptive principle of syncopation . . . [never] really disturbing the crude unity of the basic rhythm" (1967, 121), improvisation producing not an individual voice but "pseudo-individualisation" (Adorno 1941, 307–9). With his powerful, high transatlantic gaze Adorno sees jazz reception at its least critical in Europe, both because it is primitivized, as seen above, and also because "the jazz ideologists, especially in Europe, mistakenly regard the sum of psycho-technically calculated and tested effects as the expression of an emotional state, the illusion of which jazz evokes in the listener" (1967, 124). Where other critics interpret the difficulty of textualizing jazz (in musical notation and critical writing alike) as evidence of its intangibility or transcendence or mystery, Adorno contends that its "most passionate devotees . . . are hardly able to give an account, in precise, technical musical concepts, of whatever it is that so moves them" (1967, 127) and wonders whether this is actually compelling evidence of its vacuity or, worse, its inarticulate and dangerous illusion of expression, liberation, and self. Another, more damning aporia.

Webster points out that in general, fears of Americanization as cultural imperialism may be unfounded: "Instead of the homogeneity of the same, [British] youth culture finds the diversity of difference" in its appropriation and sometime transformation of pop Americana (1988, 185). And this observation may apply to not only the overprivileged category of youth in popular music: many long-standing enthusiasts and musicians (for jazz can be a music form for life in its entirety) have been able to identify *a distinction rather than a contradiction* in their choice of preferred or rejected American cultures, as have political activists. In Japan, jazz musicians were involved in the Anpo campaign, a series of mass protests against the renewal of the security treaty with the United States in 1960 and 1970: "an artistic revolt against the hegemony of American jazz was afoot, coincident with the Japanese left's strident critiques of American-style industrial capitalism and imperialist brutality in Southeast Asia" (Atkins 2001, 248). Less dramatically, it is worth considering the peace and anti–nuclear weapons movement of the 1950s and 1960s in Britain for its positions on American exports, both because of some strands of anti-American sentiment expressed within it and because jazz played a significant role in its soundtrack. For instance, Nuttall, a marcher and musician for the Campaign for Nuclear Disarmament, told me: "no, we were not anti-American. [On the other hand, i]t's true that we *were* against Admass, which can be seen as American, and our desire for authenticity and purism manifested itself in embracing trad, which was another form of America!" (personal interview, 2001). The trumpeter John Minnion, coming from a family background of fellow-traveling communists, was involved in organizing jazz brass bands on the early Aldermaston CND marches, as well as running a jazz club and promotion group as fundraiser for peace campaigns in the 1960s. He also co-edited the book *The CND Story* (1983): "Anti-American, no. That's dangerous. Reminds me a little of the discomfort I felt around the folk scene in the wake of the skiffle boom: I thought there was a potentially xenophobic line in their insistence that you must play British folk songs. But with the USA bombing around the world today, in the wake of September 11, 2001, well, yes, you *do* sometimes wonder why you're playing American music, if you have a peace campaigner's background. One of the points of CND for many years was that it managed to get away from the Cold War, by being against the military machines of *both* sides. It may be the situation now that that's more difficult because the US military machine is the sole dominant one" (personal interview, 2001).

For Ewan MacColl in the second folk revival of the late 1950s, British folk music would remove the American threat in a way that embracing, even if also reinscribing, American jazz simply could not do: "I became concerned that we had a whole generation who were becoming quasi-Americans, and I felt this was absolutely monstrous! I was convinced that we had a music that was just as vigorous as anything America had produced, and we should be pursuing some kind of national identity, not just becoming an arm of American cultural imperialism" (quoted in Denselow 1990, 26). The national identity sought by MacColl in the folk revival would in fact be a complex set of identities, each expressed and celebrated through its own folk tradition. So Scottish and Irish musics became particularly successful, while English folk would become strongly regionalized. Each of these many white folksong cultures across the country contributed to an effective culture of devolution, many years before the political devolution of Britain would take place at the turn of the millennium. It may also be that folk and regional music identity has fostered British jazz developments. The primacy of music in Scottish popular culture may help to explain why Scotland has produced so many fine jazz musicians.[15] Bill Ashton, who has seen many British jazz musicians through their early years in the National Youth Jazz Orchestra, has another theory, namely crossracial identification confirming a romanticized, or heroic, or suffering culture of struggle: "the greatest jazz musicians come from oppressed peoples. The blacks have their blues, the Scots, their pibroch and the Jews have their Jewish minor scales" (quoted in Robertson 2003, 116). Welsh jazzers have delved into their own musical tradition for connections. The pianist Dill Jones, for instance, has spoken of his childhood experience of Methodist church music: "the feeling of 'hywl' predominant in Welsh music, is akin to what black Americans call 'soul' — and I think this later influenced my jazz playing" (quoted in Worsfold 1983, 8). The feminist jazz archivist Jen Wilson was in part motivated to establish the Women in Jazz archive in Swansea, South Wales, in recognition of the historic contribution of South Walians to multiracial understanding through music.

Interestingly, the influential British folk music magazine *Folk Roots* launched what was effectively an updated boycott of American culture in early 2001, a position which was significantly *not* withdrawn or revised in the autumn of that year.[16] Similar rhetoric has been familiar in other leftist music manifestations as well — and again it is notable that positions are taken at critical moments of hegemonic military action, as musicians adopt an antiwar agenda. In *No Sound Is Innocent*, his book about free improvisation in Britain, especially around his own longstanding ensemble AMM, the drummer Eddie Prévost explores many of the connections and tensions with jazz music in particular. It is significant for the idea of jazz as liberation, though, that Prévost only mentions the notion of American cultural imperialism in the context of John Cage's perceived ab/use of the European tradition (not that this is Prévost's argument: he is as concerned to focus on the restrictions of jazz and the ways its formulaic structures and voicings limit improvisatory possibilities in spite of its avowed improvisatory core). It is curious to read Prévost's traces of European élitism, as well as (an associated) perfunctory anti-Americanism, in a book which elsewhere is much more careful in its arguments. Prévost critically describes "standard issue American imperialism; where foreign notions are adapted superficially, and reduced to trash. A mickey-mouse orientalism echoes from discarded car brake drums. Screws, bolts, bits of wood disfigure the proud grand piano which resonates like a super Cadillac version of an *mbira*. Cage was disrespectful of European sensibilities" (1995, 97). Accusations of superficial orientalism sit uncomfortably coming from AMM, whose political aesthetic included as central features Imagist texts, a fascination with Eastern philosophy (think 1960s), and an espousal (from some members) of revolutionary Maoism (think 1970s). Yet such a negative view of some aspects of the United States resonates through AMM's improvisational legacy: the pianist John Tilbury, a member of the ensemble since 1980 and a strong defender of the Marxist composer and sometime AMM musician Cornelius Cardew and the avant-garde, responded publicly to the threat of a second Gulf War led by the United States in 2003 by boycotting American appearances. As Tilbury explained: "By going to the US at this point in time . . . and playing music, by contributing to cultural life, it does send out a message that—however the musician may rationalise his act and its consequences—in the US, when it comes down to it, 'everything is all right'; that culturally, pluralism and normality reign. More contentiously, going to the US might even be construed as an act of indifference to US crimes against humanity" (quoted in Olewnick 2003, 12).

From its beginnings the reception of jazz outside the United States veered erratically: "The world these days seems to be dividing itself into two camps—the pro-jazzers and the anti-jazzers," explained an anonymous reviewer of the Original Dixieland Jazz Band's first performances in London in *Era* magazine in 1919 (quoted in Godbolt 1984, 9-10). For the anti-jazzers, an intriguing range of minor proscriptive curiosities is found in the British reception of jazz: the banning of hot jazz in English public schools (Godbolt 1984, 93), the granting of work permits for an African American big band in 1937 with the stipulation that musicians must remain immobile on stage, "apart from those movements necessary to operate their instruments" (Shipton 2001, 371), the granting of a dancing license for a public hall by local authorities on the condition that no saxophones were played (Godbolt 1984, 45). Jazz was also understood as a political culture, as an American culture, and the ambivalence in its pleasures for those on the left is evident in, for example, Iain Lang's British Marxist analysis of jazz and blues and society, published by the Workers' Music Association during the Second World War. The pamphlet *Background of the Blues* contains a short foreword that qualifies the main text. Lang explains to his (political) readers: "Certain passages in the following pages express or imply criticism of some American institutions and attitudes. I should like, therefore, to underline the obvious, and emphasize that my interest in jazz is inseparable from, and merely a part of, my admiration of the American people" (Lang 1942, 2).

There may well have been a diplomatic imperative on the publisher's part here, not wanting to appear too critical of a valued ally in the time of the common struggle against fascism, but it also illustrates the residual problematic of America for the British. In fact, in spite of the various proclaimed deaths of jazz, in spite of the rhetoric of postnational globalization, jazz and the United States today can still be intertwined as statements of power or focuses for resistance. The novelist and campaigner Arundhati Roy has recently asked: "Anti-Americanism is in the process of being consecrated into an ideology. . . . What does the term mean? That you're anti-jazz?" (2002, 2).

"THOSE WHO ARE NOT WITH US . . ."

I want to conclude this introduction by raising some necessary wider questions about the foreign policy and export cultures of the United States, especially as viewed by the British left. I am conscious that I may appear already to be losing sound of jazz. I will try to keep our ears on it. To what extent have the American origins of jazz complicated its political engagement? Consider for a moment the British left's international campaigns in the postwar period. These include, in approximate chronology, the early CND, opposition to the Vietnam War, solidarity campaigns with Chile, Cuba, and Nicaragua, positioning during the cold war generally, campaigns against the Cruise missiles and for European Nuclear Disarmament, opposition to genetically modified crops and fast food culture, and to the Iraq wars—all these movements in various ways, directly or indirectly, attacked the United States, its policies, or its actions. (It should be noted that other international campaigns have been less Americocentric: the anti-apartheid movement and other postcolonial struggles, some of 1968 in Europe, Solidarnosc, the global anti-capitalist movement of the 1990s and beyond. Further, yet other British- and European-based liberatory campaigns took a tremendous impetus *from* social movements in the United States: second-wave feminism, gay rights, civil rights in Northern Ireland and for British blacks in the 1960s and 1970s.)

Jazz seemed to blossom in Britain alongside the development of the New Left. I claim no privileged place for this music among others, but it is interesting to note that in their analyses of Americanization, some early British cultural studies texts did acknowledge jazz and other American popular musics of the time. While opening up what would become a characteristic interdisciplinarity of scholarly approach, in 1957 Richard Hoggart in *The Uses of Literacy* also condemned the destructive inauthenticity of American popular culture in Britain. In Dennis Dworkin's view, "Hoggart turned Leavis's historical mythology upside down, displacing the organic society of Merry Old England with the working-class culture of his youth" (1997, 85). There is already something of this urge in *The American Threat to British Culture* (1951), the conference proceedings of the Communist Party of Great Britain published as a special issue of *Arena*. In this E. P. Thompson writes: "Let us always remember that it will be useless to try to resist the American threat if we can only replace it with a vacuum: and that, while we may win some local gains of a negative kind, the only lasting victories will be where—whether in scholarship, *or dance-tunes*, or philosophy—the American substitute is driven out by a development of the living British tradition" (Thompson 1951, 29; my emphasis).

But by 1964 a key text such as Stuart Hall's and Paddy Whannel's *The Popular Arts* could distinguish between American popular music forms, and in fact Hall and Whannel would value jazz music—and go so far as to defend what they termed its "commercial" branch: "The conditions of production in pop music so nearly resemble those of the assembly line that it would be unfair to compare this music with folk music or early jazz. A more revealing comparison is with commercial jazz. . . . A good deal of commercial jazz has been produced by groups as keen as the teenage performers to become popular and to make money. . . . The difference between commercial pop and commercial jazz lies . . . in the fact that commercial jazz seems capable of inner growth and change . . . [it] has provided for the slow maturing of individual talent" (Hall and Whannel 1964, 307–8).

There is again, though, a residual narrative in their writing: *The Popular Arts* was a transitional text still conceived in an acceptable methodological framework that distinguished between high and popular culture, as Dworkin explains: "Hall and Whannel were undoubtedly attracted to jazz because of its roots in popular experience, but they justified its value in terms derived from their training as critics: jazz was preferable to rock 'n' roll because it was as creative as classical music. Despite their best efforts, the authors reflected the standards defined by high culture" (Dworkin 1997, 120). My wider point is not that

jazz music has been an active presence in all of the above campaigns—
thought actually in some it has—but to accentuate the potential problematic of this American accompaniment to freedom (a standard jazz
lovers' claim) when placed alongside some of the other exported American rhetorics and practices of "freedom." I am afraid I have in mind
here a litany that includes war, death, shock 'n' awe, poisoning, oppression, the overthrow of democracy, environmental pollution, ignomin-
ious future actions from a nation in the new world which had mobilized
powerfully in the anti-fascist struggle of the old world in the 1940s.
Terror. Yet for Duncan Webster, merely suggesting such a relation (of
American export culture and foreign political activity) is to trip once
again on "a persistent stumbling block for the [British] left": "Political
analysis is blunted as questions of power become entangled in a discourse of 'Americanization,' and opposition to foreign policies collapses
into arguments about 'cultural imperialism' . . . : cheese-burgers and
cruise missiles, TV cops and US bases, Hollywood and Nicaragua are
blurred together whether [British] people are mourning lost empires
or lost working-class militancy" (Webster 1988, 24).

A classic example of such anti-American paranoia from a section of
the British left is expressed in *The American Threat to British Culture.*
In his introductory essay Sam Aaronovitch reminds his largely leftist
readers

> how much of the American "way of life" is directed at young people.
> The reason is clear. Our young lads are to be trained as Yankee can-
> non fodder. They are to be militarized. And to aid this process, they
> are to be Americanized. Militarization and Americanization cannot
> be divorced.
>
> Our youngsters are being brought up to know no other films or
> songs than American. They are being encouraged to wear Ameri-
> can clothes, speak with American accents, ape American ways.
> (1951, 13)[17]

And yet when we look at the actual practice of military-cultural
relations by the imperial power—Webster does not, of course (I am
uncertain how many academics connected with the American studies
community in Britain interrogate either the propagandist origins or the
power framework of the discipline)—it is clear that there has been a
project precisely to blur the distinctions. For instance, the overt propa-

gandizing prerogative of the cultural cold war in Europe—when even erstwhile "radical" American cultural practices such as contemporary jazz music or abstract expressionist art were co-opted by the State Department for propaganda—may problematize the distantiation of the political and cultural spheres called for by Webster. The key rhetorical signifiers in the cultural cold war, concepts and appeals around which so much activity was framed, were "peace" for the communists and "freedom" for the capitalists. What better music for the export of "freedom" than jazz, whose enthusiasts, as we have seen, heard freedom inscribed in the very form and history of the music? Personnel at American military bases in Britain (which, to the horror of British anti-nuclear campaigners, from the 1950s held nuclear weapons controlled thousands of miles away in the United States) were encouraged by the U.S. Navy's plan (1961) "in appropriate ways to reinforce and support political, economic, *cultural*, technological, ideological and psychological measures" of the cold war (quoted in Campbell 1984, 145; my emphasis). To achieve this, bases organized "such events as band shows and baseball 'Little League' matches, which were reported by the US Air Force in Britain to have produced 'a desirable mixing of American and British youngsters of impressionable age' " (Campbell 1984, 145). This small last point illustrates the military march of American music in Britain. Jazz pumped out on the radio broadcasts of the American Forces Network (AFN) during and after wartime; Glenn Miller, in uniform, saying on Allied Expeditionary Forces radio that "America means freedom, and there is no expression of freedom quite so sincere as music!" (quoted in Kater 1992, 173);[18] more white big bands (Stan Kenton's in 1953, Woody Herman's in 1954: Godbolt 1989, 184–85) playing at U.S. Air Force bases in defiance of the transatlantic ban on American musicians in Britain—certain constructions of American jazz could contribute comfortably as propagandist discourse to the Second World War and the cultural cold war alike. During the Second World War the Nazi propaganda minister Joseph Goebbels targeted the radio as an essential tool for his mass work, concerned that many Germans were tuning in to the BBC for jazz and dance music—programs which would always of course be followed by news bulletins in German. His eventual response was, in spite of his own taste, to permit attempts at "German-type jazz" to wean listeners away from Anglo-American sounds. This meant the formation in 1942 of the state-sponsored DTU, the German

Dance and Entertainment Orchestra (Kater 1992, 127). So even the Nazis recognized, and more importantly actively sought to capitalize on, the appeal of jazz.[19]

But it is vital to qualify the grand, maybe just crude view here, of propagandized European subjects duped by jazz into embracing North American consumer capitalism. Peter Taylor observes of the 1920s, his "incipient" period of Americanization in Europe, that "while other countries were developing their propaganda arm of the state with 'official' cultural institutions, *Americanization proceeded through essentially private means*. . . . (The State Department only set up a cultural relations division in 1938 and Voice of America only began broadcasting in 1942 as part of the war effort.)" (Taylor 1999, 112; my emphasis). Many Europeans actively sought out American culture, not as cultural dopes or dupes, nor as naïve or depoliticized consumers. It was their *pleasure*, a term, an experience that some European Marxist critics have had difficulty with. Webster correctly reminds us that "pleasure and desire cannot just be seen as fainting into the arms of consumerism" (1989, 73). The AFN, for example, established in London with help from the BBC in July 1943, was aimed at American service personnel, not British civilians. When the Allied invasion began, "mobile stations, complete with personnel, broadcasting equipment, and a record library were deployed to broadcast music and news to *troops in the field*," moving and broadcasting across Europe as the front line shifted. Many Europeans also wished to hear jazz on the radio. Both Zwerin and Kater tell of the "Luftwaffe ace Werner Mölders, a swing fan, [who] would switch on the BBC as he crossed the channel, hoping to catch a few bars of Glenn Miller before bombing the antenna" (Zwerin 1985, 31).[20] AFN would play more than a few bars of American dance band and jazz music, which contributed further to its attraction for European listeners. In postwar England, Colin Barker remembers, "the local suburban record shops hardly had any jazz anyway. If you were lucky, you could sometimes get your valve radio to hit the AFN stations in Germany, on which they played a lot of jazz, especially swing" (personal correspondence, 2002). Half a century later there was still a significant number of listeners unaffiliated with the American military (with the caveat that the following quotation is taken from an official U.S. military website): "the US defense drawdown began in earnest after the Gulf War, and impacted AFN stations across Europe. Even though the Europeans are not our primary audience, many of their feelings are summed up in a German newspaper article in the early 1990's that stated 'the U.S. military can leave Europe, but AFN must stay' " (AFN 2002).

Of course jazz musicians (including Louis Armstrong, Count Basie, and Dizzy Gillespie) *were* sponsored for trips to communist or non-aligned countries—Ralph Ellison notes in a sardonic demolition of overenthusiastic claims of radicalism in black jazz (warning heeded) that "while a few boppers went to Europe to escape, or became Muslims, others took the usual tours for the State Department" (in Campbell 1995, 100). Thus were "musical revolutionaries [transformed into] quasi-official ambassadors . . . in the service of U.S. foreign policy" (Atkins 2001, 174).[21] But the overall position with jazz and cultural propaganda in Europe is more complex, not least because of the strong distaste toward jazz felt by some of those directing the cultural cold war from within the United States itself. In an error of judgment—in terms of the initial success of the American propaganda offensive in the late 1940s and 1950s in Western Europe, at least—jazz would frequently be rejected as an unacceptable form for projecting an ideal, official image of the United States. There seemed to be little understanding of the process of re-creation of music by local musicians, which arguably could produce a more impressive propagandized subject: jazz was not only consumed as a cultural product—musicians internalized and then reproduced it, debatably reinventing themselves as pseudo-Americans, with clothing and language to match. But would-be dance band musicians were not the constituency that the cultural cold warriors sought to reach. According to Hugh Wilford, in an illuminating discussion of the editorial policy of one cultural cold war magazine in Europe, *Perspectives*,

> It was a cause of constant vexation to Americans who cared about their country's cultural standing abroad that European intellectuals appeared not to know about the existence of high cultural traditions in the US yet were aware of the mass-produced forms of American popular culture. . . . One of I[nternational] P[ublications] I[nc.]'s main purposes was, as the American poet and "literary consultant" to *Perspectives*, Delmore Schwartz, phrased it, to publicize "the most admirable aspects of life and culture in America, but also to play down those aspects which Europe admires and are not highbrow." In

one instance this meant an article about American jazz by Anatole Litvak being "knocked out" of an issue of *Perspectives*. Litvak, incidentally, challenged this decision on tactical grounds, arguing, "We can't justify our popular culture by ignoring it. They know all about it, and they think jazz is the only good part, so we ought to play it up." (Wilford 1994, 318)

The article was not published — the spread of American jazz in Western Europe, feted in postwar Paris and desperately desired in London, was to be discouraged by official intellectuals. Mel van Elteren observes in particular of some black jazz and blues artists who exiled themselves to Europe that a "significant part of the export hits of American culture drew its appeal from popular traditions which were, and are still marginalized or even considered 'non-culture' by the cultural elites of the United States" (van Elteren 1994, 7).

Such a policy would differ with that prevailing in Eastern Europe, where jazz would become, in James Campbell's phrase, "a *samizdat* of the soundwaves" (1995, 7). A report in the *New York Times* in 1955 was headed: "United States Has Secret Sonic Weapon: Jazz" (Belair 1955, 240; see also McKay ed. 1998, 172). A regular jazz radio program on Voice of America reached eighty million listeners in communist countries in the late 1950s (Walser 1999, 240). In Poland through the 1980s the Jazz Jamboree, an annual festival in Warsaw that featured leading jazz and blues performers from the United States from across the full range of styles, was funded with money "largely from the cultural wing of the American intelligence services" (Campbell 1995, 6). When a jazz fan in communist Poland said in the 1980s that "anybody who likes jazz cannot be a Communist," repeating the earlier claim of a German in the 1940s that "anybody who liked jazz could never be a Nazi" (Zwerin 1985, 68, 24), jazz was presented as an escape route from the consensual destruction of history and tradition, a new cultural expression that would reveal a route to freedom, or compensate for its lack. As a signifier of the struggle for Western "freedom," or at least against communist oppression, a single relevant word itself could suffice: the *Shtatniki* (named after the States) in the Soviet Union was a small subcultural movement of jazz lovers in Moscow in the 1950s and 1960s (see Ostrovsky 1993), while the *Jazz* Section of the Czechoslovakian Musicians' Union, which had such problems with the communist state in the

1970s, consisted more of rock than of jazz musicians. The Polish writer Leopold Tyrmand, in a lecture at a conference called "On Freedom" in the early 1980s in Frankfurt, a period when at home the cold war was trying to freeze out the people's uprising around Solidarnosc, recalled his wartime love of the music and its significance as a social text, as a social model: "for most of us *the collective improvisation of a dixieland combo came to mean*, if only subliminally, *the perfect emblem of freedom* and all the necessary energy to defend it. It was an image of liberty whose dynamics, at the time, seemed invincible, the ultimate representation of free utterance" (quoted in Zwerin 1985, 86; my emphasis).

What is noteworthy in all these discussions is the extent to which jazz has sounded the clashing of empires and ideologies, was a twentieth-century music that signaled one shift in imperial center (from British Empire to American hegemony), was employed to culturally facilitate others (the Second World War, the cold war). Its powerful branding has been regularly understood in this framework—in Australia, for instance, part of its attraction was that that it possessed "the aura of innovation surround[ing] the United States *as an alternative to imperial traditions*" (Johnson 2000, 24; my emphasis). To parochialize once more, jazz in Britain, while it has been celebrated (though not uncritically) by its musicians and enthusiasts, has also been approached by British cultural establishments and by social critics and political activists—sometimes the same people as the musicians—in inconsistent and contradictory ways. As we have seen, and will see again, organizations ranging from the Arts Council to the BBC (called by Simon Frith "the most explicitly anti-American institution" in the British media: 1988, 51), from the Musicians' Union to the Communist Party (not always so very far apart at the executive level), promoted or resisted jazz, could read it as pleasure or threat. And these debates are not only historic—for they are concerned with the continuing presentation and negotiation of what it means to be British, and the extent to which *that* might mean being American. The example of statistics of financial support for British jazz from some leading cultural organizations illustrates the currency of the debate. In 1993–94 the Arts Council of England and its Regional Arts Boards spent 1.88 percent of their music budget on jazz; in the same year the British Council in London spent 21 percent of its music budget on jazz (ACE 1995, 34–35). These are just two statistics plucked for an argument, but how should such a huge disparity be read? It is in part a question of recognizing and defining national culture: the Arts Council of England, as evidenced here, has an established hierarchy of cultural value in place which *deprivileges* jazz and improvised music, for reasons which may be influenced by still-existing discourses of Americanization within British cultural élites (British jazz is an inauthentic, secondary form, and, worse, its imitatory model comes from the United States). Intriguingly, though, the British Council, an organization charged more explicitly with identifying and exporting culture that represents *Britishness* in some way, nominates precisely the same inauthentic, secondary form of British jazz as one of its key musical representations. What follows in this book are detailed explorations from jazz of the relation between culture and politics, between the global and the local, between the imperial or hegemonic and the postcolonial, between white and black, male and female. The jazz problematic and jazz energy are examined in the social and cultural context of Britain during a period of rapid change and shifting consensus, when there was a working-through of new social issues (larger-scale migration, postcolonialism, nuclear weapons, the blurring of class), forms of thought and action (the New Left, British cultural studies, second-wave feminism), and types of pleasure (festivals, the counterculture).

ONE

New Orleans Jazz, Protest (Aldermaston),
and Carnival (Beaulieu)

[A] sociology of jazz would be an absurd conception, and yet . . .
why should the Aldermaston marchers have followed a *jazz* band?
—PHILIP LARKIN, reviewing Eric Hobsbawm, *The Jazz Scene*,
1959 (in Palmer and White 1999, 41; emphasis in original)[1]

Focusing on the jazz boom of the 1950s in Britain, which primarily revolved around traditional and revivalist musics of early New Orleans, this chapter looks at a particular moment in the relation between popular music and social protest, and at a specific founding annual event in the subcultural history of pop festivals. The research has a number of aims. It is to reconsider a form of jazz dismissed or misrepresented by many critics and academics. Here as elsewhere I employ material from personal interviews with activists, musicians, and fans of the time, focusing on the political development of the New Orleans parade band in Britain, which I present as a *leftist marching music of the streets*. I seek to shift the balance slightly in the study of a social movement organization (the Campaign for Nuclear Disarmament, or CND, founded in 1958), from considering it in terms of its "official" history toward its cultural contribution and innovation. CND's early subcultural politics mainly happened during the annual three-day Aldermaston protest marches, to a soundtrack of jazz and folk (see McKay 2003). It is to look at the other contemporaneous social manifestation of jazz and carnival in Britain, at the negotiation and contestation of youth groups and music enthusiasts surrounding the earliest jazz festivals at Beaulieu, Hampshire (which began in 1956) (see McKay 2004). Many jazz fans and musicians were involved in both carnivalesque moments. What do Aldermaston and Beaulieu together tell us about the meanings of jazz for British youth and left politics during that decade? Larkin's characteristic contrariness in moving through the "absurd" to the astute—a "sociology of jazz"—indicates a wider theoretical and historical uncertainty in the fragmentary readings that are available on traditional and revivalist jazz in Britain of the 1950s,

3. Contesting empires? Ken Colyer's New Orleans ensemble the Omega Brass Band marches past the Royal Albert Hall for the Campaign for Nuclear Disarmament, late 1950s or early 1960s.

and that I want to counter. Finally, I want also to look further at some of the questions around Americanization and jazz music, in terms of resistance, imitation, and the idea of the past.

Definitions are necessary. According to George Melly, there developed two clearly identifiable forms—or factions—of musical retrospection in Britain, both white. The first was traditional jazz, looking to explore the music of New Orleans before the First World War. Its most visible proponent was the purist New Orleans cornetist and bandleader Ken Colyer, whose "wavery vibrato and basic melodic approach was based on Bunk Johnson. He sounded, and intended to sound, like an old man who had never left New Orleans when they closed Storyville" (Melly 1965, 46). For David Boulton, "the avowed policy of [Colyer's groups] was to re-create the archaic jazz of the Storyville period" (Boulton 1958, 79). The second was revivalist jazz, which preferred Chicago jazz of the 1920s, clustered around Louis Armstrong. Melly asked: "What was the difference between revivalist and traditional jazz? . . . What the revivalists thought of as 'New Orleans Jazz' was the music of Armstrong, Morton and Oliver—New Orleans musicians but based on, and recorded in, Chicago during the Prohibition era. . . . The basic difference between the two sounds is that revivalist jazz includes arranged passages, solos, and considerable emphasis on the individual musician, whereas traditional jazz is *all* ensemble" (Melly 1965, 160–61).

A particular British pop moment saw the so-called trad boom, in which bandleaders like Acker Bilk, Kenny Ball, and Chris Barber featured high in the charts in Britain and sometimes in the United States, in full swing in the few years on either side of the decade (see Berg and Yeomans 1962; Matthew 1962; Wallis 1987). The trad boom's subcultural and commercial success rivaled that of rock 'n' roll for a while, the hit records beginning with Monty Sunshine playing "Petite Fleur" with Chris Barber's Band in 1959. This had been preceded by the skiffle craze, during which Lonnie Donegan had a hit with "Rock Island Line" in 1956 and Chas McDevitt played his hit "Freight Train" on "The Ed Sullivan Show" on American television in June 1957 (McDevitt 1997, 102). Events such as the Beaulieu Jazz Festivals contributed to as well as benefited from the new and mediated music craze. Not too much imagination was required to jump on the, well, bandwagon: the BBC broadcast a series featuring live bands called "Trad Fad," while the final boom year of 1962 saw books like Brian Matthew's *Trad Mad* and Richard Lester's film *It's Trad, Dad!*

On the few occasions when British traditional and revivalist jazz has been discussed by academics, the orthodoxy has constructed the music and the movement as conservative, retrospective, unimaginative, and worse. Iain Chambers foregrounds "the hermetic conservatism of revivalism" (1986, 148), the "homely" nature of British traditional jazz, and the CND beatnik style, which for him is neither as "finger-snapping" as Kerouac's Beats nor as "sharp" as the mods will be in a few years' time. He continues: "The domestic mixture of New Orleans jazz with cups of tea, warm beer and lawn-mowed suburbia rarely pushed British bohemia towards the spirituality of modernism and movement" (Chambers

1986, 148). Rather too easily positioning the politics of traditional and revivalist jazz within the cozy space of English counter-modernisms of the kind expressed by George Orwell or, later, Prime Minister John Major, Chambers offers a dismissive gloss which, among other effects, obscures the music's political moments. Nor have rapid evaluations helped the music's cause: in Kevin Morgan's view, "the jazz revival . . . ended in the awful apotheosis of the Trad Boom" (1998, 138), while for Eric Hobsbawm "the New Orleans revival was essentially a *non-musical* phenomenon" (1998, 241; my emphasis).[2] Neil Nehring zones keenly in on the innate conservatism of traditional and revivalist jazz during what he calls "the puerile fifties" (Nehring 1993, 210), his suspicions retrospectively confirmed by some musicians' actions twenty years on (though I am not sure these jazzes are unique in pop music in featuring musicians who politically disappoint with age, with waning popularity). That Nehring dislikes the music so intensely seems only to confirm (his pleasure in making) his political judgment about "hideous trad New Orleans jazz by the likes of Acker Bilk": "It seems fitting that trad jazz, the favourite music of [Philip Larkin and] the Movement, would in its death throes invoke the Edwardian period, seemingly confirming how wrong the literary were about both popular music and English society. (By the late seventies [1976], former trad jazz stars Kenny Ball and Chris Barber played benefits for Margaret Thatcher, their politics consistent with the conservatism of that music's proponents, literary and otherwise, in the fifties.)" (Nehring 1993, 208).

The critical problem here is that Nehring wants to read the trad boom with later eyes—as a residual culture rather than one capable of possessing an emergent, even oppositional phase. Helen Taylor employs a similar problematic framework in *Circling Dixie: Contemporary Southern Culture through a Transatlantic Lens*, one of the very few academic books to include any detail about the extraordinary contribution of Ken Colyer to British jazz.[3] In a short section on the export culture of New Orleans music, Taylor looks at traditional jazz—but Colyer is presented through the prism of the Ken Colyer Trust, set up by aging fans in the year he died, 1988. Taylor's version of traditional jazz is represented by "a particular group of white Englishmen: middle class, financially comfortable, having repaid their mortgages and now with time on their hands" (Taylor 2001, 113). The "sweet sadness" of "nostalgic emotional appeal" is the defining feature for Taylor (2001, 115,

113), and she emphasizes that the "Colyer Trust musicians and members are not very interested in the racial and social history of this music or its evolution into other forms; their concern is with saving it as a pure music, undiluted and unhybridized" (Taylor 2001, 115). The significance of this critique is that Taylor herself presents a depoliticized sweet sadness: by looking only at the trust in the 1990s rather than, say, also the musician's projects of the 1950s and 1960s, Taylor misses the more complex situation, in which Colyer's own Omega Brass Band, for example—as I show below—frequently appeared at left-wing demonstrations.

Cultural critics of the left have expressed surprise at the links between jazz and the left during what became the cold war. In *The Land without Music* Andrew Blake identifies but does little to interrogate the "odd conjunction [of New Orleans jazz, CND, and trade union marches], given the importance of the Communist Party to union militancy, and the Soviet hatred of jazz" (1997, 114). Writing of the slightly earlier relation between the Communist Party and the Musicians' Union in Britain, Kevin Morgan notes "the contingencies of communist politics in a period swinging, if one can so put it, from a broad-minded progressivism to the bigotries of Zhdanovism" (1998, 124). It may be that both Blake and Morgan overlook the contribution of the non-state left, the anarchists rather than communists, for instance, to radical activism and alternative cultures. Overall, though, what is striking about the effort of cultural studies to read traditional and revivalist jazz is its limited nature, and its lack of interest in the music's political role. I want to interrogate and chart this "odd conjunction," to use Blake's term, to explore what may well be, after all, *a leftist marching music of the streets*. In doing so I acknowledge the lengthy tradition of music and mobilization in Britain—Stephen Yeo has argued that the "main cultural thrust of the early socialist movement was in music," for example (quoted in Waters 1990, 97). Early British activists aimed to create "a socialist musical structure that stressed the importance of communal participation and offered a unique blend of songs written for the movement and works appropriated from other cultural and political traditions" (Waters 1990, 189). This much is evident in the presence at socialist gatherings like May Day festivals of organizations such as the Clarion Vocal Union (founded 1894) of radical choirs (Waters 1990, 121), or in the songs sung at socialist Sunday schools in Scotland. More pertinent for the discussion of Aldermaston is the British brass band tradition of street music, as exemplified from Victorian times by both the Salvation Army and local industrial bands, mainly in northern England. Trevor Herbert notes that the industrial bands formed a strong working-class music movement and that this "became aligned with events such as May Day, trade-union demonstrations, and miners' galas, which epitomized working-class identity and behaviour" (Herbert 2000, 67).[4]

Clearly there are ambivalent political positions within both critical readings and the pleasures of New Orleans jazz, which may have contributed to a suspicion of it by cultural studies. This ambivalence is delineated by Robert Hewison, who identifies New Orleans jazz of the 1950s as managing to be both conservative and anti-élitist. On the one hand, *the writers* "John Wain, Kingsley Amis and Philip Larkin developed a side-line as jazz critics. The critical conservatism of their poetry coloured their preference for traditional jazz," a preference also displayed in John Osborne's work, in particular *Look Back in Anger*. On the other hand, traditional and revivalist *musicians* produced "an earthiness, a rawness, that was definitely, to use Nancy Mitford's phrase, non-U, and it had a proletarian, non-Mandarin vigour" (Hewison 1981, 114–15). For the British left, the cultural politics of jazz in the 1940s and particularly the 1950s were influenced by the revivalist movement in the United States a decade or two earlier. Projects collecting and recording traditional and folk music were organized by the Library of Congress, and in 1938 Jelly Roll Morton recorded his New Orleans classics from twenty years before for Alan Lomax. That same year other veterans such as Sidney Bechet were also recorded. In 1945 the first recordings of New Orleans parade brass bands were made, by William Russell. Recently researched recordings and publications contributed as well, and inspired groups of young white musicians to revive the early music, most notably perhaps Lu Watters's Yerba Buena Band in California. Bernard Gendron writes that "the anticommercial stance of many of the revivalists played into, and reinforced, their promotion of authenticity, folklorism, tradition, and affect, set against a vaguely left-wing, antifascist background" (Gendron 1995, 50).[5]

The mass as well as specialist media were swiftly successful in the national and international spread of this new-old music (as we will see, the *first* formal British parade band would be called the *Omega*). In England in 1943, George Webb's Dixielanders surprised everyone with their authentic-sounding music, played on Monday evenings at the Red

Barn public house in Barneshurst, Kent. According to Jim Godbolt, most of the band "had worked in the local Vickers-Armstrong factory. Sociologically minded critics with various left-wing and anarchist associations saw this as an expression of working class culture and likened the band's endeavours to those of the early US black jazzmen, whose art flourished despite their subservience, socially and economically, to the white boss. The Young Communist League promoted the Dixielanders in a series of concerts at the Memorial Hall, Farringdon Street under the banner of the Challenge Jazz Club. In their paper, *Challenge*, they heavily emphasized the socio-political overtones of this phenomenon" (Godbolt 1984, 202–3).

There *were* class implications in the scene as it developed through and after the war, often revolving around working-class communist organization. Some communists received the Dixielanders as "authentic jazz, arising from the English proletariat and offering a new vocabulary for its attenuated musical traditions." Others recognized that the anti-commercialism and avowed amateurism of Webb and most of his band effectively subverted the Musicians' Union's continuing campaign on minimum payment, so that ironically there was a "threat of this new people's music to musicians' unionism" (Morgan 1998, 136). In Melbourne musicians such as Graeme Bell and Ade Monsbourgh had been forging their own links between early jazz, wider cultural formations, and leftist politics, cultural work that would have an important impact on postwar jazz in Britain. Their magazine *Jazz Notes* "increasingly urged the claim of pre-commercial folk authenticity, and became a musical rallying point for artistic and political groups who opposed what was felt to be the philistine commercialism of Australian culture" (Johnson 2000, 15). When the Graeme Bell Australian Jazz Band made its extraordinary journey to Europe, finally to London in 1947, it was at the original invitation of the Eureka Youth League, a communist-affiliated organization in Australia, to attend the first international communist World Youth Festival in Prague (see Johnson 2000, 147–57). Its wildly successful appearance in Czechoslovakia was very well timed by the band, for jazz more generally perhaps, as Johnson notes: "the three years between the end of World War Two and the Communist coup retain a wonderful aura of freedom and possibility. . . . The soundtrack of that . . . is the dixieland which was introduced by the Australian band led by Graeme Bell" (2000, 136). In Bell's trajectory jazz is initially embraced by communism, only to be ideologically repositioned subsequently: "These circumstances had invested the music with an aura of subversive anti-totalitarianism, implicated in complex ways with the idea of local sovereignty. . . . The Bell band virtually started the jazz movement as such in Czechoslovakia, providing a working model for a music already deeply inscribed with socio-political meanings" (Johnson 2000, 149, 150).

The Crane River Jazz Band, founded in England in 1949, is important because it saw the first success of Ken Colyer, and it provides a further instance of New Orleans music sitting comfortably within a working-class, leftist prism. The *Daily Worker* reported the band's invitation to appear at the third World Festival of Youth and Students for Peace in East Berlin in May 1951: "Britain's leading jazz group, the Crane River Band, is going to the festival. The average age of these young workers is twenty-two-and-a-half. The improvised jazz they produce with such vigour and single-mindedness is going to rock Berlin solid, as the jazz fans would say. This sort of popular music has nothing in common with the canned American dance music of which the BBC is so fond" (quoted in Godbolt 1989, 16). The correspondent manages, in that final, single sentence, to position the paper, the festival, and the music produced by the Cranes as outside (and better than) both the popular music privileged by America and that privileged by Britain (the BBC).

New Orleans jazz had practical attractions too for the young in Britain: it was relatively easy to play passably, to listen to—and to move to, and it was an accessible form of musical expression in keeping with the democratic sympathies of many activists and cultural workers of the time.[6] Its partial origins as a marching music helped as well, not least for brass bands at demonstrations and other gatherings. Writing at the time, Eric Hobsbawm outlined the socialist correspondences of New Orleans jazz: "It was a self-made music, or at least music made in the image of the amateur. Its bands—in Britain at least—resisted professionalization for the best part of ten years. Moreover, in Britain and Australia, to a very marked extent, they had and maintained links with the political left. World youth festivals, anti-nuclear marches, May Day demonstrations, or other expressions of hostility to the social *status quo* have rarely lacked their quota of imitation New Orleans jazz players" (Newton 1959, 76).

In summary, Paul Oliver is perhaps most accurate about the cultural politics of the music in his observation that it "symbolized what its proponents chose to find in it that supported their own aims and ideologies" (1990b, 81). He elaborates on the music's ideological multivalence: "To the communists the ensemble improvisation of the traditional band symbolized the sharing of responsibility and skills of collective creativity without individualism; to the anarchists the traditional line-up meant freedom of expression and the loose, unshackled federalism of 'head' arrangements; to liberals the music spoke of responsibility and selflessness; to conservatives, the strength and continuity of traditions ensured the basis for the individual enterprise of front-line soloists" (Oliver 1990b, 81).

This is neat, but it lacks the essential tension of such factionalizing discourses as those of the left and of jazz alike. In the United States, for instance, vehement arguments took place between modernists and revivalists, the modernists going so far as "to accuse the 'moldy figs' of 'musical fascism.' They variously vilified them as the 'right-wingers of jazz,' 'the voice of reaction in music,' a 'lunatic fringe' " (Gendron 1995, 46).[7] In Britain, Kevin Morgan suggests, "despite its rhetoric of the people, early British jazz appreciation shared with so many forms of left-wing culture an eschewal of the popular, a comradeship of the elect, which was the secret at once of its richness and its marginality" (Morgan 1998, 139). By the 1950s British jazz was torn not only between revivalists and traditionalist purists but between both these and the relatively new modernists, so much so that trouble among fans at the Beaulieu Jazz Festival in 1959 merely presaged the festival's Saturday night riot in the following year between fans of the trad clarinetist Acker Bilk and of the modernist alto saxophonist John Dankworth.

JAZZ IN THE STREETS:
NEW ORLEANS BRASS BANDS
ON THE ALDERMASTON CND MARCHES

You want to know why we came here? Well, the simple reason is we
are lovers of good music for one thing, and if this hell of a lot goes up,
we're not likely to hear good music any more!—CND marching
musician, *March to Aldermaston* (1958)

In *March to Aldermaston*, a short documentary film of the first Aldermaston march of Easter 1958 directed by Lindsay Anderson and others,

I counted eighteen shots of jazz bands playing (the first three are of the uniformed Omega Brass Band), and on ten occasions New Orleans jazz forms the soundtrack. The production team evidently thought jazz the key musical accompaniment to the event, though it is folk music which has more commonly been recognized as providing the accompaniment for the campaign generally (Boyes 1993; Brunner 1983). Georgina Boyes traces distinctions as well as connections between the two musical forms: "although jazz bands provided much of the music for the marches organised by the Campaign for Nuclear Disarmament, it was folksong which became synonymous with protest. . . . Shared ideology also created links between performers of the two musics— [Humphrey] Lyttelton joined [A. L.] Lloyd as a Vice-President of the Workers' Music Association and prominent jazz and folk musicians appeared on the same platform at political events" (Boyes 1993, 214–15).

CND was formed the year of that first Aldermaston march, 1958 (see Hinton 1989; Taylor 1988). Although there had been small-scale campaigning in Britain against nuclear weapons before, it was the development of the super-destructive hydrogen bomb by the United States and then the Soviet Union in the early 1950s, followed by the British government's decision in 1955 to produce its own H-bomb, that really sparked what would become CND. In 1957 the first British H-bomb test took place at Christmas Island in the Pacific, while later the same year the government announced that American Thor nuclear missiles would be sited on airbases in East Anglia. Against such a backdrop, and with cold war paranoia fully in the air, CND was formed from an extraordinary alliance of supporters, including many artists and musicians, across generations and belief systems, religious and political. Its activities included mass national demonstrations and international campaigning, and related groups were involved in local direct-action protests and extensive civil disobedience. The second great wave of support for CND in Britain came in the 1980s, with the introduction of cruise missiles controlled by the United States on British and European territories. Again mass national demonstrations featured, but there were also developments in the wider movement: the peace camp movement, a much stronger articulation of the relation between gender and militarism, the use of the pop festival (Glastonbury) for fund- and consciousness-raising, a greater awareness of environmentalism.

The idea as well as organization of the first march to Aldermaston actually came from an existing group, the Direct Action Committee against Nuclear War, but CND quickly realized the potency of mass street protest. It was this event, this performance of mobilization, that caught the imagination — indeed, Meredith Veldman goes so far as to argue that "without the march, CND would have been just another largely left-wing protest movement" (1994, 137). The town of Aldermaston in Berkshire was chosen as the focus because Britain's Atomic Weapons Research Establishment was there. In "William Empson at Aldermaston," the poet Alan Brownjohn describes the contrast between "all the bands and singing" of the marchers as they arrived and the "deathly offices" of the government's military buildings:

> An absurd fete of life, in one Friday field
> For which no pass was needed. The effect:
> Two sorts of carnival clashing: on this side
> The mud, or grass,
> The boots and stoves and caravans; that side,
> The trim, discreet pavilions of the State. (Robson 1969, 36)

CND's characteristic mix of (sub-)cultural and political protest would become more familiar in the 1960s, as David Widgery recognized: Aldermaston 1958 was "a student movement before its time, mobile sit-in or marching pop festival; in its midst could be found the first embers of the hashish underground and premature members of the Love Generation" (Widgery 1976, 104). When one recognizes the improvisatory spirit of the first march in those hectic few months, it begins to appear less surprising that jazz should have been playing. John Minnion was a volunteer at CND's national office in London during the period leading up to each march. A long-time CND activist, Minnion explains his role in the organization and motivation of jazz on the marches: "CND realized that bands were springing up spontaneously along the march, and so thought they'd use them. Flyers sent out to prospective marchers asked for addresses etc., but also had a line for people to complete: 'I can play . . . and am willing to be in a band.' So if we at national office knew we'd be getting several bands' worth of musicians we'd use them. CND identified a fundamental flaw in conventional politics: let's live, not destroy the world. So: let's have a good time. So: jazz and dance!" (personal interview, 2001).

The Easter marches became the annual spectacle of the nuclear disarmament movement, recognized nationally and internationally and attracting thousands of mostly middle-class protesters from constituencies as varied as anarchists and MPs, clerics and beatniks, the New Left and the Woodcraft Folk—"a decent British sort of protest," in Widgery's words (1976, 104). In CND there was rapid recognition of the possibly innovative cultural identity of the movement, and the importance of culture for energizing campaigners and maintaining a high public profile. The Aldermaston marches, and their musics, were constantly referenced. In her autobiography *Left, Left, Left*, the campaign secretary Peggy Duff recalls a characteristic CND politico-cultural event at the Albert Hall in London from November 1961: "we wanted to run something more than a meeting, to hold a mirror up to the movement, to show its variety, its confidence, its ebullience, its political content, its diversity. . . . We had moving coloured lights on a great white backcloth, and Humphrey Lyttelton (who really understood what we were trying to do) and his band, and George Melly, the Polaris singers from Glasgow, and, real old Aldermaston March stuff— the Alberts who had always led the early marches with whippet and trumpet. *It was a crazy mix up of jazz and folk and farce, and colour, and speeches about the Bomb—hard and soft politics, but which was the hard and which the soft I am still not sure*" (Duff 1971, 210; my emphasis).

This political meeting, this self-regarding "mirror," is already a retrospective on the movement community's part, celebrating its energetic, near instant history, and the "crazy mix up" of performance and politics became central to the CND style. This was also very clearly an *organized* chaos, capturing the moving spirit of Aldermaston within the confines of the Albert Hall.

Jazz music and musicians played their part in the campaign. The trumpeter, critic, and broadcaster Humphrey Lyttelton, who had started out in the New Orleans revival in George Webb's band of the 1940s (the upper-class exception to the band's predominantly working-class membership), was a regular supporter, and indeed, according to Jeff Nuttall, a member of the Barnet branch of CND (personal interview, 2001). In 1960 the jazz singer George Melly was an original member of the Committee of 100, and he was arrested and fined at one of the movement's mass civil disobedience sit-ins in central London (personal interview, 2002). Ian Campbell, better known from the folk scene of the 1960s, traces the development and intertwining of music and

4. Humphrey Lyttelton (far left) and Jeff Nuttall blowing for Barnet CND and *Peace News*, London, 1960.

movement: "It is significant that 1958, the year that saw the climactic boom in jazz popularity, also produced the first Aldermaston march. The jazz revival and the rise of CND were more than coincidental; they were almost two sides of the same coin. Similar social attitudes and positive humanist values informed them both. At any jazz event a liberal sprinkling of CND badges, and perhaps even leaflets and posters, would be in evidence; conversely, at every CND demonstration live jazz music set the tempo for the march" (Campbell 1983, 115).

The live jazz that set the tempo for the Aldermaston marches was invariably provided by some form of brass band, however loosely that might be defined: marchers "stepped to the parade jazz of a New-Orleans-style marching band beneath the black flag of Anarchism" (Oliver 1990b, 81). Is it too fanciful to suggest that Aldermaston was a (greyer, colder) British Mardi Gras, "our own brisk little wrong-end-of-the-telescope version of New Orleans," in Philip Larkin's description (1985, 78)? The promenading into Trafalgar Square at the end of the march beginning in 1959, when marchers and sympathizers formed huge crowds led by the uniformed parade stepping of the Omega Brass Band, with behind them any number of bands and musicians blazing out jazz and other musics, must have felt powerfully carnivalesque.

Playing his own cornet loudly, Jeff Nuttall was attracted to the youth contingent of "Colyer fans . . . [who] appeared from nowhere in their grime and tatters, with their slogan daubed crazy hats and streaming filthy hair . . . blowing their antiquated cornets and sousaphones. . . . It was this wild public festival spirit that spread the CND symbol through all the jazz clubs and secondary schools in an incredibly short time. *Protest was associated with festivity*" (Nuttall 1968, 51; my emphasis).

On the marches there was a mixture of professional, ad hoc, and amateur New Orleans brass bands. Steve Lane, a cornetist with over fifty years' playing experience who had been a member of the Communist Party before the Second World War and after the war relaunched *Jazz Music*, then the moribund magazine of an anarchist-influenced organization called the Jazz Sociological Society, led a band on "three or four" marches: "John Minnion rang me up and asked if I could put a band together. I would ring around a bit and get some good musicians together. Some might have been going on the march anyway. One year, the first we did it I think, going to London [*viz.* in 1959 at the earliest], they put the band at the back of the march, so that all the people would be able to hear it—there didn't seem much point in having us leading it, blowing ahead to no one. After one or two of those, they decided to have the band marching from the front, give it a bit of focus. *Then* came the innovation of us playing on the pavement, as the marchers passed by. That made it a lot easier for us as musicians, not having to play *and* march for hours" (personal interviews, 2001, 2002).

Jeff Nuttall's experience of brass band playing at Aldermaston was characteristically less authentic still, blurring British military and American jazz band traditions, and taking advantage of the satirical opportunities of performance and place: "I was part of the so-called Aldermaston Jazz Band. We played 'Land of Hope and Glory,' badly and ironically. It was our aggressively satirical version of the tune, played at Parliament Square at the end of the march in I think 1959. We set up outside the Ministry of Defence as part of the Aldermaston show. Ours was a Portsmouth Sinfonia version, as only [the cornetist] Dougie Gray knew the tune! It was received by the passing marchers with the understanding the Woodstock audience would have a decade later listening to Hendrix playing 'The star-spangled banner.' We were anti-royalist, anti-military, anti-pomp, but no we were not anti-American. We were not pro-empire either, a sort of 'comic' nostalgia maybe" (personal interview, 2001).

5. The Aldermaston Jazz Band, including the English eccentrics the Alberts (brothers Dougie Gray on pocket cornet with whippet, Tony Gray on piccolo trombone), with the Temperance Seven's Martin Fry (between them on sousaphone) and Jeff Nuttall (trumpet, their left), CND Aldermaston march, 1959 or 1960.

In their different ways, Lane and Nuttall foreground the importance of repertoire and setting for the performance. For Lane's band, the initial choice was between being heard and being seen, combined with the choice whether the music was primarily for participants or for observers: playing at the rear of the march meant that the music projected onto the marchers, for their benefit, while playing at the front meant that there was a visual focus, more oriented to outside observers. Nuttall's was more of an informed, contumacious gesture: playing Elgar's Victorian march at the end of a kind of peace march seems both to question and to confirm the mock (post-)imperial position of many of the younger CND-ers, and playing it *badly* outside the Ministry of Defence was a critical defamiliarization. More than that, it marked a moment when British jazz praxis engaged with African American signifying. On other occasions too, musicians displayed sensitivity to their surroundings through their performances. For example, the film *March to Aldermaston* shows the marchers walking in silence as they leave Trafalgar Square on Good Friday and again on the approach to the nuclear facilities at Aldermaston on Easter Monday (the narrator explains the significance of the silences). The musicians' use of dynamics underlines the marchers' reflexive awareness of performance, the carnival's undermining of the distinction between outsider and participant. It is important also to stress the very space of performance, and its accessibility to people who wanted, and others even who did not want, to hear the music: open-air music in the streets destroys the enclosure — (re)claims the street — and challenges the hierarchy of concert and club. Colin Barker recalls experiencing a brass band led by Colyer as a teenager in Essex in 1958 or 1959: "It felt like a rebellion [just] marching through respectable Barkingside High Street with that band" (personal correspondence, 2002).[8]

The ad hoc nature of the bands led by Lane and Nuttall militated against the formal wearing of uniforms, and Colin Bowden, one of the surviving members of the Omega Brass Band, explains that the Omega's early efforts at such authentic New Orleans touches were less than convincing: "We never practiced the shuffle or stepping. No, none of that. In fact it was a shambles, that side of it! In the very early days the effort at being authentic, with uniforms and performance and all, was absolutely minimal — it was always, for the musicians, the music first and foremost. The uniform was basically black trousers, white shirt and tie, and a peaked cap. Ken worked for London Transport at the time, and he managed to get a load of London bus drivers' or conductors' caps, and we used them for the uniform. [Laughs]" (personal interview, 2002).

The terrifically mundane combination of signifiers recalled by Bowden — New Orleans parade band topped by something from a red double-decker bus — may stand as an emblematic moment in transatlantic cultural exchange around jazz in Britain, not unlike the English bowler hat adopted by "pre-atomic" Acker Bilk (Melly 1970, 60) and identified by Philip Larkin as curiously iconic. Yet I think Bowden underplays the visual impact that even a limited uniform and choreography could have: in photographs of marches the Omega always stands out, partly because the band always led — but then it may have deserved to lead precisely because of its visual and musical confidence. Also, it was not strictly a marching music: rather a step-march or shuffle was the aim of the band — perhaps the "syncopated sensibility" that Les Back suggests as an anti-totalitarian movement of the jazz body (Back 2001,

6. The Original Superlative Omega Brass Band, with Ken Colyer (far left) and Colin Bowden (snare drum), CND Aldermaston march, late 1950s or early 1960s.

193). The music did attract people too: the jazz historian and photographer Val Wilmer was an enthusiastic member of "the second line" on two Aldermaston marches: "We joined the 1960 march on the final day, as it came into London. Ken Colyer's Omega Brass Band played — that was a good occasion for them. The bowler hat with a CND symbol on the front was a big fashion item on the marches then — after Acker Bilk was no. 1 in the charts at the time. In 1961 I did the whole march, sleeping in school halls along the route. Lots of brass bands played — there were always bands playing. They made the event more appealing. I did go on the march for CND, but the bands were an exciting extra. We'd always try to be behind a band on the march, we'd position ourselves with an ear on the music" (personal interview, 2002).

The awkward, stubborn figure of Ken Colyer reappears in different people's narratives of New Orleans jazz and Aldermaston. Though he had led an informal parade band in England before his American adventure, Colyer was inspired by the funeral parades he saw in New Orleans in 1952–53, featuring the Young Tuxedo Band and the Eureka

Brass Band (Colyer 1970). This experience produced within a couple of years of his return the Omega Brass Band, its members uniformed and capped (with OMEGA on their hatbands, and LEADER on his), step-marching in time, playing what was thought of as a wide and authentic repertoire. Bowden, the Omega's original snare drummer, traces its origins and practice:

The Omega Brass Band was formed for the first Soho Fair, held on 1 June 1955. The way it happened was Ken [Colyer] and Sonny Morris, who'd both been together as trumpeters in the Crane River Band a few years before, each now led a six-piece New Orleans band. They put these two together to produce a marching band for the Soho Fair, with musicians swapping instruments as necessary.

There had been street bands before, and the Cranes had done things like carnivals and fairs, but that was sitting on the backs of lorries, or playing at the side, with banjos and so on. There had never been marching jazz bands up till then, not proper New Orleans style, like the ones Ken had seen doing funerals in New Orleans. So yes, we were the first—Ken's band set the pattern for the whole British scene. Others like the New Taeo Brass Band came along later.

The lineup of the Omega varied considerably—but would generally feature some mix of two trumpets, two trombones, clarinet, E-flat horn, tenor and alto saxophone, sousaphone, and snare and bass drums. Head arrangements were the main repertoire. We didn't have books of arrangements written out for us to read as we marched. We played by ear. The brass band played what the ordinary band played, so we knew all the tunes from our normal repertoire. (Personal interview, 2002)

Aldermaston was a grand occasion for the Omega Brass Band, evidenced by its expansion for the occasion, and the presence of a significant "second line" of CND-ers and parade marchers following along, as Bowden remembers: "when Omega turned up to play the last mile of those marches, we would try to have a bigger line up than normal—three trumpets, three trombones, that sort of thing. And on the Aldermaston marches we'd always have a mass of fans behind us, marching with us" (personal interview, 2002). Writing in 1958, David Boulton speculates on the cultural and political potential of the parade band, of this *jazz in the streets* of Britain: "Ken Colyer's experiments with the

Omega Brass Band and his attempts to establish a British marching style could spark off such a new music. If we were to bring jazz out into the streets of our towns and cities, reviving the functions and parades which characterised old New Orleans, then jazz might once again develop a music of the people, moving perhaps from jazz as we know it to a new and self-contained urban folk-music" (Boulton 1958, 137).

As we have seen, the reinvigorated "music of the people" that Boulton desires (presumably after Finkelstein 1948) was, in its original African American form, precisely that. It is clear that Colyer and the many other musicians who played jazz in formal and ad hoc brass bands for anti-nuclear and left demonstrations and rallies were not only importing and imitating an exoticized practice, they were also recognizing, even *extending*, the sociopolitical tradition of that type of music making. John Hutnyk makes a useful distinction between the negative hermeneutic of "imitation" and "derivation" in global music and a less reductive, potentially liberatory acknowledgment that *solidarities* can be recognized across quite different sociocultural formations (Hutnyk 2000, 214).[9] Colyer felt that he was taking on the mantle of the New Orleans parade tradition, and trying to create a new audience for that music, a gesture of solidarity: "As I watched the street parades in New Orleans I noticed the reaction of the different age groups. The older people really enjoyed the music, and the children were just crazy about it, laughing and dancing along the roadside. But the teenagers and young men showed no emotion whatsoever. . . . Unless a new generation comes up that can break away from this pattern and look at things objectively and realise the social bug is not important, the genuine home grown New Orleans jazz will die with the last of the old masters" (Colyer 1989, 62).

The excited second line following Omega at the Soho Fairs and the Aldermaston marches is compelling evidence of Colyer's fulfilled ambition: there was some success in his project to present parade music to a new generation of teenagers and young people. They embraced it then, and the enthusiasm spread. Provincial political cultures in Britain show that it is possible to trace significant leftist jazz street music. In Bristol, for example, the Great Western Marching Band would often be found accompanying political demonstrations, while "the Pioneer Jazzmen played in the cellar of the Communist Club in Lawfords Gate. The band started around 1961 . . . [and in brass band form] were much sought after to be the vanguard of the many gatherings that took place

7. Omega Brass Band, CND Aldermaston march, with grand
marshal (far left) and rather stylish "second line" (right), late
1950s or early 1960s.

in the city at that time. Supporters of Anti-Apartheid, Human Rights,
CND and Trades Union activities were often cheered by the band's presence" (Hibberd 2000, 29).

Modern jazzers would become interested too. In the early 1970s
Mike Westbrook's Brass Band project developed into a conscious effort
to re-present some elements of the earlier New Orleans street band
tradition, interestingly crossed with the British brass band tradition.
Looking to aspects of community theater and the carnivalesque, the
Brass Band, soon including more sophisticated arrangements by the
likes of the free jazz trombonist Paul Rutherford (who had started out
in the 1950s playing around in amateur New Orleans bands: Wickes
1999, 42), began to play further outside the jazz circuit—at communist
gatherings, in housing estates, outside factories, as well as at theater and
community festivals. (See also chapter 4 on the relation between performance and environment in the late counterculture, and for greater
detail on the Westbrook Brass Band.)

It is possible to see in this important but hitherto neglected part

8. The Pioneer Jazz Band, regulars at the cellar of the Communist Club, preparing to accompany an anti-nuclear demonstration, Bristol, late 1950s or early 1960s.

of the traditional and revivalist scenes of the 1950s not (just) the sub-urban "safe" mentality of Little England, not (just) tea on mowed lawns, conservative nostalgia, and a bleaching or romanticization of a culture of struggle, but also an early contribution to what Baz Kershaw, in *The Politics of Performance*, has called "the typical counter-cultural thrust of celebratory protest" (1992, 68) characteristic of the 1960s. One can also see an influence on movements, through the efforts not only of the Westbrooks as described above but also of someone like Jeff Nuttall, who moved from blowing his cornet at Aldermaston to taking part in the People Show, a quasi-"happening" that from the mid-1960s fea-tured the improvising People Band. As one of several carnivalesque developments in Britain at the time—the Soho Fairs of the mid-1950s, the Beaulieu Jazz Festivals of 1956–61, and an early Caribbean carnival in Notting Hill, London, in 1959 are others associated with popular music (see McKay 2000a)—Aldermaston stands out as the most clearly politicized, and it was New Orleans jazz that most noticeably accom-panied the protest. In *Bomb Culture* Nuttall argues that the choice by

British musicians and activists of this organic music "was a natural re-action after the harsh metal of war" (1968, 42).[10] Nuttall elaborated to me on "*primitivism* as a mode of the times. For CND-ers, for trad, it sig-nified in the nomadic gesture of Aldermaston, in the barefoot dancing to acoustic music. . . . A great cult of dirt—black jeans, duffle coats or donkey jackets, straggly hair, unkempt" (personal interview, 2001).[11] The embracing of New Orleans jazz exemplifies the strong backward-looking tendency of CND and the early Green movement. In many ways traditional and revivalist jazz did blow against "the presentist bias of modern society" (Veldman 1994, 306). But interwoven problemati-cally within this reading is the position of that presentist society par ex-cellence, the United States, and its export cultures, and related British fears of Americanization and standardization. From Veldman's choice of J. R. R. Tolkien to the communist-inspired folk music revival, tra-ditional national cultures are reemployed for a new or alternative na-tional identity across romantic protest, which in the 1950s and early 1960s meant CND. "The sense of national identity," Veldman continues, "was often accompanied by anti-Americanism. To these romantic crit-ics the United States represented the future to avoid, a society devoted to growth and speed and endless change, a nation without a sense of tradition, a collection of individuals rather than a community. . . . Anti-Americanism linked the concern for Britain's identity and role in the world . . . [to] antimaterialism" (Veldman 1994, 306).

As we have seen, jazz complicates this one-way gaze (see McKay 2000b). "Traddies" and CND-ers found in their version of this Ameri-can music the very attributes that Veldman suggests they thought were missing from American society: not speed but walking, continuity, tra-dition, community, anti-commercialism. There is at least one further irony. While one brass band culture in Britain began to flourish, an-other was wilting. The long-standing British tradition of working-class and Salvationist brass band playing seems not to have been of any inter-est to the novel New Orleans bands like Omega, New Taeo, and Great Western that formed after 1955. In fact, Dave Russell notes, "under the impact of the 'Americanization' of popular music, the brass band, that most British of musical institutions, had lost its privileged position in the popular musical culture of industrial Britain" (2000, 108–9). The composer Hubert Bath observed of the national brass band festival in 1930, "It was a joy to me as a musician to know that the musical back-

9. "British youth say NO to nuclear suicide": Nuttall (trumpet) leads an ad hoc trad jazz ensemble on a CND march, late 1950s or early 1960s.

bone of our country, north of Luton, is not and, it is hoped, never will be at the mercy of the American invasion. The breath of our good, honest, fresh brass air from the north was, and always will be, an invigorating tonic to the jaded, Americanised southerner" (quoted in Russell 2000, 112). A quarter of a century and a world war later, it was those Americanized southerners, led by Ken Colyer, who were blowing their own "good, honest, fresh brass air"—new musicians, new audiences, new brass band music, New Orleans.

BEAULIEU JAZZ FESTIVALS (1956–61): THE PAST AND THE PASTORAL

We're festival crazy!

In the past five years, we have gone Festival crazy. From Lord Montagu's late-lamented brainchild, the Beaulieu Jazz Festival, a whole industry has grown. Bands, which used to look upon the summer as the slack season, now find themselves on a dozen or more well-paid Festival dates. . . . The National Jazz Festivals at Richmond,

Earlswood and Ringwood are now among the firmly established
annual events. —*MELODY MAKER*, "Guide to a Swinging Summer"
(2 June 1962)[12]

It is not a coincidence that some of the first seeds of alternative and
youth culture in the context of festival were themselves beginning to
germinate during the late 1950s.[13] It is easy to lose sight of that decade, the 1950s, to caricature it as one of austerity or conformity, or to
be blinded by the psychedelia that came after it. Yet it is important to
consider the extent to which festival culture as it is understood today
originates during that time. Music (New Orleans jazz, later skiffle),
youth, radical politics (CND, direct action), and the festival or carnival itself (Beaulieu Jazz Festival, the Aldermaston CND marches)—
we are seeing that all four familiar features found a crucial early expression and combination in Britain during the 1950s. In the summer
of 1956 Edward John Barrington Douglas-Scott-Montagu, known as
Lord Montagu of Beaulieu, held a modest open-air jazz concert in the
grounds of his stately home within the ancient royal English landscape
of the New Forest, in Hampshire, to an audience of around four hundred local jazz fans. Montagu was an unorthodox young peer of the
realm, recently released from prison after two sensational homosexuality trials and a conviction in the early 1950s (see Montagu 2000).[14]
He had loved jazz from an early age: while at Eton during the Second World War he attended jam sessions featuring his older friend,
the trumpeter Humphrey Lyttelton, who was convalescing from battle
injuries (Montagu 2000, 52). In the same year that Ken Colyer was enjoying his authenticating initiation to New Orleans jazz *in situ*—on a
Merchant Navy ship and in the local jail—Montagu experienced Mardi
Gras 1953, but from a very different class position: "Since I was staying at the British Consulate I tried to behave circumspectly but I was
virtually forced to go to the formal balls. . . . I tried to get away from
these events as soon as I could and used to leave a bag with jeans and
casual clothes in the cloakroom, then change and go on to the more
amusing bars and jazz clubs in the city" (Montagu 2000, 92–93). To
escape his class, even in America, required dressing down and digging
out the jazz.

Over the next five years Beaulieu would become one of Europe's
earliest and highest-profile jazz festivals, and certainly the prototype

for many of the events and problems associated with pop festivals and youth music gatherings in Britain over the following decades. What follows are glimpses of an alternative originary narrative of British pop, not from the Beatles via Germany and Liverpool but from deepest green Hampshire, not so much through the blues and rock 'n' roll but through New Orleans jazz, not so much embodied by Teddy Boys dancing to rock 'n' roll as by the "rave gear" of "traddies." Though they have usually been overlooked, the Beaulieu festivals fit (or perhaps they set) the carnivalesque template of youth, music, protest, and identity developments of the time (in approximate chronological order): the Soho Fair, Teddy Boys, the Aldermaston marches, the beginnings of Trinidadian carnival in London, and early mod and rocker clashes. Iain Chambers describes some of the developing youth cultures of the period as "an attempt, if you like, to show that what is recognizable in British life need not be bound to [George Orwell's] 'solid breakfasts and gloomy Sundays, smoky towns and winding roads, green fields and red pillar boxes.' . . . These youth groups adapted their styles from consumer objects, . . . their cultural insubordination was allied to consumerism that touched a very un-British hedonism as it 'squandered' its money on extravagant clothing, pop records, scooters, overpriced frothy coffee, motor bikes, drugs, clubs, and attempts to create a perpetual 'weekend' " (Chambers 1986, 53). Beaulieu touched, was touched by, both these versions of Britain, the past and the future, rural nostalgia and urban clubbing, sensible breakfasts at party weekends.

I have written elsewhere of the revivalist aspects of pop festival culture in Britain, of the ways in which many new festivals and carnivals sought to authenticate and *atavize* their existence by echoing or re-presenting now-lost traditional events or rituals or indeed myths (McKay 1996, ch. 1). This pattern is evident in some of the most significant urban and rural festival events in Britain today (see McKay 2000a). For example, the Notting Hill Carnival has twin early strands: Trinidadian carnival in London first organized by West Indian migrants in 1959, and the revived (with a twist) Victorian fair at Notting Hill, in part organized by the alternative community in the mid-1960s. Glastonbury Festival, first held in minor form in 1970 but really an event that began in the 1980s, was invariably timed for the weekend nearest the summer solstice (21 June) and marketed with a heady mixture of medievalism, from Arthurian legend and Avalon to ley lines, and as late as the 1990s a newly constructed stone circle in Neolithic style. As Hobsbawm's and Ranger's classic *The Invention of Tradition* (1983) has taught us, such *faux past* gestures of reference or invention are not only variously ahistorical or nostalgic or utopian—or just cod-folkloric—they can also be signs of competing versions of Englishness, possibly even reclamations of alternative traditions or visions of the past.

The first Beaulieu Jazz Festival was something of an echo, a conscious revival of the local Beaulieu Fairs of the nineteenth century which had, perhaps ominously, been finally ended owing to the "loosely organised rowdyism" of fairgoers (Montagu 1973, 72). *Melody Maker*, keen to puff the jazz festival because of its own organizational links with it, identified some of its retro appeal in 1958 in a description of the festival as "the blending of the music of today with memories of centuries gone by" (9 August). But Montagu, taking control of the estate at the age of twenty-five after it had been held in trust for the two decades following his father's death, was eager to revive other defunct local customs as well: in 1959 an audit dinner was held again for tenant farmers on the estate, and plans for the revival of Beaulieu Easter Fair were announced in November 1960. For Montagu, reaching into the past was a way of bridging the interregnum—while the lengthy period until he inherited direct control of the estate effectively magnified the past's significance. His motivation for such gestures was strongly to revivify manorial authority and his place at the center of that: after all, other stately homes in the interwar period had been in financial crisis, or architecturally crumbling, or, worse, would be handed over to the state in lieu of taxes. The young Montagu, who had only relatively recently inherited, would have to be flexible if he was to survive and prosper through the partial "collapse" of the upper class, the "relative decline of the significance of landed wealth, and the increasing diversity of wealth" (McKibbin 1998, 42). He saw those twin icons of transatlantic modernity, cars and jazz, as the means of diversification to protect his privileged patch and past of England, his eight thousand acres. Old English and New World cultures would be brought together at the festival—not quite the dairy imperative and pastoral promise of Max Yasgur's farm at Woodstock in 1969, or even Michael Eavis's farm at Glastonbury in 1970 come to that. But for a time it worked, to the extent that the jazz critic Benny Green could observe in 1962: "It seems likely that the festival has now superseded the concert as the highest degree of respectability in the jazz world. To the evolutionary progress from brothel to ginmill to dancehall to podium must now be added the greensward" (*Observer*, 19 August).[15]

Of course the past was everywhere at Beaulieu, in the New Forest. This landscape and community formed an atavistic social and cultural space all its own. Beaulieu was an extraordinary, and extraordinarily rural, site for the continued negotiation with modernity that was taking place during the period in Britain (possibly more especially England): a slow embracing of speed cultures. A key visual and functional icon of modernity (the motor car) was championed, but for its vintage, its heritage; a key sonic signifier of modernity (jazz music) was championed, but with a major glance to its past forms, specifically traditional and revivalist jazz, which Kevin Morgan has described neatly as "the newest and the oldest sound in British jazz" (Morgan 1998, 123).[16] This incongruity, achronology, remains part of Beaulieu's charm today, for motor car enthusiasts at least: visitors to the motor museum gaze at a record-breaking speed machine inside, while a New Forest pony walks through a wooded glade framed in the picture glazing outside. For other visitors, the extraordinary romantic landscape of wild ponies, open heathland, and willow, oak, and birch forests and glades is a powerful touristic experience of a *special*, *boundaried*, and *historic* rurality.

So the stately home of Beaulieu is better known today for its motor museum than for its early flourish of festival culture. Yet Beaulieu, like Woburn in the 1960s and the better-known Knebworth Festivals of the 1970s (Cobbold 1986), began a connection of aristocratic privilege and popular music, of private means and mass entertainment, that characterized a certain social stratum of those swinging times. "A combination of blue blood and the blues" was the Beaulieu motto in 1957, while a banner over the festival stage read, "Harmless amusement for all classes." Partly it was generational (Montagu was around thirty years old at the time of the first Beaulieu jazz concert), partly a social shift, as Christopher Booker recognizes: there was "intimate cooperation between members of the crumbling old order and of the rising new — each fascinated by the powerful image of the other: the insecure lower or less 'established' group longing for the style and stability of culture and breeding, the insecure upper group mesmerised by the life and vitality of the *arriviste*" (Booker 1969, 95). For Jeremy Sandford, in the

BEAULIEU JAZZ FESTIVAL

29th and 30th JULY, 1961

ON THE LAWNS OF

PALACE HOUSE
BEAULIEU

IN THE HEART OF THE NEW FOREST

AMONG THE BANDS AND ARTISTS APPEARING ARE THE FOLLOWING

SATURDAY

AFTERNOON	EVENING
2.30 TO 5.30 p.m.	7.30 p.m. TO MIDNIGHT
	JOHNNY DANKWORTH AND HIS ORCHESTRA
	JOE HARRIOTT QUINTET
	DOWNBEAT BIG BAND
CHRIS BARBER'S JAZZBAND	TUBBY HAYES QUARTET
WITH OTTALIE PATTERSON	HANS KOLLER (German Guest Star)
	ANITA O'DAY (American Guest Star)

SUNDAY

AFTERNOON	EVENING
2.30 TO 5.30 p.m.	7.30 p.m. TO MIDNIGHT
JOHNNY DANKWORTH AND HIS ORCHESTRA	KENNY BALL'S JAZZ BAND
THE VIC ASH—HARRY KLEIN JAZZ FIVE	FAIRWEATHER-BROWN ALL-STARS
ALLAN GANLEY—KEITH CHRISTY JAZZMAKERS	DICK CHARLESWORTH AND HIS CITY GENTS with Jackie Lynn
ANITA O'DAY (American Guest Star)	TERRY LIGHTFOOT AND HIS NEW ORLEANS JAZZMEN
HANS KOLLER (German Guest Star)	MICK MULLIGAN & HIS BAND with George Melly
	BOB WALLIS AND HIS STORYVILLE JAZZMEN
	BRUCE TURNER JUMP BAND

ADMISSION

SINGLE   AFTERNOON 7/6d.   EVENING 12/6d.

PARTIES (15 or more)   AFTERNOON 6/–d.   EVENING 10/6d.

SEASON TICKETS (Admit to all four Performances £1-12-6d. not transferable)

10. Advertising the pastoral appeal of the final Beaulieu Jazz Festival of 1961: "on the lawns of Palace House . . . in the heart of the New Forest."

first book to chronicle the British pop festival movement, *Tomorrow's People*, the Beaulieu in 1958 was "the first British festival proper, a two-day event that attracted 4,000 people" (Sandford and Reid 1974, 14). In the following year five to ten thousand people attended, and the first vocal complaints about the inconvenience and the type of person the festival was attracting were heard from Beaulieu and other nearby villages. But as I have explained, by this time British jazz was torn not only between revivalists and traditionalist purists but between these together on one side and the relatively new modernists on the other—and a battle was going to be held.

The new romantic lifestyles, rural excursions and incursions, musics and fashions, temporary communities of festivals and marches, competing versions of Englishness and the past that I am writing of and that I have linked as Beaulieu and Aldermaston do not always behave. For peace is not always easy during carnival, not when subcultural contestation imbricates carnivalesque transgression: "The near riot at the Beaulieu Jazz Festival on Saturday . . . was a disgraceful affair. There are those who criticise Africans and who say that such people will never be fit to govern themselves. But a tribal dance to the sound of a tom-tom has a more civilised air than this modern wreck and roll to the beat of the jazz drum" (*Bradford Telegraph and Argus*, 1 August 1960).

At the festival in 1960 the trad clarinetist and somehow pop star Acker Bilk entered on a Model-T Ford, courtesy of the Motor Museum. By the end of Saturday night, vehicles had been targeted by festival goers for destruction—I resist calling this an early anti-car protest—that is too utopian an argument even for me. While Acker played, *jazdup* youth climbed a scaffolding lighting rig and removed horses from the roundabout stage, mounting them on rigging as they climbed.[17] A storage shed was set alight, and a 1921 fourteen-seater charabanc had its hood burned. Over the Saturday night riot thirty-nine people were injured, none seriously, though two people were subsequently jailed for assaulting police officers. For George Melly, however, "it wasn't a vicious riot. It was stupid. The traddies in rave gear booing the [modern jazz John] Dankworth Band. A young man climbing up the outside of the palace in the floodlights waving a bowler hat from the battlements. Cheers and scuffles" (1965, 239). Others viewed exuberant youth quite differently. Kenneth Allsop in the *Daily Mail* asked his readers:

Why do the Ravers rave? At which point do enthusiasm and high jinks twist into the urge to hate and destroy? . . .

Whacky dress and wild fun do not necessarily spell delinquency. Yet for a certain product of our Affluent Society this seems to have become a rebel's uniform of viciousness—and the degree is fine between beating-up a jazz festival and beating-up Negroes in Notting Hill and Jews in Germany. (1 August 1960)

For some of those activists and idealistic jazz fans who had been on the Aldermaston march a few months earlier it must have come as a surprise to be now compared to racists and fascists. But Allsop's point is perhaps more a symptom of a common English unease with American popular culture (it was Teddy Boys, apparently inflamed by the new sounds of rock 'n' roll, who beat up London's black youth), or with unfamiliar mass events such as these new youth festivals. Montagu himself said that "You'd need a policeman in every garden" in Beaulieu village if the festival was to be held again (Beaulieu Film Archive, 1961)— hardly the image of pastoral promise to transmit.

Beaulieu in 1960 was important too because it was an early example of the mediation of subcultural panic. Jazz from the festival was filmed and broadcast live on BBC television, and on the BBC Light Programme radio network. During the riot on Saturday night, the live broadcast was cut by six minutes, an interruption prefaced by an anxious BBC live commentator saying: "Things are getting quite out of hand. [pause] It is obvious things cannot continue like this." A commandeered BBC microphone was used to broadcast a shout from one fan for "More beer for the workers!" An apologetic spokesperson for the BBC was quoted in the next morning's press: "We have had a lot of telephone calls from viewers who thought the scenes were disgraceful" (*Sunday Express*, 31 July 1960). On the other hand, the *News of the World* was happy to report to its readers that its switchboard had been jammed with calls from television viewers wanting to know what was happening (31 July 1960). The "BEATNIK BEAT-UP," as it was headlined in one newspaper, was reported in the Commonwealth and world press—in South Africa, the United States, Argentina, Gibraltar, Australia, Kenya, Canada, Italy, Germany, France. The combination of aristocracy and jazz madness was an outstanding popular story of English eccentricity run, literally, riot. The Battle of Beaulieu was in part a symptom of jazz purists' investment in their particular form: subcultural tensions between traditional jazz fans and modernists were evident, as in the infamous traddies' slogan on placards held up at concerts, "GO HOME DIRTY BOPPER."[18] We would do well here to remember, as E. Taylor Atkins observes wryly, that "our comfortable characterization of jazz as a 'universal language' fails to do justice to the conflicts the music ignited around the world" (Atkins 2001, 121). This may explain the irreparable damage inflicted on the instrument of Acker Bilk's banjoist: the banjo was truly despised by modernists. The riot was also a demonstration of the cumulative sense of empowerment that the collective identities of groups attending the event each year developed with it—the carnival beginning to blur the distinction between participant and observer, as well as to challenge and invert the social hierarchy. Here the minor manifestations of transgression at the festivals of 1959 and 1961 should be acknowledged too. Also important, though, was the presence of the media—the camera as inflaming device—and its privileged space at the event in 1960—the camera as intrusion. Jeremy Sandford notes this: "Montagu had been criticised for giving too much space to T.V. cameras, and of thinking too much of the T.V. technicians and too little of his audiences. . . . The BBC had also been accused of a prissy and somewhat condescending attitude 'to unsafe things like Youth and Jazz' " (Sandford and Reid 1974, 14). For Mick Farren too, the Beaulieu festivals were "primitive mini-Woodstocks that reached media attention when *the audience took offence at being filmed as though they were sociological exhibits* and turned over BBC TV cameras" (Farren and Barker 1972, no pagination; my emphasis).

From the beginning of the 1960s the Richmond Jazz Festivals, organized under the aegis of Harold Pendleton's National Jazz Federation (NJF), illustrate the trajectory of jazz as a precursor of festival culture. Not unlike Michael Eavis in subsequent decades with his Glastonbury Festival (see McKay 2000a, ch. 5; Elstob and Howes 1987), Pendleton was skilled in identifying changing tastes in popular music, and in booking newer bands. As he observed of the Richmond festival of 1965, "Over the past year or so the hit parade has been getting crowded with groups whose roots are in jazz" (quoted in Sandford and Reid 1974, 20). He learned this through his involvement in both the Marquee Club in Soho and some of the later Beaulieu Jazz Festivals. The Richmond Festivals are significant, as they encapsulate the musical and social trans-

11. Poster for the festival, 1960, which saw inflamed jazz fans conduct the "Battle of Beaulieu" in an early manifestation of subcultural tensions.

formation of the time; in the space of a few years in the early 1960s, the shift is from the New Orleans jazz and blues of Acker Bilk, Ken Colyer, and Alex Welsh toward the new popular music—and audience—of the blues-oriented bands such as the Rolling Stones, the Yardbirds, and Manfred Mann. The NJF festival in 1965 marked the moment when this change in youth consciousness, music, instrumentation, and style became most clear, as the festival publicity articulated: "Something unheard of is happening at Richmond . . . for the first time . . . the pure jazz-men are outnumbered by beat and rhythm-and-blues groups who are no stranger to the hit parade. . . . [The festival is] something of a teenagers' Ascot, the only social occasion on a national scale when they can 'try out' new clothes" (quoted in Sandford and Reid 1974, 20). The shift from jazz to rock music is identified as a wider manifestation by Dennis Dworkin: "Rock music in the sixties and seventies came to express the experience of a generation as powerfully as any form of artistic experience in the twentieth century; during the same period, jazz was more acclaimed in art circles than in the urban neighbourhoods in which it originated" (Dworkin 1997, 120). The guitarist with the Who, Pete Townsend, perhaps combining nostalgia with retrospective self-criticism, saw weaknesses in this move: "Something happened between the trad age and rock. In the trad age there were great people doing great things, founding CND or Amnesty, and trying to mobilize young people. But then the whole subject of politics and the power of the individual to effect change was buried under this tidal wave of rock" (quoted in Denselow 1990, 93).

The events at Richmond featured most of the familiar elements of festival culture, for both its proponents and opponents, as outlined by Michael Clarke in *The Politics of Pop Festivals*: "The invasion of large numbers of young people into the pleasanter parts of the countryside for a weekend or a week in the summer, to camp in the open, listen to music, usually loud, sometimes to consume drugs, and in the context of the espousal of overtly bohemian values, involving attitudes to property and sexuality, for example, that are at gross variance with those of the local population, is inevitably a strong base for opposition" (Clarke 1982, 11). It should be emphasized that the majority of these common features were inherited from Beaulieu, and expected by audiences as a result of their experiences at the festival or their mediated images of it. Christopher Booker's claim in 1961 that the "prospect for the pro-

moters of jazz festivals during the sober sixties seems happily 'cool'"
was only partly correct: jazz festivals did indeed wane, but the decade
was hardly to be characterized (or mythicized) by sobriety, and festivals were to become a central form of social expression and gathering
(*Sunday Telegraph*, 23 July 1961).

There is a (retrospectively) intriguing coda to the Beaulieu Jazz Festivals. For 1962, an article in the *Daily Mail* describes the extraordinary
early invention of a proto-free festival, of the kind organized extensively
in Britain in the 1970s and early 1980s. The description indicates the
distance between festival organizers and festival goers, and the increasing autonomy of carnival:

> Like Frankenstein, Lord Montagu of Beaulieu has created a mon-
> ster from which, it seems, there is no escape.
>
> After the beatnik riots last year Lord Montagu vowed: "There
> will never again be a jazz festival at Beaulieu."
>
> But last night he told me that he has had to appeal to the police
> for protection from the jazz beatniks, who threaten to descend on
> the picturesque, Hampshire village again. Thousands of leaflets have
> been distributed in Chelsea exhorting the "trads" and "moderns" to
> turn up in force on August 4 "for a free rave to the bitter end."
>
> The leaflets, signed "Pete the Brolly," read: "If you can play any
> musical instrument please bring it with you and help make a suc-
> cessful weekend for every one. Spread the news and rave on." (*Daily
> Mail*, 16 May 1962)

The uncertainty of this putative Beaulieu free festival's countercultural or subcultural construction — it veers in its embryonic way between an alternative gathering or "free rave" and a showdown "to the
bitter end," of the mods-versus-rockers variety, between competing
jazz fans — should not detract from its importance as an early manifestation of more radical DiY youth culture (see McKay 1998). It also
provides evidence of the emotional and social investment that the audiences at Beaulieu developed in making the festival their own over the
years when it ran, even to the extent of claiming it as their own autonomous event. The newspaper returned to the story a month later, when
the real identity of the white beatnik Pete the Brolly (complete with
goatee beard and a small signifier of English eccentricity, a monocle,

though no umbrella, I think) became clear at a court appearance after, of course, a drug bust. Outside a London court, having been fined £10 for possession of cannabis found during a raid on the candlelit Chelsea jazz club Café des Artistes, Pete the Brolly owned up: "I am the cat who has been distributing thousands of leaflets in Chelsea and throughout the country exhorting anyone who can play a musical instrument to come to an unofficial Beaulieu jazz festival on August 4" (*Daily Mail*, 9 June 1962). Pete the Brolly, also known as Peter Dawson, aged thirty, said from his office in Holborn just after being visited by two police officers: "This is really awful man, but awful. . . . [The police] told me if I persisted with the plan I would be the first to be carried off. When I wrote to Lord Montagu I pointed out that to combat any trouble I would organise a beatnik police force. There would be little risk of damage. This rave would have lasted a while. We planned to live in the forest while it was on" (quoted in the *Scottish Daily Mail*, 16 June 1962).

Wild, pastoral living, self-policing, DIY music making, and a noncommercial economy—many of the ingredients of the free festival movement are glimpsed here up to a decade before its popularization in Britain. The poor or political in the free community of Desolation Hill (also known as Devastation Hill) outside the fences of the Isle of Wight festival in 1970, the *IT* financial "fuck up" in the same year (*IT*'s own description: quoted in Nelson 1989, 98) that became the free festival of Phun City, the free festival of Glastonbury Fayre organized and financed by upper-class dropouts like Andrew Kerr and Arabella Churchill in 1971—these were the significant early manifestations (see McKay 2000a). But as an ideological social movement of sorts in Britain, free festivals came into their own with Windsor People's Free in 1972 and then the best-known, Stonehenge Free, from 1974 to 1984.[19] In a way, with Pete the Brolly, Beaulieu was present at the lost beginning of the movement, and also at its most notorious arrest, the "Battle of the Beanfield" near Stonehenge, where the large convoy of New Travellers on its way to the stones for the festival in 1985 was violently ambushed and broken up by police (see McKay 1996, chs. 1–2). As the head of English Heritage at that time, Montagu was responsible for preserving national monuments like Stonehenge, though he was not absolutely opposed to some sort of gathering: "My desire was to turn the festival into some sort of controlled event, which meant it could still have happened. I would have loved to have made a sensible event—in fact, one year we offered four hundred tickets to the alternative community to attend the stones during the solstice, but they said no, we'd rather stay outside. I did then think they were anarchists, you see: they'd rather riot really. Were there anarchists at Beaulieu, too, among the trad jazzers, beatniks, and CND-ers? Oh yes, quite possibly" (personal interview, 1999).

At Beaulieu in 1960 (also, in leaflet form at least, in 1962), and at Stonehenge after 1985, the aristocratic imperative to grant and control freedom-of-festival was challenged and rejected. Montagu himself recognized this connection, as he used the language of Stonehenge to describe his memories of jazz festival goers at Beaulieu participating in a "Hippy invasion of the village" (Montagu 2000, caption, 146–47). As is its wont, carnival would not be so easily limited; it *required* its potential for social inversion to be fulfilled. And so it was—as the *Daily Mail* delineated the carnivalesque trajectory of the Beaulieu Jazz Festivals for its readers:

> At first audiences were sprinkled with famous faces. Gerald Lascelles, cousin of the Queen, was one who made the trip to Beaulieu.
>
> Then the rowdies moved in and last July there were riots, nude bathing parties, fights with broken bottles, beatings-up of innocent bystanders and drunken orgies. Fifteen ambulances were called.
>
> "I was disgusted and flabbergasted by the drunken youths and girls lying on the ground," said Lord Montagu. (*Daily Mail*, 16 May 1962)

As in the Victorian Beaulieu Fairs banned by his grandfather, the transgressive purpose of carnival, in the highly encoded and hierarchical social setting of an English stately home, burst out with energy, without apology, once more. That the febrile Americanisms of jazz should now be carnival's accompaniment compounded the "disgust," or the pleasure, or both. For as Baz Kershaw reminds us, "carnival inverts the everyday, workaday world of rules, regulations and laws, challenging the hierarchies of normality in a counterhegemonic, satirical and sartorial parody of power. And, like the counter-culture, carnival *appears to be* totally anti-structural, opposed to all order, anarchic and liberating in its wilful refusal of systematic governance" (Kershaw 1992, 72–73; my emphasis).

What [Britain] did develop, however, probably in close association
with American New Deal radicalism, was a powerful bonding of
jazz, blues, folk and the extreme left, mainly communist but also,
marginally, anarchist. For such people jazz and blues were essentially
"people's music" in three senses: a music of folk roots and capable of
appealing to the masses, a do-it-yourself music which could be
practised by ordinary people, as distinct from those with technical
training, and lastly a music for protest, demonstration and collective
celebration.—ERIC HOBSBAWM (1998, 272)

For Andrew Blake, "the notion of a popular festival [can be] a way of
proposing, trying to create, a truly vital cultural politics, one which
has involved thousands of people and their pleasures, generating a far
greater level of enthusiasm than other political events" (1997, 191). The
Beaulieu Jazz Festivals of 1956–61 did no such thing, of course—one
could perhaps more convincingly argue that the aristocratic mien of
the peer of the realm Montagu and the topos of Palace House *maintained* privilege and Little Englanderism,[20] while other signifiers of traditional Englishness were present annually too: the commission in 1959
of *Festival Suite* from Kenny Graham, for instance, one part of which
depicted the hunting of a fox (the fox's part was played by the tenor
saxophone), or the Sunday afternoon cricket match between Lord Montagu's team and a team of jazz and showbiz personalities. Yet a "people's
music [of] . . . protest, demonstration and collective celebration" *could*
be heard, even here.

Montagu explained to me that he was aiming for "a British version
of the American Newport Jazz Festival, if you like, but I think I saw
the festival ideally as the Glyndebourne of Jazz, or hoped it might become that" (personal interview, 1999). (Glyndebourne Festival Theatre was opened in 1934 in a private estate in Sussex. Its critically acclaimed opera festivals started again after the Second World War, in
1950.) So although musically looking across the Atlantic, Montagu's
ambitions were modeled much nearer home. In spite of the American origin of virtually all the music played at the festivals, as well as
the role that the Newport Jazz Festival played as a partial template,
signifiers of Englishness at Beaulieu would differentiate its identity. In
these ways, Beaulieu became more than, in Benny Green's harsh but
not unfair judgment of other British attempts at festivals of the time,

"a watery imitation of their American counterparts" (*Observer*, 19 August 1962). And yet, in what became the final festival, in 1961, Anita O'Day appeared on Saturday evening and Sunday afternoon. For fans such as Val Wilmer there was a direct echo here of the Newport Jazz Festival of 1958, at which O'Day's performance was documented in the film *Jazz on a Summer's Day*. Wilmer elaborates on the imitative aspect of jazz in the United Kingdom: "It wasn't just Beaulieu that was imitative, UK jazz as a whole was. In fact, all people on the jazz scene *were* essentially imitators at that time. But that can also be seen positively — jazz is (partly) about the development of an individual style, so there became the possibility of developing through the stage of imitation towards something more individual, more original. But lots of copying too. British musicians played under a cloud, and were trying to shift it, but I'd say it wasn't until the early 1960s that they began to move away from the strictly American model really" (personal interview, 2002).

Even the Battle of Beaulieu in 1960 was understood in this imitative framework by many. A few weeks before the troubled British festival, there had been violence at the Newport Jazz Festival in the United States. Over 1–2 July martial law was declared, and there was a fatality along with 150 injuries when a large number of fans were unable to gain admittance. A British correspondent for the *Washington Post* wrote of Beaulieu that "the riot was a fair copy of America's recent Newport, R.I., bangup. And the doings at Newport probably contributed to the British brawl. *Almost everything in popular music in the United States is repeated here*" (1 August 1960; my emphasis).

In the jazz setting of the earliest festivals at Beaulieu and the NJF events at Richmond, the energy was sparked by transatlantic cultural exchange that combined with an eccentric, indigenous take on tradition and a pastoral articulation of the new. As we have seen, other, more socially democratic and politically engaged counter-modernisms were being expressed and explored in the increasingly shifting society of Britain at this time too. Meredith Veldman argues that "whether it was E. P. Thompson's alternative version of history with its stress on the antiauthoritarian tradition of the freeborn Englishman or the more familiar orthodoxy of the Whig interpretation of the steady unfolding of democratic rights within a stable democratic system, the British, or at least *the English past could be and was used to criticize and challenge the nuclear present*" (Veldman 1994, 203; my emphasis). The concurrence of the first Aldermaston CND march of 1958 with the first "proper" festival at Beaulieu is important: New Orleans bands playing for the camping marchers, packed with youth, through green Berkshire at Easter 1958, New Orleans bands playing for new audiences, packed with youth, in the ancient New Forest of green Hampshire a few summer months later. Montagu of Beaulieu has recently acknowledged this: "The Campaign for Nuclear Disarmament's Aldermaston March and the Beaulieu Jazz Festival were foremost among the high days of the alternative society. Now they have been consigned to history. Still, in a small way, I can claim that the Beaulieu Jazz Festivals helped make that history. . . . I have left it to others to continue the music festival tradition originally established at Beaulieu. Such annual fixtures as Glastonbury, Reading and Knebworth were, I believe, Beaulieu's natural descendants" (Montagu 2000, 273–74).

Val Wilmer told me that she experienced the jazzy festival events of Aldermaston *and* Beaulieu in 1960 and 1961: for her they were part of the same social and musical scene. This conjunction was more widely acknowledged as well: the *Glasgow Herald* wrote of "all the usual *Aldermaston-cum-Jazz-Festival* uniforms—tight jeans, baggy sweaters painted with the CND symbol, bowler hats, long hair for all sexes" (31 July 1961; my emphasis). According to George Melly, who sang at the festival regularly with the Mick Mulligan Band, sometimes worked there as a compère, and was also an intelligent commentator on pop music and the changing world of Britain, the eccentric "rave gear" fashion worn by subcultural members "came into its own at the festivals or at the gargantuan all-night raves which were held under the echoing dome of the Albert Hall or among the icy wastes of the Alexandra Palace. Another marker of the raver was the CND symbol. Among the musicians there were some, myself among them, who were actively committed to the cause of nuclear disarmament, but I rather felt that for most of them the symbol was anti-authoritarian rather than antinuclear, not that I found this in any way unsympathetic" (Melly 1965, 221–22).

There were, then, significant connections between the developing scene around Beaulieu (as its audience began to take over) and the Aldermaston marches, in terms of youth, music, subcultural identity, and to an extent a political articulation (see McKay 2000b). This last would soon be shaped and more forcefully articulated within the New

Left as well as the counterculture more generally. In *Bomb Culture*, Jeff Nuttall traces some of the motivations and context for the embracing of traditional and revivalist jazz, which he views as part of a postwar "cult of the primitive." The eccentric tribal gathering in the deep, green, ancient New Forest that began to characterize the Beaulieu Jazz Festivals, the collective springtime excursion through the English Home Counties countryside that was the Aldermaston march—both were accompanied by the "small-band collective improvisation of twenties New Orleans jazz [in order to satisfy] a hungering . . . for the pastoral" (1968, 41–42).

TWO

Whiteness and (British) Jazz

I . . . still feel surprise at the extent to which jazz has
entered the psyche of the allegedly cold-blooded Anglo-Saxon.
—JIM GODBOLT (1984, xii)

British means English means white for Godbolt, in Lawrentian mode in the first volume of his *History of Jazz in Britain*: "the pulse of this music throbs healthily in the Anglo-Saxon" (1984, 272), though the music was embraced by, for instance, some of the Celtic parts of the nation too, in particular the urban belts of Scotland and Wales. I want to explore a number of areas around the whiteness of British jazz, beginning with some of the articulations and silences around the subject—which is more than the familiar invisibility of whiteness as an ethnic marker. The initial remarks on the contemporary reticence to discuss whiteness should balance the more positive view of jazz as standing against white racism that I offer later, signaling some limit to jazz's capacity to refigure whiteness. I go on to explore the early reception of black and white American jazz music by white fans, and the extent to which it set or confirmed a template for the reception of later African American musics by British enthusiasts. This frequently mapped on to, and was used to confirm, imperial and post-imperial understandings or rhetorics of the dominance of the white race. The political responses in white jazz to the available and developing constructions of whiteness during the Second World War and in the postwar years are important too. How did jazz contribute to the challenges to the white racist or supremacist ideologies of Nazi Aryanism, the American segregationist South, and South African apartheid, for example? What interests me is teasing out ways in which jazz enabled white British enthusiasts to reject and (partially, tentatively) to figure and reconfigure what it meant to be white—abroad, and at home—in what was rapidly becoming a post-imperial setting. Here I use jazz history to look back and to look forward, to revisit some of "the points at which the arterial system of the political body had been blocked by immigration, imperialist nostalgia and post-colonial melancholia" (Gilroy 2002, xvii).

The book begins now to take on a greater historicity in this chapter — which is also relevant to the next — because, as Simon Frith correctly observes, "The colour of jazz was an issue in Britain from the start" (Frith 1988, 55). This was illustrated in 1919 when the white Original Dixieland Jazz Band and the black Southern Syncopated Orchestra visited within a few months of each other, and reviews and commentaries of their reception were written in a racialized framework which contributed to later understandings about the pleasures of jazz. While whiteness has been the dominant color of British jazz (for reasons including the obvious demographic one that whites have always been the majority population),[1] there has been no sustained articulation or conscious expression of producing *white jazz*, with the kinds of signifiers of ethnicity that might accompany such a form (a distinctive repertoire, instrumentation, and subcultural style of bands and audiences, for example). Debatably the nearest that British musicians have got has been through the efforts of the English jazz critic Leonard Feather to introduce the European dance form of the waltz into the developing jazz canon in the 1930s (Feather 1986, 33), or the Dixieland side of the trad boom of the 1950s (reviving and imitating *white* American practitioners), or the rejection of African American swing and other musical genres by some of the more experimental European free improvisers beginning in the 1960s. I am not overly concerned with evaluating "whether 'white' and 'black' traits or methods of approach can still be discerned" in jazz (Sudhalter 1999, 746); I *am* interested in charting and exploring how this music contributed to the social and cultural understanding of the shifting terrain of racial identities in Britain. If jazz has predominantly been understood by its white British fans to be a black American form, (how) has it helped them to negotiate one compelling dynamic of modernity, race?

I understand that there is a danger in the structural approach I am taking at this moment in the book, and a danger that in relation to the following chapter on blackness(es) in British jazz, I am maintaining or reasserting a simplistic binary opposition. Partly I am, and doing so may appear more naïve because it is in the context of a hybrid cultural form like jazz. *The simple facts are that there are questions about whiteness in jazz in Britain that need to be explored, that have not been explored in the past, and that there are also striking black contributions to the development of the music in Britain which themselves warrant—demand—serious critical appraisal.* The structure does not contain the entire argument, and I hope that readers will recognize the complexities, energies, and ironies of the cross-cultural mix-music that is, maybe was, jazz in Britain in the book as a whole, while being aware too of the important and often neglected specificities of particular situations, scenes, sounds, and colors. Leonard Feather has written of the "white curtain" draped over black jazz in America (Feather 1986, 8); before peering through the version of the curtain that exists in Britain I want to look closely at its materials. My aim is to explore rather than simply maintain what Gilroy has recently termed "the crude, dualistic architecture of racial discourse" (2002, xxiii)—or, rather, my aim is to critically consider how jazz music has facilitated the exploration of that dualistic architecture, and contributed to its construction and, perhaps, political deconstruction. I am conscious of the danger of, in Gayle Wald's words, through Kobena Mercer, "reinstating the racial binary through critical gestures that disallow any possibility of acknowledging the strategic 'impurity' of resistance itself. . . . Given that it is one of the hallmark desires of 'whiteness,' it may be equally important, in other words, to resist 'purity' as a prerequisite of antiracist struggles" (Wald 2000, 79).

In concluding remarks in *Crossing the Line* Wald observes that "the durability of the black/white paradigm may in certain cases be abetted rather than undermined by its instability, insofar as this quality lends it a discursive mobility and flexibility" (2000, 187). That paradigm, helpfully characterized as durable *and* unstable, is a starting point for me in this chapter and the next. In an initially obvious way, perhaps, these chapters may seem to be writing the reverse of the situation in the United States, where according to Richard Sudhalter in *Lost Chords: White Musicians and their Contribution to Jazz*, "Jazz, says the now accepted canon, is black: there have been no white innovators, few white soloists of real distinction; the best white musicians (with an exception or two) were only dilute copies of black originals, and in any case exerted lasting influence only on other white musicians" (1999, xvi). Sudhalter's statement is offered as a justification for his historical corrective to that thesis, and presented as a stark position in order for him best to write against it. All too briefly touching on what he calls the "rage for 'multiculturalism,'" Sudhalter identifies and seeks to revise the history of early American jazz as a predominantly black cultural achievement, and with it the concomitant disregard for the white contribution: "The history of jazz, particularly its growth in the racially segregated America of the early twentieth century, offers fertile ground for such hindsight-generated assessment. As an element of popular culture, jazz inevitably reflected the prevailing system: if musicians themselves were relatively colour-blind (and indeed they were), their managers, agents, customers, employers, audiences—and particularly critics—were not" (1999, xvi).

Sudhalter's is an effort to claim an autonomy for jazz from social concerns, but this theoretical position is the weakest part of an otherwise impressively researched history. He points to the context of production of early American jazz documentation to explain the overstated importance of race in jazz, arguing that "the first, formative jazz criticism of the Depression years was shaped—and skewed—by ideas that were ideological before they were musical" (Sudhalter 1999, 744). In fact jazz did not simply reflect but also sought to comment on, to maintain or change, the prevailing system (in ways that ranged from Garveyite interventions in popular music and black nationalism to the infamous claims by Nick La Rocca of the Original Dixieland Jazz Band that jazz was a white culture in its origins). For me, the ideological use of jazz is the core interest; nor could it be entirely autonomous, pure, and unadulterated by ideology. And as we will see, a significant proportion of early jazz writing presented the music as *white* anyway.

One more initial point. It is important to acknowledge that the whiteness(es) I am writing of are social constructions, not biological or racial essences. I concur with Jonathan Rutherford: "Whiteness and blackness are not racial categories of intrinsic, self-contained meaning. They are not biologically determined. They are social and cultural distinctions, founded upon physiological differences, whose meanings are dependent upon their relation to each other" (1997, 154). The variability—"slipperiness" is Ruth Frankenberg's word (1997, 13)—of a social construction like whiteness may be seen in some American views of the transformation of Europeans in the United States. Charles Mingus once said of Charlie Mariano, who was then a saxophonist in his band, "He ain't white. He's Italian" (quoted in Collier 1973, 103). George Lipsitz writes of how the European immigrant experience of transformation in the United States was "based on identification with the fiction of 'whiteness'[, helping] people who left Europe as Calabrians or Bohemians become something called 'whites' when they got to America, and how that designation made all the difference in the world" (quoted in Fishkin 1996, 267). Frankenberg cites research on "the post–World War II transformation in the status of Jews [to join] . . . an expanded sense of white American identity" (1997, 7). Whatever else is touched on in this brief parable of (in Susan Gubar's term) *racechanges*, one point is clear: racial identity is not fixed or stable, but is dependent on and contributes to social context.[2] This is not only true of that transformative society par excellence, the United States; it is as true for the historically white-majority society of Britain, and for the Britain that underwent significant colonial and postcolonial changes in the social and cultural fabric of the country throughout the twentieth century. (In the new millennium a new focus for traditional British racism has raised its profile as British fair play's B side has turned on East European refugees and asylum seekers, breeding white-on-white racism and violence, and further problematizing simplistic constructions of whiteness: what musics are coming from this mix, I wonder?) And as we have seen, while the massively energetic cultural industry of the United States was, in the process of Americanization, a key transformer of British society during that period, jazz in particular stands out from many of the other forms because it was an identifiably black American form *consumed and then practiced* by European and British whites. What, if anything, has it meant to be a white (British) jazzer?

ARTICULATION AND RETICENCE

I was born about sixty years too late, the wrong colour, and in the wrong country. — KEN COLYER (1989, 21)

As far as I know, I'm about as white as you can get.
—DICK HECKSTALL-SMITH (1989, 145)

These statements by two white jazz men from Britain at least acknowledge that white is a color in British jazz. Colyer was the great white purist of revivalism, yet never a Dixieland player: that was too white for him — it had to be original New Orleans. Heckstall-Smith, stalwart of modern jazz and blues crossover, is one of the relatively few British musicians to have explored what being a white jazz musician involves and signifies. Broadly speaking, in this chapter whiteness is discussed in relation to blackness: to be white in British jazz was to be very black, to paraphrase Robert Farris Thompson.[3] Yet other British musicians and enthusiasts do not much want to talk about being white in jazz. I do not mean that they evade the topic, more that they feel there is not much to say about it. By and large British jazzmen (it usually is men) do not articulate their whiteness. This may not be surprising, since whiteness in a majority-white society with a long history and cultural tradition dominated by white work has become invisible and immutable across society in general. This invisible whiteness may be a relatively recent phenomenon — the doxa of "whiteness as norm, as transparency, as national/natural state" (Frankenberg 1997, 16) — yet in a cultural form so strongly dominated by black presences in its innovations (if not always in its early commercial successes), I do find it intriguing. Jazz musicians spend a lifetime on their cultural work, which should leave a little space for considering their own social position, their place in the history — if only the spontaneity of improvisation were not used by them to skirt analysis, if only the masculine template of bluffness, deflective irony, or taciturnity were not so popular, I suppose.

While some discovered their own whiteness through American jazz, for others, as noted, there seems to be an elision. It is emblematized by Colyer's revivalist drummer from the 1950s, Colin Bowden, who said, when I tried to pursue the issue with regard to their music (after all, a deeply racialized, reinvented form — Dixieland is white, revivalism black New Orleans): "We never thought about ourselves being white. I do think that when you get into black and white it's a dicey area for jazz" (personal interview, 2001). Plainly, Colyer at least *did* occasionally think about being white, as the epigraph above illustrates; perhaps being called a "nigger lover" and advised to "play with white musicians more" while in New Orleans in 1952–53 focused his thoughts on his color (Colyer 1989, 200). Bowden played snare drum in the Omega Brass Band, Britain's first formal New Orleans parade outfit — he sought to step like a black man from the American South, and was recognized and valorized for that effort by the white second-liners at leftist demonstrations and other processions. Thus the silence exists although, as Bernard Gendron notes of America, "the revival-ist movement, whatever its racial tastes, was initiated and propagated only by whites with an almost exclusively white audience" (Gendron 1995, 47). Does this fact confirm the potency of the invisibility of white-ness, even — *especially* — in a music in part about hybridity and black-ness, often used in the cultural struggle of black expression? What is most striking is the lack of interest in their own whiteness by white exponents of this black music. Why do white British jazz musicians not think about their color, not want to talk about it? Partly because they do not know what to say: it is a symptom of lacking an accept-able language of whiteness. However, that is the situation for all white Britons: ours is an invisible ethnicity, all- or once-powerful in, because of, its silence. For British jazzers, white reticence is also located in their understanding of the blackness of the music, in its appeal for them. For some — perhaps — a reluctance to discuss whiteness could be inter-preted as a reverse sensitivity, displaying their special awareness of the "color problem" in American jazz, or justifying their claim that jazz is a special cultural case of colorblindness (see below). For others — per-haps — to discuss or acknowledge their whiteness is to highlight their own inauthenticity, their imitative project. As Heckstall-Smith won-ders, surely plaintively: "am I forever condemned to inauthenticity as a jazz-stroke-blues-stroke-whatever musician by the colour of my skin? That is, by my culture's history, of which my skin stands as an indelible sign? Then every time I go on to the stand I am part of no tradition whatever; I have no history; I represent no cultural voice. Unlike white classical musicians and black jazz musicians I have nothing and no-one behind me, I represent nothing and no-one by myself; I have no bank-roll of authenticity to draw upon . . . [I am] literally, a Pale Imitation" (1989, 152).[4]

It is to admit unoriginality as a poverty of both imagination and — once a good white British word, when capitalized — Heritage. Heckstall-Smith's compensation, in his litany of negatives in which he sees or fears that he has no tradition, history, or culture, "nothing and no-one behind" him — except a rhythm section, and further back, a privileged education at Gordonstoun public school and Cambridge University, so "nothing" is relative — is a traditional modern male one of the existential solo hero. Perhaps some remaining sense of his in-authenticity of class in producing vernacular music fosters a sense of displacement as well.

Another reason for reticence on the part of white musicians is that whiteness has been tainted — is that the correct word? — by suprema-cism. Jonathan Rutherford has sharply pointed out that "the prob-lem with intellectually disowning white English ethnicity was that the left never got round to working out what it was, and what our own emotional connections to it were. We left that door wide open for the New Right" (1997, 5–6).[5] That neglect is especially important in a study such as this one, which foregrounds questions of politics and engagement in the music. British musicians of the political left asso-ciate questions of white identity with right-wing racism and extreme nationalism, ideologies that they may frequently have campaigned and played against. Heckstall-Smith does this himself: "to label jazz Black Music . . . almost says, along with the N[ational] F[ront], that race is fundamental" (1989, 152). It is also responsible for some of the anxiety identified by the improvising pianist Steve Beresford in our discussion about the racial politics of the music: "I think there's a danger of im-posing an issue here, from where I am now in the improvising scene (it might have been different in the early days of jazz in Britain, with the ODJB and white jazz from America): to break it down into black *or* white is too rigid, simplistic, and very dangerous. You've got to look at these things individually. Consider the case of the development of American free, or experimental, jazz in Europe: look at guys like Steve Lacy and Roswell Rudd, they're absolutely central to that bridge be-tween modern Monk and something much looser, and also to its rise in Europe, especially Lacy, and they are white. That says to me, that jazz is one of the places where we might be able to transcend modern problems around the issue of race" (personal interview, 2002).

While articulated in a more sophisticated language of race, Beres-ford's view may nonetheless fall comfortably back on utopian white colorblindness.[6] He manifests what Phil Cohen calls the " 'alternative' whiteness" of the period since the civil rights movement, which has sought to present an informed, visible, and critical construction of itself. This effort has worked through some of its problematic of "un-consciously reproducing, and sometimes actively promoting, a new form of colour-blindness in the name of political unity" (1997, 244–45).

On the other hand, the whiteness or otherwise of Jews is interestingly negotiated in British jazz history. A number of cultural markers and practices may signal a certain, possibly valuable, ambiguity in Jews' social positioning—and outsiderdom, the experience of social prejudice, diasporic identity, and the musical (and sometimes improvised musical) culture are features that invite (easy) correspondence with the black diaspora. Some of these features may help to explain the appeal of jazz for white Jews. While Constant Lambert is confirming in 1934 that "the importance of the Jewish element in jazz cannot be too strongly emphasized" (1934, 153), he has in mind the American situation, from Al Jolson in blackface in *The Jazz Singer* to the popular songs of George Gershwin. In Britain many of the early professional dance band leaders were London Jews, including Geraldo, Ambrose, Sidney Kyte, Joe Loss, and Harry Roy (Godbolt 1984, 222).[7] The parents of dance band musicians like Billy Amstell, Harry Gold, Ivor Mairants, "and other left-leaning musicians, were Jewish immigrants from Eastern Europe, their culture of self-improvement and educational achievement finding one outlet in the rich inherited traditions of music-making. This involvement of Jews in jazz was much remarked on by contemporaries. . . . On Archer Street [where London's musicians would congregate to find bookings] that presence met with a certain amount of anti-Semitic feeling. . . . What seems inescapable is that the politicisation of these young musicians was part of a wider process of Jewish radicalisation to which the rise of Fascism was fundamental" (Morgan 1998, 126).

The targeting of Archer Street for the distribution of leaflets by the likes of Oswald Mosley's British Union of Fascists in the 1930s was criticized by *Melody Maker*—"a welcome change from Edgar Jackson's days as editor," Godbolt notes wryly (Godbolt 1984, 127). Jackson— real name Cohen—had been the first editor of the magazine in 1926, and his reviews were characterized by what Godbolt calls a "consistent" "bias against black jazz" (1984, 29).[8] We will see more of the contribution of the important jazz critic and English Jew Leonard Feather in the United States, where his work over six decades led him to be described by Robert Walser as "one of the most prolific and influential critics jazz has ever had . . . one of Feather's favourite themes was the impact of racism on the lives of jazz musicians and the power of their music to cross racial barriers" (Walser ed. 1999, 302). In fact, on the first page of his autobiography, *The Jazz Years*, Feather explains his lifelong interest in social equality by reference to his early experiences of London Jewry: "It was in the synagogue that the seeds were planted. . . . The sight of women all seated in the balcony, like some lesser breed not fit to associate with men, taught me a lesson, not only about sexism but about segregation in whatever form it might appear" (1986, 5). But other British Jews made highly significant contributions to the transatlantic development of jazz as well, not least Ronnie Scott, whose club in London has been an internationally recognized venue for visiting American musicians since the 1960s. Scott's first tenor saxophone, given to him as a teenager during the Second World War in London, represented the glamorous profession of his long-absent father, the dance band saxophonist Jock Scott (real name Joseph Schatt). But as Scott's biographer, the jazz critic John Fordham, writes with a generous dash of sentimentality, it was also recognized by Scott as "the instrument of Jewish social life, performed on by balding moustachioed men with twinkling eyes, delivering the pop tunes of the day, mixed phlegmatically in with the music of the Jewish dances" (Fordham 1986, 8). Jackson, Gold, Scott— Cohen, Goldberg, Schatt: perhaps these are white invisibilities too, of a different sort.

With the advent of bebop in the United States in the early 1940s and then in Britain in 1948 (first at the Club Eleven in London), the issue of whiteness became more compelling—because bebop was understood as an avowedly racialized cultural form in New York. Its complexities, secrets, language, and semiotics of style were expressions of black masculine authority, originality, exclusivity. As bebop was taken up mostly by white musicians in Britain a very few years later, the social issues inscribed in the technique and performance of the music were surely inescapable. Bebop was translated into an underground outsiderdom (the sonic urban underground is almost always literally underground, the sweaty dingy dark cellar or basement the preferred space of the subcultural pleasure van), embraced for its aestheticized alienation and deracinated—but not entirely. White British bebop threatened existing scenes and forms, and the sense of threat can be gleaned in the racial terminology that its critics employed: Humphrey Lyttelton, who would in due course carve out a middle space between modern and trad with a more sympathetic ear, referred to bebop solos in 1948, the year when Club Eleven began, as "funny little pygmy phrases"; the dance band leader Ambrose, forced to pick some technically proficient young beboppers for a later version of his band, referred to them as "savages" (both quoted in Godbolt 1984, 222, 224). Bebop in Britain, and its leading figures Scott and Dankworth, contributed to a new musical practice as part of an altered social landscape and shifting cultural consensus.

Other popular music forms have different relationships with whiteness; it may not always be that whiteness needs to be "unfrozen," in Frankenberg's term (1997, 1). A brief comparison of the jazz boom of the 1960s, which covered the last of trad and post-bop, blues and free jazz, with the second folk revival of round the same time is illuminating.[9] The jazz historian Val Wilmer told me that "folk offered another approach to these questions of national culture. Sometimes this crossed into jazz — particularly with the spasm bands and skiffle music side of the trad movement — though a lot of people in the jazz world don't like folk music at all, they think it's trite and unadventurous" (personal interview, 2002). Elsewhere Wilmer found a route to white folk culture by initially stepping outside music, and indeed outside her class. Her path should remind us that in important ways aspects of class map on to debates about race and national ethnicity.[10] Researching for a proposed book project about British coal miners (in the wake of the miners' strikes of 1972–74), Wilmer recalls, "the process took me away from the Black-centred world . . . and made me take a hard look at my own people's culture and history. I realised that I was as ignorant about working-class history as my friends were of gospel or blues" (Wilmer 1989, 275). In a small, revelatory political moment in Birmingham, Wilmer freshly experienced the music of someone like the white blues singer Alan Price. When he sang "Jarrow Song," about the hunger march in 1936 to London from the industrial Northeast (his own home patch), "Alan's song, previously without context for me, suddenly put it slap-bang in the pages of history. His past was there, and it was *our* past. It was folk-music still, but modern and relevant, carrying within it the story of who we all were, just as the blues did for blues people. How extraordinary that I'd been attracted to Alan in the first place because he knew how to play the blues. Now, here he was, the trenchant Geordie fellow, bringing me back home as well" (1989, 278).

Folk could be comfortable in its whiteness, even if it did not always feel the need to articulate or explore that whiteness.[11] Writing of skiffle, Iain Chambers argues that "while it was possible in the folk song movement to enforce the criteria of 'authenticity,' to the degree that Ewan MacColl insisted that singers sang only material coming from their own national repertoire, the paradoxes of white men seeking to reproduce faithfully a black folk music, of Britishers *slavishly* imitating a now largely extinct Afro-American cultural form, drew it up short of such artificially purist closure" (1985, 49; my emphasis).[12]

When I discussed white national culture with the Scottish singer and improviser Maggie Nicols I had a sense that she was more excited with her small Berber background connection (a great-uncle was North African) than with the much stronger possibilities of exploring her own Scottish folk music tradition. How could Scotland—of grey skies and pasty complexion (some of my childhood memories now, not Nicols's)—compare with Africa, for a *jazz* lover? And here the ontology of whiteness, when raised in an interview with a white jazz musician by an awkward academic hoping to be—what? shown the light?—is defined by reference to blackness. Whiteness is acknowledged only in the context of discussions about the blackness of the music, which is a common event: David Roediger has observed, regarding the situation in the United States, that "whites are assumed not to 'have race' " (quoted in Fishkin 1996, 257). Yet other jazz musicians in Britain have tried precisely to explore what they view as this common landscape— Ken Hyder's Talisker (named after the Scottish malt whisky) moved between free experiments and pieces working from Scottish folk songs in the early 1970s, the West Country saxophonist John Surman has often explored folk motifs in his compositions, while the double bassist Danny Thompson employed his experience with the leading English folk band Pentangle in the 1960s to effect an unlikely collaboration with the free drummer John Stevens and the singer-songwriter John Martyn in the mid-1970s.

From Melbourne in 1947 came the Graeme Bell Australian Jazz Band, presenting another (and another white) New World version of a trad revivalism, complementing Lu Watters's Yerba Buena Band (1940) on the American West Coast and George Webb's Dixielanders (1943) in England. Godbolt explains, "As Empire citizens they had no problems in obtaining the work permits denied to the musicians with whom they most wanted to be associated and whom a legion of enthusiasts wanted to hear" (1984, 213). Bell's manager was careful to explain to Godbolt, at the time working as the manager of Webb's Dixielanders and publicizing various concerts, that "the billing is Graeme Bell and his *Australian* Jazz Band and in your publicity they're to be described as a *New Orleans* band, not Dixieland. You got that, son?" (quoted in Godbolt 1984, 212). Here the white tradition of early jazz is rejected in favor of a reconstructed black authenticity, ostensibly from the American South, by a *white* band from Australia playing for overwhelmingly white audiences in Europe. So apart from folk music, trad's links with music hall culture in Britain, evident from the dress style of Acker Bilk and the comedy routines of many bands, offered another route back to an earlier white entertainment tradition in Britain. It is interesting to note that some traditionalists had no problems performing music on the television program "The Black and White Minstrel Show"—I doubt that British modernists would have been so accommodating—or indeed that some old tradders had no problem "accompanying" the Conservative Party leader Margaret Thatcher for that notorious publicity shot in 1976 at a right-wing fundraising event. At moments like these are visible some of the small, public manifestations of what could be considered a less than inclusive whiteness on the part of white British jazz.

"(WHITE MAN) IN HAMMERSMITH PALAIS":
JAZZ, RACISM, WHITE EMPIRES

Tasting a bit of the Other becomes nothing but a sound bite.
—SUSAN GUBAR, *Racechanges* (1997, xxi)

While several studies remind us that there were numerous precedents in forms like ragtime, blues, and vaudeville songs for the export of what would become jazz in Europe (see Goddard 1979, ch.1; Rye 1990; Shipton 2001, 358–59), it is nonetheless true, as suggested above, that 1919 was a groundbreaking year in Britain, and for two reasons in the form of two important American bands arriving separately to play in London. These were the white New Orleanians the Original Dixieland Jazz Band (ODJB) in April and the black Southern Syncopated Orchestra conducted by Will Marion Cook in June. Promoters wished to capitalize on the audiences available again in Europe in the wake of the First World War, and perhaps too on the popularity of Americans after their intervention in the war. An influx of American bands was a sign of Europe's continuing fascination with the modern craze, and of the shifting hegemonic structures of the West. These unrelated tours have dominated histories of the origins of British jazz (Boulton 1958; Godbolt 1984), and for the same reasons I introduce them at this point: the concurrence of their arrival, the proclaimed southern-ness in the names of both bands (though in the United States Cook's was first called the New York Syncopated Orchestra: Walser 1999, 9), and their highlighting, even dramatizing, the issue of the color of jazz. The *originality* of the Originals (and they also publicized themselves as "the creators of jazz": Shipton 2001, 102) is questionable in Britain: they were not even the first American band that sought by its choice of name to make the bold claim to be playing *Jazz*. A year previously, the entertainment magazine *Encore* reported, "A new American invasion is heralded by the appearance 'fresh from the United States' of the Jazzbo Band" (quoted in Godbolt 1984, 5). With their success boosted by the East European–born Jewish singer and blackface artist who cham-pioned them, Al Jolson, they *had* made the first jazz records, in the United States in 1917 — significant less for the music recorded than for its having changed the mode of consumption of popular music.[13] But the musicians were *white*, and they caused a sensation among white audiences in Britain, on the dance floor. The importance of the Southern Syncopated Orchestra lies not in its foregrounding of rhythmic differ-ence, of syncopation — the African American drummer Louis Mitchell had toured the music halls with a band of British musicians called the Syncopating Sextette in 1917, while the pianist Joe Jordan's Syncopated Orchestra had toured two years before that (Rye 1990, 47). Its reper-toire was hardly jazz, anyway: the classically educated violinist Cook (who had studied in the nineteenth century in Europe under Antonin Dvořák) presented a mix of classical pieces, his own compositions, and some blues and "plantation melodies" (Goddard 1979, 32). The real significance of the Southern Syncopated Orchestra was, in the often-quoted words of the Swiss classical conductor Ernest Ansermet in his review of a London performance in 1919, that it featured "an extraor-dinary clarinet virtuoso who is, so it seems, the first of his race to have composed perfectly formed blues on the clarinet. . . . I wish to set down the name of this artist of genius; as for myself I shall never forget it — it is Sidney Bechet" (Ansermet 1919, 11). In the context of the develop-ment of jazz in Europe there are two important points here: Bechet *and* Ansermet, the young New Orleans Creole musician playing identifiably jazz solos for European ears, but also, for jazz criticism and reception in Europe, the classical conductor, representing European musical tradition, who recognizes and valorizes in print "the germ of a new style" in rhythm, the overall sonority of the band's arrangements, and the characteristic blue notes, "thirds which are neither major nor minor and false seconds" (1919, 11).

The *London Daily News* previewed the arrival of the Original Dixieland Jazz Band by explaining to readers that "in view of the unkind and disrespectful things which have been said about Red Indians and Negroids and West African Savages, it should be stated that the players are all white — white as they can possibly be" (quoted in Godbolt 1984, 9). The ODJB's brash strategy for success would become a familiar one through the Americanizing century, especially in the popular music industry. As noted, the band embraced embryonic mass communications media for the first recordings of jazz; it exploited the specialist press — its members were outstanding self-publicists, La Rocca in particular giving good copy for British entertainment magazines with his provocative utterances. At the same time the musicians ignored regular criticism in the daily press and worked instead on building a populist audience through their live playing; they were a dance band combining the promise of aural and corporeal pleasure for their audiences; their shows combined musical novelty with (comedic) performance and visual awareness, evident in publicity shots as well. Their directness, even in the form of contradiction (mediated but "live"; La Rocca's claim that "Jazz is the assassination . . . of syncopation": quoted in Goddard 1979, 30), demanded a response from audiences and critics alike. And they took a predominantly black music form and popularized it for white consumption: forty years later the veteran New Orleans clarinetist Albert Nicholas, who had recorded with Bechet and Jelly Roll Morton, exploded at a meal one evening in England with the white English agent and historian Jim Godbolt and the critic Max Jones when the ODJB came up in the conversation: "*Bastards!* White shit stealin' our toons!" (Godbolt 1989, 238). For these reasons, which are not all concerned specifically with jazz but with the development of popular music more generally, the ODJB matters.[14]

But the ODJB in London, soon to become resident band at the newly opened Palais de Danse in Hammersmith, did inspire local musicians too.[15] For example, the bass saxophonist Harry Gold was taken by his father to see the band as a youngster. He remembered the event eighty years later: "[It was] one of the most important influences in my musical life. . . . Although I didn't understand what they were doing, the effect was electric. Then and there I resolved to be a musician. To this day that sound of the band has never left me . . . the music that captivated my imagination at the Hammersmith Palais" (Gold 2000, 11, 13). The London musician Billy Jones took over the ODJB piano chair in October 1919—and when George Webb's Dixielanders formed in 1943, Webb would invite Jones to sit in, in recognition of his brief, historic role in British jazz. Shipton considers the attraction of white over black jazz in the very early 1920s: "During the time that Bechet was in London, various British bands set themselves up in imitation of American groups, but perhaps because Bechet's daunting virtuoso playing was seen as something exotic and foreign, or perhaps for straightforward reasons of racial identification, these generally looked to the Original Dixieland Jazz Band rather than the Jazz Kings [which featured Bechet] for inspiration" (Shipton 2001, 363).

The "staggering erasures required by the invention of whiteness" (1996, 71) that Joseph Roach identifies in his study of circum-Atlantic cultures, *Cities of the Dead*, are present in the earliest white jazz criticism as well as in the early practice of white jazz itself. Henry Pleasants points out, for example, that Henry Osgood's *So This Is Jazz* (1926), the first American book on the music, names no black musicians at all (Pleasants 1961, 140). Chris Goddard describes "the first seven or eight years of jazz history . . . [as] a record of the frantic attempts by white jazz fans to purge the music of its black influences and clean it up for middle-class consumption" (Goddard 1979, 164–65).[16] Observations like these are important not only for American jazz historiography, and American sociology; such misrepresentations also contributed to the understanding of jazz by its new and largely *white* audience in Europe. In terms of jazz practice, Goddard is particularly critical of the ODJB's role in the early reception and understanding of jazz in Europe. The cornetist and leader La Rocca, a self-proclaimed "musical anarchist," is Goddard's lead villain, because of his repeated claims that his band originated the music: "In 1920 it was the ODJB which made headlines, partly because they loudly discounted any black influences.[17] . . . [La Rocca's] starring role with the band was more as an *unscrupulous liar* who gave interviews not merely ignoring, but *explicitly denying the black contribution to jazz. . . .* The influence exerted on the history of jazz by the Original Dixieland Band seems to have been crucial if confusing. Their records show unmistakably that they were inspired by authentic New Orleans jazz, so that their explicit denials of any black influences did a great deal to mislead people about the true origins of the music. This was particularly true in Europe" (Goddard 1979, 31, 27; my emphasis).

Twenty years later, efforts were still being made in Europe to rewrite the origins of jazz from a white perspective, as one striking example from wartime France illustrates. André Coeuroy published in Paris in 1942 his book *Histoire générale du swing*, in which he argued: "It has been assumed for a long time that jazz is specifically Negro music. My theory is the opposite. Jazz became Negro by chance. The principal elements are not only white, but European. Its history and its material both *belong to us*" (quoted in Zwerin 1985, 151; my emphasis). Charles Delaunay and other Hot Club jazz enthusiasts had been trying to present a French version of jazz, emphasizing the French strand of New Orleans in the music, as well as the indigenous stylistic originality of the Quintet of the Hot Club (a difficult position in wartime, bearing in mind that the guitarist Reinhardt was a gypsy), in order to simply allow the music to continue being played under the Nazi-controlled regime. But even Delaunay thought Coeuroy went too far with his proprietorial posi-tion, criticizing him in a review in *Jazz Hot*: "Perhaps to try and remain in step with the current political state of affairs, the author adopted a thesis which he pushed to the absurd" (quoted in Zwerin 1985, 151). Evidently whiteness, and social and cultural power, could be compel-lingly contingent upon shifting political context — in Nazi Germany or Vichy France, or in other imperial situations. Thus part of the story is that rhetorics of white jazz criticism or history regularly sought to confirm a privileged racial ownership of the music.

There were white supremacist strands in British imperial culture. Concurrent with the American musical imports of 1919 that we now know sounded a hegemonic shift (perfect timing) was the late, last high point of the British Empire. In that year the League of Nations de-vised its Mandate system for allocating the spoils of victory from the First World War, which saw the transfer of German colonial territo-ries and Turkish provinces to, in particular, France and Britain. Includ-ing its effectively new African colonies from defeated Germany, the British Empire would consist of over 600 million people ruled from

London. Over the next decade many of the predominantly white or white-governed territories of the empire—Ireland, Canada, Australasia, South Africa—successfully negotiated or fought for varying degrees of home rule or independence, while any significant decolonization for nonwhite imperial territories occurred in the wake of the *Second World War*. White colonials were entrusted with freedom a quarter of a century before black colonials. The saxophonist Heckstall-Smith makes this connection too: "Racially and nationally prejudiced beliefs are an appallingly deep-rooted, long-established and serious disease of our ex-imperialist culture" (Heckstall-Smith 1989, 12). Heckstall-Smith turns the mirror of white anti-black racism around to perceive how that defines whiteness (in jazz), to nail the colors of whiteness. Through the 1920s, the Jazz Age, those in the business—of music education, and the burgeoning jazz and dance criticism—arranged themselves to present a solid white line of outrage, a certain sign that consensus was in crisis, transition imminent, and not only in the cultural arena.[18] Jazz was the musical metonym of hegemon. Uniting the authority of Christianity and of an ancient university for the benefit of assembled music teachers, the Rector of Exeter College, Oxford, welcomed delegates to a summer school in 1926 with this advice: "Don't take your music from America or from the niggers, take it from God, the source of all good music" (quoted in Godbolt 1984, 29). The public racialized discourse of the consumption of jazz in Britain was frequently channeled through the (dancing) body, (black) masculinity, and the fascinating threat to white female sexuality. This much is evidenced in an article from the *Sunday Chronicle* from June 1924 by one Violet Quirk, in which she describes for her readers her "disturbing impressions" of a jazz dance: "The negro musicians knew well how to recapture the inflaming noises made by their far-back ancestors, and which are still enjoyed by cannibals during their most important ceremonies. . . . The *animal* devotees of jazz, who like to be maddened . . . see how it *whips* them about! They obey it like *slaves*. . . . These women . . . shuffle round the room with striding *legs too far apart*, rigid bodies, and fixed staring eyes" (quoted in Godbolt 1984, 32–33; my emphasis).

Animals, slaves are whipped. Young white women are enslaved, sexualized, narcotized, through the bodily experience of dancing to that primitive, cannibalistic music. The transcendent music transports them to Africa, a colonial Africa of white nightmare (the horror), the jazz dance functioning as some kind of voodoo rite. At this time in Britain black jazz was articulated as a threat within the framework of the imperial experience. It had less to do with America *per se* than with continuing white anxieties about the blackness of empire, and how to control it.[19] Moreover, the crisis in whiteness was explicitly gendered and generational: it was young (fertile) white women that were depicted as threatened, through an implied miscegenation. Being white and weak was not an acceptable combination in a discourse of British imperial masculinity, but John Bull's flapper granddaughter, who held the future of the white race if she would only realize it, if she would only protect her privileged position as well as her virtue, was the ideal(ized) chosen symbol for the transmission of such neuroses. In a further sign of the extent to which black jazz had entered the white imagination and was beginning to influence what it meant to be white, two years later a controversy led to the withdrawal of a painting from the spring show at the Royal Academy in London. John B. Souter, a member of the Pastel Society, submitted a painting called *The Breakdown*, which showed a naked, young, white woman dancing as if in a trance to the music of a saxophone played by a formally dressed black man sitting on a broken, white, classical statue (see Godbolt 1984, 114). The first editor of *Melody Maker* (founded in that same year, 1926) was Edgar Jackson, real name Edgar Cohen, a Jew born in London. Because of the signified jazz of the saxophone, and probably also for the pragmatic reason that he wished his new publication to be recognized as a voice of conscience, Jackson felt it his duty to speak out against the painting—on behalf of all British jazz musicians: "We jazz musicians . . . protest against, and repudiate the juxtaposition of an undraped white girl with a black man. . . . We demand also that the habit of associating our music with the primitive and barbarous negro derivation shall cease forthwith. . . . 'Breakdown' is not only a picture entirely nude of the respect due to the chastity and morality of the younger generation but in the degradation it implies to modern white woman there is the perversive danger to the community and the best thing that could happen to it is to have it . . . burnt!" (quoted in Godbolt 1984, 28).

An annual report of the Royal Academy describes what followed: "At the request of the Secretary for the Dominions an oil painting (No. 600) entitled 'The Breakdown,' by J. B. Souter, was removed from the exhibition on May 8, as the subject . . . was considered to be obnoxious to British subjects living abroad in daily contact with a coloured population. The gap was filled by a portrait of Lady Diana Manners, by Sir J. J. Shannon, R.A., lent by Violet Duchess of Rutland" (Royal Academy 1958, 13). The justification for the painting's withdrawal was that it would make difficulties for white officials in the colonies, and indeed the academy's council minutes explain the removal as "due to a reason of state and not of art" (Royal Academy 1926, 223). That the painting should have been replaced by such an establishment piece as a portrait of a Lady painted by a Sir and lent by a Duchess suggests an ostentatious desire to reestablish the dominant order after its temporary breakdown.

Do denigratory or racist or exoticizing narratives such as these set a template for the subsequent reception of other black musical forms by white-majority populations? David Meltzer argues that because of the exoticizing and mythologizing practices of white enthusiasts, and because many who exploited jazz as a commodity were white, the reception of jazz during the twentieth century is a catalogue of "forms of permissible racism." In a poetic critique (Meltzer, a white American Jew, had a background as a Beat poet, having read at the Jazz Cellar in California in the 1950s), he writes of the situation facing African American music in the United States: "The trope . . . that is jazz is essentially a white discourse, a white mythology, a white form of control over its production, reproduction, history and economics; a white reverie over blackness sustained and contained within the cultural plantation-system of late capitalism" (Meltzer ed. 1993, 11–12).

The prominent early Anglo-Irish jazz critic and double bassist Spike Hughes could identify "a sentimental, patronizing doting on all things Negro which characterized the negromania of some sections of British society during the late 20's" (quoted in Godbolt 1984, 73). This "negromania" was predicated above all on the musical and performance cultures of African Americans, and it is deeply ambivalent: while its enjoyment of black culture clearly negated any obvious racist or anti-black agenda—compared with the white fear of black music outlined above—its "patronizing doting" on all (musical) things black could also efficiently function to maintain a solid, consensual, imperial white identity.

And at this stage it is necessary to go further back (then forward), before jazz, before mass communications media. In the specific context of music and performance in the United States, from blackface to Norman Wailer's White Negro—and other hip white jazzers like Mezz Mezzrow or the Beats—to wiggers, whites have sought "simultaneously [to] figure and disfigure" African Americans in processes of "racial masquerade and racechange" (Gubar 1997, xiv–xv).[20] According to John G. Blair, blackface minstrelsy was "the first American performance innovation to have notable success abroad" (Blair 1997, 53–54). A little like black jazz in the 1920s, in Britain during the Victorian period American blackface performances were understood in relation to the Empire, to "distinctive British concerns . . . notably Africa" (Blair 1997, 56–57). But at the same time, in a sign of the complex political readings of racial performances, illustrating what Shelley Fisher Fishkin has called the "complex blend of appreciation and appropriation of black culture" (1996, 256), they were also exploited by the abolitionist movement in Britain as part of the campaign against black slavery in America: "The association of minstrels with this moral cause conferred on them an indirect stamp of approval" (Blair 1997, 57), and white British audiences sympathized with the blackface character Jim Crow when he sang flatteringly about England:

> Now I say, look here white folks,
> De country for me,
> Is de country whar de people,
> Hab made poor nigger free. (quoted in Blair 1997, 59–60)

"The fact is," W. T. Lhamon writes of this song, "that Jim Crow was singing out for freedom on both sides of the Atlantic" (1998, 205). While it may not always have been so straightforward a "pantomime dramatisation of white supremacy" (Gilroy 1993, 89), blackface has had an extraordinarily lengthy career in Britain: St James' Hall in Piccadilly was a venue that specialized almost exclusively in blackface from the 1840s until its demolition in 1910. In 1929 the guitarist Ivor Mairants gained early experience in his musical career, his "fifty fretting years," in a production in London of Cole Porter's *Wake Up and Dream*, as a member of a banjo quartet: "The show lasted ten months and all we did was to play two choruses of *Wake Up and Dream* on stage, blacked up and dressed in the period costume of San Francisco before the earthquake and fire" (Mairants 1980, 19). After this Mairants joined his fellow dance band musician Harry Gold, performing blackface in the early 1930s in Marius B. Winter's orchestra (Gold 2000, 39, photo 48). A society band, Winter's had been the first dance band to broadcast on the new British Broadcasting Company radio program, in 1923 (Gold 2000, 38 n. 11), but by the 1930s it was playing, Gold remembers, "regular performances on the roof garden at Selfridges store, in Oxford Street, playing for teas and dancing. Incredible as it may sound, we dressed up as minstrels, complete with wigs and with our faces blacked with burnt cork. It wasn't so bad putting on the black make-up but getting it off was another matter, particularly as we didn't have a dressing room" (Gold 2000, 39).

In the 1950s, while Britain's social mix was shifting in part because of migration from the West Indies, while white Britons responded with what was reported as racial violence in Nottingham and London,[21] while postcolonial developments changed the vestiges of empire as independence swept through the old colonies, while reports of civil rights activism in the American South filtered through the media, and while music like jazz from white bebop to black experimentalism was creating new British sounds, the country's culture industry did what it was good at—looking backward to a time of consensus. The BBC *did* innovate in the area of transatlantic and seemingly cross-racial cultures in the late 1950s and early 1960s. From 1957 it produced the avowedly retrogressive and avowedly apolitical award-winning television production "The Black and White Minstrel Show." The program's early champion, Kenneth Adam, CBE, director of BBC Television, wrote in the 1960s: "The first summer holiday I remember was at Bridlington in the year 1914 when my parents . . . allowed me to go down to the beach to watch a concert party calling themselves 'The Black and White Minstrels' . . . [featuring] gay and melancholy coon songs. . . . 'Nigger Minstrels' were still very much part of our entertainment tradition. It was a perfectly honourable and uncondescending convention. Its revival in part on BBC Television in the 1950s . . . was no kind of insult to the Negro, though some misguided critics tried to make a political issue out of it. . . . We have herein a very lively heritage on both sides of the Atlantic, and we can exploit it in such a way that it will not grow stale" (Adam, Maschwitz, Davies, and Mitchell n.d., 2).

This show, which won a Golden Rose at the first Montreux world television awards in 1961, ran for around two decades. It was extremely popular: sixteen million viewers watched its spring run on Saturday

PROGRAMME
ONE SHILLING

The
BLACK
and
WHITE
Minstrel
Show

Based on the popular
B.B.C T.V Series

12. "Some misguided critics tried to make a political issue out of it": theater program for the hugely popular television show, Victoria Place Theatre, 1965.

13. Robertson's Jams golly saxophonist, lapel badge sent out in return for three tokens from jam jars and £1. Issued in 1998.

evenings that year, and an album of its songs featured in the record charts. The routines frequently employed backdrops, costumes, and repertoires of the American South—a nostalgic gesture—and there were regular appearances by a traditional jazz band led by the Scottish trombonist George Chisholm—further nostalgia. (Chisholm was later awarded an OBE, Order of the British Empire, by the state.) The set designer beginning in 1959 was a white South African, Stanley Dorfman. Interestingly, there *was* a development in this show from the minstrel tradition: it was called Black and White in reference to the televisual (monochrome) contrast between the black(ed up) faces of the men and "the 'white' element to be provided by attractive show-girls" (Adam, Maschwitz, Davies, and Mitchell n.d., 6). For Gladys H. Davies, writing in the official album of the show published by the BBC in the 1960s, "In combining white dancers with black-faced singers [the producer George Inns] has produced a show whose butterfly colours and constant movement have the perpetually unexpected beauty of a kaleidoscope. A new dimension has been added to the age old charm, a dimension which weds the warmth of humanity to the complexities of modern techniques" (Adam, Maschwitz, Davies, and Mitchell n.d., 22).

There is an intriguing foregrounding of color here. Evidently the negotiation of black and white—framed by a literally underlying normative whiteness—is the social narrative. The pantomime performance of a gendered, pseudo-racial dialogue of white female purity, the stepping and singing that confirms a racial expectation, the contribution (I originally wrote "complicity") of some white jazz in the show, and the infantilizing location of the director of television's memory of minstrelsy in his formative, Edwardian, pre-war childhood—these features speak of a process of negotiation through avoidance, distantiation, even denial. In a photo section in the book called "Let's make up a minstrel," one caption over a half-made-up white man's face reads: "The make-up mirrors supply the answer—am I black?" (Adam, Maschwitz, Davies, and Mitchell n.d., 57).

Minstrelsy resonated more widely too in the white British imaginary. The foodstuff company Robertson's Jams, founded in 1864, used its trademark figure of the "golly" (golliwog) as a central part of its publicity strategy. From the 1920s Robertson's gollies were distributed as free novelty collectable badges, all wide eyes and fuzzy hair. As Anandi Ramamurthy has shown, "The only dominant representational reference to black people in a British context during this period was that of the golliwog. This image, which originated in children's storybooks by Mrs Upton written between 1895 and 1908 (the heyday of colonial and imperial aggression), sanitised and domesticated Empire. The figure was never copyrighted and was used to advertise everything from Mansion polish and geysers, to soap, toothpaste, marmalade and cream" (Ramamurthy 2003, 151). The Robertson's Jams golly badges included over the years a guitarist, a saxophonist, and a singer—and a related series of promotional gollies in the form of small standing dolls formed a jazz band, with drummer, double bassist, saxophonists, trumpeter, and other instrumentalists. The very last official Robertson's golly was *made in 2002.*

The whiteness of the traditional jazz boom in Britain in the late 1950s has been touched on by cultural critics. For instance, Iain Chambers writes that white trad—at the time of bebop and the beginnings of free jazz in the United States—could "conveniently overlook" the "new, black militant musical consciousness" of the times by "nostalgically evoking a mythical New Orleans of around 1900" (1985, 48). With specific reference to minstrelsy and trad jazz, Simon Frith has explored the processes by which African American music was "made safe" for suburban consumption in Britain. The only way British jazzers up to the 1950s could attempt or claim to play authentic music was, according to Frith, by making "the music a matter of feeling, *expressive of personal not social identity*, of sensual not cultural need" (Frith 1988, 58; my emphasis). I show elsewhere that there was an important social and political aspect to this music, but because of its frequent affinities with the British music hall and the American sentimental South, of all the exported forms of jazz, trad is nevertheless the nearest to blackface, to minstrelsy. Frith continues: "black Americans became coded as the 'other' of lower-middle-class [British] relaxation, a source of musical access to one's heart and soul less daunting than bourgeois concert forms. This was to be highly significant for later attitudes to jazz and blues. If the minstrels were an easy-listening version of strong feeling, black masks were later put on with more excitement—by British jazz musicians from the thirties to the fifties, by British blues and soul bands from the sixties to the eighties" (Frith 1988, 49–50).

Susan Gubar offers a helpful and rather positive model for the white "modalities of racial impersonation," and the historical development of that process—which goes from mockery to mimicry to mutuality, "eventually playing out all three" (1997, 45). Using this model, it is possible to see that the (almost entirely) white performance of trad jazz itself could work to exclude a black audience in Britain, because of the profound uncertainty of the performance. At what stage of Gubar's were white tradders? Ken Colyer, white purist champion of original black New Orleans music, would no doubt have claimed something between mimicry and mutuality. But the jazz singer, anarchist, critic, and CND and Anti-Apartheid Movement member George Melly, renowned for his *larger-than-life* renditions of blues and trad songs, his melodrama, camp, and accent, can perhaps be seen to veer uncomfortably between mimicry and mockery. I asked him about the whiteness of trad, and he acknowledged the problematic of his own performance: "I didn't like white jazz at all. The modern jazz scene attracted lots of black people. We thought that it was because modern jazz was more contemporary, more cool and cutting edge, and that's what London's blacks wanted, whereas ours was too old music. I think as well now that black audiences may have perceived some element of Uncle Tomming in our performances. Yes, that's possible, yes" (personal interview, 2002).

RECONFIGURING WHITENESSES: PLAYING AGAINST NAZI ARYANISM, THE AMERICAN SEGREGATIONIST SOUTH, APARTHEID SOUTH AFRICA, NOTTING HILL "RACE RIOTS"

The amalgamation of variant white identities under the master-sign
of England may have been conducted in the pursuit of racial truth,
but the practice has always been promiscuous. . . . For all its breath-
taking conservatism English culture has at the same time been
extraordinarily dynamic, its very dynamism generating new spaces,
new contact zones, inside its own field of sovereignty.
—BILL SCHWARZ (1996, 190)

So far I have looked at ways in which jazz was understood or employed within a sociocultural framework that largely confirmed a normative or dominant whiteness. I want to turn this around now, to look at how jazz was a cultural space for the contestation of whiteness—by rejecting racist and supremacist whitenesses—and to explore the more inclusive or tolerant possibilities that jazz could offer to its white British communities. Ruth Frankenberg has argued that "it is only in those times and places where white supremacism has achieved hegemony that whiteness attains (usually unstable) unmarkedness" (1997, 5). By looking at some of those social mass movements and moments that achieved or aimed for white supremacism we can begin to make British whiteness more marked, more visible. My examples are not random choices. Aryanism, segregation in the American South, apartheid in South Africa, white racism on English urban streets in the 1950s—each of these ideological and social battles is also a cultural one, and jazz at its peak from the 1940s to the 1960s was a, perhaps the, primary cultural space for negotiating and transforming British understandings of whiteness, even if this is tentative and incomplete.

A Marxist rather than ethnically centered view of jazz history was offered quite early on by Iain Lang, providing evidence that British jazz critics were grappling with race too, but also that they sought to bring about a wider political understanding and thus to move beyond what they perceived as the limitations of race, toward an awareness of universal oppressions and the need to combat them. Lang first introduced this class-oriented perspective in a short wartime publication, *Background to the Blues*, published by the communist Workers' Music Association (Lang 1942)—this was the second in a series, after *Twenty Soviet Composers*. He expanded this into the book-length *Jazz in Perspective* after the Second World War, an edition of which was also later published by the Jazz Book Club. The book was an effort to privilege class over the hitherto largely accepted racial narrative of the music, to counter the romanticizing "All-Black obsessionists," as Lang put it, but there is also a careful distancing from Soviet aesthetics, perhaps a sign that "personally Lang was more closely associated with the J[azz] S[ociological] S[ociety]," the anarchist wing of leftist jazz enthusiasts at the time (Morgan 1998, 132)—and in fact *Background of the Blues* carried an advertisement for the JSS, with an endorsement by Lang for the JSS Bulletin: "I think I have read practically everything of the kind produced in this country, France and America during the past few years, and I don't know of any jazz periodical which approaches the subject so intelligently" (Lang 1942, 56). In Kevin Morgan's words, Lang presented a "categorical repudiation of ethnic or racial interpretations of jazz and its origins" (Morgan 1998, 133). In a chapter in *Jazz in Perspective* called "Black and White Blues," Lang develops his thesis: "One reason, then, why Negroes have been conspicuous in jazz is that most American Negroes are proletarians. . . . Jazz is not the music of a race, black or white, but of a class—of a proletariat which includes black and white. This view has nothing to do with any political 'party line' and it is, most emphatically, not an attempt to conscript jazz under the dreary and sentimental banner of Socialist Realism. . . . A new, independent and dynamic musical language [was created by] . . . these Negro and white Dead End Kids" (Lang 1957, 32, 30–31, 34).

Clearly Lang was prone to the odd romanticizing moment himself. More starkly, writing of Harlem in the 1920s, Lang argues that "blackness was only skin deep" (1957, 81). Morgan explicates Lang's position by contextualizing it around fascism, as a rejection of all racial classifications and their evident associated dangers. As one communist fan put it, at this time in history the "negrophile purist" was not so very far away from "the petty racialism which in the long run destroys culture and which stems purely from the Nazi-Fascist cultural mentality" (quoted in Morgan 1998, 133). This was a view echoed in the thinking of the British saxophonist Bruce Turner after the war: "I wasn't aware of any fine distinctions between black and white music. I had thought we were all through with racial categories now that Hitler had been defeated in the great ideological war" (Turner 1984, 96). Turner describes the invention of the jazz musician as an emblematic, globalized figure of the new world—"a new kind of human being, a sophisticated world citizen who simply did not fit into the old racial patterns" (Turner 1984, 111). This utopian[22] construction of a post-racial, post-national aesthetic being may be heroic (or self-heroizing) and unrealistic—and with due respect to Turner his own jazz career was not really characterized by the fulfilment of such global ambitions—but it gives an insight into what some white British musicians desired out of the cultural space of jazz.[23] Also, and perhaps altogether more problematically, the blankness of whiteness is acknowledged by blanking out blackness.

According to Ingrid Monson, "since whiteness tends to be a sign of inauthenticity within the world of jazz, the appeals of white musicians to universalistic rhetoric can be perceived as a power play rather than genuine expressions of universal brotherhood. If jazz is one of the few cultural categories in which being African American is evaluated as 'better' or more 'authentic' than being non–African American, a white musician's appeal to a colourblind rhetoric might cloak a move to minimize the black cultural advantage by 'lowering' an assertive African American musician from his or her pedestal to a more 'equal' playing field" (quoted in Atkins 2001, 18). I want to explore *blindness* a little, colorblindness as a metaphor for racial tolerance and inclusion:[24] In what ways has it manifested itself in British jazz? I find it interesting that when the Beats discover God in Jack Kerouac's *On the Road*, as Dean Moriarty and Sal Paradise sit in a jazz club in Chicago, God turns out to be the expatriate British white sub-bebop pianist George Shearing, recently emigrated to the States, "listening to the American sounds and mastering them for his own English summer's night use" (Kerouac 1957, 227; Morton 1984, 43). This moment of jazz religiosity, epiphanic, lasts one single paragraph in the novel. The whiteness of Shearing, mirroring Dean's and Sal's, goes unremarked, except for a reference to "his pale hand." However, his blindness—one of his first jobs as a teenager was playing in the National Institute for the Blind Band in London (Chilton 1997, 292)—*is* employed by Kerouac to exaggerate the myth of improvised creativity, the pathos of such individual genius: after an hour playing "innumerable choruses with amazing chords that mounted higher and higher . . . and everybody listened in awe and fright," Shearing is "led off the stand . . . back to his dark corner" (1957, 227). Shearing is a very odd choice for the Beats' jazz deity, and little more convincing in a role as a Mezzrowesque or Maileresque white negro. He would appear to operate successfully only as a marker of how *uncool* (neat, untheoretical word) these novelistic Beats were. Really, how could a *Brit* possibly show these guys the way? Playing modern *jazz*? It must be Shearing's blindness, the blindness of a white jazz musician from London, England, that signifies.

One of jazz journalism's more curious innovations was the so-called blindfold test, introduced by Leonard Feather, first for *Metronome* and then for *Down Beat* in the United States in the 1940s. (When Shearing moved to the United States about this time, Feather helped his new career with some introductions—a few clubs were reluctant to book a blind pianist, fearing that audiences would consider his disability unappealing; Feather had heard Shearing a decade before at a London Rhythm Club. He also wrote an article about Shearing's arrival in the States, entitled "Even a Londoner Can Have a Natural Feeling for Jazz.") The idea was that a well-known musician would listen to, comment on, and grade (with points out of five) a number of recordings by other musicians, the identity of which would be secret (hence the blindfold, which actually was used in the early tests, as photographs accompanying the published results evidenced). A transcript of the musician's comments would form the basis of the published article. Feather explained the very first blindfold test as follows: "To allay all prejudices, to cut through all the vast variety of points of view in jazz, we propose to play a series of records each month to a noted figure in the jazz world. With these records, we will test his or her reactions to all kinds of music, from Dixieland to Bebop. And we will test all kinds of musicians. . . . Mary Lou Williams, first musician to be Blindfold Tested, is a great pianist, arranger and composer. She is also a great person, one who is genuinely alarmed by the ignorance that prevails in the dissemination of jazz knowledge. Her signed statement, attesting to the complete accuracy of this article, is in our possession" (Feather 1946).

I think the pseudo-scientific features — objectivity, blindfold, grades of performance, the "signed statement" — were of less interest to readers than the entertaining possibility that a musician might mess up in comment or identification, but in his obituary of Feather in the *Village Voice*, published in 1994, Gary Giddins saw in the test more than novel entertainment: "It added a . . . new dimension to our understanding of critical authority, demonstrating that people often judged a work of art differently when they didn't know who signed it. Over decades, Feather embarrassed scores of musicians who thought that race and gender were audible, or that studio men can't improvise, or that big names are invariably identifiable" (Giddins 1994).

It is important that Feather was English, or rather that he was a non-American white: after all, from the beginning his blindfold test aimed "to allay all prejudices." There is a certain utopian colorblindness in this project, which may have been easier to propose for someone like Feather, an outsider in America (a Jew, in fact, though an agnostic one). As he acknowledged of his early reception by black musicians in New York in the 1930s, "Not being an American . . . fortified my credentials" (1986, 18). Feather became a staunch supporter of civil rights, and also sought to raise the profile of women in American jazz.[25] He could utilize his expertise about the music in Europe on occasion to gently remind American jazz fans that striking early examples of blacks and whites playing the music together "were invariably found outside the US. The first truly interracial big band in history, its personnel comprising West Indians, English, Scottish and Continental musicians, was assembled by Benny Carter for a summer season at a Dutch seaside resort in 1937" (1974, 303).

I do not wish to equate the permanent condition of blindness (when Shearing was asked if he had been blind all his life, he replied: "Only so far!") with a temporary game of blindfolding, and yet, though very different, British blindnesses may not have meant (only) lack of vision, but *a refusal to see in the American way*. These white blindnesses contributed to racial debates within jazz—if only because, as Les Back has reminded us, there is an "important distinction between the visual regimes of racism and whiteness and the utopian possibilities of sound" (2001, 194). The subtitle of Feather's autobiography describes him as an "*ear*witness to an era" (1986). In the 1960s, while Pink Floyd was building a reputation in the London counterculture for new rock less on its music than on the mind-blowing light shows that accompanied its performances, the group on a number of occasions shared a bill with the experimental improvising ensemble AMM. This band, in a negative gesture of visual excess, would sometimes play with no lighting, in pitch blackness. Performing in the dark, AMM sought to *unidentify* egocentricity[26] and even human agency in the production of the music (all sounds were acceptable), to question musical technique, to erase the hierarchy of audience and performer—and I am only pushing it slightly to suggest a tentative connection with the lacks of vision in music above. AMM's drummer Eddie Prévost told me of his own social and musical colorblindness, if you like: "National and or ethnic identity is of no importance to me at all. Even when we were starting out [playing jazz], in our young romanticising way we probably were expressing our own alienation, but we didn't want to bolt that on to African-American experience in their music. I have been running a weekly workshop in London now for over three years in which time there have been musicians of at least twenty different nationalities. Never has there been a particular problem in musical communication. Quite the reverse" (personal interview, 2002).

Brian Ward expresses the paradox of many white Americans' enthusiasm for black soul and rhythm-and-blues in the United States during the 1960s, that period of civil rights mass protest: "genuine admiration for black music did not necessarily challenge basic white racial beliefs and assumptions at all, but frequently served to reinforce them . . . associated with the unremittingly physical, passionate, ecstatic, emotional, and, above all, sexually liberated black worlds of their imaginations. Paradoxically, in so doing, white fans of black music neatly fitted black music, style and culture into much the same normative categories so dear to the most bigoted opponents of black music and black equality" (Ward 1998, 12).

We have seen a not dissimilar argument made for the reception of black jazz by white Europeans. Yet it is very important also to acknowledge that other white jazz musicians and enthusiasts wished to make unambiguous political statements or engage in uncompromising social actions about racism against blacks, and not only that originating from the United States. That is to say, they sought to employ the racial codings they saw at the core of their preferred culture — jazz — in order to identify and (re-)shape their own white identities. Les Back explores the correspondences and ambivalences of the white reception of black jazz between British, American, and Nazi societies during the Second World War. For Back the correspondence between the practice of the three countries (that is, Allied and Axis forces alike) worked to confirm a normative whiteness that constructed itself in part through anti-black racisms, so that there were "uncomfortable similarities among Jim Crow, John Bull, and the racial phobias of Nazism" (Back 2001, 170). The Nazis attacked jazz as degenerate culture, and used aerial propaganda to build fears of a black male presence, specifically mentioning jazz and dance, among Europeans (Back 2001, 189); the Americans segregated their black and white servicemen, trying to maintain in Britain the racist social divisions and attitudes of home (not least since many of the black GIs in Britain were from the South), and British military and political leaders struggled with trying to accommodate what one general called "the historical background of the American attitude of the colour problem" (quoted in Back 2001, 186). Back points to the radio broadcasts of the white bandleader Captain Glenn Miller's Allied Expeditionary Forces, in which "music was invoked as an icon of American justice at the very time when racial segregation in the Allied armed forces was prevalent" (Back 2001, 188). Yet, and at the same time, "The British, confronted with this spectre of racist violence and the institutionalized military segregation, more often than not took the side of the black soldiers. . . . For many black GIs, coming to England resulted in their first experience in being treated with respect and friendship by white people . . . [and] *the dance hall became a new social sphere for integration*" (Back 2001, 185–87; my emphasis).

Black regiments formed their own big bands and held dances to which white British women would be invited; in East Anglia, where there was (and still is) a very strong American military presence, there would be multiracial dances deep in the English countryside; as I explore in detail in chapter 3, the Jamaican bandleader Leslie "Jiver" Hutchinson would bring his All-Coloured Band from London to play at black GIs' dances (Back 2001, 183). As so often occurs (thankfully), the attempted censorship backfired and highlighted the evidence: photographs of black GIs and white English women jitterbugging together accompanied American newspaper and magazine articles in 1943. The American military's Bureau of Public Relations stepped in to end the publication of such provocative images of pleasure and freedom. As Back comments, "Black soldiers could sacrifice their lives in the fight against fascism, but they could not be seen dancing with the natives!" (2001, 187). Similarly, for a significant number of white British soldiers—across the ranks—and civilians, there was a compelling sense that if they were fighting against fascism, an ideology predicated on the myth of white superiority, the freedom that they envisaged and struggled for would not contain continued racial categorization, segregation American-style.[27]

The argument that white British musicians and audiences worked to avoid the militant or cutting edge of current black American music, and by implication politics—the taming of jazz, the masking of whiteness through blackface—offers an incomplete conclusion to the complex past and politicized pleasures of the trad movement of the 1950s. For instance, and notwithstanding the performances of Freddy Randall's British Dixieland band before segregated audiences in the United States mentioned below, that there was an extraordinary enthusiasm in Britain for a music of the American South that originally was largely black, and at the very time when the civil rights movement was advancing there, provided another arena for at least sympathetic interest in that political struggle. Colin Barker was a suburban trad fan whose experience of what he understood as the implicit politics of the music is illuminating and, I suggest, not unrepresentative: "When I went to university in 1959, I just gravitated towards CND. It kind of went with what I wanted to be, and though there had never been any formal 'politics' in the jazz scene in [my home town of] Ilford, and there were no black people around our area in that period, it was taken for granted that we all wished we could hear black American jazz musicians. I read in the newspaper about the early civil rights movement in the States, and automatically identified with it without ever thinking why. So jazz did imply a kind of connection with anti-racism, even though the term was unknown then" (personal correspondence, 2002).

In the mid-1950s the joint ban by the American Federation of Musicians and the Musicians' Union on overseas musicians, which had done sterling work over two decades in keeping professional British jazz and dance music white, was finally being lifted. In its place was put a transatlantic exchange agreement between American and British musicians, organized by the unions of the two countries. The key mechanism was to be reciprocity—the number of American musicians touring Britain to be equal to the number of British musicians touring the United States. That the United States, with jazz booming and rock 'n' roll beginning, was producing almost all the energetic innovation in popular music at the time made the early attempts at reciprocity ludicrously unbalanced. In practice reciprocity meant that British musicians made up the numbers in any way that promoters could manage to achieve targets: for example, a bebop band led by Ronnie Scott might tour with a rock 'n' roll package in the States, playing one number a night, or Vic Lewis's big band would play six-minute sets to uninterested audiences as part of a touring package featuring Bill Haley and his Comets (Godbolt 1989, 240–43). Concerts were frequently booked in the South, where segregated audiences watched, or protested outside, or worse. Leonard Feather reported in 1956 in *Melody Maker*: "The white citizens of Birmingham, Alabama—who were responsible for the attack on Nat King Cole during [the British bandleader] Ted Heath's concerts—again caused trouble when Freddy Randall appeared at the Civic Auditorium. The Randall band . . . played before a segregated audience. . . . Council pickets paraded outside the hall carrying signs reading: 'Down with rebop. Christians will not attend this show. Ask your preacher about jungle music'" (quoted in Godbolt 1989, 241).

Randall's band actually played Dixieland, and Godbolt notes the irony of these "white men from east London who, in essence, played white men's jazz, suffer[ing] abuse from southern rednecks for playing 'nigra' music. There was even a bomb-scare" (1989, 242). When critical reports of the workings of reciprocity for British bands that toured America began to appear in the British music press — Feather was most scathing in his reports home — other British bands began to approach the opportunity more warily, and with a greater understanding of the social implications. John Dankworth in particular refused to be part of the farce, rejecting the offer of an American tour in 1958 and explaining to readers of *Melody Maker* that his band would tour America when three conditions had been met: "First: when we are well-known enough to mean something out there. Second: when we are guaranteed a fair showing — to a jazz audience; and regrettably, I was forced to add a third condition: when we are assured of a tour that will cause no embarrassment to negro musicians or enthusiasts" (quoted in Godbolt 1989, 244).

Many of Dankworth's bands had been multiracial — singers and percussionists like Frank Holder and Bobby Breen, the baritone saxophonist George Tyndale, the singer Joy Marshall, and of course the singer Cleo Laine. Laine was born in Middlesex of mixed white English and Jamaican parents, and had sung with the band for some years. Three months after Dankworth's public refusal to play for segregated audiences as part of a reciprocal tour of America, he and Laine were married, and they went on to become Britain's best-known multiracial jazz partnership, with, as their biographer Graham Collier points out, an active interest in "social causes — particularly, as might be imagined, those concerned with racial prejudice" (Collier 1976, 54). In fact, already before this Dankworth and Laine had articulated political positions around race, being critical of the construction of whiteness and blackness in the policy of apartheid in South Africa, for instance. Dankworth had played there once, to white audiences, as Laine recalls:

> In 1954 John had made a solo trip to South Africa, playing with local musicians. The fact that he could not play to black audiences appalled him: his musical mentors were black, he was playing the music created by them, but to white audiences, while the black fans had to sweep the stage, clean the toilets and hear the music in the background. . . . Clandestine meetings [between Dankworth and

black South African musicians] . . . were loving gatherings between like souls, but dangerous for all if found out. John was asked to go back several times after that first visit, with requests that I accompany him. As it was illegal for a white and a person of colour to cohabit, let alone be allowed into a white hotel as a guest, at that time the request for me was made in ignorance of my heritage. JD had no desire to return under these circumstances, and he never went there again. It was John's South Africa experience that made us aware of this offensive law and brought us into the Anti-Apartheid movement in Britain. (Laine 1994, 167–68)

The South African government cracked down on the dissidents responsible for the Freedom Charter of 1955, a document claiming racial equality, who included Oliver Tambo and Nelson Mandela of the African National Congress. Many activists were tried for treason, in a series of trials that lasted over five years. There was an international response of opposition to the treason trials, not least in Britain, which maintained strong colonial links to South Africa even though it had been for many years an independent dominion. (In fact the treason trials were undertaken in South African courts in the name of the British monarch.) In October 1957 Dankworth's big band was a highlight of a jazz benefit concert at the Festival Hall in London, as part of an impressive transatlantic bill also featuring Lionel Hampton, in aid of Christian Action's South Africa Treason Trial fund, which supported those being persecuted by the state there.[28] Just as interestingly, Laine and Dankworth were among many jazz musicians sensitive to anti-black racism among white youth in Britain, dramatized by the riots of 1958. Along with the author Colin MacInnes, leftist jazz critics like Max Jones and Francis Newton (Eric Hobsbawm), and jazz musicians like Humphrey Lyttelton and Ken Colyer, they established the Stars' Campaign for Inter-Racial Friendship in London.

The pianist Manfred Mann and the double bassist Harry Miller were among those jazz musicians who made the journey to Britain to escape their designated roles as whites in apartheid South Africa. Miller would go on to be an important player in British free jazz, while Mann, after working as a jazz musician and critic for a period in London, found great success in the blues boom and subsequent pop-rock crossover. He charted for me his observation about South African and British whitenesses, particularly in relation to white racist ideologies:

14. The Pioneer Jazz Band leads an anti-apartheid demonstration, Bristol, *ca.* 1962.

Harry and I came over to England together on the same ship, in September 1961. The situation was this: South Africa was leaving the Commonwealth—and a small percentage of that generation of whites had *always* wanted to leave the country anyway, and we left because we didn't like the situation there. Who would want to bring children up in a fascist state, when there was a way out? I hated South Africa with a vengeance. The idea of my children being racist, conforming to that, was a nightmare. There was a period of a year I think when you could come to Britain without any problem, as part of a Commonwealth arrangement. We came to London because it was less frightening than New York [*laughs*], but of course because of the Commonwealth connection too—it was the place to come to.

Speaking from a white perspective, merely to conform in South Africa was to be a racist—the horror of it all was that for everyone this was the normal state of affairs. You simply carried on calmly, you could be—quote—*a decent human being*, you were white people calmly having tea, that was the norm. The British or European racist is different, and particularly awful. They have gone *outside* the social conventions, *against* the news, the priests, the politicians, and so on.

Initially it was an enormous relief to be away from South Africa. Partly London was so big, it was not limited to a single kind of scene either. But in England I was amazed to find a lot more racism than

I expected. I saw NO BLACKS signs and that made me feel uneasy here. You do become incredibly coloured — to use a phrase — by your South African experience. (Personal interview, 2003)

Susan Gubar identifies one engine of cultural production which may be of special relevance to jazz outside the United States in her observation that "white remorse about racial inequality . . . turns out to be a more significant motive in twentieth-century aesthetic production than many critics have realized" (Gubar 1997, xviii–xix). Remorse is an inadequate term or activity in itself, and must be, as seen here, extended to articulation, action, engagement. What it meant to be white in Britain was altering, and one of the key soundtracks both accompanying that shift, and sounding it in praxis, was jazz. I have found that particularly in interviews, there have been marked ambivalences and reticence around articulations of whiteness on the part of many British jazzers. Despite these inhibitions, I have looked at how jazz did make available and accessible a framework for maintaining a dominant colonial and post-colonial whiteness, often within a normative anti-black racism. I have then charted other geopolitical and local moments during which jazz functioned as an ideological cultural arena for the *rejection* of white racist or supremacist social practices. Through experience or knowledge the competing ideologies of whiteness — the supremacist ones of Nazi Aryanism, of the American South and segregation, of South African apartheid — were being found wanting. Even in Britain, the reaction from the jazz community to white racism directed at new black migrants in the 1950s stood as a rejection of white intolerance. White *colorblindness* is at work in each of these readings. There is the depoliticized colorblindness which refutes difference and refuses to acknowledge the possible privileges of whiteness. There is the engaged colorblindness, *à la* Feather blindfold test, which employs it to bypass accepted racism. Of course these are inadequate responses in themselves: Wald alerts us to "the difficulty of choosing 'blindness' as a political strategy" (Wald 2000, 186). As visions they can only fail. But as gestures or positions they do bear traces — whether of disengagement or negotiation — and as staging posts they offer something to work with politically. Did jazz in Britain halt its contribution at this halfway (perhaps) stage? It may be that jazz's innovative cultural and political possibilities were exhausted by the time debates about whiteness

15. African American and white British musicians play at a CND March for Life in tribute to the recently assassinated Dr. Martin Luther King, April 1968. From left Jon Hendricks, Philly Joe Jones, Pete King, on the steps of St Paul's Cathedral, London. © Val Wilmer.

were ready to progress. In this reading, jazz in Britain functioned historically during the period discussed in this chapter as a transitional culture, one which opened up *some* space for the denial, the assertion, the contestation, and the reconfiguration of whiteness.

Bill Schwarz has argued that "the rediscovery on the part of English people in this period of themselves as 'white' is as forceful a historical fact as any of the other more conventional ethnic discoveries of the 1950s and 1960s" (1996, 199)—and it is important to acknowledge that sometimes, to an extent, as in these jazz circles, white discovery was also a political rejection of other white categories. The popular appearance and experience of jazz, from big band to traditional-revivalist *and* modern jazz from the 1940s to the early 1960s, as multiracial statements at social and political demonstrations, or at events in the beginnings of alternative culture, the New Left, and the white understanding of colonialism and racism, indicate unmistakably that in Britain, the largely white practice of jazz figured as a significant accompaniment to shifting social identity and political praxis. While there remains a problematic lack of an acceptable and accessible language of whiteness in British culture and society—especially on the left[29]—it is also true that in Britain, theories of difference have not substantially percolated into jazz discourse. It may be that discussion in the field is further inhibited by the reluctance of British musicians, critics, and enthusiasts to follow the American route of the culture wars or the politics of identity. What we *can* conclude is that in Britain throughout the twentieth century, the popular, long-lasting, and largely black American culture of jazz was demonized, resisted, enjoyed, and musically participated in by whites, and that it was employed in both global and local contexts to foster or to contest differing configurations of whiteness. Jazz was a very important cultural arena in which these kinds of debates and struggles happened. What Gilroy has called "the central Manichean dynamic—black and white" (1993, 27) can be more constructively approached, and I want the next chapter to extend further the dialogic opportunities between the two.

THREE

Jazz of the Black Atlantic and the Commonwealth

There are large questions raised about the direction and character of black culture and art if we take the powerful effects of even temporary experiences of exile, relocation, and displacement into account. . . . Whether their experience of exile is enforced or chosen, temporary or permanent, these intellectuals and activists, writers, speakers, poets and artists repeatedly articulate a desire to escape the restrictive bonds of ethnicity, national identification, and sometimes even "race" itself.
—PAUL GILROY, *The Black Atlantic* (1993, 18, 19)

have shown how what might be recognized as "jazz," during its early reception in the watershed year of 1919, when British audiences felt the impact of the sonicity of American modernity in the figures of the white Original Dixieland Jazz Band and the black Southern Syncopated Orchestra, was articulated and understood in Britain within a racial framework. I have shown how the perceived dominant blackness of jazz subsequently played a role in the shifting configurations of what it meant to be (British) white. But also, how significant was jazz in the cultural construction of black identities in Britain? There were important contributions from African American musicians playing ragtime, jazz, or something a little like it in Britain before this often-identified year of 1919, and Howard Rye traces the lineage back further, arguing that "there is no clear dividing line, either in fact or in public consciousness, between the [black rather than blackface] minstrelsy of the nineteenth century and those forms of Afro-American music which have been known since 1920 as jazz and blues" (Rye 1990, 45). In the first decades of the twentieth century black American music was present: the African American mandolinist Seth S. Weeks recorded in London in 1900, while other black attractions included the cakewalk musical show *In Dahomey* (1903), the ensemble ragtime of the Musical Spillers (1912), and the Jamaican-born pianist Dan Kildare and his Clef Club Orchestra from New York (1915) (see Rye 1990). In Alyn Shipton's view, the syncopated orchestras, playing ensemble ragtime, based in New York, and then traveling to *Europe*—France rather than Britain— "played an equally crucial role in disseminating the music that became jazz" outside the United States (2001, 33). He offers a corrective: "The majority of jazz histories draw attention to the Original Dixieland Jazz

Band, as white New Orleans ensemble arriving in London in April 1919 and 'bringing jazz to Europe.' In reality the syncopated orchestra had got there first" (2001, 35). By this Shipton means James Reese Europe's Hellfighters and Will Vodery's black band in the war theater in 1918, and then Will Marion Cook in London in the following year.

Jazz practice is historically characterized by the adoption of local or indigenous forms of music, of working within international musical frameworks. I have touched on some of the negative and positive aspects of the familiar narrative of jazz as a universal language already, although there is more to be said. The language of jazz, if it is a universal one, is subject to localizing as well as globalizing imperatives, owing in strong measure to its definitive production-oriented identity: jazz is not merely a consumed music, but one played, made, produced in each locale. Alyn Shipton writes that "perhaps the most high-profile integration of folk and traditional music with jazz has come from Latin America and the Caribbean" (2001, 833), and this has been so throughout (American) jazz history (see Roberts 1999). Consider the "Spanish tinge" talked of by Jelly Roll Morton in early New Orleans, the Argentinian tango and ragtime piano and dance crossover between 1910 and 1930, the Cuban bebop developments of Dizzy Gillespie and Chano Pozo beginning in the 1940s, or the working together of modern jazz with Brazilian bossa nova in the 1960s by Stan Getz and Antonio Carlos Jobim. John Storm Roberts suggests that analysis of even the earliest New Orleans jazz betrays a complex and already lengthy musical culture in which "it is tough to disentangle the Latin influences from European-Spanish on the one hand and non-Latin Caribbean elements on the other—tough, and at times self-defeating, because all the various Caribbean idioms (including in all probability New Orleans idioms) had already been influencing each other for a century or more" (1999, 1). Britain itself had an alternate network of social and cultural—and economic—relations which has been highly significant in the development of British jazz sounds. The circulatory global framework that was the British Empire, and then its successor or residue—the Commonwealth—has played a fundamental role in British jazz. For this reason Andrew Blake argues in *The Land without Music* that in British popular music history, "the Anglo-American angle is not the only one" (1997, 79). He elaborates: "There are more voices in play than the American and the British: it is and has been since the 1950s less a dialogue than a *multilogue*, a mixture of musics intersecting in the various urban centres to produce, among other things, many new local forms of Caribbean-derived music, such as reggae and the 'new ska' of two-tone; Asian musics reworked through the use of technology and the influence of Western pop to produce Bhangra and Indi-pop. . . . The examples of Joe Harriott and Bob Marley point to the second reason for the importance of Britain as the site for the transformation of pop musics: the nature and extent of post-war, post-colonial immigration" (Blake 1997, 103–4, 107; emphasis in original).

This chapter is concerned with mapping out the jazz-inflected soundscapes sketched by Blake, with two important addenda. First, I consider the "prehistory" of British pop, to demonstrate a longer political and cultural interrogation than is usual of what it meant to be black in Britain. Doing so involves looking at significant black music production in Britain *pre*-1950s, *pre*-war, and therefore *pre*-post-colonial, because jazz was used, was played in the considered cultural figuration of blackness in Britain earlier in the twentieth century. I explore this phenomenon with particular reference to the contribution of Caribbean musicians at that time, and not only because there is a revealing link to be made with the pan-African activism and rhetoric of the leading black activist, the Jamaican Marcus Garvey (who lived in London in the years leading up to his death in 1940). Second, I explore differences in black culture, identity, and origin, which signal the extent of the imperial legacy and shift the contemporary focus toward the Caribbean and Indian innovations in British popular music described by Blake. Here I am thinking of the powerful contribution of exiled South African musicians in London in the 1960s that I discuss in the second half of the chapter.

I am acutely conscious—once more—that in framing this chapter around the twin Commonwealth routes of the black Atlantic of the Caribbean-British relation and the black exiles from South Africa in London, there are significant potential exclusions and problems.[1] For example, the musical experiments of the Jamaican alto saxophonist Joe Harriott's later career involved the Indian violinist John Mayer and the Goanese guitarist Amancio D'Silva. The central organizing personality of both the South African Blue Notes and the later Brotherhood of Breath big band in Britain and Europe was Chris McGregor, a *white* South African. Other Commonwealth nations at different times supplied important white musicians who invigorated British music too—Australia (Graeme Bell Jazz Band), Canada (the trumpeter Kenny Wheeler), Zimbabwe (then called Rhodesia: Mike Gibbs). These few examples betray the instant complexity of hemispheric, let alone global, cultural circulation, a complexity that is multiplied in the context of jazz's doubled outernationalism—both American and British structures and power and exchange contributing. As in the chapter on white jazz, my purpose in structuring the discussion thus is not an essentializing or reductive gesture: I hope rather to be *opening* a space for discussion, for exploring jazz's (neglected) role in social change in Britain, specifically around race, which has been a central dynamic of jazz culture. To achieve this requires the luxury of detail, and a detailed analysis of the black jazzes of Britain is what follows.

In considering the historiography of British imperial and colonial relations, Mary Louise Pratt has written of the way the "periphery determined the metropolis" (quoted in Ward 2001, 1)—the imperial center being *shaped by* cultures from the colonies, rather than simply or only the other way round. The material that follows also contributes to that development in cultural history, in both colonial and especially postcolonial times, but because jazz—the music of a new hegemon during the twentieth century—is the cultural focus, there is this further complexity to charting the shifting locus of culture and power. By listening to jazz from the Commonwealth one can trace the operations of its global, circulatory networks of culture and power, but one can also identify and evaluate the extent to which the center was shifting. It is important that much of the music considered in this chapter was being played by *black* musicians in Britain, during a period when government, through its changing migration and citizenship policies, sought covertly and overtly to strengthen the connection between Britishness and whiteness—what Kathleen Paul has called the "whitewashing" of Britain (see Paul 1997). This much is evident from changes in the right of access between white and black Commonwealth peoples, beginning with the Nationality Act of 1948 and continuing with the Commonwealth Immigrants Acts of 1962 and 1968, and beyond. As Paul has argued, "successive governments of both major parties expended a great deal of energy trying to devise a means by which black Britons could be kept out" of the United Kingdom (Paul 2001, 191). There was a complex balancing act attempted by British politicians, between (casuistically) protecting their version or vision of a predominantly white Britain on the one hand and maintaining their vision or illusion of a multiracial Commonwealth on the other. Interestingly, and not unlike the jazz musicians below, government officials began to look to the United States and to the Commonwealth *at the same time*: "ministers weighed up their fear of developing a US-style 'colour problem' against the potential dangers to the Commonwealth and Empire that would surely result from the introduction of [colour discriminatory] migration control" (Paul 2001, 192). Yet according to Paul, around all this a "focus upon a white skin as a prerequisite for both imperial migration and membership in the real British family was . . . evident" (2001, 185). As the left-wing MP Tom Driberg put it at the time: "The real problem is not black skins, but white prejudice" (quoted in Sinfield 1989, 127).

"LONDON IS THE PLACE FOR ME": CARIBBEAN CONTRIBUTIONS TO BRITISH JAZZ

The post-war Caribbean immigration would later enrich the London jazz milieu with Joe Harriott, trumpeter Shake Keane, guitarist Ernest Ranglin and others. But the pioneering black British swing artists set the stage for subsequent stars of more recent times. The black community's struggle for equality and justice is still lumbered with the historical irony that so many of their jazz ancestors are under-documented if not outright undocumented today. — ANDREW SIMONS (2001, 35)

The entry of blacks into national life was itself a powerful factor contributing to the circumstances in which the formation of both cultural studies and New Left politics became possible. It indexes the profound transformations of British social and cultural life in the 1950s. . . . — PAUL GILROY (1993, 10)

The Caribbean has a set of familiar and important contributions to the development of popular music globally, seen in terms of its relation with the United States in Cuban jazz, or in Paul Gilroy's privileging of the role of the Jamaican sound system in the origins of hip-hop. In Britain most people would readily identify reggae music and some of its various antecedents (such as ska) from Jamaica, or calypso and the socio-musical practice of carnival from Trinidad. What I want to consider here are the jazz traces and practices that form a background to the British experience of the black Atlantic, in Gilroy's influential phrase, through the twentieth century (acknowledging the tension between national and global once more): "Foregrounding the role of music allows us to see England, or more accurately London, as an important junction point or crossroads on the webbed pathways of black Atlantic political culture. It is revealed to be a place where, by virtue of local factors like the informality of racial segregation, the configuration of class relations, and the contingency of linguistic convergences, global phenomena such as anti-colonial and emancipationist political formations are still being sustained, reproduced, and amplified" (Gilroy 1993, 95).

Doing so involves looking at early jazz—where there are tremendously important links of some sort between the powerfully influential black nationalist ideology of the Jamaican Marcus Garvey and the rise of jazz in black America and a little in black Britain; at the role of jazz in the calypso boom of the 1950s, which was an early cultural and social expression of the new black settler generation in a soon-to-be postcolonial world; at the extraordinary achievement of the Jamaican innovator and alto saxophonist Joe Harriott in the 1960s, and the neglect of his contributions then and since; and at the significance of the modern jazz boom of the 1980s for a newer generation of British blacks seeking a musical voice that they considered suitable for articulating their lived experience.

Owing to geocultural facts such as transport links on cruise liners and the proximity of American radio stations, Andrew Simons argues that "unlike their white cohorts in England, Caribbean players were actually closer to American jazz influence" (2001, 12), while the placing of American military forces on Caribbean islands, particularly Trinidad, during the Second World War had a significant impact on local musical development too (Cowley 1990, 73). The region also had a strong international awareness because of imperial and colonial structures from Europe, a situation acknowledged by Mike and Trevor Phillips: "The problems of race, class and identity in the Caribbean had another, more positive, aspect. In all the islands, as in British Guyana (Guyana) and British Honduras (Belize), the inhabitants were always conscious of being part of a structure that stretched around the globe.

So the context of Caribbean life was never parochial" (1998, 17). Such a relation of globality, modernism, and empire in the region was not unique to Britain: French Caribbean colonies contributed in important ways to the development of surrealism and its anti-colonial politics in Paris and in the Caribbean itself (see Richardson 1996), while the evolution of France as a "revolving door for the musical genres of the world," with specific reference to African and Caribbean sounds, is charted by Frank Tenaille (2002, 39 n. 3). (It should be remembered too that these are intellectual and cultural categories as much as geographical ones.) When people emigrated from the region to settle in Britain, the internationalization of their roots/routes was not forgotten, even by subsequent generations. Their persistence is articulated by the bassist and bandleader of the Jazz Jamaica All-Stars, Gary Crosby, a second-generation black Briton who outlines some aspects of his own musical and social development in relation to the Caribbean:

> I was totally aware that there was a Caribbean culture—for a start there would be lots of family members coming from and going to there all the time. Jamaica was called "home," we all used that word—and I think lots of youth of my generation got hung up on that term, it made it difficult for us to locate ourselves. There were a couple of family members around who were sort of Garveyites on the quiet—one in particular did introduce me to those ideas. He would occasionally talk quietly to me about Garvey, and he was a DJ too, had an amazing record collection. It was him who introduced me to all the music coming from Studio One. The first improvising I took notice of would have been the solos in Jamaican music—Rico on trombone, Roland Alphonso on sax. In my late teens, 1972–73, I was still in my Rastafari phase, and we would have long and many discussions and arguments about colonialism and civil rights. You know, the Vietnam War was still resonating then, and we went on all the marches. And there was a whole group of issues during that time more generally—the New Cross fire, the Mangrove 10, the Spaghetti House siege, black power at the Olympics. At the same time I heard jazz then, and that did turn me on. A lot of young blacks born here felt that we didn't belong in Britain, and one way we dealt with that was by looking to our own black heritage, for comfort, for inspiration. The element of black nationalism in jazz was attractive to

me at that time, it spoke to me in my position in England. (Personal interview, 2002)

The West Indian contribution to the development of jazz (as a political culture) in the United States is important in relation to the Jamaican black activist in the States, Marcus Garvey, and his Universal Negro Improvement Association (UNIA), and in the particular musical form of Trinidadian calypso. According to Ted Vincent, in his book *Keep Cool: The Black Activists Who Built the Jazz Age*: "Recently-arrived West Indian immigrants composed a majority of the Garveyites in the United States during the UNIA's growing years of 1917–21. During this 'acculturation' period a test of Garveyite interest in 'jazzy' music would have to include a look at their members' relationship to the 'hot' music from the islands, such as Trinidadian calypso. . . . The recording session in New York City on 20 June 1912 by Lovey's Trinidad Band marked 'the first Black "hot" music from any English-speaking country' to get on record" (1995, 127–28).

The lyrics of the popular song "West Indies Blues," issued in no fewer than eleven recordings in 1923–24, mentioned Garvey by name, and he himself wrote the lyrics for another popular song of 1927, "Keep Cool" — "(written while in prison)," as the sheet music announced, in Atlanta Penitentiary in 1925. Vincent writes that "while it was unusual for a political figure controversial enough to be imprisoned and exiled to author pop music, it was also unusual for such a figure to get so many stars of jazz and blues to record a song giving him publicity, 'West Indies blues,' including as it happens Fats Waller and his Jamaican Jazzers" (1995, 129, 132).[2] On release from prison two and a half years later, in December of the year of that hit song, 1927, Garvey was deported from the United States. He returned to Jamaica for a short time but then made his way to London, where he was active in black politics, established a newspaper called the *Black Man*, spoke regularly at Speaker's Corner in Hyde Park, and died in June 1940.

Here, with Marcus Garvey in London during the final stay of his life, it is possible to identify small but important direct links between an overtly political black consciousness and the development of black British jazz. It is simply inadequate to state, as Jim Godbolt does in his mainly excellent *History of Jazz in Britain: 1919–1950*, that "the black contribution to British jazz was slight" during the 1930s and

1940s (1984, 188).[3] According to Andrew Simons, in his liner notes for a recent compilation of music from the time entitled *Black British Swing: The African Diaspora's Contribution to England's Own Jazz of the 1930s and 1940s*, "although black racial concerns have often been excised from jazz history, Jamaicans were especially race-conscious because of Marcus Garvey, who . . . inspired the London jazz career of Leslie Thompson" (Simons 2001, 12). It may be that there was significant black music around some sort of jazz during the period, or it may be more significant that some of the music that there was was informed by pan-African or black nationalist or anti-colonialist ideologies—Bill Schwarz reminds us that during the 1930s and 1940s, leading (or soon to be so) black intellectuals and ideologues were based in Britain, including C. L. R. James and George Padmore from Trinidad, Paul Robeson from the United States (while W. E. B. Du Bois visited too), Garvey himself, and future African leaders like Kwame Nkrumah from Ghana and Jomo Kenyatta from Kenya (Schwarz 1996, 177–79). Some of these were centrally involved in the Pan-African Congress held in Manchester in 1945. Their presence would offer an alternate, more complex, or perhaps competing explanation for the popularity among bandleaders and musicians of all-black ensembles, from big bands down, in Britain between the 1930s and the 1950s. The demands of white audiences for exoticism and authenticity in black entertainment did not constitute the entire story. Alyn Shipton draws attention, for example, to the friendships developed between visiting black American musicians and black Caribbean musicians in Britain: "[Louis] Armstrong had an equally significant effect on the community of Caribbean musicians living and working in London, in particular Leslie Thompson, the trumpeter who was to play lead in the European big band that backed Armstrong in 1934. Thompson also met and got to know members of the Ellington and Calloway orchestra on their visits to Britain. The musicians were pleased to meet, as Thompson put it, 'another coloured fellow who played trumpet and lived in Britain'" (Shipton 2001, 367).

Early musicians came across on the banana boats, or in the case of Thompson and Leslie "Jiver" Hutchinson, were in the West Indian Regiment band that won a competition at home in 1924 "to play a six-week season at the British Empire Exhibition at Wembley. They played on open-top buses and grandstands, and had numerous female fans and race-curious white English onlookers" (Simons 2001, 12). After this they returned to Jamaica, going to England permanently and separately a few years later (Wilmer, personal correspondence, 2004). According to Simons, Thompson had a "Garvey-inspired dream"; he "was further influenced by the then American-deported Marcus Garvey, who, although known as the 20th century's first important pan-Africanist, was no stranger to the music business himself. . . . By the 1930s, Thompson was well aware of Garvey's messages, delivered frequently at the Speaker's Corner in Hyde Park, and possibly of his British newspaper, the *Black Man*. Consequently, Thompson's dream was to form an all-black dance band. And although there were African-American jazz musicians who frequented Europe[, h]is idealised ensemble was a solely West Indian one" (Simons 2001, 8–9).

Thompson's ambition to form an all-black band would be realized in 1935 in a band that he led with Ken Johnson, unfortunately never recorded, that was sometimes called the Jamaican Emperors of Jazz. Jeffrey Green notes that the band had "no Americans. The instrumentalists were of African descent but born in Jamaica, England, Trinidad, Wales" (Green 1990, 40).[4] (Thompson's career also saw him working with white classical and avant-garde musicians interested in jazz, including Constant Lambert and Spike Hughes.[5]) Within two years Johnson took over full leadership rights and formed what was eventually billed as Ken "Snakehips" Johnson and His West Indian Dance Band. When the first version, led by Thompson and Johnson, employed white trombonists such as Freddie Greenslade, they had to black-up their faces (Simons 2001, 28)—not in a minstrel gesture, like Harry Gold and Ivor Mairants, but to maintain the all-black stage image of the ensemble. This is itself an interesting and complex moment: in the 1930s in Britain, the blackface of white performers is employed to strengthen the visual impact of a performance partly rooted in the ideological project of black nationalism. Of course there was a novelty aspect to such an "all-colored" band, as well as an appeal to authenticity in jazz as a primarily *black* music, and an exoticizing gesture, but this was as well a kind of *political* statement, in Britain, in a music recognizably part of jazz.[6] It was perhaps tinged with a sense of Jamaican pride on Thompson's part too, a recognition of the international achievement of his fellow countryman Garvey, who would come to be seen as one of the most influential black activists of the century. Thompson ac-

16. One of Britain's leading early all-black dance bands, Ken Johnson's Jamaican Emperors of Jazz, opening at the Old Florida Club, Mayfair, London, 1936. Leslie Thompson (3rd from left) is the bandleader. © Val Wilmer Collection.

knowledged the importance of Garvey in his autobiography: "I had no colour consciousness, but reading *Negro World* punctured my thinking. In Jamaica we had been duped: no, given a palliative, so that we accepted a peaceful and uneventful life. A radical was needed, and Marcus Garvey was that man. . . . In the 1930s I used to see Marcus Garvey at Speaker's Corner. At that time you would see coloured chaps: Indian students on their soap boxes, attacking Britain's colonial system; and Marcus would stand there, watching them: with an expression on his face that indicated to me that he had done that, what—ten and more years ago—in America" (Thompson 1985, 36, 94).

The place of Marcus Garvey in black popular music in Britain would not be so prominent again until the more significantly Garveyite reggae of Rastafarianism in the 1970s.[7] After Johnson's death in 1941 in an air raid that hit the Café de Paris in London where the band was playing, Leslie "Jiver" Hutchinson later revived the all-black British swing band as his All-Coloured Orchestra, with music stands featuring the band's image of a spade from a playing card (Simons 2001, 28, 31).

In the 1950s Hutchinson led a band called the Ebony Knights that played the American military bases in England, where the audiences were largely black.[8] The modernist trumpeter Harry Beckett, who arrived in Britain from Barbados in 1954, was in this band.

The Jamaican bassist Coleridge Goode was a member of Leslie "Jiver" Hutchinson's All-Coloured Band (the name on billings varied slightly) at its founding in 1944, but he left soon to work with the Trinidadian guitarist Lauderic Caton and the German-born pianist Dick Katz, a Jewish exile from Nazi Germany, at the Caribbean Club in Piccadilly, London, during and after the Second World War. In that casual diasporic way of things, Goode knew the club manager because his brother was Goode's family's dentist back in Jamaica. For Goode, "the Caribbean Trio was a highlight of my career," and not only for musical reasons. As he explains in his autobiography, *Bass Lines*: "It was a genuinely mixed club in terms of race and class. . . . We put together intricate arrangements, using all the resources you could get from a piano-guitar-bass trio. And each of us was musically curious and adventurous, . . . and tried to make everything fresh with new voicings and textures of sound. . . . But there were other things too that were perhaps as important as the music. The Caribbean Club was a kind of ideal of how people could mix without tensions and trouble. As the war ended we were looking ahead to the way things might be better" (Goode and Cotterrell 2002, 45, 47, 51). Ironically, Leslie "Jiver" Hutchinson's orchestra, which Goode had recently left, was making a public storm in the music press about a widespread "color bar" that it felt itself struggling against—as in the bookings policy of some of the ballroom operators: "The same was observed regarding hotel seasons (i.e. fortnight bookings) and even BBC broadcasts. . . . 'Jiver' 's complaint against the BBC was undoubtedly justified," Simons concluded (2001, 31).[9]

TRINIDADIAN CALYPSO AND THE "OTHER PIANO"

In the late 1940s and 1950s there was a further West Indian contribution to popular music in Britain, and again one significantly involving black (and then also white) jazz musicians. Melodisc was a new British record label that released American bebop on license and produced some British jazz too—it was behind an infamous, illegal, union-busting recording by Sidney Bechet with Humphrey Lyttelton's band in London in 1949, only a few months after its formation (see Godbolt 1989, chs. 14 and 15). Melodisc also played a key role in recording and releasing calypso for what would be known in Britain, from 1948, as the Windrush generation. The ship *Empire Windrush* (which left Kingston, Jamaica, on Empire Day, 24 May) carried among its passengers two well-known calypsonians, Lord Kitchener and Lord Beginner, as well as the Trinidadian vocalist Mona Baptiste. John Cowley writes that "it was the presence of these authentic calypsonians together with the pool of musicians already available and, indirectly, the Empire dollar crisis, that led to the recording of indigenous British Caribbean music for export and local consumption" (1990, 65). "In London they joined a milieu of fine band musicians familiar with Caribbean musical forms, and already represented on numerous recordings crucial to the development of British swing and jazz music. Travelling with their own core audience, the Trinidadian calypsonians brought with them the vocal music of Carnival. . . . During that decade [of the 1950s], certainly, it was the enthralling soundtrack of Black Britain" (Noblett 2002, no pagination).[10]

Interestingly, part of the impetus for early calypso sessions in London came from the key producer in British jazz of the period, the white Briton Denis Preston, who had been in New York in 1948 and heard Trinidadian calypsonians performing there.[11] The products of artists recorded in the United States were also sold under export to the West Indies—but Preston saw an opening in the market for a new black audience in Britain too, where there were difficulties because of American and Empire currency and trading restrictions (Cowley 1990, 65–66). Cowley suggests that it was Preston, with his interest and contacts in the jazz world, who extended the musical repertoire of the calypso recordings, through the introduction of such devices as jazz breaks and African percussion. The jazz singer George Melly told me that "Preston, producer and entrepreneur, was a very important figure in [the new musics]. Very commercially oriented. He recorded me in all kinds of settings, country and western, calypso, and so on. Denis played a big role in turning traditional [jazz] into trad" (personal interview, 2002). As an indication of his sheer musical range (as well as interests ranging beyond commercial entrepreneurialism), Preston also maintained a career-long studio relationship with the Jamaican innovator Joe Harriott—Harriott's bassist Coleridge Goode said of Preston, "Without Denis all that music would have been lost" (Goode and Cotterrell 2002, 156).

Lord Kitchener's records were almost immediately a hit with West Indian audiences in London, as well as in English-speaking West Africa. Music produced in London bridged the black Atlantic, making its way to the Caribbean and also exported back to Trinidad *and to Commonwealth West Africa*. Calypso records made in London formed a new culture of triangulation, one key musical instance of what Gilroy has called a "new structure of cultural exchange . . . built up across the imperial networks which once played host to the triangular trade of sugar, slaves and capital" (Gilroy 1987, 206). Two of Lord Kitchener's songs illustrate this point: "London Is the Place for Me" (1951) and the specially commissioned "Birth of Ghana (6th March, 1957)" (1956), the brown paper sleeve of which was decorated with the new Ghanaian flag and the statement SOUVENIR OF GHANA'S INDEPENDENCE. Stapleton and May describe the impact of developments in popular music on Ghana, the first African nation to gain independence from British colonial rule under President Nkrumah: "The dance-band revolution chimed in with Kwame Nkrumah's cultural revolution in Ghana. Highlifers serenaded the CPP Party with songs like 'Padmore,' dedicated to the early nationalist hero, and the Broadway's 'Nkae,' a song which listed the prominent CPP men who'd died in the struggle for independence. As the new flag was raised, Lord Kitchener's calypso . . . echoed throughout the country" (Stapleton and May 1987, 38). This black Atlantic could involve Joe Harriott too, providing early evidence of his musical curiosity. According to Roger Cotterrell, Harriott "appeared on various now almost forgotten recordings of highlife music . . . by Buddy Pipp's Highlifers [which] were recorded for the African market, the band being made up of West Indians and West Africans" in 1954 (Cotterrell 1997, 5).

Calypso recording sessions in London employed Caribbean Commonwealth jazz musicians, a significant number of whom, like Bertie King (clarinet, sax), Freddy Grant (clarinet, sax), and Clinton Maxwell (drums), had played in the all-colored bands of Johnson and Hutchinson in the previous decade, while key future modern and experimental black musicians such as Harriott and Shake Keane could also be found

17. Melodisc calypso recording session, London, *ca.* 1953. Includes Lord Kitchener (second from left), Clinton Maxwell (seated, bongos), Shake Keane (trumpet, far right). © Val Wilmer Collection.

on some sessions. (Grant would move to the United States within a few years, leading his own calypso band there under the name Sir Freddy Grant.) The Trinidadian guitarist and trumpeter Cyril Blake, who led a number of recording bands including his Calypso Serenaders, and backed Lords Kitchener and Beginner, had an exemplary provenance: he had played with the Southern Syncopated Orchestra on a tour of Britain in 1921, is rumored to have backed Josephine Baker in Europe, played with Leslie Thompson's Emperors of Jazz, the group inspired by Garvey, in the 1930s, led his own mostly black small band at leading venues favored by London's black communities, including the Jig's Club in the early 1940s, and went on to play an important role in the calypso recording boom (Chilton 1997, 33). In fact, around 1950 Leslie "Jiver" Hutchinson's West Indian Orchestra provided the backing for the Jamaican singer Louise Bennett's recordings of folk songs, which are among "the first releases of authentic black music from Jamaica made in Britain" (Cowley 1990, 68).[12] Kitchener sang about the cross-musical influences on one of his remarkable recordings from the time,

"Kitch's Bebop Calypso" (1951), recorded with Freddy Grant's Caribbean Rhythm. This number manages to be a celebration of bebop (with a series of short bop-styled instrumental breaks), an educative *introduction* to the music for new listeners (several leading American musicians are named and explained, and in the lyric below the listener is told what to listen for), *and* a simple statement of the African side of bop:

> If you listen carefully
> You will surely enjoy the melody
> It sends you in a dancing heat
> With the drums that give you the Afro-beat. (Kitchener 1951)[13]

There are important circum-Atlantic cultural traces here, which are articulated through jazz and related music in Britain, from the Jamaican Leslie Thompson and his "Garveyite dream" of an all-black big band in the 1930s to the Trinidadian Lord Kitchener's piercing criticism of the paths of negotiation taken by some diasporic blacks trying to "pass" for white:

> You hate the name of Africa
> The land of your great-grandfather
> The country where you can't be wrong
> The home where you really belong.
> You'd rather be among the whites
> Than stick up for your father's rights. (Kitchener 1953)

It is essential to remember that the period described above, from the big bands of the 1930s to the calypso of the 1950s, was also the period of the transatlantic unions' mutual ban. Some of these developments in black British music may have been possible because other black musicians—the innovative African American jazzers in particular—were mostly being kept out. Subjects of Empire nations had greater access than some other blacks (though this would begin to be checked by legislation such as the Commonwealth Immigrants Act of 1962). Did the actions of the Musicians' Union have any racist motivation, as well as effect? Howard Rye cites one union official arguing the case before the ban was implemented: "There are something like two thousand of our union out of work. Many of them are unemployed because of the introduction of American negro bands, now in favour with certain dance clubs. British musicians could play quite as well" (quoted in Rye 1990,

52). As Rye goes on to observe, "denial of the cultural uniqueness of Afro-American music would be central to the Musicians' Union's policy in the coming years," but in fairness, it should be clarified that the ban affected black *and* white American big bands of the time. Even the Musicians' Union of Australia reiterated the concerns of the British union, complaining to the minister for home and territories in 1924 about the threat posed by American jazz bands to the employment opportunities of Australian musicians, with specific reference to the importation of "coloured musicians" (quoted in Johnson 2000, 21).[14] This complaint built on a motion incorporated into the Australian MU's rule book the previous year: "To uphold and maintain the White Australia policy, and prohibit the admission of coloured races as members" (quoted in Bissett 1987, 44). What is most striking is the impact that the timing of the ban had on the British experience of the largely black innovations of American jazz: it meant that for the two crucial decades that saw every stylistic and technical development in jazz from Armstrong to Miles, virtually every one of the music's practitioners, nearly all of whom were black, was kept out of Britain by an overwhelmingly white organization, the Musicians' Union. Even if the ban was instigated first by the American side and the MU's response was merely retaliatory, it is difficult not to see a color bar functioning. At least one effect of the ban was that there may have been more work opportunities for the black musicians who were in Britain, while Paul Oliver carefully outlines other ramifications: "Ironically, while denying entry to American musicians the Musicians' Union ban may even have assisted to a certain extent, in the creation of an audience for black musicians, by helping generate a demand for them" (1990b, 82).

Links between the West Indian community and white jazzers in London were being formed, exemplified by the Grant-Lyttelton Paseo Jazz Band, as described by the bandleader Humphrey Lyttelton: "A Mardi Gras celebration was held in an hotel off Russell Square in the February of 1952. Since the Mardi Gras carnival is an event common to the West Indies and to New Orleans, the idea was to have a combined celebration with my band furnishing New Orleans-type jazz and a group of London-based West Indian musicians playing the music of the Caribbean. Two stars in the calypso field—Lord Beginner and Lord Kitchener—were on the bill, too. . . . Towards the end we had a . . . wild jam session. . . . The result was sensational" (Lyttelton 1958, 107).

From this Mardi Gras surprise Lyttelton, the ex-dixielander and now mainstream trumpeter, worked with the Guyanese bandleader Freddy Grant, and percussionists. Their band toured the country, a multi-racial outfit attempting to meld together two identifiable traditions—jazz front line and West Indian rhythm section—as well as, in Lyttelton's words,

> to reintroduce the rhythmic variety of Creole jazz into our music, and also to inject new life into the worn jazz repertoire by drawing on the folk-music material, still quite contemporary and fresh, which exists in our midst in the West Indian community. . . . On tour we were a cosmopolitan lot. Freddy was from British Guiana, and his musicians were drawn from all over the West Indies—Tony Johnson from Jamaica, Fitzroy Coleman from Trinidad, Neville Boucarut from Barbados and Mike McKenzie from British Guiana. Leslie Weekes, the bongo player, came from India. Calypsos were sung by George Brown, Jamaican mentos by Tony Johnson and, for a while, we had a singer called Bill Rogers from British Guiana who sang leggos [a form of calypso]. (Lyttelton 1958, 109, 112)

Oliver identifies the anomaly that the popularity of the calypso in Britain "was scarcely acknowledged in the jazz press, *which was deaf to the black music in its midst*" (1990b, 82; my emphasis), but the Grant-Lyttelton Paseo Jazz Band provided one of the occasions during this period when (white) jazzers did acknowledge what was now indigenous black music practice in their realm. A probably more significant achievement was that of Cleo Laine, who from the 1950s made an international reputation for herself with her husband, John Dankworth. According to Laine, her father "was known as 'Darkie' in Southall" (Laine 1994, 18), which he claimed had little impact on him, though he was a strong atheist: "He felt that he'd been ostracized by the whole of Christian society because of his dark skin" (Laine 1994, 21). Clearly there were some aspects of his blackness and whites' responses to it that were unacceptable, and in fact her father would stand on a soapbox at Speaker's Corner in Hyde Park, "spouting out his grievances to all who would stop and listen" (Laine 1994, 18). The family would socialize with other multiracial couples, and this had a significant effect on their egalitarian politics and inclusive worldview, as Laine has explained: "I seemed to be more aware of the world and its problems than a lot of other working-class children in my class: my Pa saw to that. We could not escape being influenced by him, by the multi-racial households all around us and, most important of all, by our own parents' mixed marriage. . . . [My mother] was a woman who all my life had never turned anyone away from her door if she had a bed to offer—the list of different nationalities reads like the United Nations Assembly—Africans, Indians, Irish, French, Polish, Czechs, Jamaicans and Germans as well as all the British" (Laine 1994, 48, 67).

I have shown that as they themselves became more successful in British jazz in the 1950s, Laine and Dankworth were active in promoting racial understanding, supporting civil rights in the American South and opposing apartheid in South Africa and racial tension in Britain. Laine's first acting roles in the late 1950s were in plays concerned with race relations, set in Jamaica and in South Africa (Collier 1976, 60–62). But I think it also fair to say that Laine's and Dankworth's high-profile mixed-race relationship, in the cultural context of British jazz, was viewed by them as their most positive statement about multiracialism.

During the 1950s Trinidad supplied one other hugely successful export to British pop. Winifred Atwell (1914–83) was a ragtime pianist from Tunapuna who gained tremendous popularity in Britain. She appeared frequently on television and topped the charts with million-selling singles such as "Poor People of Paris" in 1956, as well as numerous medleys of party songs, other rags, and pop classics. Her first big hit single was a version of George Botsford's historic "Black and White Rag," recorded in 1951. As Jeffrey Green has noted, by this period British "promoters and the audiences wanted Blacks performing black music. And so it was that the schooled pianist from Trinidad, Winifred Atwell, earned a living in Britain from the early 1950s by playing a pastiche of ragtime, selling thousands of discs of a superficial version of a music of black America of the 1890s" (1990, 42). Atwell is more interesting than this—and as a ragtime player, she fully warrants her place in British jazz history. Though she mixed genres with commercial zeal—ragtime, boogie-woogie, and honky-tonk, and tried her hand at the twist and rock 'n' roll when they arrived—Atwell was nonetheless a skilled instrumentalist playing a kind of ragtime, which had been "the first original African-American style to emerge as a genre in its own right" (Shipton 2001, 31). After a period studying music in New York

City, she had arrived in London in 1946 to study classical piano at the Royal Academy of Music, while supporting herself by playing ragtime and boogie-woogie at clubs and hotels in the evenings. This splitness, of music, of audience, of day and night, she intriguingly introduced into her subsequent performances, with an extraordinary gimmick that effectively dramatized the choices open to her as a (female) black musician. Atwell would open her act with a piece of classical music played on a grand piano. She would then transfer to what she called, and what audiences came to know as, her "other piano": a bashed and battered upright, carved with fans' initials, detuned to give an authentic "honky-tonk" sound.[15] On this she would play her hit rags, and her record covers would also foreground the instrument the recordings were made on: an EP recorded for Decca in 1958, "Let's Have a Ball," gave near equal billing to "Winifred Atwell and her other piano" (Stevens 2004). So this part of Atwell's music became a defining feature; the "other piano" became her (vandalized) brand, her trademark. Because she was a woman musician too, Atwell's cross-musicking may signify. Her publicity materials showed her wearing a stage costume consisting of formal, only slightly flamboyant, concert dresses, a jeweled necklace, and usually a generous, knowing smile. Transiting from the finery of the curved grand piano to the pub or club upright (legend has it that she bought the original "other piano" in a junk shop in Battersea, London), on which she played the associatively patriarchal night sounds of honky-tonk music, Atwell lightly confounded gendered musical expectations. Her single recordings did include, after all, titles such as "Let's Have a Ding Dong" and "Raunchy" / "Dugga Dugga Boom Boom."

Atwell's simple, nightly performative gesture, crossing the stage or television studio floor, swapping instruments, taking her allotted seat at her piano, speaks volumes about racialized cultural hierarchy and access. From the polished grandeur and equal temperament of the European historic tradition to black American primitivized and atavized popular music (even while she was Trinidadian), Atwell moved obediently and successfully to the sound of white British applause. In November 1952 she played for the new, young Queen Elizabeth at her first Royal Variety Performance. In the new pop discourse of *Souvenir Album of Winifred Atwell*, Wyn Carter describes the evening: "For this memorable occasion she wrote the 'Britannia Rag,' which she played on her now famous 'other piano' to close her act. She hoped the Royal party

18. The Trinidadian ragtime pianist Winifred Atwell, the first black musician in British pop music to have a million-selling hit single, played her "other piano."

would enjoy the novelty of being entertained on such an ancient instrument, and it seemed that she was right . . . It is a well known fact that both the Queen and her sister Princess Margaret are extremely talented pianists themselves, so imagine Winnie's delight when Princess Margaret graciously commented on her records and told her how much she enjoyed them" (Carter 1953, 5). Her timely hit singles included both "Britannia Rag" and "Coronation Rag" (1953), so there was a certain positioning around Commonwealth patriotism and the British monarchy, in contrast to other Trinidadian musical successes of the decade like the calypso mini-boom. As we have seen, kaiso (calypso) had a more ambivalent, even critical positioning regarding London and Englishness, as well as being a powerful celebration of the moments of colonial independence. Atwell was not a Caribbean migrant of the Windrush generation. She had professional training in her father's pharmacy business and had studied music in both New York and London, which may have marked her as a member of a relatively privileged class in Trinidadian society. But what of that repeated short journey of hers, from piano to "pi-anna" (as termed on a release from 1960: Stevens 2004)? Her commercial success in music was striking, and it needs to be acknowledged that Atwell was *the first black artist to have a million-selling record in Britain* (*Making History* 2004). Did she know her place, and step to it, on cue? Is Atwell's "other piano" the heart of a sad story, or of a conscious one? Atwell left London in 1963 and went to another new world, Australia, where she picked up her classical music playing with symphony orchestras. Confirmed by her process of becoming a global diasporean—Trinidad, United States, England, Australia—it is worth noting the internationalism underlying the marketed version of her life experience. Rather than a fan club, Atwell established "her very large International Club—which has thousands of members spread all over the world. The aim of the club is Winnie's own wish, to further International friendship and understanding between people of all nations regardless of race or creed. The club is, of course, completely non-political" (Carter 1953, 6).

"IF IT CLASHES, WELL, THAT'S PART OF IT": CARIBBEAN EXPERIMENTS FROM JOE HARRIOTT TO . . .

I now turn to Joe Harriott, to consider in greater detail the crucial work of a singular musician. With, among others, his Caribbean accompanists the trumpeter Shake Keane and the bassist Coleridge Goode (named after the celebrated black British classical composer Samuel Coleridge-Taylor), Harriott was responsible for a series of brilliant experiments in new music in Britain through the 1960s. Writing in *Melody Maker* in 1960, Bob Dawbarn anticipated as much: "Some decidedly odd sounds have been issuing from London's Marquee Club recently. Patient tracking will reveal the Joe Harriott Quintet rehearsing what Joe claims to be something completely new in jazz. . . . Harriott is on the track of something new . . . [which] may well prove important to the development of British jazz" (quoted in Cotterrell 1997, 7). Harriott arrived in Britain in 1951, aged twenty-three, part of the migration by a group of similar-minded musicians, including the trumpeter Dizzy Reece and the saxophonist Harold McNair, who "saw the pulling up of roots for a move to Britain as essential for any West Indian musician wanting to play jazz" (Cotterrell 1997, 5)—no work permits or immigration documents were required at that date.[16] Even as he played conventional bop in his first years in London, there was something recognizably different in Harriott's saxophone tone. Brian Nicholls wrote in

1957 that "Joe's playing came as a tensed surprise to the fans. . . . His alto was often hoarse in its urgency and he presented a strikingly new sound to British jazz" (1957, 154). But Harriott's musical experiments, bold in Britain, were in two main areas: the near free music of his quintet in the early 1960s ("abstract" and "free form" were his preferred terms, and became the titles of two of the albums), and the jazz and Indian classical music crossover of a double quintet a very few years later. Much of the initial groundwork of constructing a new *group* sound around his alternative conception of improvised music was made possible because of the five-year residency that the quintet held at the newly opened Marquee Club in London, managed by the National Jazz Federation. Elsewhere I write of the importance of particular performative spaces in the 1960s in providing pivotal developmental opportunities for new music —spaces that have themselves become legendary within British jazz discourse, like the Little Theatre Club and the Old Place. But Harriott's own essential practice was crucially allowed to formulate *and* to create an audience at the Marquee from July 1958 to 1963, with periodic breaks. In mid-1960 "the audience at the Marquee had its first experience of the new sounds. The reception was understandably mixed and the Joe Harriott Quintet instantly became the most controversial group on the London jazz scene . . . disturbing . . . the conventional derivative sounds to be heard elsewhere in London jazz clubs" (Cotterrell 1997, 7). Harriott's chosen lineup regularly featured black and white musicians, the blacks generally being Caribbean musicians based in England, in particular Goode and Keane but also Reece and Frank Holder (bongos), alongside the white Scottish musicians Bobby Orr (drums) and Pat Smythe (piano), or the Englishman Phil Seamen (drums).

In his "free form" recordings beginning in 1960, Harriott initially explained that the aim of the quintet as a collective was "to create sounds, moods, effects, textures in music. Just that" (Harriott 1961). There would be an occasional rejection of jazz itself in his utterances: "I am not thinking of jazz at all, not in the known sense. I'm thinking of an artist, a musician, free to paint sounds, colour and effects *as the ideas come to him*" (quoted in Cotterrell 1997, 9; my emphasis). While the reference to abstract painting was often repeated by Harriott (and other improvising musicians such as John Stevens or Mike Westbrook would come to employ visual tactics and metaphors in their performances in a few years),[17] it is the centrality of spontaneity in this

19. Joe Harriott Quintet, Richmond Jazz Festival, 1963.
From left: Shake Keane (trumpet), Pat Smythe (piano),
Harriott (alto sax), Bobby Orr (drums), Coleridge Goode
(bass). © Val Wilmer.

statement that is striking. The collectivity of music production was significant too—Cotterrell identifies a shift in Harriott's approach from effectively that of a frontline soloist pre-1958 to that of an ensemble player with his quintet: "Harriott's most important innovations concern the group rather than the soloist. . . . What was really new was the freedom the *whole* quintet had to develop a musical performance. The five instruments ceased to be constrained by the role traditionally assigned to them in jazz" (Cotterrell 1997, 8). As Harriott explained on liner notes to the album *Free Form,* "The more we play together, the more we sense what the next man is up to; the better we know each other musically, the more we can anticipate what comes next. In one sense, of course, this means that the rhythm section overshadows the soloist: they have more of a fixed path. But there is a two-way traffic here. While a soloist is playing, the rhythm can suggest a new or different line of attack—and the soloist can leave the line he has been pursuing and adopt the new one. Or, conversely the soloist can musically direct the rhythm to take up a new line he is exploring. *In this way, any member of the group is free to utilize ideas stemming from any other member*" (Harriott 1961; my emphasis).

Within a few years the collective improvisatory practice of a group such as John Stevens's Spontaneous Music Ensemble would be identified as a pivotal social and musical development, yet in some ways it was here already in Harriott's quintet (Blackford 1997, 24–25). For the bassist Coleridge Goode, this was an essential part of the quintet's project, and in his view it was also an important difference from the free jazz work of Ornette Coleman in the United States:

> I don't think there was any connection between what Ornette did and what we were doing because his music then was strictly a solo effort. It was a soloist playing free, not a group playing free. . . . Coleman avoided using a piano after his first recording session but we were making a group music where harmony was spontaneously produced with the piano as an integral part. . . . The bass player's role in Coleman's music was different from mine with Harriott. In Ornette's quartet the bassist—Charlie Haden, say—would usually be playing against a soloist, listening to one solo voice and playing according to that, but in our group there were several voices. . . . It was always a relation of the whole group, something the five of us tried to construct at every moment together, not a relationship between a solo voice and an accompanist. (Goode and Cotterrell 2002, 151–52)

In another way, the quintet's pianist, Pat Smythe, could articulate a more radical position than Harriott himself in terms of the impact that such musical freedom could have. While for Harriott rehearsals could lead to anticipating what the other players were going to do, for Smythe aleatoric discordancy within the performance had its own attraction and role: "If it clashes, well, that's part of it," he said in 1960 (quoted in Cotterrell 1997, 7). This casual statement really did presage free improvisation, and Chris Blackford is correct when he observes that in this passing comment, "Smythe acknowledges the existence of a significantly different soundworld created through free improvisation, where so-called 'discords' and 'dissonances' are an integral part of the musical fabric" (1997, 21). According to Roger Dean, "Harriott systematically explored breaking down conventions relating to each of the major musical materials" (Dean 1992, 134), and Harriott explains his tactic of what he calls on several occasions in this text "escape" (from rhythmic pulse or melody, for example) in his liner notes to *Abstract*: "Of the various components comprising jazz today—constant time signatures, a steady four-four tempo, themes and predictable harmonic variations, fixed division of the chorus by bar lines and so on—we aim to retain at least one in each piece. But we may well—if the mood seems to us to demand it—dispense with all the others" (Harriott 1963).[18]

Evidently there is a transitionality here in Harriott's experimental work, and Roger Dean elaborates on this musical approach, which seeks to retain "one jazz element. . . . So he recorded modal pieces with no fixed mode; pieces with no pulse; and pulsed pieces with complex, unconventional harmonic structures. At the same time his two recordings in this mould still retain some very traditional elements and sound not far removed from the atmosphere of [Miles Davis's] *Kind of Blue* from a year or two earlier" (Dean 1992, 135). While with hindhearing one can readily identify the transitionality of the work, at the time the quintet's exploration of new soundscapes could be tremendously shocking. Goode describes the reaction from a significant section of the jazz community in London to the "free form" work: "When we played free form [at Ronnie Scott's Old Place], the musicians listening or drinking at the bar would creep out and stand in the doorway, looking aghast. You could see those puzzled—'What on earth are they doing?'—expressions on their faces. . . . A lot of musicians acted in a completely negative way.[19] They couldn't understand at all and many were openly scoffing. . . . It was criticism from established musicians that was so demoralising. . . . Often their reaction was one of astonishment and sometimes complete mockery. Their experience of music was a strict regime of barlines and chord sequences and if you strayed from that they didn't think you were playing music at all" (Goode and Cotterrell 2002, 154, 156).

Two solid beboppers left the quintet when Harriott introduced his innovative ideas, and the resistance displayed by others gave the lie to the notion that Britain's jazz was on the cutting edge. For Blackford, this conservatism is evidence of a period of moribund music, and he views Harriott's experiments alongside the rather different route taken by other British musicians to escape a certain jazz malaise: "while disillusioned jazz musicians like Graham Bond, Dick Heckstall-Smith,

Jack Bruce, and Ginger Baker departed from an uninspiring British jazz scene for the burgeoning blues scene, later to carve out the beginnings of blues-rock and jazz-rock from rhythm 'n' blues, Harriott, Keane, Seamen and a few other kindred spirits persevered with British jazz but were determined to go beyond the stale 'chord-bound' approach, even if it meant going out on a limb and incurring the hostility of some critics and jazz fans" (Blackford 1997, 20).

In fact, when he had developed a significant and innovative musical approach Harriott *did* make efforts to explain his ideas to audiences — and perhaps to other musicians too, through interviews in the music press and liner notes. This was part of his conscious and for a while mildly successful effort to build an audience for the new music. He also wrote on his notes for *Abstract* of the importance of the heuristic and spontaneous in playing (which is seen again a few short years later in the free improvised musical practice and subsequent explanatory texts of a group like AMM and the drummer and writer Eddie Prévost). The pieces "should be taken *as* the audience hears them, not in relation to anything else. . . . Such an approach to modern music, I am well aware, . . . is partly a hit-or-miss affair; but then so is everything else. Conventional musicians, too, can play badly! When it comes off . . . it is arresting: you have to stop, look and listen. . . . I am not saying that Free Form will replace the music which makes up the general scene. But it will build up quite a following. It's here to stay" (Harriott 1963).

Ironically, given this bullish conclusion, the third and last album in the series, *Movement*, signaled an attenuation of the project: its musical approach veered less than convincingly between postbop and free-form pieces. Harriott was acutely conscious of the problem, as reported in 1965: "it is when [Harriott] is communicating to a larger audience via records or radio that he feels the restriction of consumer control to be most galling, for it is here that he would rather be represented by his 'own' music. His dissatisfaction with the format of schizophrenia imposed on a recent album of his was obvious and understandable" (Martin 1965, 14). But even in later recordings Harriott would still offer some free improvisation: duets in particular were a favored form — with Smythe ("Abstract Doodle") and the drummer Bryan Spring ("Spring Low Sweet Harriott"), for example.

Within a couple of years, though, Harriott would once more be distancing himself from the main (African American, swing) jazz tradition. The black Atlantic met the Commonwealth in the old heart of empire in Harriott's experiments with Indian improvisers in the *Indo-Jazz Fusion* series. Alyn Shipton acknowledges the importance of this project for the further exploration of new ethnic sonicities and traditions of improvised music within jazz: while American jazz from John Coltrane to Don Ellis had its own interest in Indian music, "one of the first bands to investigate the cross currents between Indian music and jazz was Indo-Jazz Fusions" (Shipton 2001, 834). A chance meeting with the Indian violinist John Mayer in the office of the producer Denis Preston in 1965, which followed earlier discussions between Harriott and his pianist Smythe on the fusion of Indian and jazz improvising traditions, led to what was called a "Double Quintet" of Indian classical musicians and Harriott's jazz improvisers (surely without question along the Ornette Coleman model this time—consider Coleman's *Free Jazz* project for "double quartet" from 1960). Roger Cotterrell describes the creative dynamic: "Although the Double Quintet was billed as being jointly led by Harriott and Mayer, and although Harriott's powerful personality shaped the jazz content of the performances, the musical concept behind the Indo-Jazz experiment was clearly that of John Mayer. The fusion, in so far as it was successful, was brought about primarily through Mayer's compositional skills . . . and by the adaptation of styles and techniques by all the musicians involved" (1997, 9).[20]

Three albums were released, with some commercial success—no doubt in part because of the coincidence of the sitar in this British jazz with the sitars appearing in British pop of the time, especially the music of the Beatles.[21] For once, pop may have helped jazz, the Eastern exoticizing prevalent in the counterculture of the period permitting the rarefied structures and improvisations of the Indo-Jazz Fusions to survive. The ensemble even played at the Isle of Wight rock festival in 1969. Harriott pursued nonwestern sounds in collaborations with the Goanese guitarist Amancio D'Silva in the same year, and with British jazzers from outside his established lineup, including the drummer Bryan Spring and the singer Norma Winstone, on the album *Hum Dono*. Working with D'Silva, who had developed an indigenous mix-music of jazz, Indian, and Portuguese traditions (he was sometimes compared with Django Reinhardt as a result of such musical reappropriation: see Kamalu 1996), signaled further old (as opposed to new, that is, American) empire influences and interest on Harriott's part.

Harriott's relation with the United States was a curious one: he never toured there, and as his career developed in Britain and he became less a postbop instrumentalist in the Charlie Parker mold and more of a composer and experimentalist, he was almost ostentatiously uninterested in American musical developments.[22] This remained his position even when there was unprecedented recognition for his work in the American jazz press, as when *Abstract* famously received a five-star rating in Harvey Pekar's review in *Down Beat*, the first such occasion for a British jazz recording.[23] Harriott's distancing was in part due to the frequently stated claims made that his experimental works from the early 1960s were imitative of Coleman's. He explained to readers of *Melody Maker* in 1960, "I haven't picked this up from anybody. . . . It's all my own. My music is really no nearer to Coleman than Basie to Ellington" (quoted in Cotterrell 1997, 7). Blackford writes that one of the reasons why Harriott was marginalized or excluded from a significant place in accounts of the music was "the overwhelming bias towards American musicians in virtually all histories of free jazz" (1997, 17). Perhaps Harriott's own softly articulated but identifiably resentful critical stance toward the perception by both Americans and Europeans that American jazz was innately superior contributed to this. On BBC radio in 1963 he explained: "I also have a pet hate that one couldn't think for oneself unless one emigrated to a place like the United States. . . . Unfortunately, I find—I hope I am wrong about this—that jazz musicians, American and otherwise, seem to think that, well, one could only be a good musician by being in the United States. And I'm sure there is a lot of very bad musicians there like any other place. It's not the place, it's you" (quoted in Robertson 2003, 129).

This sentiment would be echoed by Harriott's bassist Coleridge Goode on behalf of other members of the quintet: "We felt it wasn't always necessary to look to America for the next idea in jazz. That was a revolutionary idea then but it became a widespread view among the most adventurous young European jazz musicians over the following years" (Goode and Cotterrell 2002, 158).[24] Goode was older than Harriott, and his reluctance to overvalorize the United States was also a residue of his experience of racism through direct contact with white GIs playing at American bases in Britain during wartime: "All this made me think about these attitudes, all that vileness, which the Americans brought over here and about what it would be like to live in America. I couldn't have taken all that vicious, racist behaviour. No self-respecting person could. . . . Later on in my career these reactions that formed in my mind became decisive because some people suggested to me at various times that I might do well over there. . . . But I was very sure that I wouldn't go. In fact, I never really have spent any time there" (Goode and Cotterrell 2002, 39–40).

Blackford takes issue with the standard historical narrative of the development of free jazz and free improvisation in Britain, and he does so in two important ways in order to restate Harriott's place at the center of things. First, he dismisses any heroic narrative of experimentation, and with it any voiced criticism of Harriott precisely for his transitionality, his musical "schizophrenia," by pointing out that "moves towards a greater freedom of expression were gradually achieved and not by some gigantic leap into the unknown, the common misconception of how so-called "radical" music is instigated" (1997, 23). Second, Blackford moves outside the more familiar framework of white free jazz in Britain, that of AMM, the Spontaneous Music Ensemble (SME), the Little Theatre Club, and so on, which dates to the *mid*-1960s (see chapter 4). By this date Harriott's quintet had developed a sound and a vocabulary that explored freedom within and outwith the jazz tradition, *and* recorded three ground-breaking albums.[25] For Blackford, writing almost a quarter of a century after Harriott's death, "the pathbreaking free form work of the Joe Harriott Quintet opened the way for successive generations of British musicians in the field of free jazz and, perhaps more importantly, for those concerned to create a radical new language within non-idiomatic free improvisation. That this point has had to be made with such fervour here demonstrates the extent to which the achievements of this significant quintet have been undervalued and overlooked by too many people for too many years" (1997, 22).

Why would this be so?[26] Is it fair to ask if we could possibly have here some version of the "great music robbery" talked of by Amiri Baraka, the drawing across of Leonard Feather's "white curtain"? Harriott's outstanding oeuvre is neglected in some way because of his blackness? Is it fair *not* to ask that question? Why is it never asked? Because it's too obvious? Because it manages both to impugn the longstanding and in many senses socially aware white jazz community *and* to maintain the black victim thesis? In fact this is part of his bassist and fellow Jamaican Coleridge Goode's final, reluctant explanation: "All of us involved in his projects felt his pain. We felt it was a terrible shame that the people who had the power to present, broadcast, explain and publicize his music often ignored or neglected it. In the end, unfortunately, *one puts it down to the fact that Joe wasn't a white Englishman.* Had he been, things would have been different. There can be no other explanation. A similar thing happened years before to [the Trinidadian guitarist] Lauderic Caton. . . . In America, black musicians have received some recognition. They are a majority in jazz there, whereas in Britain they are a small minority and what they have done has been easier to ignore" (Goode and Cotterrell 2002, 183; my emphasis).

For Goode it is not simply Harriott's blackness, his nonwhiteness, that signifies — it is also his non-Englishness and, by implication from his comparison with the earlier experience of Caton, who retired from professional playing in the mid-1950s, his West Indianness. On a number of occasions Harriott explored his own West Indian musical roots. This may go some way to explain his regular choice of musicians, including fellow West Indians like Goode and Keane. As noted, he played on several of Denis Preston's calypso recordings of the 1950s, but even within the free form recordings there is, for example, a piece entitled "Calypso Sketches," while the album *Movement* contains a calypso called "Revival" and the album *Personal Portrait* (1967) contains the piece "Saga," described by Cotterrell as a "simple calypso theme" (1997, 11). The comparison with the situation of black musicians in the United States must have been particularly difficult for Goode to articulate, bearing in mind his earlier stated refusal to consider working in America because of anti-black racism. How significant is this, particularly in view of the British jazz community's perhaps warmer reception of the black South African exile musicians whom I look at below, only slightly later than Harriott's first vibrant experimentations? Perhaps Harriott in some way, for some white people, was too identifiably a member of the expanding post-Windrush migration to Britain from the Caribbean, in a way that the easily exoticizable and authenticizingly extrovert African musicians were not? An uncomfortable, uncompromising, technically superior, creatively experimental black man from Jamaica, who talked about modern painting and ancient philosophy, and had neither wish nor need to follow the latest music trends from America?[27] I recognize a slippage here, on my part, from color to personality and attitude — and Goode reminds us of the pitfall of undifferentiating black experiences when he writes that "shared West Indian origins weren't enough to overcome everything else that was different about our backgrounds and outlook" (Goode and Cotterrell 2002, 192). Life history too: how far is there an urge to read the premature death (in 1973, aged forty-four) of the indifferently treated black innovator, orphan, migrant, of frail health, autodidact in painting and philosophy, as a confirmation of (black, or jazz) cultural suffering? Writing in the wake of his death, Ian Carr suggested that Harriott "was defeated and worn down and out more directly by the system, the hostile environment. From being one of the leading pioneers of 'free' jazz, and the co-creator of the Indo-Jazz Fusions which made such an impact in the 1960s, for the last two years of his life he had been reduced to the obscurity of the provinces where he wandered about working as a soloist with local rhythm sections" (Carr 1973, 1–2). Such a narrative, especially one with a *legacy* — the back catalogue — can (too readily) confirm the masculine jazz tragedy, but for Paul Gilroy, "the identification of black musical genius constitutes an important cultural narrative. It tells and retells not so much the story of the weak's victory over the strong but the relative powers enjoyed by different types of strength" (1993, 107). It can also stand as a lesson, if a harsh one. The next hugely lauded black saxophonist, Courtney Pine (of Jamaican parentage), has referenced the treatment of Harriott — a "nightmare" — as something for his generation of black musicians to avoid, starting with the Jazz Warriors in the mid-1980s: "I had this thing about Joe Harriott, and how in ten years time all that we're trying to do here . . . will be eradicated from history. You won't be able to find the books, our records will be deleted" (quoted in Sinker 1992–93, 48). Harriott's Indo-Jazz Fusions collaborator John Mayer has looked back at their musical and social struggle: "We took all the stick from everybody because I was an Indian and he was a Jamaican . . . if it hadn't been for Joe Harriott, all the [world music] people . . . would not be doing what they're doing" (quoted in Robertson 2003, 167). Finally, though, it is difficult to disagree with John Wickes when he writes that "at a time when most of his contemporaries still insisted on the intrinsic superiority of American models, Joe Harriott, a black Jamaican immigrant, had stood British jazz's self image on its head" (1999, 15). And the *tensed surprise* of the "free form" music remains, a hemispheric achievement that no one else was thinking of, that took from America, to the Caribbean, to London, in an experimental sonicity of the black Atlantic—and *then* its creator improvised fusions with Indian classical musicians or a Goanese guitarist, blanking the Atlantic.

Harriott's achievement *was* recognized by a subsequent generation of black jazz musicians in Britain, who contributed forcefully to the modern jazz resurgence of the 1980s in Britain, in particular around the Jazz Warriors, the big band based in London. During this period there was a tangible sense that young British black musicians were reclaiming or reinventing an African American connection (which may contrast with the Eurocentric approach of many white British free jazzers), as well as paying homage to neglected black figures in British jazz: for example, a tour by the Warriors in 1989 was called "Homage to Joe Harriott" (though apparently none of Harriott's tunes were played: Blackford 1997, 26). For a critic like Gilroy, such a gesture can be read as part of black music's formal, intertextual historical strategy, like reggae's reworkings of classic tunes, or hip-hop's sampling of the black sonic archive: "The premium placed on history has been carried over into the form of jazz by an aesthetic valuation of quotes and references to preceding styles and players" (1987, 283). The nineteen-piece Jazz Warriors made their début in London in 1986. Originating from Abibi Jazz Arts, the band featured musicians like the new, mediagenic saxophonist Courtney Pine and the Tanzanian trombonist and composer Fayyaz Virji, and was guided early on by the hustling authority of the saxophonist Gail Thompson, born in England of Trinidadian parents. Once more a statement of black cultural confidence and presence was heard and seen, an all-black big band in the mode of Leslie Thompson and Leslie "Jiver" Hutchinson half a century before (see Sinker 1990). The British modern jazz boom of the 1980s saw the introduction of another, predominantly white big band, Loose Tubes, and thus British jazz reception seemed almost effortlessly to slip back into a racial framework.[28] The bassist Gary Crosby of the Warriors, later the bandleader of the Jazz Jamaica All-Stars, explored this reception with me, and what it elided:

> There weren't really two camps, but some things did get said that were probably regretted later, and they were quickly seized on. Actually I think the press *wanted* there to be separate black and white jazz scenes, even a split, it confirmed something for the critics. It's

true that there were stylistic differences: the Jazz Warriors played original music from the black diasporic experience, I think the only standard we did was "A Night in Tunisia." Loose Tubes were more beginning to explore new European sounds. The more important factor really from those two big bands is not so much that one was black and the other white—actually I . . . can hardly remember a gig when there wasn't some white presence in some way—but that *our parents were working class*, we were descendants of poor immigrants. They came over to Britain in the mid-1950s, early 1960s, and not many of us were encouraged by our parents to become musicians. There was no money or desire to pay for private lessons, to go to college, no extended family support networks so that an uncle would find you an old instrument to learn on, none of that. Even my uncle [the guitarist] Ernest Ranglin, he acted as an inspiration, but he was in the States. So quite a few of us in the Jazz Warriors were self-taught, and a number of musicians couldn't read that well. . . . That got picked on by some sections of the jazz scene, there was a bit of criticism from the pro[fessional] side, . . . the established British jazz scene. And to be honest, there was some hurt in the band because of various comments. There was resentment because it appeared that we weren't having to pay our dues like all the other British jazz musicians had! You have to remember too that we *were* allowed to jump decades of experience because of the interest in us because we were black. (personal interview, 2002)

While for the media and the newly vibrant jazz PR machines the blackness of the Warriors was the focus of interest (especially alongside the predominant whiteness of Loose Tubes), for some of those musicians in the band, like Crosby, their difference was understood at least as much in terms of class. Their working-class status dictated that music education would not be a top priority or family expectation—unlike, in their view, for the students at the Royal Academy of Music, who made up much of the membership of Loose Tubes, under the initial tutelage of Graham Collier. Their music education happened instead in workshops at art centers and community clubs. The jazz legacy as constructed by its predominantly white enthusiasts in Europe and Britain seemed to want the reconfirmation of the black-white dynamic, and Crosby notes that young blacks were granted a certain legitimacy in

20. Courtney Pine, at the forefront of media interest in the new British jazz boom of the 1980s, *Wire*, 1986.

jazz simply because of their color. But their musical experiences differed too, with reggae being a foundational presence for many: Crosby had his Rastafarian phase in the early 1970s, while the tenorists Pine and Steve Williamson met in a reggae band in Brixton, London, before joining the Jazz Warriors (Cook 1987–88, 49).

It is clear that many jazz musicians of Caribbean origin in Britain have employed indigenous music from their personal or family backgrounds — Harriott in using calypso for experimental music, Crosby in his work with the Jazz Jamaica All-Stars, Pine by combining sounds from jazz, instrumental dub, and reggae. Pine made this point very early in his career, in his first cover feature for the leading magazine surfing the new wave of British jazz in the 1980s, the *Wire*: "there will be a black British style because a lot of guys getting into it here come from the reggae thing or the calypso thing, *which is very different from the New York musicians*. A sound will evolve" (quoted in Nicholson 1986, 32; my emphasis). Remarkably, alongside the blue ska thinking of Gary Crosby, Pine has indeed gone on to produce a body of work that explores and extends the improvisatory soundscapes of black Britain. Imruh Bakari develops this amalgamation into a black musical aesthetic which is constructed outside the dominant jazz framework of African America, from Du Bois through patois to dub-ois: "Jamaican music in general, and dub in particular, gave African-Caribbean music produced as a reflection of the British experience its most definitive characteristics. The modality of dub with its cultural and political discourse has determined the framework within which all other influences would be incorporated and syncretized. . . . Within the African diaspora paradigm as a whole, however, this separates the 'British' music of [Roni] Size and Pine into a subaltern discourse, distinct from the hegemonic 'American' music of [the black jazz tradition exemplified and celebrated by Wynton] Marsalis" (1999, 109). Over all, from Leslie Thompson and his Garveyite dream to the post-Rastafarian bassist Crosby, from first-generation Caribbean migrants like Harriott and Goode to second-generation black Britons like Gail Thompson and Pine in the Jazz Warriors, and a further generation in Soweto Kinch — and with a musician such as the Barbadian trumpeter Harry Beckett carving out a career that would see him playing with Hutchinson in the 1950s, the South African Brotherhood of Breath in the 1970s (see below), and the Jazz Warriors in the 1980s — it is clear that black jazz was an important combination of musics for sounding the growing presence of the Caribbean in a changing Britain.

BLOWING KISSES, IN TIME, TO CONDUCT THE BIG BAND: SOUTH AFRICAN JAZZ IN BRITAIN

I suppose we tended to overestimate the jazz scene [in Britain]. . . .
From South Africa it looked pretty good and of course the liberal
attitudes were an attraction so that we could go on playing together.
We just naturally assumed that there would be the same kind of
open-mindedness to music here that there is to colour.—CHRIS
MCGREGOR, *Melody Maker*, 1967 (quoted in McGregor 1995, 96)

The second development in British jazz supplied from a predominantly black migrant culture that I want to look at is the South African contribution. With the arrival in London of the multiracial modern jazz sextet the Blue Notes from South Africa in 1965, through gigs and crises in France and Switzerland, a further set of new sounds, rhythms, performances, and personalities vitalized the scene. Most members of this group would become permanent exiles in Europe from the white supremacist apartheid regime in South Africa, which was established in 1948 and gathered force with increased repression and murderous violence in the later 1950s and 1960s. The impact of the Blue Notes in Britain should not be read as a result of their being first[29] — other South African musicians had arrived in the 1960s, and of course many other musicians from across British colonial Africa touched the imperial center of London for different purposes throughout the twentieth century, as I will briefly show — nor of their being the most high-profile in the jazz firmament — this distinction belongs to those South African musicians who gravitated toward the United States, and who, interestingly, would tend to play less experimental music than the Blue Notes during their exile careers. I have in mind the likes of Abdullah Ibrahim (earlier known as Dollar Brand), the trumpeter Hugh Masekela, and the singer Miriam Makeba. Three things set the members of the Blue Notes apart, though. First, they had a near instant impact on British jazz of the mid-1960s, musically, visually, socially, and politically. Second, they had an enduring commitment to experimental forms of improvisation, as they frequently set out to explore the possibilities of combining their township jazz styles of kwela and mbaqanga with European free improvisation, and to do this in collaboration with British and European players. Last and by no means least, the fact that the contribution of most of these musicians endured for all of their lives in Europe is remarkable: their creative, liberatory, and inspirational African cultural presence has been a vital source of energy and innovation (sometimes misunderstood and resented as well).

The African American singer and political activist Paul Robeson — no great lover of jazz himself — once stated that he "discovered Africa in London" (quoted in Rice 2003, 176–77). The capital of the British Empire did attract and provide opportunities for African artists, musicians, and thinkers, if perhaps not quite to the primitivizing or politically engaged, anti-colonialist extent of the modernist negrophilia that swept Paris in the middle decades of the twentieth century.[30] African sounds could be heard in London, but more pertinently, musicians from Africa could experience *and play* in London mixes of music, such as American(-style) jazz, English dance band music, and some of the Caribbean musics discussed above, not all of which would be available to them to the same extent in their home communities (see Stapleton 1990).[31] Through the 1940s and 1950s the Nigerian bandleader Ambrose Campbell's West African Rhythm Brothers played regularly for Africans and local black populations in London, in the early days playing authentic drums borrowed (back) from London museums (Stapleton and May 1987, 297)—playing in the heart of the empire could have some practical advantages. We have seen how the circum-Atlantic music of calypso featured in celebrations of African independence, as when the Trinidadian Lord Kitchener recorded "Ghana" in London on Melodisc for release in Ghana; the West African Rhythm Brothers too sang of their optimism for the new state of 1957 in their contribution "Good Luck Ghana" (Stapleton 1990, 95). With such musical statements, politics and pleasure, and different diasporic identities, were interwoven and dialogized as peripheries met at the (imperial) center, and used such meetings to successfully challenge the center.[32] The most compelling example of capitalizing on the capital for its colonial circulatory energies may be that of the Nigerian musician, bandleader, and activist Fela Kuti, who enrolled at Trinity College of Music in London in 1958 and fronted a successful band called Koola Lobitos for several years. Subsequently Kuti would go on to found, with the drummer Tony Allen, the Afrobeat style, "encompassing at once a 'happening,' a jazz session, a soul-funk show reminiscent of James Brown's, and Yoruba ritual incantations" (Tenaille 2002, 70). In Afrobeat, singing and rapping in pidgin English both maintained and subverted the language of colonial discourse, but it also allowed Kuti to address pan-African audiences across different African languages, and of course it provided a route to international communication and profile for his music in the 1970s and 1980s. His sounds and ideology produced a powerful black Atlanticist mix-music: from West Africa, highlife as well as Nkrumah-inspired pan-Africanism; from the United States, jazz and funk as well as aspects of Black Power; from Britain, the early education of bandleading with Koola Lobitos, an earlier family history of Christianity and classical western music, as well as a direct experience of the workings of empire and its (apparent) end. With Afrobeat's extended dance rhythms, jazz instrumental breaks, call-and-response structures, and damning critiques of neocolonialism, in characteristic masculinist heroic mode Kuti practiced and preached the view that "Music is the weapon of the future . . . music is the weapon of the givers of life" (quoted in Tenaille 2002, 76). Over all, in London it was indeed true that with both independence and apartheid key issues, "musicians joined the cause: in 1962, an 'African Freedom Day' at the Royal Festival Hall featured Ginger Johnson and his Highlife Rhythms Band, Johnny Dankworth, the Ghana Cultural Society, and Fela Kuti with his band Koola Lobitos" (Stapleton 1990, 96).

While musicians from West African British colonies and then newly independent nations were important players in and around jazz in London and one or two other urban centers in Britain, South Africa was taking a political path radically different from democratic majority rule, prompting an exodus of musicians and other cultural workers. The elections of 1948 had seen a surprising victory for the Afrikaner National Party, who appealed to white Afrikaners with a platform of extending and codifying the many existing segregationist acts, some of which had been effectively diluted as a result of increased social mobility during the Second World War. South Africa then embarked on a disastrous though surprisingly long-lasting national policy of racial discrimination, aimed at the further classification of people by race, the maintenance of a white supremacist state, the allotment of social privilege and mobility according to color, and the entrenchment of a paranoiac legislature embracing (or cloaking its actions in) the worst rhetoric of the cold war (as in the Suppression of Communism Act of 1961)—all held in place by an increasingly repressive and brutal regime. Despite internal and international pressures and protests, the system of apartheid kept the National Party that introduced it in power until the early 1990s—aided by continued high levels of financial investment from British and American interests, while the governments of both countries vetoed calls by the United Nations for economic sanctions against the regime in the wake of the Sharpeville shootings of 21 March 1960, when sixty-nine protestors against the pass laws were killed by the police (many shot in the back), and nearly two hundred were injured. Because Britain was the old imperial master, its interventions regarding apartheid were perhaps the most important international ones for South Africa—and there was a sense in which the British people sought to take a moral lead in campaigning, as with the broadly contemporaneous Campaign for Nuclear Disarmament (founded in 1958). While Prime Minister Harold Macmillan was acknowledging the force and the reality of African independence when he spoke of "the winds of change" blowing through the continent in a resonant speech in

South Africa in 1958, at grassroots level it was a meeting in London in June 1959 that effectively gave birth to the anti-apartheid movement, which embraced the New Left, radical Christians, African activists and exiles, and a coalition of culturalists. A powerful activist political context was thus the setting for what was in jazz a vital (necessary, life-affirming) cultural contribution from South Africa too.

PLAYING JAZZ IN SOUTH AFRICA

In South Africa there had long been a thriving jazz scene, much of it crossing the racial divide of official segregation and then apartheid. While strong colonial links remained with Britain, many in South Africa looked to the United States for cultural energy, the experience of modernity, the confirmation of their own political position. These issues of culture, identity, and ideology were complex and finely interwoven with the state's imposed racial codification. White South Africans during apartheid often believed, Melissa Steyn explains, that "the presence of racism in the United States showed the universality of racial thinking, the inevitability of racism, and even justified a system that was 'at least honest.' So South Africa's outright racism was actually moral virtue. The American South proved that South Africa wasn't so bad. After all, there was no Ku Klux Klan in this country, privately organized violence" (Steyn 1999, 271).

For many black South Africans, as well as white liberals and leftist activists, the United States and its civil rights movement were inspirational for social change in a way not entirely dissimilar from the international egalitarian activism of Mahatma Gandhi in South Africa in the early years of the twentieth century. And jazz was recognized during the establishment of apartheid as a symbol of both modernity and anti-racist black pride: "The history of urban black South African music is strongly linked to the history of black American music, above all jazz. . . . Both cultures were subject to massive discrimination from a white Christian establishment. . . . For South Africans, . . . black America provided a unique model" (Stapleton and May 1987, 192). A difficult relationship took shape with traditional values and music, one which would, as we will see, also be worked through by South African exile jazz musicians in Britain and Europe in years to come. One townsman exclaimed to Anthony Sampson in the 1950s: "Tribal music!

Tribal history! Chiefs! We don't care about chiefs! Give us jazz and film stars, man! We want Duke Ellington, Satchmo and hot dames! Yes, brother, anything American. You can cut out all this junk about kraals and folk tales and Basutos in baskets—forget it! You're just trying to keep us backward, that's what!" (quoted in Stapleton and May 1987, 201–2).

As Frantz Fanon reminds us, it is the colonialists that "rush to the help of the traditions of the indigenous society. It is the colonialists who become the defenders of the native style" (Fanon 1965, 195), for that reinforces the hierarchy of racial modernity.[33] The American culture of film signified modernity for the (unnamed) townsman, while black American jazz in South Africa sounded not only modernity but pleasure—and, more dangerously, the dominant blackness of jazz, the innovative culture of blackness, stood in direct opposition to white supremacy, sounded a route to black liberation and the resolution of problematic white identity also.

Apparently, regardless of the extent to which South African jazz musicians were as individuals ideologically articulate or politically active, by virtue of the music they played, which was their preferred cultural expression, they were positioned politically in opposition to the state. For the white pianist Chris McGregor, playing in a mixed-race band in Cape Town in the late 1950s—simply because they were "the best musicians I could find"—"was already a quasi-political orientation" on the part of *all* the musicians involved (McGregor 1995, 7). As a music student, McGregor had been directly politicized by the authorities' proposals to restrict access to the university for black students in 1957. Combined with the call for equal democratic rights articulated in the Freedom Charter of 1955 by the likes of Nelson Mandela, white and black jazz musicians began to play together for demonstrating crowds, holding music classes and dances in the townships, and jamming at the limited bohemian white cultural spaces still available. The drummer Louis Moholo recalls some of the absurdities of musicians' experiences of playing and socializing together in a multiracial band under apartheid, one more twist on minstrelsy, or Leonard Feather's "white curtain" closed again: "sometimes Chris McGregor would have to play behind a curtain, and vice versa, I would have to play behind a curtain if we got hired by some white cats. And Chris McGregor used to come to this place where we would drink some beer, in the Zulu quarters, but white people were not *allowed* in here; Chris would paint his face with black polish to come in there" (quoted in Scott 1991, 36; emphasis in original).

McGregor, Moholo, and the saxophonist Dudu Pukwana looked to jazz to move beyond the increasingly strict apartheid structure of racial classification and oppression that defined their whiteness and blackness. Once exposed to Duke Ellington and his big bands, McGregor stated simply that he "heard in [Ellington] a certain solution to the problem of black traditions in a white world" (quoted in McGregor 1995, 14). Primarily this solution entailed the invention of a social community—elsewhere McGregor would talk of his big bands as the creation of his "own village"[34] (quoted in McGregor 1995, 128)—a repertoire of joyous music based on African traditions, and the Ellingtonian generosity of offering in the written arrangements the style and a space to best meet the individual voice of the soloist.[35] In a country imposing a serious and violent racialized social classification—symbolized most shockingly at Sharpeville in 1960—such multiracial grouping, cultural celebration, and sensitivity *could only be political*. Micropolitically, when band rehearsals were subsequently raided by the police, it was essential to clear up the teacups, because socializing between blacks and whites was no longer permitted (McGregor 1995, 17). At the same time, when a small group began to form around one of the clusters of musicians in Johannesburg and they called themselves the Blue Notes, even the band's name was a double coding: on the one hand it clearly signaled the music of black American jazz, while on the other the very word "blue" was intended to camouflage the color issue (McGregor 1995, 25). The young white South African pianist Manfred Mann was then exploring jazz in Johannesburg, and being educated in the complex etiquette of apartheid-dominated multiracial relations: "When I shook hands with Lewis Nkosi in the street we were both very, very conscious of everyone looking at us. The simplest human action was a contrived gesture. On another occasion the brilliant saxophonist Kippie Moeketsi came to my house, I was eighteen years old, now why would he do that? It was an enormous privilege for me, but my stepmother made him come into our house through the back door. It was a terribly shaming experience . . . : Kippie himself was so used to this kind of thing, he handled it with a dignified resignation. In rehearsals it was even very difficult to argue with a black musician. So although music was a sort of space we could carve out, it was fraught with difficulty" (personal interview, 2003).

After Sharpeville, the "second phase" of apartheid in the 1960s saw South Africa subjected to growing international isolation and criticism, as well as internal entrenchment resulting from the banning of the Communist Party and the African National Congress, expansion of the ethnic Bantu homelands, curfews and other restrictions on black presences in urban areas, detention without trial, increased state media censorship, and the imprisonment of black leaders and anti-apartheid activists (Worden 1995, 108–14). Some musicians, black and white, were leaving: the pianist Dollar Brand, Hugh Masekela, Miriam Makeba, the then jazz pianist Manfred Mann, the bassist Harry Miller — all made their way to the United States or to Britain, where there was still relatively free access for some South Africans for a grace period of one year after South Africa's withdrawal from the Commonwealth in 1961. A company visiting London earlier in that year with the hit musical *King Kong*—which had a powerful musical accompaniment that itself played a significant role in disseminating South African jazz — "stirred controversy over its apparent lack of political content" (Stapleton 1990, 96). In fact, the program contained the following statement from the British producer: "Jack Hylton has received every courtesy and co-operation from the [South African] Union Government and wishes to record his appreciation" (see Stapleton 1990, 101). Such a defensive statement at least indicates the extent to which the political situation in South Africa *was* then being discussed in Britain, by activists and cultural workers as well as politicians. That so many musicians were leaving may ironically have opened up some space for those still in South Africa, of which the Blue Notes were becoming the best-known and most popular. The lineup stabilized around one white and five black musicians: McGregor on piano, Pukwana on alto saxophone, Nikele Moyake on tenor saxophone, Mongezi Feza on trumpet, Johnny Dyani on double bass, and Moholo on drums.

In the early 1960s the Blue Notes toured South Africa almost continually, a tactic described later by McGregor, somewhat naïvely (one of the more obvious drawbacks of a politics of love), as "Dance, stay on the move, and you'll beat apartheid" (quoted in Wickes 1999, 54). There were kinds of zones or gaps within apartheid at different times where it was possible for blacks and whites to make music together.

Primary among the geographical ones was the west Johannesburg residential area of Sophiatown, which in the 1950s remained one of the few areas of South Africa with black freeholders' property. In his history of African popular music, *Music Is the Weapon of the Future*, Frank Tenaille traces the influence of this suburb on global protest, the international politicization of local music practice: "Sophiatown had been the symbol of the vitality of an urban music inspired by the big bands of Duke Ellington, Count Basie, Jimmie Lunceford, and, later, bebop. . . . The destruction of Sophiatown forced many artists into exile or retirement. . . . [Subsequently] the international anti-apartheid movement focused its searchlights on the South African scene, revealing to foreign ears a formidable wealth of kwela, mbaqanga, and mbube, not to mention jazz, soul, and reggae" (Tenaille 2002, 81).

The passing of the Natives Resettlement Act of 1954 would make it possible to evict and forcibly relocate Sophiatown's inhabitants to the township of Soweto (Worden 1995, 96), while the area was demolished by the authorities (echoes of Storyville) and replaced by a whites-only residential area. In spite of this, Johannesburg maintained spaces for cultural difference: Dorkay House became an important venue for multicultural events and experiments in performance, music, and education in the 1950s and 1960s, and it was here, among many other cultural events, that the Blue Notes would regularly play. This semi-interstitial culture, in some ways officially obstructed—police lining the exits to jazz concerts, surveillance and intimidation combined—was able nonetheless to take advantage of occasional commercial playing opportunities, such as a tour sponsored by Pepsi-Cola (American jazz, American drink, American business interests), and a first big band in 1963, sponsored by a local brewery, though only to play in black townships. According to Gwen Ansell, "ironically, while the 60s were the 'silenced time' for black culture, particularly literature, with a fresh wave of repression following Sharpeville . . . the festivals provided a cultural space for six or eight years longer into the decade for some quite daring musical experiments and self-consciously African expressions" (personal correspondence, 2004).

The route to Europe in 1964 from South Africa was via Mozambique. Maxine McGregor, subsequently Chris's wife and the Blue Notes' effective manager, recalled that there, "for the first time in their lives the musicians were all free men. . . . [They] walk[ed] up and down the train, into the bar from which they had previously been excluded, with the knowledge that they could stand next to any man and not be arrested" (1995, 69). After some festival appearances in France, some busking on the Mediterranean coast, and a few months' work deputizing for Dollar Brand in Switzerland, the Blue Notes arrived in London. There was a developing sense already of the difference of their music from most other jazz, which they began to recognize with a combination of insecurity and confidence, the combination itself a symptom of their diasporic experience. Maxine identified this from the beginning, in Paris, when "the music of the South Africans was different and [resident American musicians] seemed uneasy as to how to take it; perhaps they felt in its originality some form of a threat?" (McGregor 1995, 73).

AFRICAN MUSIC OF EXILE AND
ANTI-APARTHEID PROTEST

But why go to London? With South African passports by this date, band members had no right of permanent residence (McGregor 1995, 78), would have to apply for general work permits which could take a year to be authorized, and anyway could expect to find opportunities for commercial playing obstructed because of the Musicians' Union's restrictive or self-protectionist practices. However, there was a significant exile community in London, English was the spoken language, there were some personal contacts — those affiliated with small organizations like the Transcription Centre for African culture where Maxine found work, musicians like Dollar Brand then temporarily staying in London, other musicians who had come to play in the South African musical *King Kong*, and artists and writers from across Africa — and of course there was an awareness among the musicians of the active anti-apartheid movement that had been established in Britain (McGregor 1995, 96), with contributions from sympathetic jazzers like John Dankworth and Cleo Laine. The anti-apartheid movement itself was founded in London through 1959 and 1960, while the radical priest Trevor Huddleston, recognizing the place of culture in political legitimacy, had called for a cultural boycott of South Africa as early as 1955 (Denselow 1990, 49).[36] Because of Britain's imperial legacy and its role in shaping the post-imperial organization of the Commonwealth, African independence and postcolonialism were important topics for political debate and public action. In 1960 Hugh Masekela had left South Africa to study in London and then New York. For Masekela, in spite of the American civil rights movement, there were significantly different experiences of the understanding of wider, global black politics and postcolonial struggles between the United States and Britain: in his view the United States was wrapped up in the cold war externally and McCarthyism internally. In Britain, while he found British jazz profoundly disappointing ("the music scene was dead—there was just Dudley Moore playing piano and telling jokes": quoted in Denselow 1990, 52), he could recognize the implications of mobilization around the Campaign for Nuclear Disarmament, and of activists who took on responsibility for sustained work against apartheid—the growing New Left: "When I got to New York, people there didn't know shit about South Africa. Anyone from Africa, as far as they were concerned, was a communist. . . . They were still lynching people of African origin in the States. When I came, . . . Nkrumah was just flabbergasting everybody with his rhetoric and sensibility. The week I arrived, [the Congolese leader Patrice] Lumumba went to ask people for help against the Belgians. They said, 'Fuck it, you're a communist.' It wasn't a very welcoming time. In London, there was Bertrand Russell at Trafalgar Square; the anti-nuclear thing had started. There were big rallies against South Africa" (quoted in Stapleton and May 1987, 198).

My point is not to establish some kind of political campaign hierarchy in any way (London good, New York bad)—after all, it was the African American singer and civil rights activist Harry Belafonte who would arrange a scholarship for Masekela in the United States (Denselow 1990, 52). It is rather to draw attention, through one musician's subjective experience of political and cultural exile, to societies' and governments' differing international priorities and sympathies, as well as the impact of those on the motivations and actions of exiled African jazz musicians. London, the center of the Commonwealth (notwithstanding South Africa's withdrawal from the organization at this time), still provided a locus for black cultural expression and exchange, and Maxine McGregor describes the global, mediated nature of black cultural and political energy in London then. As well as the Africa Centre, registered in 1961 but formally opened by President Kaunda of Zambia in 1964, "artists crossed frequently at the Transcription Centre whose transmissions on the art, music and literature of black Africa were broadcast locally throughout Nigeria, Sierra Leone, Ghana, Kenya, Uganda and Tanzania.[37] The years from 1962 onward were seething with activity because it was almost the first time that these artists were able to proclaim their pride in their own cultural background and history, which up until not long before had been completely denied and disavowed by the colonial and missionary thinking" (McGregor 1995, 87–88).

Anti-apartheid sympathies in Britain unlocked doors for the Blue Notes: Ronnie Scott (a Jew) offered a short initial residency to the band at his club in London, and because of Maxine's persistence the Musicians' Union "granted the band membership as exiles, as had been done for Jewish musical refugees from Hitler's Germany during World War Two" (Wickes 1999, 54). The trumpeter Ian Carr remembers the band's total impact, as local musicians headed to the club to "have a listen . . . *and a look*" (Carr 1973, 95; ellipsis in original, my emphasis). The Blue Notes were reviewed for their musical contribution (what they themselves considered a fairly straight mix of hard bop and high life at the time), but as a collective multiracial musical presence from South Africa, they inevitably appealed also to political constituencies. *Peace News* wrote in 1966 of how the Blue Notes rhythm section "outplay[ed] nearly all their British counterparts. . . . There is above all an air of 'happening' about them . . . a freshness and an unexpectedness, both in the solos and the melodies, that has disappeared from much of the music that once was revolutionary. . . . They play musically within the boundaries set by Parker and his associates, but emotionally beyond them" (quoted in McGregor 1995, 89). Interviewed in the communist *Morning Star* in 1967 by Brian Blain of the Musicians' Union, McGregor mused about the relation between politics and culture and, interestingly at this early stage, what he perceived as the tendency of that relation to get diluted in exile in Britain:

> One of the things which always fascinated us, a constant subject of discussion over there [in South Africa]—for white as well as black— was how the American Negro had got his music *through* in a white-dominated society, from people like Armstrong to today's openly defiant musicians. In South Africa the spirit behind the resistance is expressed in the music. Although there have been political setbacks, spiritually the people are definitely not in retreat, and I think the

music plays a part in this. The kind of jazz we play is not obviously political, but I think our generation were the first to make an impact on South African cultural thinking. To come from there to here, where in a strange way what you do doesn't really *matter* to anyone, is a difficult thing to adjust to. (Quoted in McGregor 1995, 97–98; emphases in original)

While Peter Buckman has argued that in the 1960s, "South Africa was too far removed from Europe for the race issue to take on the reality it had in America," he does acknowledge that the politics of apartheid had a special impact in Britain. One reason was of course that Commonwealth and residual colonial relations persisted, but another was that "the English Left came nearest to understanding [civil rights and race relations] because of the problem of *apartheid* in south Africa: . . . the Left were constantly demonstrating against the Verwoerd regime" (1970, 133). This explanation overlooks cultural input, in particular the international sports boycott that focused in Britain on games like cricket, widely recognized as a quintessentially English contribution to imperial masculinist culture (and played in "whites")— the controversy surrounding the naming of the Cape Coloured player Basil d'Oliveira by the English selectors for a tour of South Africa in 1968 was a pivotal politicizing moment.[38] The situation with regard to the political contribution of black and white exile South African musicians in London during the period was different: their very presence in the heart of the Commonwealth, *combined with their chosen music form — jazz — which connected directly to contemporary American black experience and political struggle*, raised the profile and insistence of a creative liberatory African presence in Britain. And when the energy of the anti-apartheid and anti-colonial campaigns seemed to be faltering in the 1970s, South African jazz musicians were still there: in Britain, former Blue Notes figured strongly in bands like Assegai and Jabula; the first released an album called *Zimbabwe* in 1973, the second an album supporting the anti-apartheid struggle in 1977.[39] In Denmark the bassist Dyani recorded *Song for Biko* in 1978 with Pukwana and the African American avant-garde trumpeter Don Cherry.[40] When Nelson Mandela was elected president of South Africa in 1994, watching the ceremony on television in Brixton, London, was a small group of South African exile jazz musicians, the most senior of whom was the then sole surviving

Blue Note, Louis Moholo. To great delight the cheer went up: "No more benefits!" (fund-raising concerts at which musicians generally play for expenses only; Fordham 1996, 306).[41]

Displaying unconfident insularity, some British jazzers (perhaps led —for once—by the rhythm sections snubbed above in the *Peace News* review of the Blue Notes) made it clear that the Blue Notes' music would indeed not matter to them. Maggie Nicols, in the 1960s a young singer on the fringes of the modern scene, reluctantly recalls criticism as well as a certain pressure on her to conform: "To be honest there was some resistance from the London scene towards what they were doing, because the Blue Notes weren't playing straight ahead bebop and there was some snobbery about their technique. I loved them, but I was very young then, and maybe rather held my enthusiasm back because of the criticisms some of the beboppers were making" (personal interview, 2002). As with some modernists' disparaging (and disappointing) responses to the experiments of Joe Harriott in London a few years earlier, here is confirmation, as if it were needed, that not only trad jazz was open to accusations of neoconservatism.[42] To an extent this latest difficulty was musical—but not only within this new, exoticizing critical framework of (bebop) technique *versus* (South African) "emotion," in the term employed by *Peace News*. The difficulty was a symptom of the Africanization of jazz that the Blue Notes were exploring: using local musics such as kwela, mbaqanga, and marabi as the basis for melodies and improvisations could be exclusionary. These were unknown soundscapes for many British musicians. The Blue Notes only fully realized this later: "the various musical traditions that existed in the [South African] environment (including tribal music, Malaysian music, Christian and Moslem choirs, North American jazz, even South American carnival music brought to the Cape by sailors) [—]we had no way of knowing just how 'different' it seemed to what people were used to in Europe" (McGregor 1995, 96).[43]

In a further remove from the tightness of technique, the musicians' improvisatory flexibility and musical openness could flow and flourish within the newer free music that was now being practiced by some British musicians in small London venues like the Little Theatre Club and Ronnie Scott's Old Place (see chapter 4). Also, different members of the band began to listen to, meet, and work with touring and expatriate avant-garde American players: Moholo and Dyani toured with

21. The South African exile pianist Chris McGregor on the farm at Alfriston, Sussex, 1972. © Val Wilmer.

Steve Lacy, while experimentalists like Cecil Taylor, Don Cherry, and Archie Shepp were appearing in Denmark about the time the Blue Notes had a short residency there in 1966. Albert Ayler was in Europe in 1966 and stayed with the McGregors in London for a short time. (McGregor and Pukwana took Ayler to a jazz club in London for a blow, but the manager refused to allow *that* music to be inflicted on his audience: McGregor 1995, 100.) Visual signifiers were shifting too: the sharp suits, thin ties, and short hair of the Blue Notes' early days in London in 1965 were exchanged for hippie locks and ethnic clothing, the exoticist preference of the counterculture conveniently coinciding with the arrival of these Africans.[44] As a small functioning unit the Blue Notes would soon cease to exist, having fulfilled its dual purpose of providing mutual support for the journey into exile and making each musician's international reputation (if never great commercial success). As the musicians had desired in their long pre-exile view from South Africa, there were indeed new vistas opening up, in terms of the musicians' approaches to their own playing, their repertoire, and their lineup. These innovations coalesced around the Brotherhood of Breath, the big band that evolved out of jam sessions held on Thursday nights at Scott's Old Place beginning in 1967. Nicols, who would in turn sing with both sets of musicians in Keith Tippett's mammoth project Centipede, has described how the initial "explosion . . . of new life" that the South Africans brought to Britain became a prolonged and mutually productive multiracial "interaction": "the interaction between Tippett, Elton Dean, Nick Evans and Marc Charig (a new generation of white jazz musicians) and the predominantly black South African musicians created such an exciting new music" (personal interview, 2002). Relatively fresh himself to the London scene, having come from the West Country, the pianist Tippett had found "a lot of little pockets of activity in London, not that they were separate, a good amount of cross-feeding went on. But there was Ronnie Scott's, the Little Theatre Club, the Musician's Co-operative, and the Blue Notes. Musically and socially the Blue Notes was the grouping I gravitated towards" (personal interview, 2003).

As I explore in greater detail later with Centipede and others, the phenomenon of the big band happening-gathering was an important reemployment of jazz tradition in the context of the new sociocultural ambitions and practices of the European counterculture—the big band of musicians influenced by free jazz, with entourage in tow, caravanserai-ing across Europe, would be understood by audiences within the alternative society's context of communal living, ritual, and celebration. (Reviews occasionally compared such projects with Sun Ra's Arkestra as a sociocultural phenomenon, though rhythmically the Brotherhood at least was exploring different terrain.) Recall here McGregor's solution to black and white divisions in the creation of a big band ("my own village": quoted in McGregor 1995, 128), first essayed in the early 1960s in South Africa. A small grant from the Arts Council in 1970 enabled the big band to be formally constituted as the Brotherhood of Breath, and its first performance in March of that year was at a concert in London underwritten by the Jazz Centre Society.[45] It was led by McGregor, with most of the material written by him and Pukwana. On the group's first album of 1971, alongside these two were the other South African musicians, Feza, Moholo, Harry Miller, and Ronnie Beer, a white saxophonist who had effectively replaced Moyake in the Blue Notes, and some leading British free musicians, including the saxophonists Mike Osborne and John Surman. It was this version of the band that most excitingly explored the tensions between arrangements and free improvisation, a difficult musical project made accessible for a wider audience by virtue of the kwela style of the arrangements. To emphasize the African content, the album cover shows a pair of ceremonial or fertility wooden carvings of females draped with necklaces (though there is no band photograph to indicate its multiracial lineup). The Afro-rock band Osibisa was popularizing a version of African music in the pop charts during the early 1970s, which may have aided the Brotherhood's own survival as an experimental big band. The second version of the Brotherhood was established by McGregor with a mostly newer, but still multiracial, lineup in France with an arts festival grant in 1981. McGregor's motivation remained the same, as Jane Herve wrote in a review of a concert by the London Brotherhood in 1984: "the music of this jazzman who mixes seven black and eight white musicians in his band, marries individual improvisation with collective logic (like Duke) . . . makes it possible to escape from the 'schizophrenia' of apartheid" (quoted in McGregor 1995, 197). This Brotherhood took the music back to Africa, playing in Mozambique at effectively the musicians' own expense. The third, final version of the big band significantly worked in Europe in 1989 with the American veteran radical and saxophonist Archie Shepp, known to the Blue Notes from meetings in the 1960s. McGregor spoke of Shepp in those early days: "he became a pioneer figure for us; he talked so clearly about the black music situation in the States, and naturally we saw quite a few similarities and parallels with the South African situation that we had just left" (quoted in McGregor 1995, 214–15). The legacy of the Blue Notes and the various versions of the Brotherhood of Breath continues to be heard and felt. For example, both the key big bands of the generation of British jazz musicians that came of age in the 1980s were influenced by them. The Jazz Warriors commissioned work from McGregor and occasionally included in its ranks senior black musicians such as Harry Beckett, who had played with the original Brotherhood, while Warriors played with the Brotherhood and other South Africans too. The eclectic "world music" repertoire of Loose Tubes in part explored the African free terrain opened up by the Brotherhood, the trumpeter Dave Defries played in both ensembles, while one inspiration of the young keyboard player Django Bates had been Dudu Pukwana. Most significantly for the Blue Notes and Brotherhood repertoires, the Dedication Orchestra was formed in England in 1992 and re-formed for a tour of the Contemporary Music Network a decade later. This stellar big band played arrangements of numbers written by the Blue Notes and their South African constellation in Britain, with one aim being to raise funds for music education in deprived black communities in post-apartheid South Africa. Musicians active in the Dedication Orchestra included, center stage, Moholo; original Brotherhood musicians like the trombonist Malcolm Griffiths and Beckett, and other musicians from that period like Nicols, Tippett, Mike Westbrook; second-generation free improvisers like Steve Beresford; new jazzers of the 1980s like Bates and the flautist Eddie Parker from Loose Tubes; as well as later South African exiles like the trumpeter Claude Deppa. That the cover for the first album, *Spirits Rejoice*, features an extended list of sponsors, companies, organizations, and individuals who donated facilities, skills, and money to facilitate the recording and its release indicates the jazz community's warm effort to mark the contribution of the South Africans. As Richard Williams writes in the program notes for the Contemporary Music Network tour of 2003, the Brotherhood of Breath approach to the London jazz "world of cliques (and sometimes factions within cliques) was to bring everyone together and show them that jazz was really about inclusiveness, not exclusivity. This was a lesson [McGregor] had surely learnt in his earliest days, when, as a white man, he had to cross apartheid's barricades in order to play with his black colleagues" (Williams 2003, 12).

Mark Sinker has sought to evaluate the contribution of the South Africans to British and wider improvised music, beginning with "the phenomenal energy of their actual presence: it's something like a validation of the links between the hardest and most free of 60s players, the all-embracing reach of the best 70s fusion outfits, and the deepest powers of Africa folk and pop roots" (Sinker 1987, 33). The South African musicians carried with them at least two other essential(ism)s, which they managed to combine: their energy and experimentation working with the visceral pleasure of dance, rhythm, and spectacle, and the political engagement of multiracialism in the context of a critique of apartheid. Pleasure and politics combined in a music of affirmation, blowing the winds of change, blowing the changes of the wind. Does this seem too positive, a feel-good story to be claimed by British jazz? Looking back on the cultural and political landscape of the 1960s, the producer Joe Boyd has remarked that "Britain seemed totally unprepared for the intensity of the musicianship that came pouring out of [the Blue Notes]. Britain's (and my) failure to provide a working living for that group always struck me as one of the great tragedies of music in this country" (1993, 31). That Johnny Dyani moved to Denmark in 1971, Ronnie Beer returned to South Africa in 1973 (later living in Ibiza), the McGregors moved to Lot-et-Garonne, France, to live and work in the following year, and Harry Miller became based in Holland may be a sign of the restlessness—or the easy mobility—of the exile, but it also confirms that jazz in Britain had or developed some serious limitations. Maxine McGregor writes with light damnation of London's "pervading apathy which was to prove, musically at any rate, more deadly than the [apartheid] system they had left behind" (1995, 90).

I want finally to look a little more at that continuing negotiated relationship with what the South African musicians left behind, with what they carried out of South Africa. Doing so reveals a perhaps now overfamiliar diasporic dialectic—though we should remember Minh-ha Trinh's observation that "the experience of exile is never simply binary . . . [but is a] question of fitting in a no-fit-in category" (Trinh 1994, 12–13). While, in Louis Moholo's blunt phrasing, "exile is a fucker" (quoted in Scott 1991, 37), at the same time Moholo found in the early energy of free jazz in London a musical *and* social liberty that *rejected* South Africa (this may not be surprising: he had once been sold by the South African police to local farmers to pick potatoes): "I started hearing some other vibes. I was away from South Africa and away from the chains. I just wanted to be free, totally free, even in music. Free to shake away all the slavery, anything to do with slavery, being boxed in to places—one, two, three, four—and being told you must come in after four. I was just a rebel, completely a rebel. . . . Free music is *it* man, it's so beautiful. The word 'free' makes sense to me. I know that's what I want; freedom, let my people go. *Let my people go!* And that's interlinking with politics, they embrace each other" (quoted in Scott 1991, 36).

Yet there appears to be something disturbing about the short lives of most of the Blue Notes and their constellation. I do not wish to present a simplistic or romanticizing version of the tortured African genius, nor do I necessarily concur with John Wickes in his diagnosis of "the long-term effects of internalised repression and forced exile" that they endured (1999, 214). Sometimes, for instance, "exile" was a marketing tool, with consciously employed assumptions of struggle and resistance. In 1986 a band combining politics and township jazz toured Germany, called the South African Exiles Thunderbolt, and including Pukwana, Dyani, McGregor, Jonas Gwangwa, and the percussionist Thebi Lipere alongside more recent exiles like Ernest Mothle and Lucky Ranku. But the biographical facts of the Blue Notes and early Brotherhood seem stark.[46] Nick Moyake would return to South Africa within a year of leaving to die of a brain tumor, Mongezi Feza suffered serious psychiatric problems before his death in England at the age of thirty, Ronnie Beer would give up playing (exile becoming silence), both bassists, Dyani and Miller, died young, in continental Europe, and Pukwana and McGregor died within a few weeks of each other in 1990, barely into their fifties. While McGregor's description of himself as "a bit schizophrenic, divided between two personalities, European and African" (quoted in McGregor 1995, 186) was as much a statement of his white, Christian missionary, Xhosa-speaking childhood as of his later diasporic identity, Moholo the survivor could not escape feeling the social and psychological pressures of apartheid and exile in Europe (indeed as a leader he entitled — marketed — an album called *Exile* in 1990). He articulated this in 1975, the year of Feza's shockingly early death: "Sometimes it happens that I sabotage my own concerts. . . . I feel like going home, and I become unable to tell the difference between what is good and what is not; everything becomes horrible. To be an exile is already horrible. . . . I have the sensation of being violated in the true sense of the word, and I think perhaps Dudu thinks the same as I do. There are times that anything that is said to me, even a joke, will be misrepresented in my head" (quoted in McGregor 1995, 145).

If the impulse to make music motivates and salves exile — "the grudging gift" that compensated slaves for exile and exclusion (Gilroy 1993, 76) — then unmaking it, sabotaging his own concerts by absenting himself with no notice — presenting in his place *silence* — may underscore the difficulty of the compensatory process, the fragility or unconvincing nature of the compensatory narrative. That it is the *drummer*, losing confidence in judgment, sensing violation and misrepresentation, who offers in response silence, withdraws the grounding (flying) pulse of the band, weighs heavier still in the African matrix. Here is a moment when the exile fits Trinh's category of "no-fit-in," and there is fleeting, bathetic nostalgia, even for a place where he could be, had been, bought and sold: *"I feel like going home."*

Whether or not South Africa still signified "home" for all the musicians I have been writing of, there has been reference to their African routes throughout their experience of displacement—and it should be remembered that their specific choice of musical expression, American jazz, was already a sort of cultural displacement, before their physically leaving South Africa in the early 1960s. This is the final, vital point about the Blue Notes and the Africans of the Brotherhood of Breath in Britain and Europe. What Val Wilmer has correctly called "their African reconstruction of American music" (1989, 28) was a timely project, which coincided with *and contributed to* one of the periodic Africanizations of American jazz, the political and spiritual Africanization of the music in the 1960s. Alyn Shipton has briefly made this link: "[John] Coltrane had been influential in creating a climate of Afrocentrism among American jazz musicians that was in place when the diaspora of South African musicians began in the early 1960s" (2001, 838). The Black Arts Movement championed by Amiri Baraka privileged jazz as an African American social culture, and looked to its African origins (see Thomas 1995). The saxophonist and writer Marion Brown has written of how the black experience of the transatlantic journey of the slave trade could be encoded in black music expression: "Our having made the transition from Africa to America, without the necessary cultural institutions, was a manifestation of a superior adjustment potential and an act of societal *improvisation*" (quoted in Thomas 1995, 262; my emphasis). There was a compelling, possibly righteous sense of situated authenticity in the South African musicians' understanding of the Africanness of jazz, which became stronger as they learned more about the radical black musical practice and political criticism coming from American cultural workers and activists who were increasingly exploring what they understood as their own African legacies. The Blue Notes *were* African; from that musically mixed identity of Africans in Europe they projected an increasingly confident sense that this background was valuable, even original in jazz.[47] There was thus the added attraction for African American musicians such as Don Cherry in playing with Johnny Dyani, or Archie Shepp with the Brotherhood of Breath, of a circum-Atlantic exchange between American and African jazz musicians taking place in Europe. In a radio interview with the BBC, McGregor touched on the diasporic identity of the music, his own expatriate experience, and the turn to Africa in American jazz: "It seems very significant and very serious. Of course there is very much in the music that survived . . . the long exile—which gives it a great interest. It shows to my mind a certain psychic continuity. The African remnants, if you like, and now a certain turning towards Africa, show a definite psychic continuity which is very important in the music, I think. It is something beyond any individual—almost a tidal movement" (quoted in McGregor 1995, 157).

When McGregor stated that "the piano is my favourite drum" (quoted in McGregor 1995, 138), by means of a banal truism he offered a clear African-Atlantic musical motif. The relation with African musical styles and traditions was dealt with differently by the musicians at different periods in their musical careers: McGregor would sometimes, in a nostalgic (that is, homesick) gesture that was a central part of his creative process, seek to re-Africanize, or find himself re-Africanizing, his playing (see McGregor 1995, 119, 188, 223). There was a fundamental connection for him: "One could perhaps say that African music, coming into contact with modern technological society, tends to become something which one could call 'jazz music' " (quoted in McGregor 1995, 215). Moholo, who earlier was quoted talking energetically of the liberatory power of creating free music "away from South Africa and away from the chains," would in the years following reexplore the rhythmic, improvisatory, and performative possibilities of African traditions directly in groups like Culture Shock, which effected a kind of theatrical performance of jazz and dance and costume (shades of the Art Ensemble of Chicago), African Drum Ensemble, and Viva Le Black. Most ambivalent perhaps were the reactions of the bassist Johnny Dyani who, having distanced himself from the Blue Notes and associates in Britain, was to be found in 1970 criticizing his erstwhile colleagues for "not doing what they were talking about in South Africa; they are losing their way and letting themselves be influenced by Americans and that's why I find it difficult to play with them" (quoted in McGregor 1995, 184). While this doubtless reads curiously alongside the fact of Dyani's own regular playing with members of the American avant-garde in Scandinavia, it also signals the continuing discussion of how South African music related to American improvisation. But in European minds as well Africa was inescapable for the musicians, a fixed locus in their displacement. This Africa was not only the South Africa of residual but forceful colonial racism and the anti-apartheid struggle (I recognize that I may be guilty of overemphasizing that circumstance in my own account), but also the old Africa figured on the primitivist physicality of the dancing body in rhythmic pleasure. Denis-Constant Martin has articulated this problematic in the Blue Notes' and the Brotherhood's reception: "Too often, European audiences have imprisoned them in their South Africaness. . . . [T]heir music was tremendously enjoyed in Great Britain and on the continent, but precisely because it was extremely enjoyable, it was not necessarily taken as seriously as it deserved" (Martin 1995, v).

The Arts Council of England working group on jazz in the 1990s found "a strong move among young black musicians to claim jazz as a part of the African cultural heritage deserving positive recognition from the cultural and commercial establishments of Britain" (ACE 1995, 17). Although blacks were relatively well represented in British jazz music, the ACE group expressed a difficulty for a black jazz audience: "lack of attendance at jazz concerts and limited purchases of jazz records by members of the black community were clear causes for concern. It was felt that young black people should be encouraged to see jazz not as a 'European thing' but as an African-American historical form, as relevant to black cultural history as soul, calypso, rap and reggae" (ACE 1995, 47–48).

As I have shown, to this Caribbean and American list should be added kwela and highlife — more accurately to reflect the multi nature of colonial and postcolonial jazz mixings in Britain. The identified irony that "the black community" is apparently uninterested in jazz when it is largely black musicians who have created some of the most exciting and original improvised music in Britain is, I think, questionable. It could equally be taken as a symptom of the richness of black musical culture more generally. More importantly for assessing the role of jazz, one of my aims in this chapter has been to chart ways in which jazz music has spoken to, has facilitated people to speak of, their social place and racial identity. At key international political moments concerning Britain — colonial independence, black immigration, the anti-apartheid struggle — jazz musicians have contributed to the cultural and political expression of racial celebration (black) and problematic (white) alike, and done so in a profoundly pleasureful nightly experience. I stress again that jazz particularly matters with regard to this social issue because of its history, its origins in the United States, and its perception by European audiences as culturally placed within a racial framework. "If it seems obvious," Trinh T. Minh-ha writes, "that the history of migration is one of instability, fluctuation and discontinuity, it seems also clear for many Third world members of the diaspora that their sense of group solidarity, of ethnic and national identity, has been nourished in the milieux of the immigrant, the refugee and the exiled. Here, identity is a product of articulation" (1994, 14). Here articulation has been a product of jazz. What has also become clear in this chapter is the extent to which the black innovations in jazz in Britain, thence Europe, from the late 1950s on were formed from a global music of jazz as an American export culture that mapped on to an alternative global circulatory network, the residue of British Empire in the international structure of the Commonwealth. Bill Schwarz has written of colonial London that "the metropolis functioned not only as the administrative centre for the ruling bloc, but at the same time generated the resources for the creation of a rich array of subaltern networks of the colonised" (Schwarz 1996, 178), and jazz has been an energetic soundtrack to and creator of some of those networks. Chris McGregor once described how the Brotherhood of Breath benefited from being organized from London, "a London that has become the cross-roads of the Caribbean, India and Jamaica" (quoted in McGregor 1995, 208). The Ghanaian percussionist Guy Warren and the Goanese guitarist Amancio D'Silva released in London in 1969 an improvised duet for talking drum and guitar entitled "Africa speaks, India answers." For Paul Gilroy, the busy capital junction has also been at once a point of critique of empire, of (post-)colonial national identity and color, *and* a site of energizing pleasure and engagement. "That critique is still *lived and enjoyed* as both counterculture and counterpower, formulated at the junction point, the crossroads of diaspora dwelling and diaspora estrangement" (quoted in Rice 2003, 116; my emphasis). Finally, the largely black innovations presented here—in particular the Caribbean and South African—were possible because of powerful cultural and musical traditions significantly outside the hegemonic framework of African American jazz (even, in Joe Harriott's case, to the extent of blanking America), and outside the largely imitative impulses of *white* British jazz.

FOUR

The Politics and Performance
of Improvisation and Contemporary
Jazz in the 1960s and 1970s

Together [performers and listeners] bring into existence, if only for the duration of the performance, an ideal society very different from that created by a classical performance; the performance negates the values of industrial society, disregarding the onward march of clock time, celebrating the body and its sensations, affirming . . . qualities of warmth, communality and emotional honesty. . . . [This] means only that the ideal is recognized, and that, for the duration of the performance at least, one can feel what it would be like were it a reality. —CHRISTOPHER SMALL (1984, 4)

These comments, made by Small in seemingly full utopian mode in a paper at a conference on improvisation in music at the Institute of Contemporary Arts, London, in March 1984, were swiftly rejoined in Alan Durant's paper at the same event. For Durant "improvisation cannot provide a general paradigm of human social existence," and furthermore "there are differences between participatory enjoyments and experience, and the experience which comes from listening, which is inevitably far less interactive" (Durant 1984, 8, 9). Yet I want to stay with the social issues of improvised music, focused more on the space opened up by Small because there have been important contributions, ideas, gestures, collectives, noises, and splits made by improvising and contemporary jazz musicians *in the social context of their music-making*.

The 1960s and 1970s saw a high period of innovation and confidence (if, as in general, not exactly strong economic support or success) that produced an extraordinary range of creative work in the fields of contemporary jazz and the new form of free improvisation. For the wider picture this chapter should not be read alone: developments in Caribbean and South African jazz in Britain (1960s), as well as the gendered critique of the privileged male zone of jazz by, for instance, the Feminist Improvising Group (1970s), are dealt with elsewhere in the book, but they also fit here. The relevance of these other developments is not only chronological but musical and social too. Pragmatically they are treated elsewhere to allot those musics the necessary space for detail. This was a time of extremes in cultural production, as well as a bewildering and inspiring variety of cultural activity and strategy. For example, the introduction of the seemingly austere solo work of a Derek

Bailey or the duo work of Eddie Prévost and Keith Rowe contrasts with Mike Westbrook's half-tamed Cosmic Circus (twenty-five performers) and Keith Tippett's sprawling Centipede (fifty musicians). The fetishized, semi-autonomous, enclosed small spaces of the *Little* Theatre Club or the Old Place (post–Ronnie Scott's) contrast with a poetry and jazz event attracting three thousand at the Royal Festival Hall in June 1961 and with the environmental explorations in the open air to accidental audiences of some Scratch Orchestra performances in the early 1970s. Across these extremes I identify a number of common strands, and so pay attention to the relation between improvisation and organization, and improvisation and education, for these seem to me significant aspects of the *social imperative* of contemporary jazz and improvised music, its practical politics if you like. I am also interested in ways and moments in which the energy, cheek, social idealism, and political activism of the liberationist counterculture were embraced or (occasionally) resisted.

It is already evident that in this chapter the recognizable practice of jazz music as such is being left behind, or widened out—part of the point of this book is to illustrate what jazz led to, and part is to note the continuing connections with, if qualifications of, jazz in some music experiments and innovations of the time. So in this chapter jazz is referenced alongside contemporary "classical" music, the European song and cabaret tradition, music theater and multimedia performances, the development of rock as a soundtrack of the counterculture, and to a small extent the attitudinal style of punk rock. Yet while in examining this period I interrogate the rhythmic, melodic, and harmonic conventions associated with jazz, as well as other conventions such as instrumentation and the interaction of instruments in performance—front line and rhythm section, for instance—there is one constant in the flux: the music remains characterized by an element of improvisation. I recognize that "improvisation" has a significant problematic inscribed within it. Durant, professor of English language and improvising double bassist, has considered this. "Improvisation" implies spontaneity, as in music and some other performance acts, including dance, drama, some comedy. At the same time it can be used to suggest incompletion, lack of preparation, perhaps shoddiness, carrying the "implication that the degree of preparation is insufficient": "an improvised shelter," "an improvised solution" (Durant 1984, 5). The experimental guitarist Derek Bailey, author of one of the key texts in the field, also notes the negative connotations, which critics, in his view, see as evidence that music made (composed) from improvisation can only be "a completely ad hoc activity, frivolous and inconsequential, lacking in design and method" (1992, xii). We will see how *ad-hockery* becomes a key cultural strategy within improvisational music performance.[1]

FROM THE TRANSATLANTIC LINER
TO THE CROSS-CHANNEL FERRY

Freely improvised music, variously called "total improvisation,"
"open improvisation," "free music," or perhaps most often simply,
"improvised music," suffers from—and enjoys—the confused identity
which its resistance to labelling indicates.—DEREK BAILEY,
Improvisation (1992, 83)

In some ways the new music and scenes that developed in Britain during the 1960s did construct and present the kind of "confused identity" proposed by one of their leading practitioners, Derek Bailey. Yet from another perspective the identity of the musics (in Britain and Europe) was becoming altogether more confidently expressed and explored. How far and in what ways did the new scenes and styles consciously realign themselves more within European music traditions than within African American jazz practice? I have shown already the extent to which the Jamaican innovator Joe Harriott talked of disregarding American music in both his groundbreaking "free form" music and the "Indo-Jazz Fusion" project of the 1960s. I have also detailed how the South African musicians who were clustered around Chris McGregor and Dudu Pukwana introduced another tradition into the matrix, exploring American jazz and developments in Europe within the music of kwela and mbaqanga. There are national questions which can help form a framework for understanding musical circulation and development—not, again I stress, to (binarily) fix the potentially energizing fluidity of music, nor to reintroduce an unproblematic national framework, but to facilitate the comprehension of its operation. The more interesting trajectories in British jazz typically showed a variety of strategies for turning away, for being, in the pianist and composer

Mike Westbrook's words, "very strong in one's convictions, to question the American orthodoxy and to work on developing an independent voice" (personal interview, 2003). Acknowledging a necessarily advanced stage of imitation which would enable his generation to do different, Eddie Prévost recalls that "in terms of jazz, people were so patronising about *British* jazz, even the idea of it—you weren't supposed to *play* such a thing. For instance, Tubby Hayes was one of my real heroes, a fantastic, an amazing British saxophonist at the time. But Tubby basically wanted to *be* an American jazz musician. What we were trying to do quite quickly with AMM could be a response to the difficulty of the American roots of the music: we were young men in London in the 1960s, not Harlem or Chicago, and we became more courageous with our music-making. I've often said that the music of Ornette Coleman and Albert Ayler gave us *permission to disobey*" (personal interview, 2002).

The sonic experiments being undertaken at this time in Britain (perhaps more accurately, in England) were variously happening across Europe too, such as in Germany and also in Holland. The revolutionary saxophonist Evan Parker has outlined the early national characteristics of some of these new music developments, in an exercise he freely describes as "a grotesquely over-simplified, hackneyed way of talking about the three schools, even if there is a grain of truth in each of those characterizations." For Parker, the German approach was of "music as an expression of a way of life. On-stage, off-stage, it's all one thing: an intensity of experience which has to be communicated." For Dutch musicians, it was "always about the strong idea, associated with the remarkable individual." The English was "based on a sort of group introspection. The rationale for doing anything is determined by a kind of consensus that the group itself generates" (quoted in Whitehead 1998, 46). These differing approaches quickly cross-pollinated, in Parker's view, but what is interesting is the absence of reference at a quite early stage in the free music of Europe to the previously dominant practice of American musicians.

A small example of the ambition "to get out of America's shadow," in the English critic John Fordham's phrase, is seen in the history of the Berlin Jazz Festival, Germany's largest jazz event during the 1960s. In 1964 the festival was opened by a prestigious African American guest, Martin Luther King; by 1968 German free improvisers, now grouped in

22. The Westbrook Trio on the cross-channel ferry. From left: Kate Westbrook, Chris Biscoe, Mike Westbrook.

a cooperative, were organizing a kind of counter-festival, the first Total Music Meeting, as a statement of European articulations ("Double Entrance Price for Critics" was a sign at the entrance of one venue: Fordham 1996, 112). Their actions signify a shift in relationship: not only was there no longer felt the need for a transatlantic imprimatur, but the transatlantic jazz music festival format was rejected and replaced by a meeting of enthusiasts and practitioners of the new music. In a further sign of German innovation, in the following year, 1969, the producer and erstwhile bassist Manfred Eicher established the record label ECM, with a distinctive aural and visual aesthetic, dedicated to presenting the new European, American, and other collaborative musics and musicians on an equal footing.[2] These developments and others are significant, signaling the rising confidence and ambition of European musicians—a fact that becomes clearer when compared with, say, the state of jazz in Japan at the same time. That appears to have been still in an imitative, even overawed mode, as E. Taylor Atkins explains, drawing a contrast with music ranging from Sonny Rollins to Sun Ra: "some of the best jazz ever produced in the United States was being made at precisely this time. . . . With so daring and impressive a body of work requiring digestion, in combination with the economic constraints . . . , it is understandable that Japanese felt there was little room or time left for comparably inventive projects" (Atkins 2001, 214–15).

A little more of this progression away from jazz in England is evident in the explanation of Gavin Bryars (then a bassist) of the musical development, from what was a jazz origin, of the early improvising trio named Joseph Holbrooke from the mid-1960s: "after a while it became *anti-jazz*, and after that there was a complete ignoring of possible jazz aspects in the playing" (quoted in Bailey 1992, 91; my emphasis). However, it becomes clear that a simple national framework is inadequate for this movement—it is important to acknowledge, for example, that jazz was also being rejected in the United States by some free improvising experimentalists at the time: "First," explained Larry Austin of the New Music Ensemble on the West Coast, "we consciously ruled out any overt jazz expression" (quoted in Dean 1992, 133). For Bryars too there was no rejection of America—just of African American jazz: the United States would remain his chosen space of music innovation, but it was from the John Cage catalogue rather than John Coltrane or Scott LaFaro that he now drew his inspiration. More generally, according to Roger Dean, "the radical developments in Europe which had little or no counterpart in the USA were in relation to instrumental timbre and texture, and the development of microtonal, multitimbral and multiphonic sounds and their usage in long time units (as with [Willem] Breuker, New Phonic Art, Vinko Globokar, and Evan Parker and Derek Bailey); and, in parallel, the development of electronic instruments and transformation of normal instrumental sound (AMM, [Tony] Oxley, Bailey, M[usica] E[lettronica] V[iva], Nuova Consonanza)" (Dean 1992, 135).

Of course there were pragmatic issues in the turn to Europe. Some of the impetus for building a network in London, with its own dedicated performance spaces, came from pivotal musicians like John Stevens, Trevor Watts, and Paul Rutherford. More importantly, it came from their experiences as musicians in the Royal Air Force when posted to Germany:[3] So Europe inspired by practicalities as much as the United States inspired by its jazz music. Hearing new recordings by Coltrane and Ornette in their entirety on German radio, attending and sitting in on performances by European and American musicians in a jazz club

23. Founder of Spontaneous Music Ensemble in the 1960s, musical director of Community Music in the 1980s, the drummer John Stevens in the studio recording SME's debut album *Challenge*, 1966. © Val Wilmer.

in Cologne, running their own club for a time, and seeing Coltrane, Miles, Mingus, and Dolphy there—these experiences had a massive influence on the ambition as well as the direction of these embryonic British improvising musicians. Also, they made European contacts that would stand them in good stead over the next few years as free music developed in Britain. Stevens recalls returning to Britain in 1963, experiencing a musically limited environment even for someone making a reputation for himself, as Stevens was beginning to do as a drummer: "Coming back to London, I found it strange . . . one of the first things I heard was a jazz programme on BBC radio, and they played a tiny section in the middle of a John Coltrane record. . . . It was as if he'd [the DJ] thought Coltrane had gone crazy. . . . [As for playing in London, e]ither I misunderstood jazz, or jazz wasn't being played in the right way. The feeling I got initially attracted to in jazz was its feeling of total freedom of self-expression . . . but some people as soloists just wanted a clear way—a time-keeping drummer—they didn't want to converse with the drums, or they didn't want the drums to interfere with their monologue" (quoted in Carr 1973, 43, 45).

Questions were beginning to be posed—even in the music that was still being made up and explored. Of the Spontaneous Music Ensemble's album *Karyobin* (1968), Evan Parker finds it significant that many of the instrumental "phrase shapes finished on an upward curve, *like a question rather than a statement*" (quoted in Whitehead 1998, 46; my emphasis). Trevor Watts, involved with Stevens at the Little Theatre Club and the SME from their beginnings in 1966, offers his own complex, critical reading of the chauvinistic trajectories of improvisation. Importantly, Watts also illustrates how such apparently abstract or global debates can shape the personal style and musical development of an individual musician:

> Sure, in the '60s we reacted against the jazz music scene here, and the fact that you were compelled to play jazz like an American or not at all. So the music of the SME came about from the fact that we didn't want to dote on American jazz, but [to] take the spirit of that music for ourselves, and move things along in the way *we* wanted. Quite a novel idea still in 1964! However by the '70s a lot of free and improvising musicians in Europe who began via those American jazz influences became rather anti-American jazz and [strongly] . . . pro-Dutch or -German, saying this is Dutch Music or German Music now. And [they] denied the fact that without that involvement in American jazz in the first place, they wouldn't be doing what they're doing . . . : without players like Albert Ayler and others, they wouldn't be doing what they were doing in the '70s. . . . That is when I started to lose interest in the free music scene. That and also all the rules that tacitly, and not so tacitly, became apparent for European improvising musicians. [These included a] rejection of anything to do with American jazz, or rhythm or melody. So being a rhythmic and melodic player, it wasn't on for me. (Personal correspondence, 2002)

Indigenizing jazz and its performative possibilities can take different forms. As a singer and performer exploring connections between American jazz and European music theater in her repertoire, Kate

Westbrook has found the language of much jazz song—English—inhibiting, particularly when performing in Europe:

> In order to communicate more directly I wanted to use the language of the audience if I possibly could. This interest has developed over the years since then, and now I perform in French, Italian, German. . . . I remember when a friend, at my request, translated the lyrics of Cole Porter's "Love for Sale" and I sang them in German— it somehow became tremendously political for the audiences. This was a song that had been banned in the US originally. When it was performed in the theatre there, a black woman, rather than the intended white woman, had to sing it. Us doing it in German in the late 1970s—well, there was a lot of soul-searching going on in the country still, to do with their own past, and that song really touched a nerve. We really like putting our inflection on an American standard like that. (Personal interview, 2003)

Here there is a straightforward but important attempt, from an English-language singer, to interrogate the Anglo-American imperative of much of the jazz songbook. Nor has Westbrook limited her repertoire to jazz standards; she has sought to explore the European cabaret song tradition also, with a musical approach which in a way— to reverse the pole above—imposes an American inflection (a jazz-inspired "irreverence") combined with an English "eccentricity" on a European popular tradition: "When we performed our first Brecht/ Weill in German in both East and West Germany, it was in true Westbrook style, which meant that we were irreverent not slaves to the original musical score. I think our German audiences found that pretty refreshing, our eccentric English take on this rather 'sacred' repertoire" (personal interview, 2003).

The importance of language in jazz-related song as a means of problematizing or overcoming Anglo-American linguistic hegemony is identified by Tony Haynes in his own long-standing music theater project, Grand Union Orchestra, formed in 1984. For Haynes, the cross-cultural aspects of music traditions and languages themselves, and the stories, carnivals, and rituals that form a people's culture, are woven together in Grand Union concerts and projects, to take jazz-inspired work to a more socially and culturally vibrant contemporary context:

Lyrics have always played a large part in my work. And increasingly the language of the lyrics is not English. There's only a limited amount you can do with singers in the English language—so, with us, Bangladeshi or Chilean experiences are sung about in their own languages. How do you communicate that to the (British) audience? There's a compromise for the purpose of communication, which is to use the other language *and English*. The difference between us [and other music theater approaches] is to do with time and with the *cross-cultural* nature of our work: Grand Union has twelve to fifteen years of working as a group of Caribbean and Asian and white players, and this gives us an entrée to *all* communities and audiences across the UK. This is an extraordinary social and cultural advantage. We've tried to develop our audience within the Turkish, Chinese, and Asian communities and—in the big cities at least—this has worked. By contrast, the jazz audience is small and, well, a bit miserable! (Personal interview, 2002)

FREE IMPROVISATION IN BRITAIN: AMM, SME, LMC, ETC....

The appeal of freedom in improvisational practices resonated with/in the emerging political climate of the 1960s as improvisers began to discard codified procedures, including those found in jazz improvisation, in favor of experimental practices. These practices were concerned not only with aesthetics but with political, economic, and social matters as well. Irène Schweitzer recounts that this politically charged time influenced her decision to stop playing "the changes" and leave improvisational structures and systems behind: "For me, it was a natural development. We had always played the music of the time. In 1968 a lot of things were happening in Europe. There were student revolutions. Barriers were falling. It seemed natural to want to free yourself."—JULIE DAWN SMITH (2004, 227)

I start with AMM because this ensemble was among the first and longest-lasting, because its members have produced an impressive range of autocritical texts alongside recordings and images, and because its early members set a template for an extraordinary fractured political discourse which resonates through this chapter. Here the figure of

Cornelius Cardew, the avant-garde composer with an interest in improvisation, the revolutionary Marxist, looms large. I also consider the Little Theatre Club and SME, John Stevens's vehicle for free improvisation or "spontaneous music," which had a rather different ideology of the relation between social and cultural. Both groups, AMM and SME, rose out of an experimental arena formed in London as a tangential part of the counterculture in the 1960s. The following decade saw a second wave of innovative improvisers and radical political and musical projects, and I trace some of those, in particular the ones surrounding the London Musicians' Collective (LMC).

Roger Dean notes that "AMM was and is a remarkable amalgam of social and musical endeavour. For these improvisers were explicitly bound up with social commitment and ideals" (1992, 138). AMM developed in 1965 from what the band percussionist Eddie Prévost has called "an unease with emulation" (1995, 9), the emulation of the African American jazz genres of bebop and big band: "adopting jazz as a cultural inspiration is by no means the same as taking one (or many) of the many forms it has developed, and using it as a rigid framework" (1995, 11). Where earlier musicians—and in fact many *contemporary* ones—were attracted to the improvisatory character of jazz and articulated that in terms of musical freedom, now groups of improvisers were characterizing jazz by its "rigidity" and lack of thought. Couldry traces the origins of free improvisation "in terms of an escape from what had come to be seen within jazz as certain constrictions of form and content" (1995, 5). But it was also "a hybrid of both jazz and classical traditions" (Couldry 1995, 7)—and, though this direct relation is generally overstated,[4] Couldry cites as examples of influence or active contribution Cage, Stockhausen and his one-time assistant Cardew (of the improvised projects AMM and the Scratch Orchestra), and Gavin Bryars, and to this male canon could be added women musicians such as Irène Schweitzer. Prévost historicizes the development of improvised music: "the social, educational and cultural democracy that emerged, however unevenly, from the post World War Two welfare state in Britain, was bearing this kind of fruit by the 1960s, encouraging the spirit of confidence needed to pursue a new and experimental aesthetics. In general however jazz (in Britain and elsewhere) has been content to remain the same and to perpetuate itself—all too often in an unthinking emulation of past styles" (Prévost 1995, 12).

The AMM aesthetic has since then been consciously multimedia: the visual design of records and publicity employing bold post-pop art imagery, and the textual explanations and provocations—liner notes, album titles, submanifestos—positioned skilfully between the haiku and the slogan ("Every noise has a note": Prévost 1995, 16). The music itself, quite heroically, comes from "the intuitive responses of strong-minded people," a small number of musicians having been involved over the four decades of the ensemble's existence (Prévost 1995, 25). AMMmusicians (as they termed themselves) have a pivotal role to play when "music is dead and the meta-musician is needed" (1995, 34). AMMmusic's roots in the mid-1960s are clearly within the experimental side of a thriving counterculture, and Prévost recalls the noncommercial, nonpromotional ethos of the times which the group embraced: "During the early days people only found out about 'sessions' by word of mouth or accident. There was no admission charge" (1995, 28). Barry Miles remembers the band playing with the Pink Floyd Sound (as it was then named) at Sunday afternoon happenings sometimes called Spontaneous Underground at the Marquee in London, where, "to reinforce the sense of serious scientific investigation they played in white lab-coats." It was not a good venue for this music, Miles thought, because "the audience was too stoned and out of it" (2002, 102)—but even so, at AMM concerts in London the likes of Paul McCartney and Syd Barrett would be in attendance, listening for ideas from the new European avant-garde that they could import into rock and pop. Prévost elaborated for me: "It was the sixties after all! Audiences couldn't believe we were being serious—they would be angry or dismissive or offended. If you had to deal with that playing context, and also with your own doubts about the music you were involved in, because making the music was very much a kind of process of exploration, then you had to be strong, convinced, mentally. AMM's use in performances of both silence and darkness did give us an austere aesthetic which was part of the experimentation of the times even if it appears so different" (personal interview, 2002).

Within a few years, the orientalist fascination of AMM developed, as what might be termed a shift from Taoism to Maoism was effected by Cardew and the guitarist Keith Rowe. This ensemble—like the Scratch Orchestra, as we will see, another important improvised music-making experiment involving Cardew—was effectively split by leftist politics. Prévost and Lou Gare maintained their interest in exploring what Prévost remembers the others calling their "useless bourgeois self-indulgence" (1995, 21) of internal soundscapes, while Cardew and Rowe attempted to edit out the reactionary elements of the music with a focus instead on the outside, the social. There were elements and echoes of an earlier Marxist argument about modernist aesthetics, the relation between the avant-garde and the people, the "inner turn" of modernism versus social realism. And it *was versus*: the situation culminated in a tour of Holland in 1973, on which AMM, booked as an experimental British quartet, performed as two duos. The political shift had an effect on practical music-making and sound exploration: for example, in performances Rowe now used taped recordings of Radio Peking rather than the more random samples of live broadcast radio used previously, which had supplied witty, unsettling, unpredictable counterpoints. While such a performative approach as splitting in two may sound like the limit case for the dialogic of dialectic, in practice performances also included debates between the musicians and audiences about the new and old political and cultural terrains that they were exploring or hoping to hear. "Concerts are moments of communal realisation" (1995, 33), and Prévost elaborated to me that for him, "the way you do things is important — if the civil society can't be seen in the very music you make then the music is bogus. All of this is important with AMM of course, because of the early period when Cornelius Cardew was involved, and his heavy espousing of Marxism. Cardew's idea of projecting to the workers, and from his extraordinarily privileged social position — it felt very uncomfortable at the time, and with hindsight seems so wrong" (personal interview, 2002).[5]

As a result, this version of AMM "collapsed" (Prévost 1995, 24). Among other subsequent projects, Cardew and Rowe essayed the production of music which they considered more closely in tune with the working class, as part of an effort at "leaving the avant garde clique and integrating more with musicians working in the music 'industry' proper" (Cardew 1974, 9).

There is a politics of scale in the music produced through improvisation. Here we see musicians addressing the "failure" of their music as a low-key, minor scene. The celebration of a minority culture can be interpreted as a fear of the masses, or as a call to élitism (Cardew's "avant garde clique"), but for Prévost a quietist intensity is appealing:

24. Cornelius Cardew (voice, electric piano) playing with People's Liberation Music in a protest against "British imperialism" in Ireland at an anti-internment demonstration, Lincoln Inn Fields, London, 1977. From left: Keith Rowe (guitar), John Marcangelo (drums), Hugh Shrapnel (voice, oboe), Cardew, Laurie Baker (voice, bass guitar).

"In the face of the thundering energy and giantist perspective of The Who or some Wagnerian extravaganza," he asks, "can anyone turn away to find meaning and artistic fulfilment in the sounds of a squeaking door?" (1995, 47). Loudness, scale of project ("Improvised music is a small music": 1995, 136), form of music, and size of audience are all problematized, and expected criticisms are rejected in a wilful gesture of minoritarianism from Prévost's reconfigured AMM. Derek Bailey articulates the negative perceptions of musical smallness: "to play in a manner which excludes the larger audience or, worse, *to prefer* to play before a small audience, is taken as an indication that the music is pretentious, elitist, 'uncommunicative,' self-absorbed and probably many other disgusting things too" (1992, 47). Andrew Blake's notion of the "aestheticised poverty" (1997, 115) of improvisation may be useful for understanding the white free music of AMM, SME, and similar groups at this time. Bailey observes that "external matters — aesthetics, musical fashion, even economics — are to a unique degree irrelevant to the practice of this kind of music making" (Bailey 1992, 141).[6] This would be a line taken by Steve Beresford too—in 1979, perhaps still optimistic about the politico-cultural possibilities of the London Musicians' Collective, then recently established, he had proclaimed, "The more you shore up their conditioning, the more gigs you get" (quoted in Wickes 1999, 315)—the implication being that lack of playing opportunities confirmed a musician's sociocritical status and validity. Two decades later, despite the LMC's continued existence, he was altogether more critical of the absence of recognition and support from the cultural arbiters and funders: "I have this sort of semi-jokey answer to people who ask why there's such a scene here: *it's because there's no money in it.* We don't get the grants, we get sidelined by fucking everyone in the arts establishment, the media—but we've been a continual presence for more than a quarter of a century" (personal interview, 2002).[7]

At Jean Pritchard's Little Theatre Club, the almost wilfully anticommercial music was also a response to the commodification of Swinging London. Here, just off Trafalgar Square, at first for up to six nights a week, the British free jazz movement developed and flourished. The drummer John Stevens became the organizational hub of the club, which opened on 3 January 1966 and ran until 1972. In his book *Music Outside: Contemporary Jazz in Britain*, Ian Carr states that the club "laid the foundations for what was to become a vital British jazz scene" (Carr 1973, 19)—and its temporary parallel venue (offered though not run by Ronnie Scott when his club moved to new premises), simply known as the Old Place, "changed the whole climate of the British scene" in the mid- to late 1960s. All the leading musicians in Britain who were interested in exploring improvisation during these years would play, listen, rehearse, talk, and argue at these and other more temporary venues. For Stevens himself, moving from the mock-heroic to the harsh reality, a "thing like The Little Theatre Club succeeds when the musicians stick together and carry on. It wasn't initially a political movement, but it became that—it was anti the establishment which was, of course, the Ronnie Scott Club. . . . On average when I play there I guess I would get 50p for it which doesn't really cover the fare" (quoted in Carr 1973, 47, 53).

Musically, Evan Parker remembers, "at least a year before Stockhausen wrote the so-called intuitive pieces which are just instructions about emptying your mind and not making any sounds until you hear the sounds that should be made, all those activities were things that the

Little Theatre Club group of musicians were already doing" (quoted in Carr 1973, 81). Socially, the approaches being developed by Stevens at workshops and at the Little Theatre Club would be articulated most clearly, early on, in the liner notes for the SME album *Karyobin*, in which Stevens explains his challenge to value in improvised music, to the long-standing focus on the soloist taken from jazz: "The thing that matters most in group music is the relationship between those taking part. The closer the relationship, the greater the spiritual warmth it generates. And if the musicians manage to give wholly to each other and to the situation they're in, then the sound of the music takes care of itself. Good and bad become simply a question of how much the musicians are giving" (quoted in Wickes 1999, 57).

In Joachim Berendt's view, this kind of collective approach was an identifiably European one. Writing of the experimental movement in 1973, he observed that "American jazz has until today remained—primarily—a soloistic jazz, a jazz of 'stars' and the individual; European jazz is—again primarily—a collective jazz in which the individual merges within the group" (Berendt 1976, 404). Ian Carr has gone so far as to claim that "Stevens has been carrying on a kind of guerrilla warfare against conventional musical thinking and, although he would not put it so forcefully himself, there is a degree of revolutionary fervour in his approach to musical experiment or 'finding new ways of saying things'" (Carr 1973, 49). Experimentation and musical change was for Stevens "the only constant," and the political motivation for this was relatively straightforward: "if people become more familiar with change, then automatically they become more tolerant as people" (quoted in Carr 1973, 54). Within free improvisation more widely, the correspondence between music and personal politics was not always so apparently congruous; Julie Dawn Smith has examined the limitations of its assumptions of freedom. For Smith, much of the music was "exercised within a predominately white, male improvising community existing on the margins of avant-garde and mainstream music—the move towards aesthetic freedom was a critique of class structures and power networks embedded in European music and society. . . . Neither free improvisation nor free jazz however, extended their critiques to include the aesthetic, economic or political liberation of women. For the most part, a practice of freedom that resisted gender oppression and oppression on the basis of sexual difference was excluded from the liberatory impulses of male-dominated improvising communities" (Smith 2004, 228–29).

Toward the end of his own book, Carr is also rather more critical of a certain, usually masculinist, construction of jazz persona: "if one was ignored, then that was proof of one's quality. . . . There is a long tradition of jazz musicians whose talents, however remarkable, can be bought cheaply—it is even a point of honour among many of them to be naïve and incompetent in business affairs, as if this proved the worth of their creative inspiration" (Carr 1973, 128). I will return to questions of gender within the politics of improvisation in my final chapter.

Later, flaunted naïvetés and incompetencies would not be so attractive for the founding generation of free improvisers around AMM and SME. In the mid-1970s the "second-generation" musicians arrived with an attitude that often was altogether more disdainful toward some of the musical assumptions and battles of their elders. Their contumacy turned reflexive, striking against the very music they were involved in making, and an identifiable schism opened between the first generation from the 1960s, which focused on technique and aesthetic purism— for some, like Bailey, asceticism—and the second generation from the 1970s (see Couldry 1995; Bell 1999). As a series of generalizations, the new school, which was active in the foundation of the London Musicians' Collective in 1976, was more comfortable playing a range of instruments (some lost and found), was characterized by a degree of openness to women musicians, eschewed virtuosity as an aim or even an option, and sought more fully to incorporate performative aspects, even humor—John Wickes makes the good point that "improvisation is one of the few serious . . . forms of music capable of not taking itself too seriously" (1999, 306). Steve Beresford articulated a fairly common position within the LMC, in part a reaction against what a number of newer musicians perceived as the first generation's overemphasis on instrumental technique, baldly stating, "I'm not that interested in technique" (quoted in Wickes 1999, 312).[8] For Beresford the LMC had a formative period, which contained "an intense period of discussion about politics, about technique in the music, about our relation with and difference from the so-called 'first generation.' And that was when we were doing all those things like Music for Socialism gigs—they were hilarious, Evan Parker, Sham 69, the inevitable Henry Cow, all on the same bill—when FIG were bringing the politics and music together too

25. Poster for an SME "evening of group improvisation," London, 1969.

from their position in the Women's Movement" (personal interview, 2002). Things were not always hilarious for such anti-virtuosic players as Beresford, with his toy pianos, in a field that had largely been opened up by virtuosi in the previous decade: "The story of how . . . [Beresford] was ostracised by some performers at Company Week in 1977 (Derek Bailey's annual gathering of improvisers of different persuasions) because his approach to his instrument(s)and his technique was insufficiently serious may be more rumour than fact, but it indicates at least that very real differences of approach existed among improvisers at this time," writes Couldry (1995, 11).

In many ways the narrative provided so far of the development of experimental jazz-influenced music in Britain in the 1960s and 1970s is an unsurprising one: small groups of musicians and enthusiasts intently exploring sounds in little urban venues, in the face of indifference or scorn from the cultural establishments. Such underground or backroom scenes were much the same for earlier styles of jazz, from the downstairs clubs of all-night raves during the trad boom to bebop enclaves. These are the preferred spaces of jazz, a chamber music of the cellar. But Nick Couldry identifies one of the serious weaknesses of improvisation in Britain, which continues to be its performative environment: "Most performances . . . now take place by economic necessity in drab back rooms of pubs or the like" (1995, 20). As we have seen, this generalization should be extended to qualify its presentism: the *legendary* early spaces of improvisation in Britain, such as the Little Theatre Club and the Old Place, were pretty bare and functional; the London Musicians' Collective building by the railway line in Camden famously had no toilets — "it added to our beatnik loft-dwelling cred," Clive Bell wrote sardonically (1999). There were free moments, though, that signaled a significant awareness of environment, even if that awareness was combined with the pragmatism of widening the audience, and that was particularly true of events at the LMC. Bow Gamelan Ensemble was launched there in 1983, remembered by Clive Bell as "a spectacular and downright life-threatening event." The ensemble's début was the culmination of an Evening of Self-Made Instruments organized by Sylvia Hallett, and "the place was packed for this riot of pyrotechnics and barely controlled arc-welding equipment abuse" (Bell 1999). In Couldry's view the "Bow Gamelan Ensemble have had considerable success in attracting a wider audience to their experiments. This is perhaps because they have grasped better than anyone else in

British improvising since the Scratch Orchestra and the early outdoor performances of AMM, the scope for putting improvised music into a wider physical context. . . . The Scratch Orchestra frequently played in direct contact with the uninvolved public—for instance, along the cliffs at Beachy Head or in the forecourt of Kings Cross [railway] station" (Couldry 1995, 20).

Events and approaches such as this were forming a tradition at the LMC, and carnivalesque opportunities for performance became an important part of the collective's achievement. One high point in its extraordinarily energetic early history was the nine-day Festival of Environmental Music and Performance organized by David Toop in 1978: "Warming up with a talk from Trevor Wishart and an instrument building workshop, [a number of musicians] flung themselves into a continuous 24 hour concert called *Circadian Rhythms*. Visiting performers . . . alternated with seminars ('Music/Eventstructure/context'). . . . Whirled Music played on nearby Primrose Hill, and guerrilla activities by Lol Coxhill and Michael Parsons could be encountered along the towpath of the Regents Canal" (Bell 1999).

The very fact that the popular music world was developing so enormously and rapidly during the 1960s and early 1970s significantly affected improvising musicians. Some of the established musicians in London were sensing further opportunities for innovation. For instance, Mike Westbrook formed the jazz-rock band Solid Gold Cadillac to escape jazz purity and respond to audiences' modulating expectations of performance. With more an eye than an ear on the glam rock embodied by Marc Bolan and David Bowie in the 1970s, exploring pop by wearing costumes and makeup on stage was too much for some of Westbrook's previous collaborators in jazz (Carr 1973, 35). Other jazzers' resistance to playing a bridge between pop and jazz was rooted less in a reluctance to work in cross-media or cross-cultural contexts than in a distrust of the *commercial* imperatives of the pop music world.[9] In spite of a rhetoric stressing freedom of expression in the music, or indeed the ambiguous position of jazz itself within any high-low culture frame, many performers and enthusiasts of contemporary jazz and improvised musics, like those in earlier, related forms, swiftly constructed and vigorously defended hierarchies of cultural value. On the other hand, someone like Beresford, as an admirably curious music student at York University from 1968 to 1971, was immersed in popular, classical, *and* improvised music, and heard distinctions as well as surprising similarities that would inform his own subsequent career:

> For some reason I then started wanting to listen to the weirdest music I could find, which meant Cage, Ornette. At university I came into contact with the hippie thing more, and *tried* to listen to the Grateful Dead, Bob Dylan, all that. I tried to like them, but I couldn't do it. I liked *singles*, you see, that pure pop rush of mostly black music — soul. I mostly played with people from *outside* the Music Department, I was pretty unhappy in there. We started putting on improvised music gigs in York — Evan Parker and Paul Lytton, Derek Bailey and Han Bennink, those were two of the *life-changing* gigs for me at that time. It sounds grand or pompous but it's true. There were two others, really important nights for me musically, in York. First was seeing AMM at the arts centre, when Cornelius Cardew was in it. Second was Bob Marley and the Wailers, the originals, with Peter Tosh and Bunny, on their first tour of Britain, 1972. Actually there were musical similarities between those two gigs for me: the Wailers were playing really slowly at the time, they had a fantastic simmering energy, and AMM had this slowness too, this deliberation without loss of spontaneity. So in my post-student musical life there was so much going on, and we were conscious of that at the time, were trying everything — reggae, soul, slowed down Terry Riley, et cetera. (personal interview, 2002)

As well as a transatlantic pop openness to new sounds such as Beresford's, there were a significant number of performance groupings from the counterculture and its legacy in the 1970s that worked with or from jazz. These are important in part because they provide evidence of the social criticism role of culture working over decades. Jeff Nuttall's career exemplified this tendency, beginning with his experiences as a New Orleans jazz trumpeter on the Aldermaston CND marches in the 1950s; his later work with alternative theater in the People Show (see Nuttall 1979) from 1966 involved collaboration with the People Band, which itself was a significant free music and social experiment: "This was the heyday of Happenings, mixed media events that thrived on simultaneity of disparate events, unexpected juxtapositions and levelling of aesthetic and social hierarchies. The People Show/People Band alliance at the Arts Lab, and at hip clubs like Middle Earth and UFO in

Central London, the Edinburgh Festival Fringe . . . fed into this creative surge" (Cowley 2002, 44).

The year 1975 saw the formation of Tony Haynes's Red Brass, originating from the fringe theater and agitprop troupe Belts 'n' Braces. Red Brass was a jazz-rock band with a clear leftist agenda, which sought through extensive touring to avoid state subsidies and construct or tap into an alternative network nationwide of audiences and organizations. A grant from the Arts Council to tour Scotland in 1978 has been interpreted by John Wickes as "final recognition that Red Brass had not succeeded in realising Haynes's ideals" (1999, 300), though this is a harsh judgment. Rather, Red Brass was an early effort in what for Haynes has been a long-term project to maintain a social profile for jazz and related forms, evidenced in his more ambitious and still-thriving music-theater project the Grand Union Orchestra, formed in 1984. The People's Show and Band combined elements of jazz and alternative theater in the 1960s and early 1970s, building on jazz and politics links from the 1950s; Red Brass and Grand Union brought jazz music-theater together with community arts and activism and multiculturalism across the decades from the 1970s to the present.[10]

"TUNE A BROOK BY MOVING THE STONES IN IT":
PERFORMANCE AND ENVIRONMENT BY
WELFARE STATE, THE SCRATCH ORCHESTRA,
CANTERBURY . . . AND MARXIST MUSICS

The new cross-cultural and multimedia collaborations of the counterculture created opportunities as well as problems. I want to look at a small number of collaborative organizations or moments to assess the significance of the contribution made by jazz and related improvisatory musics, and I want to do this from the perspective of both jazz musicians and other performance artists. Mike Westbrook was an early musical collaborator with John Fox and his countercultural theater company Welfare State, founded in 1968. According to Wickes, this turn took Westbrook "away from jazz clubs, concert halls and theatres, and into the thick of community activities. Committed to the then-burgeoning fringe theatre movement's radical aim to take culture out of the palaces of art to 'the people,' John Fox's Welfare State/Cosmic Circus lived a nomadic existence, travelling in convoy from place to place, staging theatrical spectacles in shopping centres, community centres, factories, church halls and homes for the elderly" (Wickes 1999, 113). For Fox, street music was an essential constituent of open public performance, and there was a jazz element to his enthusiasm. For instance, he told me laughingly, "as a young man I wanted to *be* George Lewis" (personal interview, 2004). *Earthrise* was an important and ambitious early collaboration between Fox and Westbrook, originating in Bernard Miles's offer and commission of the Mermaid Theatre in London as a jazz venue in 1969, and with repeat performances around the country over the next two years (Coult and Kershaw 1999, 236–38). A narrative of space exploration and lunar landing, with jokey sections, it featured the big band of twenty-five musicians, moving and still projections, a light show, and plans for dancing, acting, and fancy dress. While Westbrook can note sardonically, that within the jazz community at least, "from then on, my reputation plummeted even though I was really getting into something" (quoted in Carr 1973, 33), his collaborative multimedia work with Fox in Cosmic Circus continued until the summer of 1972. In June, Westbrook wrote the music for *Lot Song* with Welfare State, which presented urban decay as a prelude to nuclear holocaust, while in July the final Cosmic Circus show happened at the Tower of London, featuring "ravens, high-diver, tightrope, carnival processions and beggars and Jeff Nuttall as the syphilitic king" (Coult and Kershaw 1999, 239).

Lol Coxhill succeeded Westbrook as Welfare State's musical director in 1973, staying around eighteen months, but it is fair to say that jazz improvisation, as the source of a core music in Welfare State's practice, has attenuated in the decades since then. This shift from jazz may be a symptom of the ambivalent space of Welfare State, which both originated in 1968 in the avant-garde public happenings "pushing back musical, visual and theatrical barriers that were previously rigid and orderly" and at the same time tried "to uphold a tradition of popular entertainment against much of the mind-blown, elitist experimentation of the time" (Coult 1999, 6). Also, the emphasis on change within ritual and repetition that is characteristic of Welfare State events occurs in music too. As Tony Coult explains: "Individual arts are continually changed and transformed. In music, for instance, you can catch the flavour of a jazzband or folkband, which have a Fifties resonance, while drawing on popular music from the start of the century or earlier. It isn't long before these are transformed — by a South American bayonne rhythm, by Celtic pipes, ska or South African Hi-Life textures, by reggae or by synthesiser. The new sounds do not replace the old ones, but colour them, and move them on into new hybrid styles" (1999, 12–13).

Welfare State offers advice on the choice of instruments for street music: trumpets or cornets are "very useful outdoors for their cutting tone, but require experienced players. . . . In the rain, wet lips can be a problem"; bagpipes on the other hand "create an enormous full sound [and] immediate audience response" (Mishalle, Howarth, and Moser 1999, 45, 47). The company also addresses the problematic of music's secondary nature in street or community performance (secondary to the performance, for example, or to the political context of the production): "The company works on two levels at once, for it has a full-time professional commitment to the excellence of its product musically, and a full-time multiplicity of roles creating popular accessibility and possible amateur models. Within this dichotomy could be the seeds of destruction, were there not a constant re-assessment of standards" (Mishalle, Howarth, and Moser 1999, 57). The utopian blend of professional and amateur music making claimed here, as well as the perhaps more tense relation between avant-garde and traditional origins referred to above, illustrates how Welfare State over its existence has identified limitations in the use of a specialized improvisatory form like jazz. According to John Fox, Welfare State now uses "music that works in the street, and is not military, but has a certain kind of funky openness. . . . It's got space within it. It's not imperialist. It allows space for the beat and it allows space for the audience. It's also theatre music, and not thought of separately from the image. . . . As 'music' music, it has its limitations, but again, you see, it's about breaking categories" (Fox 1999, 28).[11]

It was perhaps predictable that the maverick individualist Coxhill should not have fitted for too long in Welfare State's established performative community of caravans and tents in a quarry outside Burnley, Lancashire, but he explains the reasons for withdrawing from the central role as musical director with Welfare State: "we reached the point where they said what I was writing was too difficult, and I didn't think it was" (quoted in Wickes 1999, 262). Contesting priorities.

26. Welfare State lays bare the military origins of the brass band with a blood-stained colonial band, including blackface and whiteface, Burnley, Lancashire, 1976.

After his sabbatical with Welfare State, Westbrook went on to establish the Brass Band, which touched on some of the same territory, though without the ritual aspects of Welfare State: performance, community, and street-based events. One early gig was as a warm-up to a hippie, anarchist rock band led by Edgar Broughton at a rock festival. Continuing his focus on aspects of community theater and the carnivalesque, and away from pure music, Westbrook explained to me what he terms "the Brass Band's musical and political stance," as well as a strategy for escaping the "restrictions" in British jazz of the early 1970s by seeking refuge in alternative theater:

> Writing and playing music for the Welfare State, among others, required a new approach. This led to the formation of the Brass Band in '73. The idea was to be able to play anywhere. So the music was acoustic, mobile, and open to all kinds of situations. We played in the streets, shopping centres, schools, hospitals, factory canteens—

anywhere that anyone asked us. To find suitable material, I drew on New Orleans, folk songs, early music, anything at all that would work with that line-up, or was suggested by a member of the band. Songs and improvisation were included. It was the most natural kind of music making, but in that rock-dominated scene, quite provocative. It was anti-elitist, democratic, populist, yet High Art— for all of us, I think, a fusion of our musical and political philosophies. We played in Community Arts events (at that time there was some Arts Council support for Community Arts), Tribune rallies, demos, benefits, and the Communist Party's Moving Left Revues at the Roundhouse. (Personal interview, 2003)

In part as a further small challenge to the orthodox reading of traditional and revivalist jazz of the 1950s as unimaginative and conservative, it should be remembered that the social action and theoretical notion of performing improvised music to uninvolved audiences in outdoor spaces was what Ken Colyer's Omega Brass Band had done with startling success a decade and more before such apparent *innovations* as the Westbrook Brass Band, formed out of the experience of working with Welfare State, or indeed the Scratch Orchestra's environmental performances. The latter group is of particular interest because of the political debates that arose from within it, and because the orchestra chose to perform, to dramatize the political positions articulated through the debates, in a subsequent piece of music. Apart from his early, temporary membership in AMM, the Scratch Orchestra was the other significant musical project of Cornelius Cardew that explored improvisation (Jeff Nuttall calls him "Corny Cardew," a neat counterpoint: 1968, 204). According to Georgina Born, of Henry Cow and the Feminist Improvising Group, "Scratch Orchestra, and AMM, emphasised changes in the social relations of music production and performance in their attempts at a new interactive, collective, and non-hierarchical group practice. The social dimension of music was seen as a crucible for experiments in collective and democratic social relations" (quoted in Hanlon and Waite 1998, 88 n. 45).

The Scratch project was devised by Cardew from his Experimental Music Class run at Morley College, London, from 1968 (see Eley 1974). For an experimental ensemble, especially with a name suggesting a permanent state of initialization (as in a "scratch" or pickup band), it was quite formalized from its beginnings: a draft constitution delineated the structure, presentation, and order of activities (Cardew ed. 1972, 10–11), and there remains an ambiguity as to whether the project was subverting or maintaining the authority of the traditional orchestra and composer. Born may overstate the nonhierarchical nature of the project: Cardew himself acknowledged, if with irony, "the domination" of his "subtly autocratic, supposedly anti-authoritarian leadership" (1972, 12). But in its "improvisation rites," its inspiring list of "1001 activities, by members of the Scratch Orchestra," as well as in some of its key personnel, there are direct links with the exploratory aspects of the improvisation movement of the time. Alongside graphic scores and doodled notation, there are pieces written by orchestra members concerned with location and environment, which consist entirely of resonant or gnomic instructions like "Tune a brook by moving the stones in it. . . . If inside play the sounds from outside, if outside play the sounds from inside" (Cardew ed. 1972, page X, page S). Early performances, from late 1969 to the summer of 1970, included two political events, a benefit concert for the Chicago 8 and a CND rally (Eley 1974, 17).

In 1971 the orchestra effected an ideological split within itself, "between the 'Communists' and 'bourgeois idealists'" (Eley 1974, 29). A not dissimilar split was shortly to happen in AMM, as we have seen. Cardew, John Tilbury, Keith Rowe, and others formed the Maoist Scratch Ideology Group, while other "Scratchers," designated anarchists, hippies, and so on, belonged to an existing subgroup of the ensemble called the Slippery Merchants. Inscribed within these ideological debates and fractures were performative ones: the Slippery Merchants were more interested in the provocative potential of happenings, a continuation of the counterculture; the Ideology Group was more interested in exploring non-Cagean aesthetics and practices of improvisation and radical musics. The Slippery Merchants inspired the more interesting environmental performances. For example, May 1971 saw several events devised by Birgit Burckhardt: "Scratch Below" involved random appearances across the London Underground network, while an attempt to "merge with Highgate Cemetery," paying homage at the grave of Karl Marx, was at the very least an effort to combine the performative and ideological imperatives of the orchestra (Eley 1974, 25). In January 1972 the Scratch Orchestra's self-reflexivity peaked with a performance in Liverpool of comic-opera extracts from Greg Bright's

Sweet F.A., "which depicted the struggle and triumph of a group of revolutionaries over a crowd of hippy students" (Eley 1974, 30)—that the Ideology Group was in ascendancy was evident from that performance, and evident as well in Rod Eley's written history of the orchestra, for that matter. Like a good Marxist, Eley understands the importance of History, and he concludes his "History of the Scratch Orchestra" as follows: "With the lessons of our past development in mind the Scratch Orchestra can begin to lay plans, and progress towards the future with hope. It must develop solidarity with the revolutionary class—the working class—in the only way possible, by joining them. That would be a noble contribution to the struggle, and the final march to victory over the decaying fascist system of monopoly capitalism" (Eley 1974, 31).

As noted previously, performers of contemporary jazz and improvised music also sought to extend the environment of performance by playing in collaboration with rock and pop musicians. There had been a long-standing connection between the two communities dating to the early skiffle of the 1950s and all manner of blues-oriented rock projects from the 1960s that worked out of a jazz milieu in some way—Jack Bruce, Dick Heckstall-Smith, and Ginger Baker all thought of themselves as jazz musicians who moved into blues and rock, while the white South African pianist Manfred Mann was one jazzer who had great success in the pop world. Not all were happy with this: the critic Steve Race railed against the multiplying liaisons between the jazz and pop worlds in *Jazz Journal* in 1968, concluding on behalf of the jazz community that it was "morally better off when jazz was a tight little world completely ignored and treated with contempt by those outside it" (quoted in Wickes 1999, 196). But for the more flexible and curious jazz musicians there were possibilities in the new sounds, audiences, and markets of rock and pop, while the newer, "progressive" rock musicians could enhance their Romantic seriousness and validate their instrumental technique (this was before punk, after all) by working with improvisers (see Nicholson 1998, ch. 2). What Andrew Blake calls "the whole genre of quietly pretentious and occasionally politically radical music known as Canterbury Rock" (1997, 152)—more a stylistically than a geographically accurate label, it should be said—is pivotal. From the late 1960s Soft Machine, King Crimson, Henry Cow, and various permutations of them were rock bands that improvised, worked with jazz musicians, and explored jazz sensibilities. After a number of years quite successfully developing a less than whimsical but still quirky "prog-rock" sound and image, Henry Cow seemed suddenly to turn radical in the mid-1970s. Perhaps this was a reflection of the band's wider European profile: its newer lineup included the German singer Dagmar Krause, and it toured European countries. The band featured over its ten-year existence musicians like the guitarist Fred Frith, who would go on to work in New York, and Lindsay Cooper and Georgie Born, who would soon be founding members of the Feminist Improvising Group. Henry Cow *had* had an interest in the politics of the music before then — the band had appeared at some of the most significant gatherings of the radical counterculture, including the legendary free Glastonbury Fayre of 1971 and the People's Free Festival at Watchfield, Berkshire, in 1975, and it had played benefit gigs for the People's Free in 1976 (see McKay 1996, McKay 2000a).[12] But involvement in the largely middle-class counterculture's efforts to construct a longer-term alternative society did not quite map on to a revolutionary workerist rhetoric and ideology. Yet the band supported from its inception the campaign group Music for Socialism, which organized consciousness-raising performances featuring a range of popular musics, and went on to front a project called Rock in Opposition with various European experimental rock bands that culminated in a collective festival in London in March 1978, the year of the band's final recordings. Fred Frith used a fairly standard Brechtian analysis to explain the band's new consciousness and practice: "We don't make political statements in a passive way. . . . It's the theoretical and it's also doing what most so called revolutionary artists aren't doing, which is expanding the form we're working in, which I think is the most important and most people get bogged down in that area. They have to make their music accessible as part of the revolutionary struggle to stop being interesting and experimental and play things everybody can understand, which is extreme boredom" (quoted in Wickes 1999, 175).

Audiences that consisted not solely of Cow fans struggled with this political aesthetic: at a concert by Music for Socialism in Leeds, Dave Laing, one of the campaign organizers, remembers a post-performance discussion with the audience, which revolved around the perception that the music of Henry Cow was élitist and indulgent and therefore politically limited (personal interview, 2002). The precisely opposite line from a radical politics of aesthetic experimentation would be endorsed by Robert Wyatt in 1985, when he was an active member of the Communist Party. For Wyatt it became essential that any ambiguity be erased, producing what he called "un-misusable music . . . that couldn't be appropriated by the Right": "I was fiddling around on the short wave radio when I heard one of my old songs being played on one of those Western propaganda programmes—the Voice of America or Radio Free Europe. Blow me, I thought, I don't want my music used in this way. So I consciously set out to make records where the ambiguity was removed, records that would have to be rejected by anyone promoting Western culture. Now I make sure I always put a spanner in the works" (quoted in King 1994, no pagination).

In the 1960s Wyatt had been the drummer—"a combination of Ringo Starr and Elvin Jones" was how Mike Zwerin put it in *Downbeat* in 1967 (quoted in King 1994, no pagination)—with the seminal English progressive rock band Soft Machine, whose music crossed over into early explorations of jazz and free music. A couple of years after a life-changing injury left him in a wheelchair in June 1973, Wyatt, like the members of Henry Cow, emerged to some surprise as a revolutionary Marxist, and would go on to release numerous political songs on the punk record label Rough Trade, covering a wide range from antiwar to anti-apartheid. It is possible that the impetus of a later and different music form—punk rock—influenced Wyatt's politicization, though there were other novel factors impacting on his life view, most strikingly his paraplegic state.[13] He finally joined the Communist Party of Great Britain in 1979, though the death of Wyatt's friend and sometime musical collaborator, the South African exile trumpeter Mongezi Feza, in 1975 had seemed to crystallize his understanding of power relations in terms of race, culture, and empire, as well as make him realize the political potential—responsibility, even—of his role as a musician: "Mongezi's death had a very dramatic effect on me. The nature of his death was that really he had come to England thinking that he had escaped the tyranny of racism, but of course in coming to England he came to the mother and father of apartheid. . . . It's very difficult for a non-white person to adjust. . . . I have a feeling that if it had been Prince Charles that [*sic*] he would not have died, if he had been white he would not have died. *I think that gave me a strong push towards a sense of political urgency*" (quoted in King 1994, no pagination; my emphasis).

Blake has described the European free music of the period as "arguably the least Americanised 'jazz' there has ever been, a minority music owing much to the Maoist and Trotskyist fringe politics of the 1960s" (1997, 149). The countercultural and avant-garde developments outside jazz—in terms of both the musics and the preferred spaces of performance—that I am looking at came together during the mid- to late 1970s in a remarkable series of leftist events in London. This was a period of high activity for campaigning musicians more generally, as attested by the establishment of organizations like Music for Socialism and Rock Against Racism.[14] The British free trombonist Paul Rutherford was an important figure in the organization of political music events, which followed an internationalist concert in January 1976 at the St Pancras Assembly Rooms, London. By this date the libertarian potential of the Scratch Orchestra had been self-critiqued into fracture, and the political People's Liberation Music was formed by Cardew instead. While the PLM played a fairly diluted jazz-rock with polemical lyrics, some of Cardew's other music was heard too: the bill included Rutherford, Evan Parker, Cardew, and others performing his *Music of Resistance*, as well as excerpts from a Chinese Maoist opera entitled *The Red Lantern*.[15]

Within the space of a few months Rutherford was involved in organizing a significant musical and political event at the Roundhouse in London under the aegis of the Communist Party of Great Britain, the first Moving Left Revue. It took place in April 1976 and featured a variety of musical turns—free improvisations by such musicians as John Stevens, Derek Bailey, and Lol Coxhill, the English rock of Henry Cow, and music that would perhaps be more familiar to communist audiences, like that of the folk singer Frankie Armstrong or, in forms of instrumentation at least, the Westbrook Brass Band (featuring Rutherford on trombone). A second Moving Left Revue took place the following year, with a similar lineup, although on this occasion Rutherford did more to consciously work together the musics of Henry Cow, Frankie Armstrong, and the Westbrook Brass Band. This one-off mix-music was of sufficient power and interest to lead to the formation of a new political and musical ensemble, as Mike Westbrook recalls: "At the Moving Left Revues we were on the bill with Henry Cow and Frankie Armstrong. We teamed up with them and formed the Orckestra. This toured in France and Italy, where the Cows were well established in the alternative scene. In these countries there was a link between revolutionary politics and the avant garde. This was never really the case in the UK—as a Brass Band tour organised by the Communist Party of working men's clubs showed. Sadly" (personal interview, 2003).

In 1977 Rutherford was the musical director for the People's Jubilee Festival, a pair of anti-monarchy gatherings at the Alexandra Palace on 12 and 19 June, to coincide with the national celebrations of (and protests about) a royal jubilee. Interestingly, this is the only one of these music events so much as mentioned in Andy Croft's collection about culture and the Communist Party, *A Weapon in the Struggle*—and then only as an example of the party's continuing pulling power: "As late as 1977 the Party was able to attract 11,000 people to Alexandra Palace for the People's Jubilee," Croft notes, a little wistfully (1998, 3). Perhaps such improvised music does not fit the (Marxist) historical template as neatly as, say, unionized dance music of the 1930s, or the second folk revival of the 1950s, both accorded chapters in his collection. Ironically— for Rutherford and other contemporary and avant-garde communist musicians at least—communist cultural historians have not been very much concerned with their contribution. I wonder whether this is a residual sign of the distrust of the avant-garde, the traditional suspicion of élitism in Communist Party aesthetics (perhaps the American taint of jazz inspiration was felt too). But for those with direct experience of the party in power, there were altogether greater reservations. Leo Feigin, who did much in the 1980s to introduce the West to the new improvised music of Russia through his releases of (frequently *samizdat*) recordings by groups like the Ganelin Trio and Sergey Kuryokhin, offers a different perspective, based on his own experience of jazz in the Soviet Union and in Britain:

> To my mind, another great misfortune of the new jazz was that its exponents from the very beginning tried to identify themselves with the political left. . . . I remember what a shock I got in the mid-seventies when I arrived in England after living in the USSR for thirty-five years. The Roundhouse, the most important venue of the time, staged a series of concerts of new jazz with all the receipts going to the Communist Party of Great Britain. I could understand that the musicians, who were dissatisfied with the attitude of the Establishment and public at large to their music, were forced to join

the leftist movement, but here there was a great paradox. On the one hand, the musicians considered themselves to be in the forefront of the counter-culture and anti-Establishment. They were in opposition and it was exactly for this reason they had leftist tendencies. On the other hand, they did not realize that where the communists, whom they were supporting, had come to power, the playing of free jazz was discouraged. (Feigin 1985, 187)

I have discussed Cardew, Rutherford, Wyatt, Henry Cow, Nicols — what was the attraction for a significant number of British improvising musicians to orthodox revolutionary parties' structures?[16] I asked this of the vocalist Maggie Nicols, whose extraordinary curiosity, enthusiasm, and energy across her life experience set her apart even within *the strange world of free improvisers* (a description of mine which I am not substantiating) — singer, educationalist, wife, mother, lesbian, feminist separatist, member of the Workers' Revolutionary Party, anarchist:

The party was putting on a performance about the Russian Revolution at Alexandra Palace and Gerry [Healy, the general secretary of the WRP] was keen that I should be free to follow through my improvisational musical ideas. I brought John [Stevens] along to talk about his unique approach. As John spoke about music and peace I became nervous about what Gerry might be thinking and then Gerry turned to me and said "Comrade, there's nothing like internal peace for waging external war!" John was a bit disturbed by that but I found that dialectic inspiring.

You can't just say that creative types can't take the discipline of the party; there are musicians who have long-standing commitments to political beliefs. And I wouldn't want to say there was an over-centralised hierarchy oppressing artists [who were members] either. The WRP for all its organisation and hierarchy I found to be much more open than the anarchist movement I had some involvement with later. You might think there would be strong links between anarchism and free improvisation, but some of them were culturally pretty conservative: if it wasn't some sort of thrashy punk music they weren't interested, didn't want to listen. In organisational and personal terms as well, in spite of the ideology, they were rife with their own hierarchies, too — you just had to look harder to find them. I think it is the case that liberation movements can quickly turn into their opposite, and for me, to overcome that, we need to maintain our improvisatory approach, so the music has certainly to that extent informed my politics. (Personal interview, 2002)

↔ IMPROVISATION ↔ ORGANIZATION ↔ EDUCATION ↔

Improvisation . . . is, uniquely, the property of disestablished classes.
No political or cultural Establishment ever improvised.
—BRIAN MORTON (1985, 5)

The first study of the new music in Britain was the trumpeter Ian Carr's *Music Outside: Contemporary Jazz in Britain*. The book was published in 1973 — in the wake of the recent and premature deaths of three of its leading practitioners, as Carr's first chapter notes with sadness: the saxophonists Tubby Hayes (aged thirty-eight) and Joe Harriott (forty-four), and the drummer Phil Seamen (forty-six). In his introduction, Carr explains the (nonmusical) meaning of the book's title, the premise that it set out to challenge: "Jazz is a music outside, a perpetual Cinderella of the arts in Britain" (1973, vii). This is a familiar, if not entirely valid, charge from musicians and enthusiasts. I want to spend a little time considering what might be thought of as *the benefits of marginalization*. Or, to necessarily finesse this, for I can hear the sound of an improviser's hackles rising (it's musical), I want to consider some of the imaginative responses and solutions to the cultural and economic marginality that people on the various scenes have experienced. As well as in the material music, it is also in the pragmatics of the everyday that social and political meaning is made. I am struck by the extent to which improvised music — not only free jazz, but possibly genres going all the way back (twenty whole years further!) to some traditional and revivalist jazz — has successfully negotiated the apparently contradictory demands of forming a specialized, in some ways exclusive culture and maintaining a grassroots, democratic social practice and vision. So I want to look at some of the issues around and achievements of *organization* itself, specifically the extramusical support, self-help, and campaign groups formed by jazz musicians, and to consider the place of *education* in jazz and improvisation, with particular reference to those pedagogic ideas and practices that are non-institutionalized.

As a largely collective form of cultural production, one characterized by its players' ability to move between groups, it may be unsurprising that improvised music should foreground organization as an activity; for a form at the cultural margins, such an imperative may be doubled. What follows is a narrative of jazz and improvised music in terms of mutual aid and the autonomy of cultural production. The cultural politics presented here are not quite the perhaps relatively straightforward ones of the organic music and leftist associations of New Orleans parade bands accompanying political processions, or the experimental sounds of the 1960s and 1970s performed at Moving Left Revues and the concerts of Music for Socialism. But there is too a cultural practice of some democracy in the surprisingly lengthy and sustained history of self-organization among British jazzers and improvisers. An important and consistent feature of jazz production, promotion, and consumption is the frequently grassroots style of organization. Consider the timeline below (inevitably partial), which contains only *extra*musical groupings, organizations *not* formed with the primary purpose of playing. Nor does it include individual venues, festivals, media, commercial publishing enterprises, union branches, musicians' own record labels, educational projects, internet distribution—all of which have played their role in the development, the survival of the music.

1933: Rhythm Clubs movement, followed by the Federation of British Rhythm Clubs (1935)

1939: short-lived Heralds of Swing musicians' cooperative

1942: Jazz Sociological Society (anarchist influenced)

1942–43: Jazz Appreciation Society (slightly more communist-leaning)

1948: National Federation of Jazz Organisations (NFJO)

1956: NFJO becomes National Jazz Federation Ltd. A private company, though also runs the (nonprofit) London Jazz Centre

1950s: Scottish Jazz Information Centre

1968: Jazz Centre Society

1968: Musicians' Co-operative (improvisers, Incus Records)

1972: Musicians' Action Group (across the range of jazz, works with the newly formed (1973) House of Commons Jazz Society)

1975: Bristol Musicians' Collective (first in country)

1976: London Musicians' Collective (the most important)

1980: Association of Improvising Musicians

1985: Abibi Jazz Arts

1980s: National Jazz Centre project (funded and then collapses)

1987: Jazz Directions (jazz and improvisers' cooperative)

I recognize that there is a variety of rationales in organizations such as these—mutual aid, the need to act as a pressure group, political commitment, self-interest, commercialism, state-subsidized art—which may contest one other.[17] I am also aware that a timeline like the one above can be read with a dismal inference, as a chronology of failure, as one group or generation after another tries to make that key breakthrough toward stability, superior funding and conditions, even complete cultural acceptance. Nonetheless there is something compelling in the continuing activity of self-organization through what is after all most of the historical trajectory of jazz and improvised music in Britain. It is illuminating to compare the situation within jazz with that of the entertainment industry, which until the 1960s saw its patterns of consumption go through a process of expansion and standardization—notably provincial cinemas and dance halls coming under the control of national corporations such as Gaumont, Rank, and EMI. "During these years leisure provision became increasingly centralised," Dick Hebdige writes, with features such as "the growth of recreation oligopolies . . . , the removal of leisure provision from popular control, a tendency towards greater specialisation in what had previously been communal or class-based rituals" (Hebdige 1988, 68).

A more minor form of centralization is identifiable in the tradition of communist organization among early British dance and jazz bands, some of it through agitation by professional musicians within the Musicians' Union. During the Second World War, while some London "communist spectacles had even come under criticism from [Communist Party offices in] King Street for featuring 'hot trumpeters' at the expense of political propaganda . . . it seemed that there was hardly a name dance band without its communist faction" (Morgan 1998, 125). Kevin Morgan locates the reason for this in the musicians' workplace experience: "The causes of this unsuspected politicisation lay not in the music itself but in the conditions in which it was produced. For many of the leading players, nightly exposure to the vile young bodies of class privilege provoked considerable revulsion" (1998, 125). Soon, from the altogether less professional end of the dance and jazz spectrum would famously come George Webb's Dixielanders, kick-starting the New

Orleans revival in 1943 after being formed at the Red Barn public house in Barneshurst, Kent—that is to say, formed for the purposes of playing at meetings of the No. 130 Bexleyheath and District Rhythm Club. And as we have seen, early appearances of the Dixielanders in London were organized under the auspices of the Young Communist League's Challenge Jazz Club (Godbolt 1984, 202–3). So beginning with the founding of the Rhythm Clubs Federation in 1935 there was within the appeal of jazz a strong impulse for regional or grassroots organization of enthusiasts. This tendency is a symptom of the democratizing impulse recognized or inscribed in the music by its adherents, but it also becomes a forceful statement of the commitment to anti-commercialism from the traditional and revivalist movement of the 1940s and 1950s, as well as, later still, a response to improvised music's non-acceptance by the cultural establishments. I follow the conclusion of Bernard Gendron here, who notes the role of the arguments between New Orleans revivalist and bebop fans in the United States: "the apparently retrograde Dixieland war played a significant role in the transformation of jazz from an entertainment music to an avant-garde music. . . . I am accentuating . . . the crucial role that the Dixieland war played at *the level of discourse*, of talk and patter in magazines, books, and radio shows, in preparing the way for the emergence of a jazz avant-garde" (Gendron 1995, 33; my emphasis). To Gendron's discourse I add social practice, and political understanding.

Surprisingly, it may be that musicians like George Webb in the 1940s and Ken Colyer in the 1950s set the attitudinal, economic, (largely) masculinist, and political template for subsequent generations of musicians in the field who stylistically were hugely divergent.[18] For example, in *Improvisation: Its Nature and Practice in Music*, Bailey describes the organizational backdrop to much performance in the field and provides a telling comment on its economics: "The bulk of freely improvised music, *certainly its essential part*, happens in either unpublicised or, at best, under-publicised circumstances: musician-organised concerts, ad hoc meetings and private performances. . . . *The more conducive the setting is to freely improvised music, the less compatible it is likely to be with the kind of presentation typical of the music business*" (1992, 141; my emphasis).

Bailey accepts, indeed privileges, the noncommercialism or anti-commercialism of the field. Trying to ply a lifetime trade producing a music that thrives only *outside* the music business is a startling, energizing, engaged, perverse, or destructive life project. Quite possibly, it is all five. Apart from free improvisation, is there a single other modern cultural realm that offers absolutely *no* possibility of significant reward for its most accomplished practitioners—*ever*? Experimental classical music, contemporary dance, the postmodern novel, conceptual visual art—all have their (relatively) powerful cultural champions, some or many financial resources or patronage, recognition and validation, some sort of career structure or opportunity. Only in improvised music (in Britain) do you start at the bottom, as it were, and stay there—even when you have reached the pinnacle. As noted, the problematic of its cultural value is inscribed in the term itself—improvisation is "spontaneous," but it is also "shoddy," "half-formed"—and perhaps the most shoddy aspect of the scene is the lack of sustained, significant economic support. In the early days, of the first-generation (1960s) and second-generation (1970s) free players, this marginal status may well have been part of the attraction—a boho, avant-garde iconoclasm, loudly or quietly knocking down (well, on) the walls of—what? the conservatoire? But radical sheen, like hair, thins over the duration, and from early on there were efforts to locate the practicalities of mutual support in the face of disinterest or worse within an ideological framework. Evan Parker articulated such a position in his discussion of the philosophy and impact of the Musicians' Co-operative that he and Bailey helped to found in 1968: "When we started the Co-op, it was much more of a socio-political expression than a musical one. . . . [Now i]t's as much a psycho-therapeutic exercise for us as it is a practical way of handling our social problems as musicians. . . . There is a move towards decentralisation, based, I think on a loss of faith in the international companies. It's an expression of basic socialist attitudes like workers' control, and also a rejection of the depersonalised, antihuman relationships that global companies tend to generate" (quoted in Carr 1973, 86, 88).

Other motivations as well as problems with a collectivist approach to organization are explored by Laka Daisical of the feminist all-woman band the Guest Stars, active in the 1980s. For Daisical, collectivity is an essential part of a gendered politics, but she also acknowledges its difficulty in such an individualistic cultural form as jazz: "We try to work as a collective . . . and I think one reason we do that is because it's been part of the experience of the whole women's movement—in which we've all been involved—to come together to share knowledge, and to break down feelings of oppression and resentment at work. . . . It may turn out that . . . collectivism and individual expression are mutually incompatible. . . . I think the collective idea is easier to pursue in a jazz context because the way you put the music together involves so much trust, improvisation means you're listening and giving. But at the same time there are certainly six very strong pulls in the band" (quoted in Lock 1985, 41).

Eddie Prévost of AMM—a unit that has been exploring improvisation sounds and processes for the best part of the last four decades, for more or less as long as there has been such music played in Britain—*does* see some development over that time: "The kind of music I play was then [in the formative period of the 1960s] frankly *despised* by those in control, the culture establishment. The Arts Council and the BBC alike have both since made minor patronizing attempts to support our 'free' improvised music, but I have rarely found their commitment convincing. Our music *is* outside the mainstream, but over the years we have developed an audience, a community, a group of people all around the world now, who believe in it. [But] the attraction, even the politics, of AMM and similar music can't just be put down to the fact that it's outside" (personal interview, 2002; my emphasis).

The notion of constructing what Prévost calls "a community" through the music is an important claim, though this may equally be no more substantive than the carving out of a specialist audience or a niche market. It is of course possible to view much of the preceding activity as a petit bourgeois practice, a minor cultural entrepreneurship, low capitalism for high cult music—so that mutual aid becomes self-help, in effect. But the social aspects of music making are important—and as much for constructing a community of musicians as for the community of the audience raised by Prévost. This is exemplified in a phenomenon such as Centipede, a cross between a big band and a temporary nomadic collective of musicians and friends, formed in 1970 from bands including King Crimson, Soft Machine, Nucleus, and the Blue Notes. The pianist and organizer Keith Tippett elaborates:

I had this idea of writing a piece virtually for all our friends to play. We knew a lot of people from different musics. Julie [Tippett] was from a soul-R&B background, there were the jazz musicians, string players from western classical music, and then those playing what goes by the label of progressive rock. Those sorts of people hadn't really worked together at that time. So we formed Centipede, featuring them all. There were fifty musicians involved, but actually there could have been a hundred — there was a lot of enthusiasm for it. It was done innocently, we were all friends, we were all young, no one was doing it for the money — actually the first gig, at the Lyceum, was a benefit, for the never-to-happen Jazz Centre. This was a time when youth had power. Of course we were in the midst of a cultural revolution at the time. People born just after the war were shaking off their parents' attitudes, and [in the 1960s] the music, the whole scene, was changing, evolving. And the world was different because everyone had jobs, you could afford to experiment, the music business allowed you to take more risks. (Personal interview, 2003)

Roy Carr reviewed Centipede's appearances in November 1970 at the Bordeaux Arts Festival in *New Musical Express*, and was evidently caught up in the utopian collective spirit of the jaunt: "A family it truly turned out to be. . . . Both on stage and off, a most amazing and spontaneous rapport existed" (quoted in King 1994, no pagination). In such a collective exercise, across musics and in grandeur of scale (underlined by the band's name), as well as in the memory of the gesture after the event (aided by re-release of the recording *September Energy Parts 1–4* thirty years on), is found a statement of, in Tippett's terms, innocence *and* power.

The kind of cultural and social organization of an ensemble like Centipede was rooted in the idealism and couched in the rhetoric of the counterculture, but within a few years a seemingly less promising subcultural music movement would be informing newer, longer-lasting developments. Primary among these was — and, as we have seen, is — the London Musicians' Collective, which shared correspondences with the emerging punk rock scene, if not musically as such then certainly in terms of attitude and accessibility.[19] The LMC emerged in 1976 from some mix of first- and second-generation free improvisers, with an important caveat identified by Clive Bell in his history of the collective: "A major difference from the Musicians' Co-op was the LMC's openness to anyone who wanted to join. Improvisers were dipping their fingers into the many pies of mixed media, dance, film, and performance art. And in fact at this time, just before punk and its DIY ethic erupted, there was a remarkable burst of energy in the underground arts scene. Dancers founded the X6 Dance Collective and New Dance magazine at Butlers Wharf, while film makers started the London Film Makers Co-op" (Bell 1999).

Steve Beresford would rail against collective organization in improvised music, based on his experience as a member of the editorial board of *Musics* magazine: "The collective is a morass of impersonality" (quoted in Bell 1999). But Beresford looks back on the LMC's extraordinary achievements rather differently now:

> It's insane: the LMC, *this* is where the real thing happens. Okay, there were no toilets in the building for years, you'd have to run over the road to the pub, but the *music* . . . The scene supports itself better now, socially and artistically. No, we don't stay in this field because it's anti-establishment or rebellious: we get really pissed off, and there are some musicians who've been doing this for thirty years, recognised elsewhere in the world, and they may be alcoholics or have psychological problems, because of the near total lack of support and respect. So we have to supply that for ourselves, from within. One advantage I suppose is that we don't need to take any of the bullshit traditionally associated with the established [visual] art avant-garde, but, like I say, we don't have the profile or opportunities it has either. (Personal interview, 2002)

I want now to consider the place of education in the improviser's social and organizational brief. In the United States, the struggle to place jazz music in the college curriculum had wider ramifications: in terms of both jazz technique and history, it was part of the development of black studies more generally, claimed and understood as a key feature of African American cultural identity and legacy. Further, there was a chauvinistic motivation, as it eventually was kind of accepted that jazz was a vital twentieth-century cultural invention of America, perhaps *the* vital invention, which should be considered as such and treated with due respect within cultural and educational institutions.[20]

It is widely recognized that teaching has long played an important role in the economy of jazz—many musicians informally offer private lessons, both as an alternate means of disseminating the music and as an essential economic support, particularly when the diary is thin. Through the 1960s and 1970s forms of more structured jazz education were beginning to appear in Britain. These ranged from the annual jazz course at Barry Summer School in South Wales (established in 1966) to the Wavendon All-Music Plan of John Dankworth and Cleo Laine (1968), from the National Youth Jazz Orchestra, with its origins as a rehearsal band under the direction of Bill Ashton, to the incorporation of jazz practice in higher education music courses, pioneered by Leeds College of Music in the early 1970s. There have been other signs that the potential of jazz in education is being recognized: in 1983 the Arts Council established a four-year scheme to fund projects involving professional jazz musicians working in educational establishments, and in 1992 the National Curriculum for all schools in England included jazz within its specified music options. It is telling that the notable big bands of the 1980s, Jazz Warriors and Loose Tubes, both had some origin in education projects.

Alongside developments such as these have been debates and alternatives from the improvising community, as we have seen with ensembles like the Scratch Orchestra (an atypical example to the extent that it combined aspects of institutional education with improvisatory practice). It is important to stress the concurrence of formal *and* improvisatory education developments. During this time projects such as the London Free School, the Anti-University, and the campaign group and publication *Libertarian Education* were all involved in the movement broadly called *deschooling* — removing the institutional regulations and (it was argued) related authoritarian methodologies from education in a practical radical critique of the system. As one class warrior, Arthur Humphrey, put it, "there will be no libertarian revolution in society unless and until our education system is liberated" (quoted in Smith 1977, 46). Within jazz and improvised music at the time, though, there was no school to de-, no formal mode of jazz and improvisation study against which to kick. As an illustration of this, while Graham Collier may have been a sole British presence in Boston, studying jazz at the Berklee School of Music (1961–63), before that he had spent five years as an army bandsman, while the likes of John Stevens and Trevor Watts met in the Royal Air Force music school. Ian Carr explains that "during the 1950s several would-be jazz musicians adopted this curious method of studying music because there was simply nowhere else where a jazz musician could get organised study and practice time" (Carr 1973, 42).

It is ironic, or perverse, that some of those who may have wished to benefit from the greater opportunities in jazz and improvised music education available today are among those senior musicians most critical of the way the education has developed. Trevor Watts, for example, announces on the limitations of formal jazz education: "*Nothing* attracts me to the current methods of teaching and regurgitating the music. I think promoters and teachers are perhaps even more to blame than aspiring musicians. They teach kids to be very proficient on their instruments, competitive and judgemental. Whereas I feel there should be some encouragement of a musician's individuality and to show the students of the music how to embrace and value discovering their own way through this music" (personal interview, 2002).[21]

Eddie Prévost describes the development of formal education courses in jazz music (in music colleges and universities) as "the flattening fifth"—a newer, fifth element supplementing the original four of musicians, promoters, audiences, and critics. The characteristic flattened fifth of much of the music is repositioned by Prévost: such education in jazz history and technique produces new generations of musicians who are what he calls "brainless clones" (1995, 52), able *and content* to emulate every nuance and mannerism of, say, a John Coltrane or Charlie Parker. This is a flattening, homogenizing, parodic, and anti-creative development, a retreat from meta-music into mannerism. It validates and is validated by an audience which is effectively, in Prévost's view, "a reformed lobby of former dissidents" (1995, 75). He continues: "The formal education of musicians in the historical techniques of jazz . . . disturbs the delicate balance within jazz life," producing "unthinking" players who "make flashy parodies of old men's dreams of great musics past" (Prévost 1995, 62–63). But what else is happening in the motivations for such common critical statements? They articulate survival and celebration of one's own route through the culture (often inscribed with a mix of the mock-self-heroic and self-effacing), and they are self-serving tactics to keep the *true* improviser on his (usually) toes.

The pivotal figure in improvisatory music education in Britain was the drummer John Stevens, whose manual *Search and Reflect*, inspirational workshops, and musical directorship of the organization Community Music in the 1980s drew on his free playing in concerts and what would become known as workshops from the mid-1960s.[22] Stevens explained that his interest in the combined educative and social potential of improvised music "started really with the audience at the Little Theatre Club which actually developed into a group. . . . [I suggested that] if they wanted to take part there was something they could do in relation to us that was simple and that would create a collective experience within the club. And they did it—and it was a nice experience and some of them, because of hearing us play and because of that experience, started taking up instruments" (quoted in Bailey 1992, 119).

From 1968 Stevens was running music workshops for nonprofessionals—marked by a Thames Television Fellowship (for him and Trevor Watts) in 1972 for making music within the community, in particular working with schoolchildren in Stepney, in the East End of London. He also ran what he termed Spontaneous Music Workshops at Ealing College in West London. Within a few years one of the activities of the proposed National Jazz Centre in London was outreach work, or jazz education in the community, and from this grew the organization Community Music in 1983, with Stevens as its musical director. As noted, the musical and social sides of a workshop led by Stevens were intertwined, to such an extent that Stevens often argued that "the quality of the music was secondary to that of the human relationships in its making" (Wickes 1999, 226). In his foreword to *Search and Reflect*, Christopher Small outlines the political imperative of Stevens's music project: "What is it that makes a musician important? . . . Is it in using his or her gifts, skills and experience to awaken and to guide the dormant musicality of those whose music has been taken from them? . . . Once people become aware that music is in themselves and not only in those who have been selected to become musicians, once they take back to themselves the musical act in a spirit of delight and self-affirmation, who knows what else they might insist on reclaiming, and enjoying, of what has been taken from them?" (1985, iv).

This is both conspiratorial and romantic, and as a social manifesto quite inadequate. And yet, and yet, consider just a very few of the various direct or indirect projects inspired by contact with Stevens, with Community Music.[23] In a way, thinking close to hand, consider this book for a start. Moving outside jazz and improvised music, the album made by Asian Dub Foundation in 1999 was called *Community Music*, for reasons explained by John Hutnyk: "The band's musical style was formed in the milieu of the music workshop located in Farringdon, and, as is often emphasised, in the East End of London: ADF's involvement with Community Music is more than as a contribution to an 'outreach' programme, but is explicitly linked to education, consolidation and politicisation work among youth of the East End. This work began with a programme in music making and media, MIDI techniques in a live situation, performance skills and mixing" (Hutnyk 2000, 185).

Maggie Nicols worked with Stevens in the early days at the Little Theatre Club, and was introduced to some of his breathing and vocal warm-up exercises. These she developed further at a series of intensive education and performance events at the Oval House arts center, Kennington, in the early 1970s. Nicols and Stevens continued to collaborate periodically, while she also took her own route through politics, gender, improvisation, and education. The social and educational aspects of improvised music making remain central to her work, her workshops, as she told me in 2002 about the Gathering:

> This is something important, an achievement. Every Monday night for twelve years we've been running what's got called "the Gathering," a kind of informal musical, social workshop drop-in, in a room above a London pub. There's no fee, and no-one gets paid. It's not a workshop and I never say it is but people always assume it is. Improvised music is at the heart of it. The Gathering isn't fixed, it's fluid depending on who shows up, and that changes over time. The fact that it has lasted so long shows its value, and that it's needed, and that it is a long-term process, commitment. I've missed maybe ten nights in twelve years, which amazes me. It originates in my experience at a very frustrating London Musicians' Collective meeting, where there was some tension, bit of bad feeling, people wanting to go in different directions. I just said, "Wouldn't it be good if we could meet in a different way, maybe a gathering." Sinead Jones, violinist and vocalist, said what a lovely word, better than a meeting. Loz Speyer (trumpeter) said we could bring instruments and trumpeter Ian Smith went out and found a pub for us to play in. The first evening no one was quite sure if we were there to talk or play and it was that very *uncertainty* that I feel has made it such an unusual combination of social and musical interaction. From that very

first session it was totally inspiring. It was LMC members to begin with but it gradually widened out, and it's still going. The Gathering has a political dimension, it's creative, it's community. It feels like home. (Personal interview, 2002)

REINSTATING THE POLITICS OF AUTONOMY

Can anarchist music be directed by a conductor? — EDDIE PRÉVOST, *Improvisation: History, Directions, Practice* (1984, 11)

In Britain and other European countries this alliance of new music with the leftist movement resulted in a total disaster for the music and musicians themselves. The leftist movement, being by nature impecunious and unsubsidised, could not give the new music either financial or moral support. And though the musicians had taken this anti-Establishment stance they could not survive without the help of the Establishment. They had to apply for grants and bursaries, but the grants were small and hard to come by and the exponents of new music had to play in dirty little pubs and badly lighted, unheated places like the London Musicians' Collective. Derek Bailey, Evan Parker, Trevor Watts, John Stevens, Barry Guy and many other fantastic musicians deserve to play on big stages in front of huger audiences. — LEO FEIGIN, *Russian Jazz, New Identity* (1985, 187)

Apart from Feigin's there are other dissenting voices to a sociopolitical reading of contemporary jazz and improvisation such as the one I am presenting. In his book *New Structures in Jazz and Improvised Music since 1960*, Roger Dean argues for an analytical approach to developments in free improvisation which privileges the primacy of the music *removed* from sociopolitical interpretation or context. Dean argues for this kind of cultural autonomy because such music is ordinately self-referential, *and* because musical developments in quite different socio-economic situations occurred, broadly speaking, concurrently. From African American free jazz on, he suggests, "one should ask how a comparable revolution occurred in other countries with very different social formulations at the time, and with relatively little sign of social change, for example, in West Germany (Mangelsdorff, Dauner, Brötzmann, Schlippenbach), England (where a black influence might also be suggested in the work of West Indian Joe Harriott, but a white was also evident in AMM, Spontaneous Music Ensemble, Parker, and Bailey), and in eastern Europe, particularly East Germany and Poland" (Dean 1992, xvii).

Its extensive musical transcriptions, descriptions of notation, and extracts from compositions make it evident that Dean's is a musicological hermeneutic, concerned with the practice and production of those sounds (mostly) called "music." This is a serious and valuable project in its own right, I agree—but music is not autonomous, or free-floating, not even a music of improvisation which survives at the cultural and economic margins. A sociologist might cite each of the countries above as in the late 1950s and early 1960s *precisely* the ones undergoing marked social change—through the impact of postwar reconstruction, communist and liberal democratic social projects, immigration, the shifting demographic that produced youth cultures, and so on. Also, the power of the hegemon is entirely elided by Dean: it may well *matter*, in sociopolitical terms, that some model of the music originates in the United States. And music, even that like free improvisation which may be understood to fetishize the heuristic, is an overwhelmingly mediated culture: records and radio and, to a lesser extent, television broadcasts were the means of swift international dissemination, and today these have been joined by the internet and other digital media. Where Dean's usefulness lies in this context is not in his argument "that sociological interpretations are as yet dangerous and impoverished as explanation" (1992, 138), but in reminding us that we do need to interrogate the social claims and purposes of the musicians' and other enthusiasts' statements and actions.

In his (overanxious) defense of the praxis, Nick Couldry deprivileges the social and especially the political in British improvised music too: "Improvisation is not a 'movement' with a programme of any sort. It is fundamentally misleading . . . to compare improvisation with anarchism. . . . If labelled in this way, it is easy to dismiss improvised music itself as an incomplete 'answer' to a 'problem' of social and musical change which it is no part of its purpose to pose or solve" (1995, 31).

A music on the margins, but lacking social or cultural critique? A music of voice and dialogue which does not seek to pose questions? Played by musicians, a remarkable number of whom have been, may

27. The jazz press revisits and repackages the revolutionary cultural politics of the 1960s in a special issue commemorating 1968 of the *Wire*, 1993.

still be, political radicals (intriguingly, as we have seen, more unreconstructed communists than apparently undoctrinaire anarchists)? Organized at an autonomous level with surprisingly little official sanctioning, recognition, or funding, but reliant instead on mutual aid, that old anarchist concept? Where education has featured as a *central* activity, as central for some important musicians as playing the music itself? I would rather *celebrate* the incompleteness of its answers to all sorts of questions, including sociopolitical ones, and do so in the face of its apparent "dismissal" as musical practice. Of course I recognize the validity of, the exasperation in, Steve Beresford's question, offered as a response to my own probing: "Is it entirely fair to talk about these, what you're calling 'limitations on the assumptions or inscriptions of liberty' in improvised music? *We're not in utopia!* It's just a music scene in a problem society!" (personal interview, 2002). But why did I seek out Beresford in the first place? *I was attracted by the articulacy of his critical and practical interventions in the field.* That is to say, he, like all the other musicians featured in this chapter, has explicitly or implicitly interrogated cultural value and social hierarchy through music making, asked the kinds of questions I am asking now. Frankly, I see nothing but worry in the effort to depoliticize the musical scene. My aim in this chapter, and of course throughout the book as a whole, is precisely to challenge such an interpretation, to illustrate its limitations and inaccuracies. What has struck me is the absolute insistence on political engagement by many musicians at different times in their careers—sometimes this is effacingly presented ("Well, someone asked us to do a couple of gigs for a campaign"), sometimes it is a core feature of a musician's social and cultural identity (Rutherford, Nicols, Cardew, Wyatt, all card-carrying members of revolutionary parties). As Clive Bell notes regarding the membership of the London Musicians' Collective in particular, and improvisers more generally: "Many British improvisers were, and still are, highly politicised, in all the different Marxist and anarchist hues. For many others, the collective spirit still expresses important truths about the cooperative and non-hierarchical nature of improvised music, and the importance of musicians taking creative control of their own music" (Bell 1999).

FIVE

From "Male Music" to Feminist Improvising

One day an argument started over something quite trivial and I grew so angry about it that I said, "Don't you realize I've just had a baby?" He retorted, "Don't you realize I've just had a band?" — Domestic negotiations between singer, mother, and wife CLEO LAINE and bandleader, father, and husband JOHN DANKWORTH, 1960 (Laine 1994, 171)

I'm really pregnant with these guys. *Pregnant* with them, they're *in* me. It's a shame. And I knew them from boys too, when we were still young. I dream about them a lot. — LOUIS MOHOLO, survivor of the South African Blue Notes, remembering (quoted in Scott 1991, 64; emphasis in original) recent analysis of British jazz musicians indicates that 85 percent are male; since the 1991 national census showed that among musicians generally 75 percent were male, the masculinist bias of jazz music practice may be even stronger than for other musics in Britain (ACE 1995, 17). John Chilton's essential reference book *Who's Who of British Jazz* contains over nine hundred alphabetical entries covering musicians from all jazz styles and periods; of those around thirty-five are female (Chilton 1997). This situation of "musical patriarchy" (Green 1997, 15) is not new: in his analysis of the membership details of the National Jazz Federation in 1958, Eric Hobsbawm found that fewer than 10 percent of members were female. Apart from the unfortunate result that the already minoritarian was further marginalized, even erased in his study, this meant that any analysis of female jazzers was impossible in Hobsbawm's view: "Only about sixty out of the 820 sample jazz enthusiasts are girls: the public of enthusiasts is overwhelmingly male. The remainder of this analysis is therefore confined to the boys and young men. . . . *There are too few girls to allow us to draw any conclusions* about their occupations and social classes" (Newton 1959, 271; my emphasis). Male musicians, male-dominated audiences (at least among those who would join organizations), male historians: a good deal of what has gone before in this book involves primarily men, a powerful exclusionary fact in a culture of liberation but one which I have largely allowed to pass without comment until now. I look consciously and critically at gender and sexuality—at jazz masculinities—to probe aspects of male culture and socialization that might vary within jazz from patriarchy to misogyny, gay sexuality to jazz as a space for some alternative constructions of masculinity (in particular, for working-class men). Men figure here in their predominant jazzed status as musicians, as audience members—and of course they are also the collectors and even curators. For the history of jazz in Britain is one of men supporting men, talking to and writing about men, preserving special male sociocultural spaces, men listening to each other's music and responding, men filling the willed silences of their daily discoursing with other sounds, men compensating for their societal inadequacy or familial indolence with a solo, men sharing instrumental secrets with each other, seeking structure or escape in a twelve- or thirty-two-bar sequence, men helping each other break out of rigid class expectations, small groups of men on stages and in corners watched, listened to, and envied by larger groups of men. The subcultural argot of jazz displays masculinity too—as Leslie Gourse has pointed out, "Everyone still says 'man' in the jazz world. It's the tradition" (1995, 13).[1] But there have been women too, even in jazz, even in Britain, and their practices and questionings form much of the chapter.

Have jazz *and* improvised music presented—preserved, even—a cultural zone of masculine liberation, masked behind a rhetoric of universal liberation? Lynne Segal has shown that "when men have written of themselves, . . . they have done so as though presenting the universal truths of humanity, rather than the partial truths of half of it" (Segal 1997, xxxiii)—but jazz's *liberatory* avowals amplify the silences and fermatas of such grand universal claims. No less interestingly, to what extent are its masculinist priorities historically specific, and at what sorts of moments have these been challenged? (I am thinking here of what Bruce Johnson terms the masculinization of jazz in Australia, of the European ladies' orchestras, all-women big bands, and the American "all-gal orks" of the war years, and of second-wave feminism's challenges to patriarchal improvisation in the 1970s.) Less critically, for men, in what ways has jazz offered opportunities to reconfigure social expectations of masculinity? It is questions such as these, concerned with *the music scene's male domination in relation to its frequently avowed "liberations,"* that I think worth exploring, because they raise issues about gender and music, about different constructions and challenges, pleasures, politics, and their limitations. At the same time, though, I am conscious of the articulation of someone like the improvising vocalist Maggie Nicols, informed by her own experience, who counsels caution about oversimplifying questions of gender and jazz. In Nicols's view, some male improvisers have been characterized by their very musical and social openness, while her extensive and committed work with other women musicians has taught her that improvisation, whether individual or collective, is enriched by female contributions: "I wouldn't want to stereotype women and men, though. Gender expectations are socialised, and if nothing else I'd say that women can play phenomenal solos as well! Dialogue and interaction are always there in the music, or in the workshop, and I learned that from a man, John Stevens. I've been lucky in that, musically, I have been supported by some great men. Dennis Rose, John Stevens, for example, and then Keith Tippett opened his heart and his music to me, filling in the gap between Dennis's bebop and John's free work. At the same time, in a music like ours, of collective communication, women have a lot to offer because of their history of social interaction and group communication" (personal interview, 2002).

GENDERING JAZZ

A good deal of research shows that music itself is a heavily gendered arena, and this starts relatively early (see Green 1997). For instance, Nicola Dibben's survey of gender identity and music research points to the importance of music education in (British) schools: even though "music in schools generally is regarded as a 'feminine' subject" by pupils, by the age of ten there are clearly demarcated musical choices and preferences along gender lines, to the extent even that children who buck the trend and opt for "gender boundary violation . . . are far less popular with their peers" (2002, 122, 123). Dibben has found that "one of the domains in which gender beliefs can be seen to operate most powerfully is in the gender stereotyping of musical instruments" (2002, 122). But is there anything in jazz specifically that makes it such a gendered form, particularly in fact when "many writers have noted a tendency for music to *feminize*" (Green 1997, 25; my emphasis)? As I explore in more detail later, it is possible that the partial origins of jazz in military music somehow resonate still, and its instrumentation may also contribute. A study from 1978 mentioned by Linda Dahl found that the drums, trombone, and trumpet were considered the most "masculine" instruments—military and jazz instruments all, though the most "feminine" included flute and clarinet, each of which also has a notable jazz tradition (Dahl 1984, 35). The different physical demands of these instruments may lead to their perceived gendering, and instrumental dynamics and tone seem to signify too. Women in jazz are of course frequently vocalists, which might lead to a tempting essentializing of body and voice (not least as men are relatively infrequent jazz vocalists). Jazz's central practice of improvisation does require consideration. The jazz solo as heroic or compensatory male autobiography is one important way of reading the music; but can its dialogic, intuitive, improvisatory impulses not equally be claimed within a female cultural framework? Roger Dean has suggested that "female musicians might introduce more 'intuition' into composed music, and probably music in general, than do males. Interestingly, a study of boys aged 10–15 found positive correlations between compositional abilities and psychological androgyny. . . . It found no such correlation with improvisatory abilities. . . . There were no such correlations in the girls of the same age range. . . . Such studies begin to imply significant differences between the sexes in relation to musical activities" (Dean 1992, 201). The improviser Steve Beresford develops this theme by identifying male domination as "a worry at the heart of the improvised scene": "There are numerous features of improvisation as a cultural and social practice that have been or may be of particular interest to women: I'm thinking of intuition in playing the music (I *don't* mean by this to suggest women are intuitive, flaky, whatever), of its non-hierarchical aspirations, of the way it offers the opportunity for cross-dialogue in music. You might think all of these would or could appeal to women looking for creative opportunities for music-making. But, in proportion, they are not there. On the other hand, go into the classical scene — which is frankly more hierarchical, more authoritarian altogether — and there are, comparatively speaking, many more women musicians" (personal interview, 2002).

I am uncertain that Beresford's very final point stands scrutiny: a recent survey of the extent to which the work of women composers was programmed in British orchestras and festivals over the period 1997–2002 produced predictably gloomy results. The Hallé Orchestra in Manchester, for instance — still remembered for banishing women musicians in 1920 to achieve a "unity of style" (Fuller 1995, 27) — played 820 musical works during those five years, only one of which was by a female composer (0.12 percent), while the annual Proms Festival Season in London featured works by 722 composers, of which eighteen were by women (2.5 percent; Women in Music 2004). Even so, extending Beresford's example dramatizes the gender gap in improvisation and jazz: go into the realm of folk—which is frequently centered in some of the very male social spaces privileged in jazz, such as smoky pubs and cellar bars—and there may well be *more* women musicians and enthusiasts than in jazz. Further comparative analyses provide conflicting information around music and gender. In *Frock Rock: Women Performing Popular Music*, Mavis Bayton seems to suggest that some jazzes have been more amenable to women musicians than rock music. Bayton also illustrates the interlinking of ideological and musical discourses at points when social movements have been highly active and aware, such as the women's movement in Britain: "In the late 1970s, there was a debate in feminist circles about the existence or possibility of a 'female music.' Although some feminist musicians, at the time, rejected electric music as intrinsically 'masculine' and would only play acoustically, it was always easier to specify what 'female music' was not (loud, aggressive, heavy, throbbing, 'cock rock') than what it actually was. 'Women's music' was *supposed* to be more flowing, less structured, lighter, warmer, softer, but beyond that there was little agreement. . . . If too many of the conventions and codes of rock are broken (because they have been created by men) then one is no longer working inside that genre. Maybe that is one reason why many feminist musicians in the UK have more of a presence in experimental forms of jazz?" (Bayton 1998, 199; emphasis in original).

Yet in a national study of women's participation in jazz in Britain published in 1998, the lack of women to emulate was cited as one of the most important factors excluding women from the music (Huxley and English 1998, 8). This factor's significance is particularly acute because in the same study, at least as many women musicians were inspired to play the music by having seen female performers (28 percent) as male performers (27 percent) (Huxley and English 1998, 13). The instructive if unsurprising observation to be made is that the simple presence of women musicians has an inspirational impact on other women—which can then have an incremental effect.

There are other social issues for both audience members and musicians: the chosen or available spaces of jazz, its pubs and underground clubs, are heavily gendered, as are their unsocial hours. I recognize more generally that leisure itself is a gendered practice or commodity,

BLOKE NEWINGTON

THE FIRST ANNUAL FESTIVAL OF MALE IMPROVISATION

A very special event celebrating men's contribution
to improvised music.
Featuring-
-Extremely Loud Saxophones
-Harsh electronics
-Bone rattling drums
-heavily amplified double basses
-a deep and brooding sense of loneliness

(artists to be confirmed, check press for details)

PLUS a heavily laden record store of rare and
hard to find vinyl recordings.
Starts 12.30 PM, Saturday 1st April
Stoke Newington Town Hall, London.
Admission £7.00 /£6.00 Concessions
Please note this is a <u>men only</u> event.

28. Patriarchal practice? London Musicians' Collective flyer for
an April Fools' Day spoof concert. Source: *Resonance* magazine,
"25 Years of the LMC."

as Stephen Whitehead has summarized: "if we understand free time
to be a form of capital, then it is apparent that women have less of it,
have reduced access to it and are less able to negotiate their actions
within it" (Whitehead 2002, 141). Nonetheless, at times of intense social movement activity normative social practice is challenged—the
women's liberation movement of the 1970s is a case in point. The jazz
guitarist Deirdre Cartwright recalls the impact of feminism on music
of the 1970s and 1980s: "The feminist politics that had been coming
over from America and changing the ways women in Britain thought
led to campaign groups, conferences and organisations up and down
the country. Even the Trades Union Congress would put on a women's
caucus event. And lots of those conferences had entertainment in the

evenings and organisers started booking all-woman bands. *To put a women-only band on the stage during these years was itself a political act*—in a positive way at things like women-only benefits, which were happening for the first time, in a more charged way at some of the punky gigs when some men would be shouting abuse at us for just being women playing guitars and drums" (personal interview, 2004; my emphasis).

Even so, from her experience as a jazz publicist Polly Eldridge has observed that the world of jazz "is still suffering from when jazz was promoted in dingy men's clubs and the only women present were ladies of the night" (quoted in Cornwell 2002, 28). Eldridge foregrounds the assumption of the possible roles available to women within jazz structures: it is a common perception by women *and* men that in its history, jazz granted limited accessibility to women, who were accepted into its clubs and other private spaces on the understanding of *unrespectability*. While this arrangement has undoubtedly been attractive to some women, including unconventional ones, many others have had to balance musical curiosity alongside social orthodoxy and expectation. As for performers, it may be that the musician's lifetime commitment in a relatively unstructured and unrewarding professional environment, such as jazz offers at its best, has not been an adequately attractive career option for many women. The perennially attractive shade of the authentic lone jazzman is a key trope in the figuration of pop music masculinity; perhaps jazz even set that template for subsequent pops to fetishize. Derek Bailey's early publicity leaflets included contact details alongside praiseworthy quotations from international reviews about his music—the latter framed in turn by quotations from different bank managers inviting him to deposit sufficient funds into his account: " 'He operates outside every accepted tradition'—*New Statesman*; 'Unless you make a sustained effort to bring your account into credit we shall have no alternative but to . . .'—Midland Bank" (Wickes 1999, 268). Here Bailey celebrates or ironizes the improviser's familiar gap between cultural profile and economic standing, the life choice of an "aestheticised poverty" (Blake 1997, 115) that may well be a masculine prerogative. The singer Elaine Delmar, though, daughter of the black bandleader Leslie "Jiver" Hutchinson, was one young woman determined to make her way in jazz. She recalled of her teenage years on the northern club circuit of the 1950s: "I'd do a gig and go home on the milk train. Sometimes I'd play two or three clubs a night. It makes today's audiences seem easy. . . . There'd be lots of booze, lots of smoke and rowdiness—the chairman of the club would come on stage saying, 'Come on, give a bit of support, give the poor cow a chance!' Dreadful" (quoted in O'Brien 1995, 77).

Jazz criticism and history, and the organization of the music, are important extramusical issues to consider. In the context of her early efforts to break into jazz criticism in the 1960s, Val Wilmer has observed that even "writing about the music was something that men did" (1989, xii–xiii), while some of the publishing opportunities for writing and reading were themselves patriarchally positioned. As she has recalled, with a critical eye informed by her later feminism, "in 1966 the 'girlie' magazines were regarded as a sophisticated outlet for jazz writers" (Wilmer 1989, 135). The "cultural intermediaries" (Keith Negus, quoted in Bayton 1998, 2) that influence success in the music industry, such as promoters, agents, and journalists, remain predominantly male.[2] Are there gender issues in jazz even about its retrospection, and this in spite of its rhetoric of nowness, even futurity? For some women involved in the business side of jazz in Britain there certainly are. An article in *Jazzwise* in 2002 showed a number of women managers, press officers, and record company executives in jazz interpreting how the past orientation of the music was perceived in terms of masculine exclusivity: "Jazz attracts an older audience, and the male/female split shifts with the type of gig." . . . "Jazz is often seen as a 'serious' music, a genre that demands total involvement and knowledge of past and present details to be enjoyed. Dare I say it, but that's rather anal, rather male." . . . "Jazz tends to be in thrall to its past and sadly retains many of the prejudices and patriarchal attitudes" (Cornwell 2002, 28–29).

Being in thrall to the jazz past can function as the formative tactic of a heteropatriarchally constructed history, even when gender or sexuality is a foregrounded social and musical question in performance. For instance, in the view of the American vibraphonist Gary Burton, who came out in the late 1980s after decades of being in the jazz closet, "a lot of jazz's present is closely tied up with its history. Many people still persist in wanting jazz to be played by fucked-up addicts and alcoholics, in cramped smoky clubs. . . . The historians have absolutely avoided the issue [of lesbians and gays in jazz], of course. . . . Too bad. It makes them lousy historians" (quoted in Gill 1995, 75, 76). A similar experience is articulated by Maggie Nicols, in a European and lesbian

29. Poster for the Women in Jazz archive in Swansea, encapsulating history. It features a shot from a Women in Jazz concert by Crissy Lee's Big Band: Lee had been a drummer with Ivy Benson.

context, in her discussion of the critical recognition allocated to the groundbreaking Feminist Improvising Group, founded in London in 1977: "I've said it before, I know, and I'll keep saying it—FIG is written out of the history: we're all socialised, and music is just another history, and it's passed down the *male* lineage, and we have been written out" (personal interview, 2002). Other women involved in jazz history confirm Maggie Nicols's critique. Jen Wilson's work in establishing the Women in Jazz archive in Wales provides a counterbalance to masculine culture. In Wilson's view, "the existing libraries and archives of jazz are already gendered: they are collected and organised by men, and they are not [as] interested in what women have done" (personal interview, 2001). There is an illuminative example in the breadth of the archive that Wilson has established; alongside the expected, familiar materials of books and recordings, the archival holdings of Women in Jazz include the stage gown collections of the singers Blanche Finlay and Beryl Bryden (see Women in Jazz 2004). For Wilson, these are not female ephemera but central jazz artefacts.

We should pause for a moment also to consider the case of Winifred Atwell, the Trinidadian ragtime pianist whose recordings topped the British charts in the 1950s. Why Atwell? Because frankly, until I came to research women in British jazz history I had never heard of her, and Atwell, the idea of her and her performance, struck me. As I have shown, Atwell's music and performance repeatedly brought black American music to a huge British public, even if it was a diluted, retrospective version. Her jazzy cross-musicking dramatized racial conformities for white Britain, and she was the first black artist in British pop history whose recordings sold a million copies. It is fair to say that in terms of chart records, *she may be the most successful jazz-influenced artist in British pop history*. Yet none of the available histories of jazz in Britain (Boulton 1956; Godbolt 1984, 1989; Chilton 1997) so much as mentions her. While the white trad scene and the new black urban sounds of the time have been or are being written about, and their various brief moments of pop success celebrated, what has become of Atwell? And while black and white British musicians have begun to pay homage to the Caribbean and African jazz innovators—the Jazz Warriors touring in memory of Joe Harriott in the 1980s, the mighty Dedication Orchestra playing the music of the South African Blue Notes in the 1990s, Courtney Pine releasing a track called "Osibisa" in 2003—I know of no such tribute from the music community across the board in recognition of Winifred Atwell's achievement. Atwell's is a compelling if predictable case study of the limitations of a male-constructed historical model in a male-dominated cultural formation. What Linda Dahl has termed a "blanket of silence" (1984, x)—surely the worst professional situation for almost any musician to endure—weighs heavily on women like Atwell, who have made some mark on the music.

The domestic character of the jazz world—jazz at the kitchen table—has seen women in important administrative roles. There have been significant, perhaps more conventional contributions from life partnerships such as husband-and-wife teams, in which the husband is the musician and the wife the organizer. One saxophonist wrote of the transformation in his private *and* professional life when he met the woman who became his "loving wife and personal manager rolled into one" (Turner 1984, 207). In the 1970s Hazel Miller (wife of the bassist Harry) was involved in running Ogun Records; Jackie Tracey (wife of the pianist Stan, mother of the drummer Clark) organized Steam Records, which released Stan Tracey's music. Hazel and Jackie teamed up too, estab-

30. "It takes two people to confirm the truth": Barbara and Dudu Pukwana, London. © Val Wilmer.

lishing Lambeth New Music Society to promote innovative live music in south London. More recently, Janine Irons co-directs Dune Records, which releases the music of her partner, the bassist Gary Grosby, while Dani White runs a management company whose clients include her husband, the trombonist Dennis Rollins (Cornwell 2002). Clearly these kinds of partnerships fundamentally confirm the male priority of cultural creativity, the view that jazz is, in Whitehead's general term, "a culture of masculinism—the cultural dominance of the male (in the public sphere)" (Whitehead 2002, 115).[3] But they illustrate as well Wilmer's point in *As Serious as Your Life* that "it takes two people to confirm the truth" (1977, 191), and they remind us that a life's energy and dedication to making jazz continue to happen come from women *non*-musicians too. This chapter aims further to tease out the complexities of the possibilities and exclusions for men and women in jazz in Britain. How far is it still true that "women's lives are accompanied by a *male* soundtrack"? (Bayton 1998, 1; emphasis in original).

In *Stormy Weather: The Music and Lives of a Century of Jazzwomen*, Linda Dahl identifies "factors that have tended to keep women from playing jazz." While Dahl is concerned specifically with the situation in the United States, many of her points stand as general jazz observations. I offer them here in part as a summary of the gendered nature of jazz, but also because they should be read contrarily, as part of the attraction of jazz for many men. The near exclusive masculine social space and cultural practice critically charted by Dahl is often what men actually receive—*want*—from the small reality as well as the grand mythography of jazz. In some ways what has put women off is also what has attracted men:

> The qualities needed to get ahead in the jazz world were held to be "masculine" prerogatives: aggressive self-confidence on the bandstand, displaying one's "chops," or sheer blowing power; a single-minded attention to career moves, including frequent absences from home and family. Then too, there was the "manly" ability to deal with funky and often dangerous playing atmospheres, nightclubs infested with vice and run by gangsters. These frequently went hand in hand with a tendency to drink vast quantities of hard liquor, or sometimes take hard drugs, while continuing to play coherently into the dawn. A woman determined not to be intimidated by such a tough, smoke-filled atmosphere (where one's peers were probably all men) often paid penalties designed to put her in her place—the loss of her respectability being high on the list, as well as disapproval, ridicule and sometimes ostracism. (Dahl 1984, x)

SOME JAZZ MASCULINITIES

Jazz has attracted more than its fair share of the fantasy of
opposition, the individualised, implicitly male, "heroism" of the great
artist working in defiance of social norms. This is a convenient view
of themselves for lonely suburban men, not gifted with great
social skills, but who can play a saxophone or trumpet—or who
have record collections and opinions thereon.—ANDREW BLAKE,
The Land without Music (1997, 113)

The regular, formal mix of ensemble and solo playing in jazz, with the intermittent accompanying percussion of its male-dominated audience, makes the live music event a fairly powerful manifestation of masculinity. More than that, being predominantly a male group performance predicated on the necessary solo contribution, *jazz has been a cultural dramatization of the poles of masculine social expectation or possibility*. The gendered dialogue or tension that it admits mirrors the social veering of men between isolate and mutualist. Jazzers: Are you playing on your own, or playing with other lads? Men: How do you move or how are you moved between individual and collective social roles? Jazz is an important space in which to pose such questions, because in its cultural practice, jazz poses them itself.

In Victor Seidler's view, there is not so much a dynamic between individual and collective identity in constructions of masculinity as there is a rejection of the collective. For Seidler, men publicly "have learned to be independent and self-sufficient. We have learned to go it alone and to do without the help of others. . . . Often there is little that prepares us for relationships, for in learning to be self-sufficient we learn to do without others. Often our very sense of male identity is sustained through our capacity for *not* needing the help of others" (quoted in Whitehead 2002, 157; emphasis in original). While recognizing that one aspect of much jazz making — its collectivity — may not convincingly map on to the solitary masculinity outlined by Seidler, it is at the same time important to acknowledge familiar figures of mostly male, single otherness in the scape of jazz: the exile, the misunderstood, the junkie, the bohemian, the dropout, the fugitive. For instance Mike Zwerin, an American jazz musician and critic in Europe, a late member of the lost generation, presents a free, romantic, explicitly male narrative of jazz desire. The professional jazz musician "automatically becomes an outlaw. There is no valid motivation for it other than love — outlaw motivation in a profit-motivated society. He leaves the crowd. It is not a worn path. . . . Improvisers tend to transpose musical values to a life-view. . . . Those who create 'the sound of surprise' for a living are not likely to plan very far ahead" (Zwerin 1985, 36). The general observation stands that the license to make the kind of life choice lauded by Zwerin has traditionally been a male prerogative. What Blake has less heroically described as "the mythology of [jazz musicians'] romantic/shamanistic cultural place" (1997, 113) is a facet of this solo masculinity, but it can be deeply uncomfortable: from Buddy Bolden to, in Britain, the saxophonist Mike Osborne, jazz has scattered psychological trauma. At the same time, John Fordham has touched on one oppressive side of the masculinity of the British jazz club demimonde, writing in the context of the saxophonist and club organizer Ronnie Scott's chronic clinical depression: "It was a predominantly male world, the inhabitants of which tended to be uncomprehending of mental difficulties, if not actually unsympathetic. Ronnie for his part found it harder to relax the cynical, freewheeling image that men admired him for enough to really let his difficulties out" (Fordham 1986, 175).

It is familiar that British jazz's suburban enthusiasts have also written narcotic, alcoholic, sexual excess vicariously into jazz legend, and these figure predominantly as male. In *Waiting for the Man*, Harry Shapiro identifies the narcotic template of jazz for subsequent pops: "the drug connection was central to the creation of the jazz (and later, rock) musicians as outlaw figures" (1988, 47). In fact the first British police drug raid on a music club took place in the London bebop arena Club Eleven, recently removed to new premises in hip Carnaby Street, in 1950 (Shapiro 1988, 105–6, 111; Fordham 1986, 49–53). Some of Britain's best modern jazz musicians would follow, fall to, the heroin addiction model of jazz inspiration: the saxophonist Tubby Hayes (died in 1973, aged thirty-eight years), the drummer Phil Seamen (died in 1972, aged forty-six). Seaman produced an extraordinary autobiographical statement of his early jazz career on side 1 of the record *Phil Seamen Story*, which consists of short bursts of solo drumming interspersed with his voiced memories, recorded in the studio. It opens with him using beaters, followed by his Beckett-like voicing: "The drums. As you may no doubt know. Well, I was asked to do the Phil Seamen story, which I didn't mind at all, because being an egomaniac it pleased me greatly, therefore here I am" (Seamen, 1973). The slurred delivery, the semi-rambling structure, the inconsequentiality of most of the monologue, in combination with Seamen's percussive breaks, even the record's posthumous release, present a kind of masculine performance, a pathetic confirmation of what another British jazz musician claimed in his autobiography: that "to be a ruined man is itself a vocation" (Heckstall-Smith 1989, 65). Just as interestingly, what was the hoped-for market for such a record? Who wanted to hear the ghoulish stripping away, the sad sound of a drummer without a band, who wanted to turn the flaunted failure of an extreme jazz masculinity into cultural counter-triumph or vicarious male fantasy?

More pragmatically and less dramatically, a report of the Arts Council of England on jazz in England locates the constructed jazz isolate firmly within the socioeconomic context of cultural production: "The fragmented nature of jazz employment means that [many musicians] will be self-employed and working part-time, or unemployed.

Most jazz musicians live by a mixed economy, supplementing their income with commercial opportunities (not always playing jazz), teaching, and part-time work of other kinds. . . . *Isolation and anxiety are fairly universally expressed by jazz artists*" (ACE 1995, 18, 19; my emphasis). As a result it may be that templates of jazz masculinity are further skewed in certain directions at the expense of others. Intriguingly too, the economic frame supplied here by ACE has been a recurring trope in masculine motivation in the music—from the male prerogative of Blake's "aestheticised poverty" to Zwerin's "outlaw motivation in a profit-motivated society." Within British jazz, we have seen it in certain anti-commercial projects, utterances, and attitudinal identities associated with *authentic* musics in *underground* spaces, *grassroots* politics, and *subcultural* pleasures. I am really thinking here of such wilful, stubborn, directive musicians and leaders as Ken Colyer, exponent of New Orleans music of the 1950s, all the way along the musical spectrum to John Stevens, free-music experimentalist a very few years later. (I nominate these two here precisely because the similarities in their jazz masculinities cut so startlingly across musical differences.)

But both the trumpeter and cornetist Colyer and the drummer (and sometime trumpeter) Stevens were also regular originators of collaborative projects—that is to say, leaders of bands—and they were men who usually inspired tremendous loyalty from the musicians who played with them. They were musicians who had strong, blunt personalities, but who really only wanted to operate within a collective situation: for Stevens, as we have seen with the Community Music workshops, that could lead to a privileging of the social experience over the aesthetic evaluation in music making. The wider point for jazz and improvisation is that the masculine social dynamic of solo and group is constantly played out, literally *performed*, in the process of a gig. Evan Parker delineates the contestation and negotiation of male power and control in the free ensemble Music Improvisation Company, which featured him and Derek Bailey among others during its life from 1968 to 1971. In its self-heroic—and possibly mock-heroic—depiction, this was a nightly music and performance of alpha struggle: "The sound of the group, its whole character in fact, would depend on who was 'leader' at the time. Who was leader wasn't a matter for discussion or democratic decision. It depended on whichever member's influence, extended through psychological alliances and conspiracies, was predominant at the time. . . . During this time the group would reflect, not always without a struggle, his preferences and performing style until, exhausted by his responsibilities, the leader would be overthrown and returned to the rebellious ranks" (quoted in Bailey 1992, 96).

Part of the pleasure of such music, for both musicians and audience, is the public performance of the masculine process of making it. Outside the gendered arena of the domestic sphere, the performance of fraternal solidarity and competition in jazz and related music history—from front line "cutting" at jam sessions to the revolutionary process described by Parker in free music—is a *public* display.[4] For as Whitehead reminds us, "the public sphere is a place that males are supposed to inhabit naturally, a place they must colonize, occupy, conquer, overcome, control. It is the site where men come to be (men)" (Whitehead 2002, 114). That most British institution, the exclusive nondomestic space known with supreme ambivalence as a *public house*, figures strongly in jazz history here. Its back rooms and cellar bars, occasionally aggrandized into the club, are where jazz still happens, where men gather to hear the band play solos. And as Jonathan Rutherford has pointedly reminded us regarding masculine collusion, "it's not just what is going on inside the pub that unites men, it's what the pub door is shutting out" (Rutherford 1988, 54).

There are other important masculine spaces or moments in British jazz history. For Theodor Adorno, jazz bands "do not by accident stem from military music" (1967, 129); unlike its fans who love the music for its individual expression, Adorno could discern through his rigorous vision that its military origins betray and confirm its standardizing urge. In Adorno's hearing, the key rhythmic "trick" of syncopation became so widespread through the twentieth century that jazz "achieve[d] musical dictatorship over the masses" (1967, 125). Within Adorno's text there is a gendered reading of jazz, although it is an enfeebled, and effeminized, masculinity that is constructed in the music—jazz fans suffer from "coming-too-soon," while "the eunuchlike sound of the jazz band" proclaims, "Give up your masculinity, let yourself be castrated" (1967, 128, 129). Susan McClary reads Adorno's jazz criticism, his "otherwise incomprehensible ravings," as fearful texts. They are writings in which "gender, race, and class identity get mapped onto each other, and they seem to become the same threatening issue" (McClary 1991, 65). But Adorno's point, of jazz in relation to the military, is worth pursuing. Linda Dahl recognizes the significant male collusion of military and music in particular in early jazz: "The trumpet would appear to be the quintessential masculine horn; whether made of shell or bone or metal, its loud, carrying and even frightening reaches of sound have made it a leading instrument on battlefields and in the military. Retaining this militaristic-masculine significance, trumpets and cornets made perfect lead and 'signifying' horns in the marching bands of early American popular music and in the New Orleans jazz ensembles" (Dahl 1984, 37).

In Britain the masculine space and idea of the military have played a strong role in jazz development.[5] In some ways this is an unsurprising observation: jazz really took off in Britain in the 1930s and 1940s, during the Second World War, when it was a key cultural import from one of Britain's closest allies. The industry profile of the dance band leader Gerald W. Bright is indicative here. Better known as Geraldo, following an attempt to ride the tango craze of the 1920s and 1930s, he was during the war head of light music for the Entertainments National Service Association (ENSA), and after it he headed a successful theatrical agency (Chilton 1997, 133). Nicknames for his bands were Geraldo's Guards (when touring overseas for Allied forces during the Second World War) and Geraldo's Navy (after the war, when his agency supplied bands for the Cunard transatlantic cruise liners). Opportunities for playing the music, or for hearing it, were framed by masculinity during and after the war: even would-be rebellious British beboppers like Laurie Morgan, Ronnie Scott, and John Dankworth who sought access to the source of the music in New York had to join Geraldo's Navy. To British musicians, access to the key space or life-changing experience of the transatlantic was essentially a masculine privilege. For Scott and others, it was playing in the cabin-class band on the recently refitted *Queen Mary* that made New York accessible.[6] For Ken Colyer, to reach New Orleans and his mythicized original space of the music a few years later, in 1952–53, meant rejoining the Merchant Navy and hoping for a job as an assistant cook, *not* as a musician (Colyer 1970, 22). Tellingly, Colyer's autobiography, *When Dreams Are in the Dust* (1989), is far more focused on characters and anecdotes from his time as a merchant seaman than on his musical career.

In the 1950s and 1960s the popularity and innovation of jazz, from trad to free music, were at a high level, and frequently dependent on young men who had either survived the war or completed National Service (a compulsory two years of military training in Britain from the end of the war until abolition in 1963). In those vital decades for British jazz, military experience and memory infused national life—the masculine half, at least. In Lynne Segal's view, National Service "played a not insignificant role in constructing the masculine mood of the moment," was in fact "the last rite of passage into manhood designed to include *all young men*" in Britain (1997, 14, 132; my emphasis). Even those of the younger generation seeking to escape the psychological and cultural aftermath of the war had to reference it, if obliquely. Captain (retired) Peter Hunter, in 2002 a committee member of the Ken Colyer Trust, explained to me how he understood the semiotic significance of the traditional jazz crowd of the 1950s: "Much of the dress was pure black, and I think, speaking from a Merchant Navy perspective, that it was in part a postwar next generation's reaction against wearing uniform. Instead young people wanted to dress down" (personal interview, 2002).

How fair is it to suggest that some of the desire for a form of (male) collective experience in improvised music in London of the early 1960s was at least partly informed by the lengthy experiences of key players in the military forces? After all, John Stevens, and other later-to-be experimental musicians like Trevor Watts and Paul Rutherford had all signed up for five years in the RAF in 1958 to obtain a musical education. Each followed a similar pattern: study at the Royal Air Force School of Music in Middlesex, and then a posting to Germany to play in the Regional Band based at Cologne. A few years before this the composer Graham Collier had signed up into the army for five years as a teenage band boy. All would anyway have been called up for National Service—but each decided to extend the compulsory period in order to receive a firm musical education. It may not be so surprising that most of these working-class musicians then went on to make significant contributions to jazz education as well, providing to subsequent generations opportunities to learn that had not been so accessible to their own. The possibility of impact on an increasingly active music scene in London, when a cluster of now experienced international musicians like Stevens, Watts, and Rutherford were demobilized after their five-year RAF period in 1963, becomes easier to understand. In this way the musicians may resemble the players in Geraldo's Navy and the likes of Colyer in the Merchant Navy, seeking out the available male spaces for creative development and expression, and perhaps also bearing the traces of these predominantly masculine formative experiences in their subsequent jazz careers. One of the "real and lasting joys" that Segal identifies as the legacy of men's experience in National Service was an "intensified male friendship and comradeship" (Segal 1997, 18), and I suggest that such an achievement could be both a contributory factor to jazz development and a continued product of it. I do think that for important generations of British musicians innovating from the 1950s and 1960s—and especially those who signed up for longer periods to gain a musical education—the male group experience of National Service and other military or pseudo-military moments facilitated a normative masculine sociocultural alignment. This link helps to explain the masculinity of jazz in Britain, and can extend to a musician like Dick Heckstall-Smith who for political reasons refused to do his National Service. Registering as a conscientious objector, Heckstall-Smith went before a tribunal that permitted him to undertake alternative public service in the mid-1950s by working as a hospital porter (Heckstall-Smith 1989, 2). But even Heckstall-Smith falls back on a kind of "militaristic-masculine" (Dahl 1984, 37) metaphor when describing his taste in jazz—that is, an avowed pacifist musician confirms that jazz is best understood as a form or expression of (male) heroic warfare. Thus are dominant masculinities internalized, even by those men who would otherwise resist certain arenas for their construction: "The kind of jazz I like—the kind of *music* I like—is strong, pushy, forward, full-blooded, free of self-imposed restrictions. It takes risks. It is not in the least afraid; it battles its way through to expression. . . . When it senses unhealthy restraint it plants a bomb under it and trips the detonator. It shows no mercy" (Heckstall-Smith 1989, 32).

As we have seen, the perception that jazz was primarily a music of black origin was part of its attraction for its predominantly white players and enthusiasts in Britain. Writing of African American free jazz at the height of the women's movement of the 1970s, Val Wilmer observed that "women musicians have been actively discouraged by most of their male counterparts on a certain level" (1989, 204). Some British jazz masculinities adopted a template from black culture, one which was infused with sexual myth and white fantasy. When African American musicians first began to appear again in Britain after the unions' ban was lifted in the mid-1950s, the excitement among local players at being visited by these bands of men was intense. According to Wilmer, "for some, the most ancient of patriarchal practices prevailed: rumour hath it that one eager musician even offered his wife" (1989, 40). Whites also looked at other black men, non-Americans. One of the most frequently repeated anecdotes about the Jamaican innovator Joe Harriott, for instance, concerns his observation of a street fight between two women after a gig (see Godbolt 1989, 112). It transpires that the women are fighting over *him*. This story is significant both because it confirms a certain expectation of black masculinity in the period, and because in its repetition it bears the weight of white male awe. Indeed, maintaining a normative, heteropatriarchal identity for black musicians has been understood by some as a central function within jazz criticism as well as in informal legend, as argued in this blast from John Gill, from his book *Queer Noises: Male and Female Homosexuality in Twentieth Century Music*: "Jazz criticism, as it is practised by white heterosexual males on either side of the Atlantic, is one of the last bastions of intellectualized homophobia, a virulent bigotry which in fact leaks back into a furtive racism. . . . Heterosexual WASP critics policed the public image of their heroes. The British critic Max Jones, for example, took a whole library of unrepeatable anecdotes about Billie Holiday, among others, to his grave. Similarly, British and American critics have appointed themselves as security guards outside the closets of many jazz artists living and dead . . . It is possible that the urge to edit and suppress information about a musician's sexuality may also be linked to unresolved tensions about race" (Gill 1995, 45, 49).

Lynne Segal suggests that popular music has been a key cultural space in which to express and assess a black or a white masculinity: "Stereotypes of white masculinity—the typical silence on feelings and inability to express emotions, for example—are so much at odds with the Black jazz, blues, soul and reggae tradition, [which are] so expressive of Black men's (and women's) feelings and emotions. . . . Through dancing, athletic and erotic performance, *but most powerfully through music*, Black men could express something about the body and its physicality, about emotions and their cosmic reach, rarely found in white culture—least of all in white male culture" (Segal 1997, 188, 191; my emphasis; see also Mercer and Julien 1988, 140).

Updating Segal's list of black musics to include "the misogynist tone and masculinist direction of hip hop"—a form on which Segal is notably tacit—Paul Gilroy offers a more problematic consideration of the black male musical achievement embodied in some rap: "an amplified and exaggerated masculinity has become the boastful centrepiece of a culture of compensation that self-consciously salves the misery of the disempowered and subordinated" (Gilroy 1993, 83, 85). For the white bassist and composer Graham Collier, visible elements of homophobia and misogyny in black culture have rather undercut some of the positive expression claimed around jazz. He told me: "This is what really annoys me in all the talk of freedom [around jazz]: the lack of women and gay men in the music speaks loudly against that. I also feel strongly that, for instance, blacks and others who do make anti-gay, anti-women remarks are not respecting the freedom they want for themselves—and which is part of *all* our heritage" (personal interview, 2004).

At the same time, there has been social space in the music for what we can term alternative masculinities.[7] So jazz and improvised music have supplied both a predominantly and reassuringly heterosexual expectation *and*, concurrently, a sociocultural space for alternative constructions of masculinity. Writing of the Jazz Appreciation Society of the 1940s, Kevin Morgan identifies "its boozy masculinity. Whatever the style or location, jazz audiences and practitioners alike were in this period overwhelmingly male. . . . Among the communist element this preponderance of young men generated a virile camaraderie that apparently was inseparable from the taproom. . . . [They] even detected in some jazz fans a 'tendency to fairyness' alien to a people's music and wished the 'precious pretty boys' and their 'abnormality' some more appropriate outlet" (1998, 132).

One member of the JAS talked of jazz as "a male music" (quoted in Morgan 1998, 132). Here class and ideology, working and Marxist, map on to constructions of masculinity (and implied sexuality), and jazz is a culture where all these are negotiated, by men. This set of beliefs and practices is contrasted with those of the vegetarian Max Jones, and of the nonsmoking teetotaler Albert McCarthy, who describes himself in the first edition of *Jazz Music*, the magazine of the anarchist-leaning group the Jazz Sociological Society, as "interested in modern poetry, literature, surrealism, classical music and Eastern philosophy, opposed to haircuts and manual labour" (quoted in Morgan 1998, 131). These

31. Jeff Nuttall performing jazz's "boozy masculinity"? 1960s.

positions were being articulated—and damned, by others, for their "shaggy hair and sandals" self-indulgence (quoted in Morgan 1998, 132)—during wartime, so the JAS's hetero critical masculinity may well be touched by contempt toward the perceived indulgence of the JSS's social unconventionality at a time of global anti-fascist armed struggle. But to an extent these maps of masculine identity remained in place after the war, and may be identifiable in some of the New Orleans enthusiasts' interest in other spiritualities. One of the relatively few Jewish musicians to take up the traditional-revivalist mantle, the clarinetist Cy Laurie, gave up playing in the mid-1960s "and travelled to India to study Oriental mysticism" (Godbolt 1989, 84).[8]

SOME BISEXUAL AND GAY MEN IN JAZZ

In Gary Burton's experience in the United States, "of all the forms of music, jazz is the least tolerant of homosexuality." He elaborates on how such intolerance is predicated on a "clear perception of masculinity and macho characteristics in jazz. . . . We want our musicians to kick ass. These are still the terms in common use. There's a kind of athletic implication, too. Playing the long solo, working it out, building and building" (quoted in Gill 1995, 75). Jazz seems on first appearance to be an avowedly, forcefully heteropatriarchal sociocultural practice—to the extent that Burton can consider describing gay musical tastes as "anti-jazz." Their preference is instead for "Show music, disco, opera, classical, k. d. lang, Judy Garland, etc." (quoted in Gill 1995, 77). While such a stereotypical listing may be tinged by Burton's frustrations at coming out in a sociosexual context that seemed to undervalue his life's music choice, nonetheless it does appear that jazz is rarely if ever one of the musics perceived as sympathetic or attractive to non-heterosexualities. From a European perspective a dominant musical masculinity is recognized too. Unsurprisingly perhaps, bearing in mind their sociocultural articulation, members of the Feminist Improvising Group have been highly sensitive to the restrictions on access and expression available to anyone outside the heteropatriarchal norm. The pianist Irène Schweitzer asks: "Why are so few jazz musicians gay? This question has never been asked. The jazz musician has a totally different image. He has to act macho: to read the notes with one eye and to peek in the audience for nice women. With improvised music the consciousness of the music has changed a little bit. There are some emancipated men . . . but gay musicians? Even if they were gay, they wouldn't be showing it" (quoted in Smith 2004, 235–36). The FIG vocalist Maggie Nicols has observed a dominant practice as well, but she also suggests that the male collective constructed in ensemble improvisation may be simply too challenging for straight men to deal with: "I think that gay men have quite a hard time of it in jazz. Most male jazz musicians declare themselves to be strongly heterosexual (I find that a bit suspicious). I wonder if they fear the intimacy produced in their own music-making. Or maybe that's just the way they get close" (personal interview, 2002).

To explore gayness and jazz more fully I want to return to the 1950s, a time when homosexuality was still a crime in Britain, because there are even in these relatively early periods of British jazz creativity important contributions to gay or bisexual masculinity that in part map on to class and race. This retrospection may appear problematic, since it overlooks what John Gill calls "the queer culture wrought by gay liberation" (1995, 35)—which in Britain began to manifest itself more confidently in the wake of the Sexual Offences Act of 1967, which legitimized homosexuality. In jazz, this post-legislation queer cultural revolution never seemed to happen for men (though, as we will see, the situation differed significantly for lesbians in the women's movement in the 1970s). In fact there was some sort of identifiable public tradition in the postwar years of gay performance, as it would be retrospectively considered. Gill writes of "that curious English music-hall sense of poovery" (1995, 100), which was most audibly manifested in the extraordinary BBC radio program *Round the Horne*, the dialogue of which was peppered with the gay secret language polari (see Baker 2002). George Melly points to the "nostalgic camp" (1970, 61) of mock-Edwardian ensembles like the Temperance Seven, which popularized early-twentieth-century white English dance music during the 1950s trad revival. Such modest performative and musical moments of sexual disruption indicate the overall strength of hetero culture, while the exclusion or denial of homosexuality may have been far from unique to jazz music. In the British classical music world, for instance, Peter Pears would write to Benjamin Britten, in 1963: "We are, after all, queer & left & conshies, which is enough to put us, or make us yet put ourselves, outside the pale" (quoted in Gill 1995, 10). That the limits of male sexuality were so strictly policed during these years was fundamentally connected with issues of national identity and power, within a transatlantic cold war framework, as Lynne Segal points out: "Associations of this kind were consolidated in 1951 with the defections of British diplomats Burgess and Maclean to the Soviet Union, and the concurrent McCarthy witch-hunt against Communists and homosexuals in the United States. There was a dramatic increase in police activity against male homosexuality in both Britain and North America, culminating in Britain in the anti-homosexual drive instigated by the authorities in the early 1950s, in which young detectives were employed as *agents provocateurs*" (1997, 17).

But others were seeing in the specificity of jazz in Britain an opportunity for some sort of social innovation. Jeff Nuttall recalls, "In both the peace movement and the jazz scene in the late 1950s we were against sexual repression. The spontaneity of jazz as a form, its audibility came from its bursting into being. And of course there was a longstanding link between jazz and fucking—the sexual lyrics, southern brothels, eruptions of desire. Contrast that with Britain at the time, which was tremendously repressed. And homosexuality was still illegal—I know now that most of my young friends from then were gay—I didn't at the time" (personal interview, 2001). One Englishman whose sexuality *was* public knowledge then was Edward, Lord Montagu, organizer of the earliest British jazz festivals at the family estate in the New Forest, at Beaulieu, Hampshire. In a pair of sensational court trials in 1953 and 1954 Montagu became the highest-profile establishment figure targeted in the British authorities' wider social campaign against "inverts" (homosexuals).[9] Montagu *was* bisexual—his disagreements at the time of the trials revolved around challenging the factual status of the events that were presented in court. In his personal account, written almost fifty years later, he also articulated his objections to the criminalization of homosexuality itself: "in other words I was innocent, but had I been guilty I would insist that I had done nothing wrong, much less criminal" (2000, 107). He has ventured that his "bisexuality" (2000, 81) was perhaps facilitated by the masculine experiences of school and the army: "In many respects the all-male Grenadier Guards was much like Eton and homosexuality was a fact of life. . . . I soon found myself being invited to all-male parties of an undeniably homosexual nature" (2000, 80). One officers' evening party culminated "when George Melly, then a young naval rating and not yet known in the world of music, arrived and proceeded to do an extremely suggestive striptease, after which some of the other guests followed his example" (2000, 80). Though he fled this night "embarrassed," Montagu was to become in future years altogether more comfortable with his bisexual identity: "although I have to acknowledge that my capacity for loving members of both sexes is still regarded by some as unorthodox it seems to me entirely natural and healthy" (2000, 81). Looking more widely at the social context, it is arguable that what Montagu has called his "prosecution, or what many felt as 'persecution,' for homosexual offences" (2000, 95) has had a profound impact on gay liberation in Britain, for "it is now widely accepted that the public reaction to our trial and imprisonment was the single most important factor in the change of the law which decriminalised sexual acts between consenting male adults" in 1967 (2000, 97). He was first charged with sexual offenses against Boy Scouts in his beach hut at Beaulieu, in 1953, and acquitted. The following year, in an extraordinary and seemingly vindictive effort by the authorities to, as he put it, "get me and prove themselves right" (2000, 105), he was tried for other homosexual acts, involving male friends and two RAF hospital orderlies, that were said to have taken place almost two years before. He was found guilty of these offenses and sentenced to twelve months' imprisonment.

Montagu has directly connected the homophobic treatment he received as a result of the British establishment's "deep vein of anti-homosexual prejudice" with the establishment's perception of him as a class "traitor," a peer of the realm who was also—in his own words— "completely unsnobbish" (2000, 98, 99). "It was not just the question of homosexuality which so irked the judge," he has written, "but his obvious concern about the class differences and the dreadful social impropriety—as he saw it—of 'upper-class' people like us consorting with 'lower-class' men" (2000, 114). Such informality across the class divide could best be accompanied by that high-low pleasure music from America he had first encountered and loved while a boy in Canada, and then attending jam sessions featuring Humphrey Lyttelton at Eton. The "unconventional life" (the subtitle of his second autobiography) of this peer of the realm would include his important jazz activity beginning in 1956. Within a year of being released from jail for homosexual acts, Montagu was organizing the first of the Beaulieu Jazz Festivals on the lawns of his stately home, and inviting hundreds of fans to come and dance under the open skies. It is reasonable on one level to think of the jazz festivals, influential as we have seen, as a response to imprisonment. The very public house party of the concert in 1956 becomes then a marker of freedom on Montagu's part, a celebration of personal survival against repression, and a contumacious gesture of antipathy toward the very establishment that had so recently jailed him. In this way, Nuttall's reading of "the spontaneity of jazz as a form, its audibility c[oming] from its bursting into being" *against* sexual repression may be validated. It seems too that the crowd played its part. Perhaps recalling his early vision of George Melly privately performing for the Guards, Montagu regularly booked Melly at the Beaulieu Jazz Festivals, as a singer and an MC. Melly told me his memory of the organizer's reception by the crowd at the first: "after the homosexuality case was over, at the Beaulieu Jazz Festival [Montagu] went on stage to introduce someone in that curious high-pitched voice of his, and everyone clapped. Rousing applause. We hadn't known what the response would be — could have been jeers and homophobic jibes, but the audience rose to him" (personal interview, 2002). I asked Montagu his view of any connection between his imprisonment and the subsequent festivals:

> I see where you are coming from but that is not how I remember it at all. There was no conscious link in my mind between what had recently happened to me and the first jazz concert of 1956. It was really a modest affair organised at Beaulieu, in fact, in response to a suggestion from, I think, the Yellow Dog Jazz Club in Southampton. It *is* true to say that following its success, the event really began to evolve. As it became annually more ambitious in scope — and what I really wanted was for it to become a kind of Glyndebourne for jazz — I did begin to have a different motivation. This was partly the entrepreneurial side of trying to offer something else from Beaulieu as well as the established connection with cars, with the Motor Museum. *But it was also trying to put a new perception of Beaulieu out there, to break the connection that was there in the public mind between Beaulieu and prison. So yes, to that rather minor extent, I think, a connection may be possible.* (Personal interview, 2004)

In some ways Montagu both exploited masculine cultures and was anyway triumphantly privileged through patriarchal tradition. The manly enthusiasms of jazz and of motor cars were Montagu's chosen entrepreneurial projects at this time (the Beaulieu Motor Museum has probably become Britain's most successful permanent automobile tourist attraction), while of course the Beaulieu estate itself, and the related peerage, were the supreme prizes for competitive aristocratic masculinity, being handed on through male primogeniture. (This meant that his elder sisters could not have inherited before him.) For Montagu, the legacy of the case also affected the Beaulieu Jazz Festivals, or rather their demise. As he has recently written, "I don't think I am being unduly paranoid when I also suggest that there were some — and this included one or two senior members of the county police force — who remembered my prosecution and who believed, rather eccentrically, that I had 'got off lightly' " (Montagu 2000, 268–69). In his view they would add to his punishment by ensuring that the festivals' success would be short-lived, an outcome which they achieved by deliberately limiting the amount of police security for the festivals each summer, until effectively they became too large and self-destructed. If it is my suggestion that these founding British jazz festivals can be seen in part as Montagu's response to a powerfully homophobic witch hunt, it is Montagu's that the jazz festivals' ending in 1961 had homophobic motivations of its own.

At the same time as the English establishment was rocking and reasserting, a young, white, working-class musician thought to extend the imminent obligation of two years' National Service and sign up into the British Army for five years as a band boy instead. The military forces were the single option to a solid musical education accessible to him, a route that would later be followed, as we have seen, by other musicians. Graham Collier would soon go on to be the first British musician to study at Berklee in Boston, an institution understood by the British jazz community as an important imprimatur of American jazz authority or authenticity. In the 1960s and 1970s Collier was a bassist and bandleader, turning increasingly to composition, and in the 1980s and 1990s he established and directed the jazz course at the Royal Academy of Music and played a key role in founding a big band of younger musicians, Loose Tubes. He has also written a number of books about jazz. Collier is one of the few "out" gay musicians to emerge from Britain. He currently lives in and works from Spain with his partner John Gill, the author of *Queer Noises*. Though broadly concurrent, Collier's experiences as a gay man, in the masculine spaces of the military forces and jazz alike, have been quite different from those of Edward Montagu: "There was nothing gay in the British Army [in the 1950s]; really any overt or known activity would have been quite impossible. When I won a *Down Beat* magazine scholarship to study at Berklee in 1961, there was a pragmatism about it: leaving the army, going to the States, focusing on jazz. In Boston in the early 1960s there were gay cruising grounds, and people went round those, but I wouldn't necessarily say that being in America at that time—or being out of Britain—meant any greater opportunity to be more free or open about being gay" (personal interview, 2004).

I asked Collier about the extent to which being gay had influenced his musical practice, and he outlined for me some ways in which it was visible, before going on to take issue with what he took as the assumptions of the questioning:

In 1974 we did a benefit gig for the Campaign for Homosexual Equality, at their conference in Sheffield. It was a one-off because I recognised that unless you were involved in an organisation it was difficult for the musicians to do gigs for nothing. In the later 1970s I remember playing with Tom Robinson for a week at the Shaw Theatre in London. That was good, playing double bass with all his pop songs, including "Glad to Be Gay." And a few years before that, the early 1970s, I put on a words-and-music event at Camden Festival, featuring a narrator reading from my personal diaries along with commissioned music. I was effectively painting a self-portrait through jazz and diary, though not all the words were mine by any count. Whitman, Cavafy, straight writers and so on. It was a self-portrait through jazz and words, from all areas of my life, not just the gay side.

But actually I think that there is much more than being gay which made me into the composer that I am. For instance, being British, from a working-class background, studying at Berklee, what I listened to, read, looked at, etc. etc. I think the stress on gay influences is wrong: as I read once, someone said "Liking [the early composer and lutenist John] Dowland has had far more influence on me and my art than being gay." Another reason I object is that it's not the sort of thing that would get asked about a straight person. [They might cite the importance of t]he family, of course — but often that's a throwaway, like "I wanna thank my family for being there" — and of course God. But good relationships of any kind form one's personality, and mine with John has been influential of course. And has led to a settled life, which has again had an influence, opposite to that if I had not had that — and might have ended up lonely and sad whatever my sexual orientation. (Personal interview, 2004)

What John Gill calls "the myth about queers versus jazz" (1995, 48) manifested itself in Collier's experience in a reverse way: "There were odd moments of homophobia. I used to review jazz records in *Gay News*, and when ECM used a quotation from one of my reviews, with the magazine credit, in an advertisement, someone did write in protest about how he would never buy any of their records ever again. Because I'd written in *Gay News* about some interesting music, and ECM had quoted from it! On another occasion in the late 1980s, a television documentary about my work included a shot of my partner John at the end giving me a requested pint of beer and a big kiss. I didn't mind at all that this was broadcast (I remember my mother objecting slightly), but there were comments about it in the jazz press" (Collier, personal interview, 2004).

Both Gill and Val Wilmer (1989, 168–69) offer their versions of the relatively minor homophobic slights that Collier experienced.[10] What is interesting about them is that they came from *within* the jazz community. Gill recalls that the critic Jim Godbolt "complained 'although John may be Graham's inamorata' what did that information add to the music?," and he continues: "passing over the feminine noun 'inamorata,' which Godbolt probably intended as a sly dig at effeminate homos, Godbolt's complaints, which were discussed at length by friends in the media and music circles, also carried a second-order meaning, . . . 'I don't mind gays but . . .', a form of wish-fulfilment censorship which I consider to be little more than gentrified fascism. The subtext of Godbolt's column . . . was an urgent need to erase this evidence that queers may have infiltrated his exclusive train-spotters' club" (Gill 1995, 71).

As we will see, throughout this time other queer noises were being made and heard in jazz and improvised musics that contributed to and were informed by the women's movement, that interrogated, subverted, and sometimes outright rejected the dominant or subdominant masculinities of the British jazz scene.

THE SISTERHOOD OF SPIT:[11]
JAZZ AS/AND (THE) WOMEN'S MOVEMENT

If it wasn't "women's lib" yet, at least it was *ad lib.*

—MARIAN MCPARTLAND, remembering her early days in
the United States in 1947 (quoted in Maher 1987, ix)

The English pianist McPartland was on to something when she punned on "women's lib" and *ad lib*: the first "lib" is from the Latin *liber*, meaning "free," the second from the Latin *libitum*, meaning "pleasure." The chance relation signifies: of course, as I go on to show, there are still-obscured histories of women playing the musics of and around jazz as well as important and considered activist contributions by engaged feminist musicians, but I want to pause first to consider the (politics of) pleasure that jazz could afford to those women brave enough over the decades to—well, what, step on to stage, or merely the dance floor? There are links in the reception of American popular music to be constructed and explored between the female body, pleasure, and liberation. Eric Hobsbawm, for example, has identified the "link between *the dance revolution*, even specifically between the new primacy of rhythm in social dancing, and the emancipation of women" in the early twentieth century (1998, 267; my emphasis), as American dance music was enjoyed in the new spaces and practices of British society. In his study of early jazz and gender in Australia, Bruce Johnson argues that the pleasure and liberation of jazz's dance "made it particularly hospitable as a site of emancipated femininity": " 'The Jazz' was imagined and practised as a dance—a process in which active participation is the actual condition of its consumption. To a greater extent than is already the case in improvised music in performance, 'the jazz' was seen to be something done by what we would now think of primarily as its audience. You didn't dance to jazz that was being made exclusively by people who were separate by virtue of instrumental ownership, competence and the space defined by a stage. You 'jazzed' " (Johnson 2000, 64, 65). This dance imaginary allowed glimpses of sexuality; as one flapper impeccably put it: "we *do* jazz in order to experience a mild—very mild—sex adventure, and to allow our repressed polyandrous instinct to get a breath of fresh air" (quoted in Johnson 2000, 66–67; emphasis in original).

The situation in Australia is relevant here because it impinges on jazz in Britain. As we have seen, in the early postwar decades Britain entered a sustained, if problematic and exploitative, period of cultural outernationalism, as it sought to capitalize both on its place at the heart of the Commonwealth and on its continuing close relations with the United States. I have touched elsewhere on the powerful impact of the (all-male) Australian Graeme Bell Jazz Band on British traditional and revivalist jazz of the late 1940s and early 1950s. Much of the antagonism toward the music as social practice as well as the enthusiasm for it was tied up with the question of whether *dancing* to it was acceptable—but it is worth emphasizing that a key part of the band's attraction lay in its "jazz and dance" policy, frequently cited as significantly counter to the respectful, analytical atmosphere of many of the Rhythm Clubs then still popular in Britain. In Bell's words: "We found this approach so stuffy. It contradicted the very reasons that attracted us to jazz in the first place; the breaking free of the restrictions, rigidity and seriousness of European music. . . . So we decided to open up our own club with the slogan 'jazz for dancing.' . . . With posters and flyers proclaiming 'Jazz for Dancing' and 'You *Can* Dance to Jazz' we opened [in London] on Monday, 2 February 1948, on a regular, once-a-week basis. . . . The people started coming in . . . the women in particular had come to jive and jitterbug" (quoted in Johnson 2000, 155).

As Johnson comments, "that moment incorporated the active participation of the audiences . . . regarding jazz, dance, and emancipative gendered practices" in particular (2000, 154, 155). In Britain of the 1950s, "still a pretty drab nation," with notable repressive tendencies, as we have seen, the other new world would finally, with the transatlantic unions' agreement on musical exchanges, be directly experienced too. Val Wilmer has well articulated the attraction for British women of black American musical masculinity: "Just the *way* these Americans looked, even wearing their band uniforms, had an enormous effect on someone used to economies, as I was. For a start, they were clearly well-fed. Well-dressed too, in mohair suiting and overcoats luxuriously lined with fur. Invariably these tours took place in the colder months, and the Black musicians' faces would be carefully creamed against the weather and ashy complexions, leaving them sleek and ageless. . . . All of them reeked of cologne. After two decades of grappling with blue serge and utility underwear, those British women 'on the scene,' as they were known, flocked around their visitors" (Wilmer 1989, 40; emphasis in original). To free and fulfil their polyandrous instincts, no doubt, as the Australian flapper had dreamed of while dancing the jazz three decades earlier. For white women of the Commonwealth, jazz offered the prospect of libidinal pleasure, even if through the corporeal practice of dance rather than sex "on the scene."[12] The powerfully charged masculinity of London a decade later is acknowledged by Maggie Nicols in her explanation of why she chose the voice as her medium of improvisation: "It's true that it was a male-dominated scene—because I didn't see many other women there, and it was also a time of awakening sexuality for me, and to be honest I did idealise the men, and I was pretty young, but it was exciting with all these men around. I was socialised—we all were: women sing, men played instruments. It didn't even occur to me that I could do something different. I'd never seen, say, [the saxophonist] Kathy Stobart, so there were very few models for aspiring women in the scene. This is probably why I came to use my voice like an instrument. All that passion for instrumental music got poured into my voice" (personal interview, 2002).

Pouring instrument into voice is the acceptable route for women in jazz, in popular music more widely, perhaps not least because, as Lucy Green reminds us, it confirms "the unsuitability of any serious and lasting connection between woman and instrument, woman and technology" (quoted in Bayton 1998, 13). Yet I want to use the experience of another vocalist, who happens also to be an instrumentalist, to move the discussion on from the Barthesian cluster of pleasure, the body, and the voice and into a historical consideration of the spaces available to women in jazz and popular music. I asked the English singer and horn player Kate Westbrook about her thoughts on women in jazz:

> The consistent lack of women in the whole jazz scene, and the wider one of which we are part, has troubled me, of course. For instance, when I first joined the Brass Band and we did festivals around 1973–75, sometimes I was the only woman playing in the entire festival. There might be one American woman singer, but often not a woman instrumentalist. The situation is improving but even so *there remains a pathetically small number of women*, especially instrumentalists, and I think it is difficult for those that are there. The way I personally address it is not by being militant, but by working through my art, and sticking at it over the years. Other women approach the situation differently—good luck to my militant sisters. We played with Henry Cow (who were from outside the jazz scene) in 1976 for some concerts and tours. There were women in the band—Lindsay Cooper and Georgie Born, both terrific improvisers—and there was something liberating and powerful in that for me. (Personal interview, 2003)

Such observations as these sound familiar, and are undoubtedly valid. It is also true, though, that all-woman ensembles and projects have had a significant, long-lasting presence in popular music. These ensembles predated jazz, were musically transformed by jazz, and in turn made a conscious political effort to transform jazz itself. That is largely the subject of the rest of this chapter.

32. The tenor saxophonist
Kathy Stobart, Great Harwood
Jazz Club, Lancashire, 1978.

In a slim volume of memoirs and family photographs written in her elderly years, *A View from the Bandstand*, Greta Kent traces from personal experience the significant tradition of ladies' orchestras in Britain from late Victorian times until well into the twentieth century. As Carole Spedding explains, "many of us assume that women's bands in this country are an invention of the contemporary women's movement. Not so. . . . 'Ladies' orchestras' were a regular fixture at holiday resorts, teashops, pavilions and concert halls. For example, when J. Lyons opened his very first Cornerhouse in 1909 at The Strand, London, these groups of professional and skilled lady musicians regularly provided entertainment for the customers" (quoted in Kent 1983, 5).[13] Indeed, when the Maison Lyons was opened at Marble Arch in 1933, an "all-ladies band" was still considered an important attraction (Kent 1983, 21). Kent's grandmother had organized an all-woman ensemble, the Anglo Saxon Ladies' Band, as far back as the 1870s or 1880s, and her mother, aunts, female cousins, and sisters would all be similarly involved. Margaret Myers's research on ladies' orchestras across Europe has found that "thousands of women instrumental musicians found employment in these orchestras. Ladies' orchestras must thus be regarded—along with music teaching—as a major source of employment for women instrumentalists" (Myers 2000, 190). In the United States too ladies' orchestras were in existence—according to Linda Dahl, the first was formed in Chelsea, Massachusetts, in 1884 (1984, 45). Sophie Fuller contextualizes the development of ladies' orchestras within emancipatory "New Woman" discourse: "One of the hardest-fought battles was for women to be accepted into professional orchestras. In the late nineteenth century women reacted to their exclusion from the mainstream orchestras by forming their own all-woman orchestras. These were both amateur and professional groups, and proved to be a vital training ground for many women musicians who were then able to take the place of the male musicians who had been called up to fight during the First World War. When the men returned, a fierce campaign to keep the women in the orchestras was waged by the Society of Women Musicians (founded in 1911) . . . [but w]omen continued to be excluded from many of the major British orchestras throughout the 1920s and 1930s" (Fuller 1995, 27).

With the Jazz Age there was some stylistic, sartorial, and instrumental adjustment, and the widespread introduction of "talkies" in cinemas closed one important avenue for employment, but experienced female musicians in the realm of popular music could still find a place. Kent's mother, Nellie Baldwin, had started on violin and piano in the nineteenth century, but fortunately for her, in the light of changing musical tastes in the new century, she "broke with tradition for lady musicians and took to playing the trombone" (Kent 1983, 7). Kent continues: "The first 'British Syncopated Orchestra and Entertainers' appeared at Kingsway Hall, London, on Monday 1st October 1921 and, according to a newspaper report, augured well for the prosperity of the latest enterprise. The writer of this report was '. . . amazed to see the inclusion of women and especially the trombonist . . .' who incidentally, happened to be my mother. Naturally the ladies had to follow suit with this new style of music, but with a less noisy and raucous style of jazz, for the stage and dance halls. The ancient Lyceum Theatre in London was soon converted into a vast ballroom with an all-feminine band. Among the many popular leaders of this latest craze were . . . Miss Ivy Benson with her All-Girl Dance Band" (1983, 36–38).

Myers identifies effectively a second wave of ladies' orchestras

stretching up to the 1940s, and it is here that there is a blurring between the early repertoire of forms like light opera, music hall, popular song, overtures, and formal dances and the later requirements of
dance bands and jazz-tinged music, even if some of the musicians were
playing an obviously gendered "*less* noisy and raucous style of jazz." As
new African American music "threaten[ed] to oust the older European
repertory," Myers writes, so "banjos, saxophones, jazz trumpets, trombones, clarinets, different types of percussion, plucked double basses,
and accordions all found their ways into the hands of women, especially those of the second wave" (Myers 2000, 196). In the United
States this same transition from ladies' orchestras to all-woman jazz
ensembles and dance bands was occurring. Dahl mentions the trombonist Marie Lucas of New York taking over the musical direction of
the Lafayette Ladies' Orchestra around 1915 and leading a number of
all-woman ensembles playing the new music in East Coast theaters,
or the multi-instrumentalist Alyse Wills crossing over from the Chicago Women's Symphony to Ina Ray Hutton's Melodears in the 1930s.
In fact, Dahl has gone further, to argue that "with groups like the
[International] Sweethearts [of Rhythm] and the Melodears achieving
broad popular appeal in the United States [in the 1930s and 1940s], it
wasn't long before the all-woman–band idea caught on in other countries as well," citing a number of British examples (1984, 57). However, it is clear that the all-woman template was in existence in Britain, in Europe, already, and had been for perhaps half a century. It
was not imported from the United States at this time; what *was* imported was the new music, which transformed the instrumentation,
repertoire, and performance style of the European ladies' orchestras tradition. There were transitional difficulties in this new repertoire, the
result of the new music's contingencies around sex, race, and commercialism. Myers charts the difficult balancing act: "to maintain their
moral reputations, . . . [women musicians] had to perform art music
and, if possible, prove themselves to be artists of the highest rank. To
maintain their popularity, they had to play jazz, making efforts at the
same time to avoid undermining their respectability and their employment possibilities" (2000, 200). Lucy Green writes of the continuing
"mismatch between women's group instrumental performance on the
one hand and feminine sexual display on the other" (1997, 70).

I want to look more closely at the all-woman ensemble identified by Greta Kent above as one of the notable British bands, for with it we can trace a thin but alluring and significant sociomusical lineage that spans the centuries: from the Victorian ladies' orchestras that have been read in part as responses to female emancipation, through the social change and absent masculinity of the world wars that permitted all-woman dance and swing bands, to the women-only world jazz projects from the 1970s that were informed by feminist and sometimes strategically separatist ideologies.[14] The big band leader Ivy Benson's unique achievement was to run an all-woman ensemble that was to endure in various forms for around forty years, gaining a national and then international reputation. Benson, born in Yorkshire, worked especially with northern musical talent, young women who were often educated in local brass bands. She had herself been playing saxophone in a local British Legion band at the age of fourteen, while brass players like the trumpeter Gracie Cole (who joined in 1945), or in the early 1970s the trombonist Annie Whitehead, brought their expertise from brass bands. Benson was interested in the transformative possibilities of music making for women — in particular, owing to her geographical origins, working-class women. She could indeed, as she claimed, transform a factory worker into a musician (O'Brien 1995, 73). Benson herself played in all-woman ensembles throughout the 1930s, including Edna Croudson's Rhythm Girls, Teddy Joyce's New Ladies' Orchestra, and then Joyce's Girl Friends, though she could be critical of the musical value expected of such ensembles: "All you had to do was toodle. . . . Once upon a time it was almost laughable when one heard a girl attempt a jazz solo" (quoted in Dahl 1984, 57). During these early years, as Brian Ravenhill informs us (2004), there was a background of some resentment from the formative Musicians' Union toward "girl players," so Benson was already experiencing gender discrimination within a predominantly masculine popular music world. According to a feature in the *Sunday Times* in 1975, her own first band at the end of the 1930s marked "the beginning of an unbroken struggle against discrimination expressed by poor payment, the contempt of musicians and other bandleaders, even arrangers who provided scores with deliberate mistakes" (Atticus 1975).[15] Benson's bands made pursuing musical ambition for women in dance and jazz accessible and possible. Sheila Tracy, for example, who joined Benson's band as a trombonist in 1956, recalled of her earlier musical education, when "jazz was absolutely taboo": "I was sitting in the orchestra as a Royal Academy student in the late 1940s, fourth desk of the second fiddle, scraping away, surrounded by women. I looked up at the brass where there wasn't a woman in sight; all men were sitting up there. I thought it'd be rather nice to sit up there" (quoted in O'Brien 1995, 75)—which she subsequently did with Benson. Though they occurred before her time with Benson, Tracy recalls that the band suffered moments of dismissal and resentment from men. Evidently these stories did the rounds with later band members, and the all-woman identity was maintained and rejustified by reference to a history of experience of discrimination: "Women [musicians] were rubbished then. . . . 'She looks pretty, but don't expect her to play the same way as a man'—that was the attitude. . . . When the BBC made Ivy their resident house band [during the Second World War], all hell broke loose, because it was the plum job in the country. The male bandleaders didn't want to know her, they loathed her guts. And the reviews for the first broadcast were vitriolic. . . . [After the war a] committee of bandleaders was set up and they all closed ranks, saying, 'We're not having Ivy Benson in.' She said, 'Don't you want me in? Forget it, I don't want to be in!' " (Tracy, quoted in O'Brien 1995, 75).

During and immediately after the war, Benson's working relationship with the BBC endured success and failure in ways which are at least in part concerned with gender. As Tracy observes above, the nomination of Ivy Benson's Ladies' Dance Orchestra as resident dance band for BBC Radio in 1943 provoked outrage among other bandleaders, in particular, Ravenhill writes, Billy Ternent, who was a leader of the BBC Orchestra (Ravenhill 2004). After the war Benson's success found her caught up in a power struggle between the established theater management and the newly programming BBC television: the band was booked for the "first post-war broadcasts on BBC television, but was forced to withdraw after the Stoll Theatre group, fearful of the repercussions of this All Girl phenomenon, threatened to cancel her contracts" with the agency (Ravenhill 2004). In a widely publicized spat, Benson was caught between residual and emergent entertainment forms—the theater and music hall quite correctly sensing a threat to their very existence from television—and she was forced to honor her theater contracts instead of benefiting from a prestigious early opportunity to lay claim to a place in the new media. Benson's alternative routes to maintaining an active band were to keep playing for British military forces overseas, and to exploit the holiday camp summer season residencies at home. But it did begin to have a negative impact on the repertoire, as the drummer Crissy Lee remembers: "When the Beatles became big, the swing side of a band was no longer popular . . . people were requesting 'Hard day's night,' and we had to do everything from country to pop. I didn't enjoy that, the band lost some of its identity. There were a lot, like Ted Heath, who dug their heels in, but their identity was more established with big bands and they were *men*. Poor Ivy, she always had it difficult. To keep her band going, she had to go with the flow" (quoted in O'Brien 1993, 34; emphasis in original).

While it is appropriate to outline how the male-dominated music organizations slighted and obstructed Benson, it is equally important to acknowledge her achievements over sixty years in the business, forty of them running an all-woman ensemble of some kind. Foremost among these is the inspiration and empowerment that Benson seemed able to transmit to her musicians around female music making. This is most forcefully illustrated in their subsequent careers: it matters that on leaving Benson, a number of her musicians would go on to lead or contribute to other, newer, all-woman ensembles. For instance, Gracie Cole (trumpet with Benson, 1945) was later associated with Gracie Cole's All Girl Orchestra, Crissy Lee (drums, 1960s) with the Crissy Lee Big Band, Deirdre Cartwright (guitar, 1970s) with Jam Today, the Guest Stars, the Sisterhood of Spit, and Lydia D'Ustebyn's Ladies Swing Orchestra, and Annie Whitehead (trombone, 1970s) with the Guest Stars, Gail Thompson's Gail Force, the Sisterhood of Spit, and Lydia D'Ustebyn's Ladies Swing Orchestra.

It matters too that in the 1980s Benson's all-woman big band template was reactivated by feminist musicians like Cartwright and White-head—for its social scale, educative process, and as a celebratory historical gesture. So big bands like the attitudinally punky Sisterhood of Spit or Lydia D'Ustebyn's gently parodic Swing Orchestra again functioned as "a training ground for a further generation of women musicians," who constituted "a significant core of talented, experienced professional female musicians, at the centre of a changing landscape of (often jazz-orientated) all-woman bands in London with an overlapping membership" (Bayton 1998, 73–74). Cartwright explained to me her view of Benson's significance and influence:

What Ivy did was something special. I do think about that. In classical music, there may be prejudice and discrimination against, for instance, women, but at the same time you know where you can go—
there are grades, exams, orchestras, structures or lines that you can
follow to get some sort of career or recognition. For young women
wanting to start out in jazz that simply was not the case—except for
Ivy. And she was so important for that, there was a sort of presence
there, and there was an identifiable route for progression. Because
she offered a professional band, with high standards—it was an
opportunity, for training, for getting taken seriously. We've talked
about this and I'm fairly confident Annie [Whitehead] feels the
same.

Lydia D'Ustebyn's Swing Orchestra was in a way a tribute. Lydia
was a fictional character of course, but she was vaguely based on Ivy
Benson—a strict, feared, and also admired bandleader. We would
have running jokes at gigs, apologising to the audience for the late
appearance of Lydia, she's missed her train or something. Not that
Ivy was ever late for a gig, but the whole thing, a twelve- or fourteen-
piece all-woman dance band, was modeled a bit on Ivy, and our
memories of working with her. . . . The Sisterhood of Spit big band
was 22–24 strong, so there was certainly an element of scale, of impact with that. . . . It probably is significant that some of the musicians involved in these large all-woman ensembles had been with
Ivy; she gave us a template, and we carried something on. (Personal
interview, 2004)

In the end it is difficult to demur from Lucy O'Brien's view that
Benson's bands were "one of the major routes for women instrumentalists into jazz and studio work in Britain," as well as "a rare example
of women musicians working in solidarity" (1995, 72, 77). But solidarity could be bluntly expressed (after all, Benson was from Yorkshire,
a county whose people are renowned for their bluntness). The saxophonist Barbara Thompson worked a summer season with Benson as a
teenager, playing lead alto in 1964. She recalls: "I had a horrible sound
on the alto. . . . Once, we were doing a Sunday concert, when we'd have
to accompany people like Cleo Laine and Ted Ray. Ivy seized the sax
out of my hands and carried on playing the part, to show me how to
do it! . . . But it was very good training. I could read anything after

33. Lydia D'Ustebyn's Ladies Swing Orchestra, 1983. © Val Wilmer.

that" (quoted in Cook 1992, 18). Over the decades, Brian Ravenhill calculates, around 250 female musicians graduated from Benson's "Ivy League" academy (Ravenhill 2004; O'Brien 1995, 73). This is indeed a significant social, musical, and educational lifetime's achievement.

Some of the women playing in later versions of Ivy Benson's bands signal the progression from female to feminist music activity. Cartwright and Whitehead are emblematic, since in the 1980s both belonged to the feminist all-woman collective the Guest Stars (a sextet which also, by the way, formed the core of Lydia D'Ustebyn's Swing Orchestra). The repertoire of this successful band ranged from jazz to Latin, African to pop, always with space for improvisation, and in their live performances always emphasizing dancing by the audience. But even in their repertoire there was a gendered position. For these women musicians, it was important to be more fluid in their musical approach, less masculinely purist (in comparison with, say, a Ken Colyer or an Evan Parker).[16] Genre-hopping or genre-mixing became an informed, gendered response to certain ideas of male jazz purity, though for the Guest Stars there was also a pragmatic issue simply about the range of musical interests that the band members enjoyed. Deirdre Cartwright recalled: "there was no female tradition as such, so yes, we had to create our own genre, and at the beginning it could be difficult. But it's probably fairer to say that our repertoire came about because of the influences we all brought to it. It was around the start of the world music scene, and we were interested in postbop jazz—Mingus and Monk; soul vocals and harmonies; and African sounds were fresh to us" (personal interview, 2004). John Fordham touched on gender and genre in a jazz piece in the *Guardian* in 1989 entitled "Woman Talk," about Whitehead and the percussionist Cheryl Alleyne: "Women instrumentalists have become more visible, more audible, in the [British] jazz world. . . . What unites them as much as their membership of a growing force of British high-class women instrumentalists in what has until recently been a man's profession, is the originality and independence that they have developed through exposure to a mixed musical culture, in which definitions of musical differences have never made much sense" (Fordham 1996, 206–7).

Bands like the Guest Stars could recognize the critical limitations of such a position, that "the white Western musician with flapping ears" (their words: quoted in Lock 1985, 41) was in danger of replicating colonial relations in a homogenizing blur of pastiche or robbery. They were also sensitive, though, to the implications of their activity as women in a male-dominated form. The Guest Stars developed out of the wider feminist movement's grassroots interrogation of the music industry in the 1970s, in particular around the feminist rock band Jam Today, which both Cartwright and one of the Guest Stars' bassists, Alison Rayner, worked in. According to Mavis Bayton in *Frock Rock*: "An outstanding example of this DIY approach was 1970s/early 1980s Jam Today, who set up their own record label (Stroppy Cow), producing, engineering, promoting, and distributing their own records. Alison Rayner: 'The idea wasn't just for our band. It was a feminist label with a specific kind of feminist politics: anti-capitalism and the straight music business, and the charts, and all that kind of stuff.' Members of Jam Today were involved in setting up Women's Liberation Music Projects, a Women's Music Newsletter, and women's music workshops. They also established an all-female P[ublic] A[ddress] company that enabled a decade of women-only bops to flourish" (Bayton 1998, 202; see also Houghton 1986).

In a feature on the band in the *Wire* in 1985, Graham Lock describes some of the "enormous" pressures on being a feminist collective in jazz:

"The Guest Stars are trying simultaneously to blaze political trails, develop musically, stay together, and remain in touch with their populist roots. On top of that, they're also in what [the pianist Laka] Daisical calls 'the cleft stick' of keeping faith with the fact that they are *women* musicians, while also wanting to be recognised as *musicians* rather than tokens" (Lock 1985, 41; emphasis in original). It seems that the danger remained the same as it had been for all-women dance bands in the 1940s, or for ladies' orchestras in Victorian times: the (sometimes unspoken) accusation or assumption that women-only ensembles were a gimmick, that they privileged entertainment over musical expression, or they were really simply arenas for second-raters and amateurs. The Guest Stars' drummer Josefina Cupido sought to address directly the issue of being a female improvising percussionist: "I'm forever trying to find the female style of playing the drums. . . . Well, I say that as a joke, but I really don't know. . . . I often think about that in relation to my instrument, because you do have to be so overtly physical to play the drums, and given the fact that all the music that has gone before has been written mostly by men — the way the rhythms have developed and so on — it *is* male music, I think. . . . I often feel inadequate on my instrument, and I know that has to do with technique, but then in a sense I don't know what technique is — like, who made all the rules and the standards . . . it's men, isn't it?" (quoted in Lock 1985, 39; emphasis in original).

Yet in music production and education, Bayton has argued forcefully for "the strategic effectiveness of *separatism* as a temporary political strategy for increasing the number of young women musicians" (1998, 193; my emphasis). This does correlate to an extent with the actual opinions of women in jazz education — Huxley's and English's survey in *Women and Jazz* found that "33% of women who want to learn jazz would be more attracted to a course led by a female tutor or organised for women only, demonstrating a clear demand for positive discrimination in jazz education." This preference is not absolute, though, which perhaps suggests a certain recognition or realistic approval of male authority in existing jazz expertise: 58 percent of the female respondents to the survey said that it did not matter whether a course was led by a female tutor, and 40 percent said it did not matter if a course was organized for women only (Huxley and English 1998, 25, 15).

FIG

Politics though are thrust upon women in jazz all the time. No one
asks a male musician why he only plays with other men, for instance,
and is that part of some social comment?—DEIRDRE CARTWRIGHT
(personal interview, 2004)

There is one further, powerful, collective statement of women in improvised music in Britain that must be looked at, one which presented
audiences with "the spectacle of so many unsupervised and unpredictable women on the stage" (Smith 2004, 238). This was an ambitious
project: it aimed to be multiracial, to draw from and contribute to pan-
European music scenes, to be inclusive of a range of technical musical
skills, as well as of a range of music styles, with an avant-garde aesthetic that sought to interrogate the distinctions between music and
performance, the limits of what was acceptably musical, to construct
new audiences from other identity communities, and to do all of these
in a discourse that explicitly was ideologically framed. This was the
Feminist Improvising Group, founded in 1977. FIG's vocalist Maggie
Nicols recalled:

> Actually we called ourselves the *Women's* Improvising Group, but
> when we got the leaflet back for the first gig we were doing, it said
> *Feminist* Improvising Group. So the original strong political state-
> ment of the band's name never even came from us! But we just
> thought, "OK, they've called us feminist, we'll work with that." We
> got all these dykes to come along. That first gig was an absolutely in-
> credible night for us, it really was, it was mind-blowing. I always *wish*
> it had been recorded. It was at a festival for a new campaign, Music
> for Socialism. The dykes we'd invited were all into disco and soul,
> but they sat there through all the other improvisers, until we came
> on. They laughed their heads off; it was performance, music, com-
> edy, a really great mixture, so liberating and open, accessible, and
> with a focus on women's experience, mundane daily things. At the
> end, there was a big discussion with the audience, a perfect musical-
> political combination. (Personal interview, 2002)

FIG included musicians from British improvisation like Nicols, from
rock and art music like the cellist Georgie Born and Lindsay Cooper

of the progressive jazz-rock band Henry Cow, and Dutch and Swiss improvisers like the pianist Irène Schweitzer. Combining this musical breadth with cultural experience from alternative theater (so that FIG's vocalist Sally Potter could make connections with the English music hall tradition, for instance: Wickes 1999, 241) and political activism (from the revolutionary left to the Musicians' Union to the Women's Liberation Movement) gives a sense of the multiple agendas that could energize or conflict in FIG events. In spite of the single gender message, for Nicols it was the diversity inherent in FIG that allowed competing or complementary codes to be expressed: these could be "even as basic as divisions between the musicians' different class, race and educational backgrounds. But also a range of musical technique, and expectations of what we might do: we were a mix. The politics of FIG were in our social and physical relationships. We were comfortable with physical intimacy. What we had was a *social virtuosity*, a way of being different, and I think we developed a confidence in that" (personal interview, 2002). That first FIG performance was at the Almost Free Theatre in London in October 1977. According to a review in *Musics*, a magazine produced by activists and musicians from Music for Socialism and the London Musicians' Collective, the political context of the evening of performances and discussions itself held serious expectations.[17] That the review was unusually co-written, by Susan Hemmings and Norma Pitfield, itself signaled a dialogic awareness of political process. Quoted here at length, it captures the sense of excitement and innovation experienced by engaged audience members:

> We expected [FIG's performance] to comment on improvisation as a form, and feminist socialist relevance of that form, and the position of women musicians within the male dominated music world. . . . The women's set began unobtrusively with a bit of cleaning up on stage—and at first this housework went unnoticed, as it normally does by those serviced. Soon, however, the servility of the [white] cleaning woman (Maggie) grew into irritation with the whiney demands of her [black] child (Corine). The tension gradually increased as the working mother tried to instil a respectful anticipation for the important middleclass lady musicians still off stage. Lindsay and Georgie then appeared suitably made-up and hairstyled as befits concert playing ladies. . . . This . . . was a welcome contrast to the

34. The Feminist Improvising Group in its début performance at the Music for Socialism festival, Almost Free Theatre, London, 1977. From left: Corine Liensol (trumpet), Maggie Nicols (voice), Georgie Born (cello), Lindsay Cooper (bassoon), Cathy Williams (piano). © Val Wilmer.

previous performances [of the evening] which had been singularly humourless. But the point lay, of course, not in that contrast, but in their use of slapstick to convey a violent response to the imposed domesticity which limits women's lives, and from which it seems *no* woman is ever set free. The male adventurist musician can use his claim to creative specialness to relieve himself of all sorts of responsibilities his female counterpoint is never allowed to shrug off. . . . The hoover, softly whirring in endless vacuity, and the kenwood mixer, grinding and circling, were shown for what they are — not liberators, but enslaving accoutrements, women-assigned instruments that allow precious little room to improvise. (Hemmings and Pitfield 1977, 20; emphasis in original)

The performative aspects of FIG could themselves militate against musical acceptance, which was a political position when what was deemed acceptable in improvisation was still largely a male evaluation. Georgie Born recalls, "We brought along a load of washing-up and we were washing plates, and we did non-sound things too, like

I had an onion which I was peeling under people's noses" (quoted in Wickes 1999, 241). Unlike a previous musically improvised domesticity—skiffle, a music of the austerity era of the 1950s, with broom handles, tea chests, washboards, and thimbles—this gendered charivari was a knowing ideological culture.[18] Even so, FIG performances were not always enjoyed, as such. Even Val Wilmer sensed a certain ambivalence toward FIG's kind of improvised performance. Wilmer recognized the difficulty that new audiences found with free improvisation, and she had her reservations about a music that seemed to be leaving (male) instrumental expression behind. She wrote about it subsequently: "the 'free music' idiom was unknown to most of the audience, and unease and uncertainty were expressed about whether, being so 'inaccessible,' theirs was an élitist concept. It was bitterly frustrating for the musicians involved to be rejected in this way. Most of them had a history of struggle against male refusal to allow them a place on the bandstand. Now, having shown that not only could they play their instruments but were equipped to handle the most demanding of concepts, they were under attack from the quarter where they most needed friends. . . . FIG's attempts to incorporate 'the sounds of women's work into a work of women's sounds,' Lindsay Cooper's description of a piece which used cake-whisk, hairdryer and vacuum-cleaner, did not necessarily endear it to me when I yearned for the dramatic lovecry of Albert Ayler or the double-clutching drumbeat of a New Orleans parade" (Wilmer 1989, 285).

Of course, Ayler's masculine cry or scream, or the uniformed jazz marching *à la militaire*, may have been precisely what FIG wished to problematize musically. Indeed, FIG members discussed the gender assumptions of improvisation, and the difficulty of moving toward a non-hierarchical music, in an article that was a self-edited transcription of a group discussion. This auto-critique spoke of the strengths and weaknesses of an improvisatory praxis predicated on an existing masculine prerogative (such as the aggressive, competitive music produced and valorized by many modern and free male musicians and fans that I discussed earlier):

SALLY POTTER: One of the pitfalls of women working collectively is that in an attempt to de-hierarchise the product there's often a sort of curiously uniform bitty quality to the product because nobody wants to soar up and take on a so-called hierarchical position — musically that can lead to one of the weaknesses I've heard in FIG which is that sometimes people don't take the space and confidence to develop a line or idea.

GEORGIE BORN: Often because other people step in and don't allow things to happen. To me it's much more to do with habits about who does what. It's not to do with the other thing which is a general grey acceptance that for anyone to take an initiative is individualistic.

CORINE LIENSOL: Who, what, solo? Me? I'm feminist — after you. (FIG 1978, 11)

Interestingly this problematic would be articulated a few years later in the feminist collective of the Guest Stars, musically a more structured and more pop- and dance-oriented ensemble, but with some similarities in terms of ideological underpinning. The Guest Stars guitarist Cartwright has described the band as "a support network," while pointing out that "though there were lots of leadership issues in that band, there were no individual leaders" (personal interview, 2004). The pianist Laka Daisical projected forward from the Guest Stars' period of success in the mid-1980s: "It may turn out that collectivism is our undoing in the end, . . . that collectivism and individual expression are mutually incompatible" (quoted in Lock 1985, 41). What is important to acknowledge is that jazz and improvisation are specifically employed during this period of high feminist activity to explore a dynamic tension at the very heart of the collective project — that between the individual soloist and the group. This tension is an alternate version of the masculine solo-group drama that jazz plays out endlessly elsewhere for the benefit of male audiences, for men in general. And "fem musikers" (actually a term used in *Billboard* in 1946 to describe the International Sweethearts of Rhythm: quoted in McPartland 1987, 156) were not working in isolation here. Outside the individual-and-group dynamic of collective musical improvisation, these issues were being explored in other feminist cultures. In Britain, performance groups like Monstrous Regiment Company and Siren Theatre Company were established to explore women's performance, challenge patriarchy, assert alternate women's sexual and social identities (in Siren's case with an initially explicitly lesbian-separatist agenda: see Reinelt 1993; Devlin 1993).

But a shift in organization and cultural production would take place as feminism developed. Lynda Hart explains that "collective authorship was an extremely important concept in early feminist companies of the 1970s and 1980s. As the utopian fervor of such collectivities gave way to a realization that they were, to some extent, based on a vision of feminist homogeneity that could not fully take into account the divisions and productive conflicts between and among feminists, the 'idea' of a collective suffered fragmentations. . . . As feminism has become feminism*s*, the very notion of collectivity has been the site of heated debates" (Hart 1993, 6, 7; emphasis in original).[19]

I am conscious that in this discussion of women in jazz there is a gender-exclusive concentration, which occasionally touches the temporarily separatist in articulation. Focusing on women-*only* projects inevitably involves a degree of overlooking those many women musicians who have not, or who have only rarely, chosen to operate apart, including those who aim for, in Susan McClary's formative distinction, "MUSIC (as opposed to 'women's music')" (1991, 19). Some of them are to be found elsewhere in the book, of course. Focusing on women-only may also be read as functioning to maintain a ghetto mentality.[20] But rather than offer a brief apologetic corrective, I want to pursue this line one small (or large) stage further. It is the view of Mavis Bayton that "during the 1970s British *lesbians* developed a coherent subculture with its own norms, values, and institutions, which represented a more radical alternative to dominant culture than any of the formations studied by subculturalists" (Bayton 1998, 73; my emphasis). Interviewed about her experiences in the International Sweethearts of Rhythm, the veteran American trumpeter Clora Bryant hinted at an unspeakable (perhaps for her generation) feature or perception of early women-only units: " 'a problem for me was that, well, the all-girl bands have had a certain—connotation for many people for a long time . . .' Her voice trails off. Pressed, she admits that a common attitude has it that women playing in all-female groupings must be, ipso facto, homosexual. Bryant was one of the few women I interviewed who alluded to the problem of women being considered not only unfeminine but even 'butch' for playing 'male' instruments and stepping outside traditional roles" (Dahl 1984, 213; ellipses in original).[21]

Val Wilmer tells a wonderful story in her autobiography *Mama Said There'd Be Days Like This* about meeting Maggie Nicols, who was surprised and embarrassed—because it was *outside* the jazz scene and *inside* the Gateways, an underground, members-only lesbian club in Chelsea in the 1960s. Nicols was then in what she called her "first lesbian period" (quoted in Wilmer 1989, 162). Wilmer had gone with her partner, a singer and percussionist from a West African background whom out of discretion she calls Stevie Tagoe in the book. Even at the Gates Wilmer could not resist music criticism: "it wasn't really until the 'smoochies' such as [Engelbert Humperdinck's 'Release Me'] and Dusty [Springfield]'s 'You Don't Have to Say You Love Me' that the majority of the women took to the floor. We missed the soulful sounds of the Flamingo [Club], the organ-and-tenor groups, the Ska and Rocksteady beat" (1989, 163–64). For Alison Rayner of the all-women ensembles Jam Today, the Guest Stars, and Lydia D'Ustebyn's Swing Orchestra, "becoming a lesbian and then getting involved in Gay Liberation" offered a way into music in the mid-1970s (quoted in Bayton 1998, 73). Nicols herself came to appreciate the significance of her lesbian identity as she reevaluated her experiences at the forefront of women in improvisation: "we [in music] are not lesbians by chance. That has something to do with autonomy. . . . *The lesbians were pioneers and had to be lesbian*" (quoted in Smith 2004, 236; my emphasis). This is a strikingly reflexive reading of one's own gender and sexuality in relation to one's cultural expression. It may even be that lesbians have made a more readily identifiable powerful and political contribution to improvisation, to the creation and exploration of what Martha Mockus has termed "sounds that are interstitial, defiant, peculiar at times . . . *queer*, in the most musical sense of the term" (quoted in Smith 2004, 226; emphasis in original). Perhaps Nicols's vocal praxis in such musical and social settings as FIG was a form of Elizabeth Wood's "Sapphonics," using the voice as "a way of describing a space of lesbian possibility, for a range of erotic and emotional relationships among women who sing and women who listen" (quoted in Green 1997, 35). In terms of the racial framework that a music like jazz has supplied to Britain, and with several caveats—prevalent homophobia in some black cultures, some white gays' exoticizing tendencies, for instance—Wilmer tentatively connected experiences and cultures of oppression: "Gay men and lesbians have developed intricate strategies for survival, in the same way that people of oppressed races have done—indeed as women everywhere do in their relationship to men" (1989, 169). We should recognize

35. Volumes from
the Jazz Book Club,
1950s–1960s.

the important role that lesbians played in reconfiguring the masculinist culture of jazz (and, by extension, their contribution to the relative acceptability of lesbian artists in today's popular music world: see Bayton 1998, 74). But we should not be surprised by it: in the 1950s the Jazz Book Club was established by the publisher Sidgwick and Jackson in London, alongside a second specialist imprint, the Science Fiction Book Club (see Collin 1991, 314). These two cultural specialisms spoke predominantly to young British men, often about America. In the 1970s, as we have seen, new women musicians and jazz critics actively challenged the "male music" of jazz — just as, in literature, feminist and lesbian writers like Joanna Russ, Marge Piercy, and Octavia Butler were infiltrating science fiction and confounding genre and gender expectations. When social change is in the air, culture is its reflection *and* its engine. The cultures most open to challenge (whether their adherents like it or not) are those which have that tantalizing combination of liberatory rhetoric — jazz and social struggle, science fiction and utopia — and a cozy, constructed consensus, in these cases around men being, learning how to be, men. Radical feminists and lesbians rose to that challenge. More widely, part of my aim has been to illustrate the role that music has had in developing women's cultures — to argue not just, say, that feminism helped create women's music but that there was a more symbiotic and diachronic relation. While Mavis Bayton shows from British rock in the 1990s that "the women's movement has been a continuous wellspring for the development of musicians and, especially, women's bands over two decades" (1998, 193), I have aimed to show — and, even if it surprises me, I do not think it a serious overstatement — that women's music making, in ways which have often been profoundly touched by developments in jazz, has functioned *over the past century* as one important nexus of pleasure and politics encouraging female expressiveness (of culture, of identity), education, dance, power.

For John Wickes, jazz men have implicitly been more open and sympathetic as a result of a reflexive awareness of their own marginal location in the sociocultural realm. Julie Dawn Smith interprets male marginality in music rather differently: "perhaps because improvisationally based music struggled from the beginning for recognition, its practices and documents have not always been liberatory, often reduplicating the marginalization and exclusion women face(d) in more mainstream musical structures and in patriarchal society at large" (Smith 2004, 229). In tracing the interwoven cultural histories of jazz and gender, with particular reference to the activity of social movements around gender and sexual identities, I hope to have shown a less stark, more interestingly complex set of themes and negotiations between these two evaluations.

CONCLUSION

> From personal observation as well as endless discussion with
> American [musicians], the USA is the most racially divided state
> I've ever been in. But it's also the case that jazz wouldn't have got
> as far as it has, or did, if it weren't for American capitalism. It's an
> ambivalent form: look at the way the Soviet Union veered towards
> it in Stalinist times: first they say it's the decadent, hedonistic
> soundtrack of the west then it's the music of the people, of oppres-
> sion. And the fact is, jazz is *both* of those. At the same time. I think
> we all have ambivalent relationships with America. I don't think
> it's just my old hippie side coming out, but I continue to believe
> that music *can* be a uniting force, and jazz is *a music that connects*.
> —STEVE BERESFORD (personal interview, 2002)

This book opened with two stated aims: to consider jazz as an export culture, engaging with questions of "Americanization" and shifting British national and Commonwealth identities, and to look at how
social and political issues in Britain have been negotiated through jazz
music. We have seen that the idea of a *Jazz Britannia*, to employ the
title of a modern album from the mid-1950s, has employed a number of "strategies of authentication" (Atkins 2001, 12). Prime among
these has been for a privileged few Brits a simple immersion in jazz
in America—either in effect permanently, as with the critic Leonard

Feather, George Shearing (being written into Beat culture), Marian McPartland (through marriage), and Dave Holland (through Miles Davis's casual life-changing invitation one night in Ronnie Scott's club in 1968), or for a temporary touch of the real thing, to be traded on for a life's time in jazz back home, as with Ken Colyer in New Orleans, the members of Geraldo's Navy who would hear bebop in New York, the working-class Scottish prodigy Tommy Smith (whose council estate in Edinburgh clubbed together to get him to Berklee in 1983), or the story of Courtney Pine being invited to join Art Blakey's Jazz Messengers.[1] Other strategies we have seen include indigenizing jazz through British folk music, or through references to local landscape and culture; exploiting the outstanding resource of musical traditions from the Commonwealth—in particular music from the Caribbean, South Africa, and Australia; looking to European music traditions, both pop (cabaret and music theater) and classical (the avant-garde); even attempting to close one's ears (Adorno's impossible act!) to the sonic spread of America—"the emancipation of British jazz from American slavery," in Ian Carr's quite extraordinary and resonant phrase (1973, 21). Interestingly for post-imperial Britain, a number of musicians have articulated their route to innovation or difference in terms of their musical *in*competence. The pianist Keith Tippett, for instance, has talked of early experiments at jettisoning structured time sequences, "getting away from the one-two-three-four beats to the bar, . . . I'm sure, came about as much from our limitations as anything else" (quoted in Wickes 1999, 109). Elsewhere a certain reserve has apparently been maintained: the Jamaican Leslie Thompson, playing with Louis Armstrong in Europe in 1934, found only "shades of urge" in European playing, not American urge or urgency itself (quoted in Shipton 2001, 368), while John Dankworth, bop revolter of the 1950s, seems to be viewed as embodying English inhibition, once being described as " 'couth, 'kempt, and 'shevelled" (quoted in Collier 1976, 5). The both comic and admired bodily characteristic of British, imperial, masculine self-control—the stiff upper lip—makes an unlikely appearance here. One might think that the purpose of jazz for British men was to loosen them up, liberate them and their womenfolk from their own repression, make them "unBritish," as the reception of the Original Dixieland Jazz Band in 1919 was described (Brunn 1961, 126). Does the stiff upper lip of the waxed-moustachioed Brit, comically written of by P. G. Wodehouse and sung of by Ella Fitzgerald, inhibit the embouchure? Or is it possible that a stiff upper lip is quite a useful asset for a reed or a brass instrument player in jazz? As I seemingly edge toward "a quiet cultural nationalism . . . [that] pervades the work of some radical thinkers" (Gilroy 1993, 4), I wish to go no further.

The improvising pianist Steve Beresford touches many of the points I have explored in detail: a(n overstated) leftist critique interwoven with an appreciation of the United States, an acknowledgment of the role of capitalist energy in the mass mediation of the music, and its impact as an export culture, an underlying belief in music's "uniting" capacity. Not long after this interview I saw Beresford in 2003 conducting the Dedication Orchestra, that stellar big band playing the repertoire of the South African jazz musicians who came to Britain in the 1960s, on a national tour of the Contemporary Music Network. I employ Beresford here not because he is a unique figure, but because he is indicative: among the other members of the Dedication Orchestra that memorable night in Kendal, Cumbria, were, center stage, the original Blue Note Louis Moholo, veteran political radicals like Maggie Nicols and Paul Rutherford, musical revolutionaries like Evan Parker, the maverick individualist Lol Coxhill, and the Barbadian Harry Beckett . . . each features in this book somewhere. Some of the musicians wore black armbands to signal their disapproval of the war that Britain was then engaging in alongside the United States. Before the first set a short introduction to the packed house placed the celebratory music to come in its historical context of South African apartheid and British activist and cultural opposition to it, *and* reminded us, to a surge of sober applause, that deadly imperial adventures were currently being undertaken in our name. And then we were presented with some joyful musical, transatlantic, postimperial outernationalism: black American jazz meeting South African rhythms with Caribbean solos punctuated by the squeaks and squiggles of white, British free improvisation. For me, in the audience, that gig, that band, was like a sonic, performative, late confirmation of the book I was engrossed in writing. The circum-Atlanticity of African people's diasporas, the affirming movement of wind through tube and over reed: circular breathing. For Geoff Dyer, such a term is useful to describe jazz's reflexive insistence. In *But Beautiful* he writes that "in an elaborate critical kind of circular breathing, the form [of jazz] is always simultaneously explaining and questioning

36. Concert program for the Dedication Orchestra's Contemporary Music Network tour, 2003: joyful musical, transatlantic, postimperial outernationalism. Great gig, too.

itself" (1991, 190). As I have shown, though, that degree of reflexivity within the music should not be subject to an over-autonomized reading. It is noteworthy that jazz, quite possibly a music past its dominant phase and into its residual one (in Raymond Williams's terms), should still be a hemispheric, possibly global and national point of reference. Could this be particularly so in times of social crisis? In the introduction I quoted Arundhati Roy, novelist and campaigner for global justice, exploring the critical rhetoric and sometimes destructive practice of reading America as an enemy. Does being anti-American manifest itself in being anti-jazz?, she asked. We have seen, historically of course, that Roy's conjunction has been a recurring question: jazz has often been understood and resisted as an exported symptom of American cultural pollution. But her question is of greater interest because it illustrates that jazz was still, in 2002, considered a suitable cultural reference for social movement activists in discussing an apparently globalizing America. From the (or an) other side, as it were, in planning for what was called the Second Gulf War in March 2003, the British military chief, Air Marshall Brian Burridge, compared the shift in military thinking and organization from little more than a decade previously. Burridge stated that during the cold war, his job was like playing "the second violin of the London Symphony Orchestra. You had a sheet of music with clear notation. . . . *{Now} it's jazz, improvising*" (quoted in Norton-Taylor 2003, 3; my emphasis). Playing *second violin* (a neat touch), one followed the score, supportively; now, surprisingly in jazz again, one is *out there*, in the military, the musical front line, in transatlantic alliance. It appears that in times of profound hemispheric and global uncertainty, especially in relation to the position of the United States in the world and different peoples' positions in relation to the United States, a key historic soundtrack of the hegemon — once febrile, clashing, intense, and now perhaps nostalgic — can still be our ear-catching culture. Even if not that many really listen to it nowadays, even if the Beaulieu Battlers and New Orleans ravers are dead and dying, the white beboppers have, as requested, gone home, the tragic early deaths of misunderstood male musicians have been marked and now memorialized, and the revolutionary free musicians are quieter and more thoughtful and still poor, jazz still seems able to speak to us. Is this so surprising? After all, one of those whose music and journey were being celebrated by the Dedication Orchestra, Chris McGregor, has reminded us that "music is in fact very, very precise; it says exactly what words are unable to do" (quoted in McGregor 1995, 5).

But even floating signifiers are heavily weighted — and as we have seen, jazz has been loaded with its Americanicity, chauvinism, and propaganda, racial questions of black and white, the legacy of triangulation, a dominant masculinity, a high-lowness of cultural hierarchy and identity, as well as significant political refigurations in the United States and when exported. Jazz has also been able to float higher — or been further weighted — by being free, that is to say, by the inscription of being liberated through improvisation and expression by its participants and enthusiasts. In Britain, Anglo-Americanicity and Commonwealth networks could map onto one another with especial cultural energy in music, and for a while, the flexible forms of jazz were where that hemispheric imbrication was most really happening. Jazz was able to embody and exploit what Gilroy has called Britain's "liberating sense of the banality of inter-mixture and the subversive ordinariness of convivial cultures" (Gilroy 2002, xxxviii). Even taking only the short-long hop of twenty years in Britain from New Orleans jazz to free music has allowed us to see a consistent social imperative. That these two other-wise divergent kinds of improvised music are often homologous in their collective improvisation, anti-commercialism, and certain attitudinal masculinities should perhaps make their common leftist political sym-pathies less surprising. As Ajay Heble has put it, jazz music has served "important cultural and political ends (desegregation, decolonization, civil rights, and struggles for equality, for access to self-representation, for control over modes of production, and so forth)" (Heble 2000, 5–6). These ends form jazz's social identity, which has been, I have argued, consistently *part of the attraction for its enthusiasts and practitioners in Brit-ain*. I have sought to trace jazzy inflections on, and direct incursions into, British communist organizations, the New Left, the anti-nuclear and peace movements, anti-apartheid and postcolonial identities and campaigns, anti-racist mobilizations, gay liberation, and the women's movement, among others. The foundational fluidity of the form, so con-firmatory for its participants of a political openness, has granted me a definitional openness: where relevant I have been comfortable with using as well as looking at "jazz" in relation to other practices of dance band music, folk, calypso, avant-garde, rock, pop. This is not to say that the liberationist rhetoric of "political" jazz should be accepted from any source, nor that my construction of such a social culture is all-inclusive or complete. Of course there are persistent and important obstacles and problems in any such reading, and I have identified and explored the limit points—jazz as American propaganda, exoticism and racism from its white British enthusiasts, anti-jazzisms in music organizations and cultural establishments, jazz as a consensual heteropatriarchal cul-ture. But I have tried to alter the *scape* of British jazz understanding to include its compelling engagement with social activisms, which forms the center of this book. Here I deliberately echo the work of Andrew Blake on the shift from a Britain once characterized as "the land with-out music" to one which understands itself "as precisely a musical land: a sounding landscape, or soundscape, whose historical continuities and vertical connections have been and are vital to the continuing recon-figuration of the musical" (1997, 178). I have sought too to problematize this kind of metaphor, by showing how one influential music form rup-tures landscape and nationhood, is in fact profoundly intercultural and outernational. My purpose has not at all been to claim jazz as some sort of purely ideological culture: *it has rather been to refigure British jazz his-*

tory to more comprehensively include its ideological assumptions and actions. For this is not only about the dissemination through much of the twentieth-century world of a new art form (if that is what jazz was). It has also been an examination of the soundtrack of empire, of how there was an extended cultural negotiation of shifting hegemonic power through the century (in this case, from Britain to the United States), of how music accompanied, articulated, facilitated that shift, and of how it could express the construction of post-imperial identities.

NOTES

PREFACE

1   If you *do* want to read the history of jazz in Britain, the following books are available: Boulton 1958, Carr 1973, Godbolt 1984, Godbolt 1989, Wickes 1999. I have relied on each of these for background narrative, and much else.

2   It is telling that among the best English-language studies of jazz as export culture — Atkins (2001) on Japan, including wartime and postwar occupation, Kater (1992) and Zwerin (1985) on jazz in Nazi Germany, Goddard (1979) on wartime France, Starr (1983) on the Soviet Union — jazz is always implicitly constructed as a culture of liberation, both because it was proscribed to varying degrees by the totalitarians and because it was in fact the music of the liberators. Kater writes in his conclusion: "It was jazz and not the Third Reich that saw the Final Victory so often conjured up by the Nazi leaders" (203). Consideration of jazz in Britain, for instance, cannot appear quite as immediately dramatic or exciting; the story is not as heroic or epochal, or sobering.

3   Though this study differs from the approach taken by someone like Tia DeNora in *Music in Everyday Life*, I do concur with her observation and conclusion that "we have very little sense of how music features within social process [or] . . . how real people actually press music into action. . . . These are large issues, but are probably best advanced through attention to the so-called 'small' details" (2000, x).

INTRODUCTION: JAZZ, EUROPE, AMERICANIZATION

1   A word of warning: in this study I am fairly open in the range of musics I am including within the term "jazz" — from sweet or wild dance music of the period 1910–1930, which may have featured little or no improvisation, to the European free musics of the 1960s on, which may have featured little recognizable rhythm originating in "jazz."

2   And not only transatlantic. The American journalist Burnet Hershey wrote a piece in the *New York Times* in 1922 which traced and celebrated the global circulation of jazz through contemporary trading links, in a period which predated mass international broadcast media: "Jazz follows the flag. Ships freighted with jazz—'Made in America'—form the newest product of export" (Hershey 1922, 26). Note the privileging of the Pacific route rather than the Atlantic one to start the journey of jazz off:

> Jazz latitude is marked as indelibly on the globe as the heavy line of the equator. It runs from Broadway along Main Street to San Francisco to the Hawaiian Islands, which it has lyricized to fame; to Japan, where it is hurriedly adopted as some new Western culture; to the Philippines, where it is royally welcome back as its own; to China, where the mandarins and even the coolies look upon it as a hopeful sign that the Occident at last knows what is music; to Siam, where the barbaric tunes strike a kindred note and come home to roost; to India, where the natives receive it dubiously, while the colonists seize upon it avidly; to the East Indies, where it holds sway in its elementary form—ragtime; to Egypt, where it sounds so curiously familiar and where it has set Cairo dance mad; to Palestine, where it is looked upon as an inevitable and necessary evil along with liberation; across the Mediterranean, where all ships and all shores have been inoculated with the germ; to Monte Carlo and the Riviera, where the jazz idea has been adopted as its own enfant-chéri; to Paris, which has its special versions of jazz; to London, which has long sworn to shake off the fever, but still is jazzing, and back again. (Hershey 1922, 25–26)

3   This heading is taken from the title of R. W. S. Mendl's *The Appeal of Jazz* (1927), which claims to be "the first book about jazz to be published in Great Britain" (v). Mendl was better known as a Shakespearean scholar, which indicates his interest in the formation of national cultures. The high-low perspective is not quite as unusual as it might appear—after all, T. S. Eliot, that American in London, had written fairly five years earlier of "that Shakespeherian rag" in the section of *The Waste Land* which includes the pub scene (Eliot 1954, 55).

4   He also at some length challenges this standard romanticized and partial history of New Orleans as "the supposed birthplace of jazz" (2001, 9).

5   Angela Y. Davis has touched on this, in considering the liberatory possibilities of analyzing the export of African American music forms. "With the globalization of music . . . feminist interpretations of blues and jazz women's legacies can contribute to an understanding of feminist consciousness that crosses racial and class borders" (Davis 1998, xviii).

6   On the other hand, Bruce Johnson charts the contribution of Graeme Bell and other pre-bop musicians to the Australian contemporary and modernist art scene in the 1940s (2000, 25–26). Graeme Bell was also a modernist painter, and he has identified strong cross-cultural sympathies in what Johnson describes as "the affinities between the jazz coteries and other radical groups in politics (the Communist Party), painting (the Contemporary Art Society), and literature (the Angry Penguins). The radical alliance of oppositionality is emphasised by the terms in which it is habitually described, and by its multi-levelled libertarianism. The network was social, artistic, ideological" (Johnson 2000, 25).

7　Though Richard Palmer's and John White's later edition of Larkin's uncollected writings on jazz seeks to challenge this: "Larkin's views on the development from diatonic-to chromatic-based jazz amount to something much more complex than mere rejection" (Palmer and White 1999, 128 n. 36). As evidence they point to Larkin's Records of the Year in the *Daily Telegraph* through the 1960s, which cite Thelonious Monk (for 1964), John Coltrane (1965), and even Ornette Coleman (1967). Miles Davis's *Miles in the Sky* is a record of the year in *both* Larkin's 1968 and 1969 columns (Palmer and White 1999, 164–66).

8　The employment of national icons in British pop music has become familiar, signaling ambivalent or perverse nationalisms. Think only of the various uses of the Union Jack flag in pop and subcultural moments: by Little Englander mods in the 1960s, by neofascist skinheads after that, in tatters by anti-monarchist punks in the 1970s, in ironic *mode retro* by the Spice Girls and Britpop in the 1990s. This appropriation reached a peak, or nadir, in the attempt by Prime Minister Tony Blair in the late 1990s to present a "youthful" parliamentary Britpop politics through the rebranding of UK plc as "Cool Britannia." But Larkin's astute comma makes it more interesting. See also Morden 2004 for consideration of the problematic nostalgia of the 1960s English eccentrics the Bonzo Dog Doo-Dah Band, who indeed released a song in 1967 entitled "Cool Britannia" (95).

9　See also Harold Budd: "About improvisation—it's a uniquely American way of making music" (quoted in Dean 1992, 131).

10　Though see Richard Sudhalter's alternative reading: "The music may not be so much a black American experience as an *American* experience, with various racial and ethnic groups playing indispensable and interlocking roles. . . . The blues has indeed been a rich ingredient in what came to be called jazz—but not the entirety, and certainly not equally indispensable to all styles. Other formative components include ragtime, Tin Pan Alley, late nineteenth-century European concert and dance music, grand opera, vaudeville and the minstrel traditions of both races, the white folk music of Appalachia, and—perhaps most of all—the concert bands so ubiquitous on village greens and in town dance halls in turn-of-the-century America" (Sudhalter 1999, xvii, xix).

11　This was far from uniquely British. Atkins argues that we "may rightly locate the 'origins' of jazz in Japan in the commercial dance hall, where the jazz community developed its own separate identity" (2001, 56).

12　Further afield, the broadcaster and bassist Honda Toshio: "There is a well-known saying that 'jazz and freedom go hand-in-hand' . . . and, in fact, in Japan and Europe after the Second World War, jazz and freedom *did* come hand-in-hand" (quoted in Atkins 2001, 124).

13　And note the sardonic comment from the British jazz critic and broadcaster Steve Race in 1961: "I like that phrase 'Anglo-American jazz.' At least it's half way to the truth" (quoted in Godbolt 1984, 195).

14　George Melly: "There was that whole group of writers called the Movement—Larkin, Kingsley Amis, Osborne, John Braine. I don't know how I would reconcile their enjoyment of jazz with the right wing views many of them held or came to hold. You know, there would be Amis and Robert Conquest having their monthly right-wing lunches, the Fascist Dinner Club or something it was called. John Braine started on the left and moved over to the right wing of politics. He was at these lunches. Once he was praising the United States and someone said, 'But you know you wouldn't have these freedoms and opportunities there if you were black.' Braine just replied in his bluff northern voice, 'But I'm not black, you daft bugger!' " (Melly, personal interview, 2002).

15   While a transatlantic gaze has elsewhere often been used by Scottish artists as a post-colonial strategy in writing against the center, viewed as London. Consider, for instance, the Scottish poet Tom Leonard, who has rewritten the technique and language of William Carlos Williams (a language Leonard calls "American") as part of a project to connect with a literary tradition outside EngLit. Or the Scottish pop duo the Proclaimers, who in the 1980s presented a kind of political acoustic music in an identifiable Everly Brothers format.

16   Here the *Folk Roots* editor Ian Anderson quotes from the editorial in question, and then goes on to explain what happened next:

"When I was an early teenager, . . . America seemed alluring and romantic. We were dazzled by it. Blues, jazz, American folk, the still-fresh roots of rock 'n' roll, . . . — all these things were hip, sophisticated, attractively different, had a depth of secret culture that we wanted to find a way into. It's all different now, of course. America has dumbed beyond belief, and the secret cultures are our own and those of all the other local communities around the world who have undergone cultural ethnic cleansing." That piece drew the biggest postbag on anything we've ever published, overwhelmingly in favour. . . . After September 2001, we and our American friends in the world roots music business widely expressed the hope that the sharing of musical and cultural experiences would be a route to reconciliation and understanding in the USA. It hasn't happened. The Bush regime have continued with political, environmental and commercial policies that are terrifying the world and have squandered much of the international sympathy that resulted from the World Trade Centre incident. They have encouraged jingoism and xenophobia at home, and have pushed the door nearly shut on world musicians entering the country. . . . We think it's time to ferment some cultural resistance, however tiny. And yes, it's possible to be anti-American without being anti-Americans. (Anderson 2001)

17   Earlier communist utterances against jazz were not necessarily framed in terms of its American origins, though. Helen Crawford, suffragette and founding member of the Communist Party of Great Britain, wrote an article in October 1921 entitled "The Jazz Period": "To-day, we are living in the *jazz period*. We have jazz music, jazz dancing, jazz frocks, jazz furniture, jazz art, jazz politics. . . . *The jazz period must end.* . . . [Capitalism's] prolongation means a jazz of death to the suffering and toiling masses. . . . *Stop jazzing and get to work. Up Labour! Organise! Organise!! Organise!!!*" (Crawford 1921; emphasis in original).

18   Though note Leonard Feather's stark Englishman-in-New-York admission: "The first man I ever heard using the word 'nigger' was Glenn Miller" (1986, 120).

19   The "Germany Calling" broadcasts of the Nazi propagandist William Joyce, known as Lord Haw-Haw, had featured an authorized dance band, Charlie's Orchestra, since 1940. "The attraction for the British, especially the servicemen whose morale was to

be undermined, was meant to be original modern jazz, played so well that Anglo-phones would have to think the programs came out of England, or perhaps neutral Scandinavia" (Kater 1992, 132).

20   Cf. the kamikaze pilot Oikawa Hajime: "How funny to listen to jazz music on the night before going out to kill the jazzy Americans!" (quoted in Atkins 2001, 127). I wonder if this can be read as confirming the life-enhancing qualities of jazz? The young man was facing his own death too, as well as that of the Americans, but he had the knowledge of the morning.

21   Frank Kofsky was outspoken on how this was being viewed in the United States itself: "I endeavoured to call attention to the cynical exploitation of jazz overseas as a 'Cold War secret weapon' at the same time that its black practitioners here were still being relegated to the status of third-class citizens both as artists and individuals" (1998, 88).

CHAPTER 1: NEW ORLEANS JAZZ, PROTEST, AND CARNIVAL

1   I have long been intrigued by the socialist historian Hobsbawm's use of a pseudo-nym for writing about jazz. I have wondered whether it was a symptom of some sort of cultural hierarchy, or indeed of a leftist ambivalence regarding such an American pop export. John Young has, too: "Perhaps [Hobsbawm's pseudonym] can be taken as an indication of the continuing low status of jazz in academic and other High Cul-tural circles, irrespective of its gains among certain artistic and intellectual minorities" (2004, 79 n. 37). Apparently we are both wrong, as Hobsbawm explained to me: "I wrote under a pseudonym because I didn't want the students to start discussing jazz with me instead of the history they were supposed to be studying. After I retired I used my own name. Why should I have wanted to 'distance myself' from the 'unrespect-ability' of jazz? And I would have been a half-wit had I tried to distance myself from its American origins. It cannot be done" (Hobsbawm, personal correspondence, 2004).

2   Nor has the fact that traditional and revivalist music was an early space for a signifi-cant number of modernist and experimental musicians. The pianist Keith Tippett's first jazz influence was a local West Country hero, Acker Bilk. Early on, that fero-cious experimentalist Evan Parker was "absolutely fanatical about Lonnie Donegan" (quoted in Carr 1973, 71). The bassist Jack Bruce, the trumpeter Ian Carr, the free im-provisers Paul Rutherford and Eddie Prévost—all had some early experience with the New Orleans style. As we will also see when discussing free improvisation of the 1960s and 1970s, the collective improvisation, exploration of musical effects and unusual in-strumental sounds, for some an anti-technique, as well as an anti-commercialism, are among the mutual features in this apparently surprising correlative.

3   Conscious of the irony of complaining about neglect in a note, I should neverthe-less point out that in the space of a very few years up to the mid-1950s, the cornetist Ken Colyer championed purist New Orleans ensemble jazz and played a key founding role in three significant areas. With various bands before and after his New Orleans adventure in 1952–53 he led the traditional movement—his musicians Acker Bilk and Chris Barber went on to take the commercial plaudits; second, he introduced skiffle between sets, and his musician Lonnie Donegan took the hit singles; third, he

introduced to Britain what I believe to be the first New Orleans parade band, the Omega Brass Band. At the 100 Club in London, Colyer's contribution is seen in an entire wall of photographs, with a large commemorative plaque (compare the fact that opposite, photographs of the likes of Mick Jagger and Pete Townsend onstage at the club are altogether smaller and more poorly presented, while the now legendary Sex Pistols concert there in 1976 is allotted no wall space whatever). Bands such as the Rolling Stones and the skifflers the Quarrymen—who went on to bigger things as the Beatles—played in between sets at Colyer concerts. Taylor notes that Colyer's achievements have been acknowledged or formally recognized by Paul McCartney, the New Orleans City Council, and the British government (Taylor 2001, 111–12). Academia has been less kind.

4   Note Ian Whitcombe's reservations, though: "No regiment of dance-band boys marched off to the Spanish Civil War. . . . No dance or jazz bands accompanied the Jarrow Marchers" (quoted in Morgan 1998, 124). Yet, and so as not to replicate an overly retrospective view, let me point out that leftist marching musics of the streets are not only historical: we will see that later jazz musics also took to the street, while the Big Red Band marched in demonstrations in the 1980s. The sociologist Ben Crow—a BRB member who had started out as a teenage politico trying to play trumpet with jazz bands on the CND marches—remembers the band playing at "pickets, demonstrations, occasionally festivals and pubs. Mostly demonstrations. My shining memory [from 1984–85] is playing the Internationale standing at the entrance to Downing Street when Maggie [Thatcher] was P[rime] M[inister] as the foundation for many tens of thousands of miners from all over the country. There was an extraordinary elation to being drowned out, at our most extended volume, by the rich, harmonious voices of thousands of miners. It was great music at a very emotional event" (personal interview, 2002). In the 1990s samba bands and cycle-powered techno sound systems accompanied political mobilizations of the anti–road building and pro–rave culture varieties, while a uniformed avant-garde ensemble called Infernal Noise Brigade accompanied anti-capitalist activists in Seattle in 1999 (see Whitney 2003).

5   In origins, the New Orleans marching brass band was a significant feature of black and Creole culture in the city, not least because, as William Schafer notes, "the brass band emerges as a major source, a gene pool, for jazz" in the late nineteenth century (Schafer 1977, 8). He continues: "This band music was born of an intense, emotionally charged desire for freedom and recognition. Its militancy is not of the battlefield or the church, but of the political arena" (13). The brass band parading with a procession of supporters alongside ("the second line") was also a black cultural expression of urban presence and power, of reclaiming the streets.

6   Using homemade instruments from domestic materials, the do-it-yourself form of skiffle would open wider still access to pop music performance in Britain (see McDevitt 1997, for example).

7   The influential English critic Leonard Feather popularized the term "moldy fig" in the American jazz press, and often led the way in attacking the moldy figs' politics. From *Metronome* in September 1945, for instance: "Just as the fascists tend to divide group against group and distinguish between Negroes, Jews, Italians and 'real Americans,'

so do the moldy figs try to categorize New Orleans, Chicago, swing music and 'the real jazz.' Just as the fascists have tried to foist their views on the public through the vermin press of *Social Justice*, the *Broom* and *X-Ray*, so have the Figs yapped their heads off in the *Jazz Record*, *Jazz Session* and *Record Changer*" (quoted in Feather 1986, 88). He later acknowledged that this kind of discourse was "venom[ous]" and "mean-spirited" (1986, 88, 89).

8   I should acknowledge that not *all* young trad fans felt this contumacy, though it is interesting, I think, that even those from a conservative background could articulate their response to the music in terms of some sort of progressive agenda, however qualified. One undergraduate enthusiast in the 1950s, Ken Hayton, explained to me:

> As far as political alignment was concerned I seem to have largely bucked the trend [of your argument about jazz and leftist sympathies]. I had no patience with CND and viewed their activities with great suspicion. I suppose my youthful leanings were towards a liberal viewpoint away from my upbringing of true blue conservatism but in any case the emotional response I made to the music was linked to the appalling racial prejudice, nay persecution, which I read about in my study of early jazz roots, rather than any left wing feelings or anti-fascism. Like many others in my circle I viewed the efforts of the [British] Trad. musicians as a sort of homage to the great originators and their stand against commercialisation was somehow bound up in this attitude, a refusal to be deviated away from "the truth" by the possibility of commercial gain! (personal correspondence, 2004)

9   It should be noted though that jazz clubs are cited by Hutnyk as one among many examples of the derivative nature of European culture. His point about solidarities is directed more at different black musical formations.

10 Other postwar British jazzers understood differently the war's continued shading of the cultural landscape. The drummer Laurie Morgan explained the attraction of bebop for the Club Eleven groups in London from 1948 on: "The war was just over and this music reflected the new thinking. It was aggressive, vibrant; it wasn't apologetic" (quoted in Godbolt 1989, 47).

11 This primitivism is wonderfully captured in Clive King's classic novel for children, *Stig of the Dump* (1963). Stig is apparently an otherworldly wild boy from the Stone Age whom the twentieth-century children Barney and Lou come across in a chalk pit where rubbish is dumped. On a moonlit Midsummer's Night near some standing stones, at the novel's end, Barney and Lou witness Stig and his people at a ritual.

> "Listen! Music!"
> "That's not music!" said Barney.
> "Well it's jazz or something. Or one of those skiffle groups. . . ."
> But there was yet another sound which the listeners could not quite understand, a kind of BLOONG, BLUNG, BLONG, BLOONG, not always on one note as most of the singing was, and not really taking much notice of the rhythm of the log-drum and jawbone. It was as if someone who had never heard a tune was trying to play one for the first time with a tea-chest, string, and broomstick. . . . Barney nearly fell off his branch. "It's Stig!" he almost shouted. (King 1963, 197, 200–201, 202)

12　All newspaper and magazine quotations in this section are taken from the Beaulieu Jazz Festival press cuttings files of the Beaulieu Motor Museum Archive, Hampshire.

13　Books devoted exclusively to British pop festival culture are Sandford and Reid 1974, Clarke 1982, Hinton 1995, and McKay 2000a.

14　As I explore in more detail in chapter 5, a police drive against homosexual acts in 1953–54 led to a number of trials and convictions. Writing in the *Independent* in 1999, Philip Hoare called the Montagu case "the highest profile gay trial since Oscar Wilde's" (quoted in Knitting Circle 2002).

15　Montagu lent his name and the reputation of Beaulieu Jazz Festivals to the Manchester International Jazz Festival of June 1963, which featured the most impressive trans-atlantic bill of headliners to date for a jazz festival in the United Kingdom (much more ambitious than Beaulieu ever was), including Dizzy Gillespie, Buck Clayton, Bud Freeman. It was a financial flop—partly because the jazz boom was at an end, while the headliners may have been too modern for some tastes. Also, perhaps it indicated the importance of the *genius loci* of Beaulieu and the New Forest: when offered the industrial urban north of Manchester instead, audiences, ironically prompted by the presence in publicity of Montagu connecting this festival with the earlier Beaulieu ones, refused.

16　Montagu's enthusiasm for linking music and motors reached new depths a few weeks before the 1958 festival. With an eye on publicity for his ambitiously expanding motor museum, Montagu performed on 17 July 1958 at what was billed as a "Midsummer Madness" event, a pre-Prom romp at the Royal Albert Hall in London. It included a performance of Antony Hopkins's *Concerto for Motor Car and Orchestra*, with movements called "Ritual Tyre Dance" and "Carburettor Waltz." For the first Montagu danced round a car; for the second the car, specially fitted with six tuned horns, was played by Montagu. Surprisingly critical, the *Daily Express* called the performance "a new low in musical buffoonery" (28 June 1958).

17　*Jazdup* as in "jazzed up"; cf. the 1990s neologism *luvdup* for "loved up," describing the Ecstasy-generated group experience in dance culture.

18　When Bruce Turner was introduced into Humphrey Lyttelton's band in 1953, replacing trombone with the heretical (for New Orleans purists) alto saxophone, the response from those defending territory against an invader was swift: "Humphrey whispered: 'Look over there!' and nodded his head incredulously in the direction of a row of seats some distance back. At the start of my solo, the occupants of this row of seats had raised a long white banner on which had been inscribed the words 'GO HOME DIRTY BOPPER.' Every time I took a solo, throughout the entire concert, this banner was raised aloft, and the strange slogan displayed there for all to see" (Turner 1984, 132).

19　In fact there had been earlier jazz scares and informal youth gatherings at Stonehenge for summer solstices. In the 1920s and early 1930s crowds partied through the night among the stones to gramophones and occasional live jazz bands, while in the 1950s the local and national press published letters complaining of the pollution of Stonehenge during the solstice by young rowdies playing loud live skiffle music (Worthington 2004, 20–27).

20　It may be important not to overstate the purity of the English aristocracy, and this is particularly so in the context of the reception of American cultural exports such as jazz music. As long ago as 1933 one Lady Londonderry was complaining that Society was becoming "Americanised" (McKibbin 1998, 24), while Ross McKibbin writes that through the twentieth century, Society hostesses increasingly "saw their role as the integration of Anglo-American elites. 'Society,' as it was understood at the time, was in any case a significantly Anglo-American affair" (1998, 27).

CHAPTER 2: WHITENESS AND (BRITISH) JAZZ

1   There is a telling distinction between recent American and British historiography of the music in this context: in America a small number of studies are dedicated to exploring the marginalized contribution of white musicians to jazz history and development (see Sudhalter 1999); in Britain, as shown especially by Val Wilmer's journalism (sadly often in the form of obituaries) and work-in-progress on Ken "Snakehips" Johnson, it is research on the marginalized contribution to early jazz of black musicians based in Britain that is uncovering lost chords.

2   Though note Wald's comment on Gubar's term, which in her view "potentially reinscribes the *stability* of racial categories" (2000, 203 n.16; my emphasis).

3   Farris Thompson: "To be white in America is to be very black. If you don't know how black you are, you don't know how American you are" (quoted in Fishkin 1996, 252).

4   The first couple of times I saw Heckstall-Smith live, he played a feature on two saxophones simultaneously, tenor and soprano I think, and yes, like other audience members I *did* think of Roland Kirk.

5   The classic punk–white reggae song by the Clash, "(White Man) in Hammersmith Palais," that I use below as an imperfect Original Dixieland Jazz Band update, sort of, became a favorite on neo-Nazi National Front youth dance floors (Gilroy 1987, 161; Sabin 1999, 210). It was easily co-optable for espousers of racist "swamping" rhetoric. The song's lyrics narrate the experience of a white fan attending a concert of reggae musicians playing for a massively black audience in London, "for the first time from Jamaica" (Clash 1978).

6   And there remains the plea to America for authenticity in the referencing of Lacy and Rudd, an avoidance of a potentially inauthentic, imitative white British praxis.

7   See Colin 1977 for the British dance band history of this period.

8   A joke by Edgar Jackson from a record review signals an English awareness of titular propriety, and an implicit criticism of its misuse (by Americans): Duke Ellington is "Massa Ellington" (quoted in Godbolt 1984, 35).

9   British rock too would begin to inform these musical and social questions. The American jazz composer Carla Bley has spoken of how listening to the Beatles helped her to negotiate an understanding and a musical creativity from her position as a white woman in a largely African American jazz community: "I started hearing the possibilities of not borrowing from black culture. Actually finding substance in white culture. The Beatles's best stuff was taken from Anglo-Saxon roots. I was amazed because up to then I thought only black music was important" (quoted in Dahl 1984, 207).

10   I was myself forcibly reminded of this during correspondence with the saxophonist

Trevor Watts, of Spontaneous Music Ensemble and later Moiré Music. I had asked Watts a sensitive question about the Moiré Drum Orchestra's lineup (single white man front line blowing long solos over the backing of a black African group of drummers), and whether it could be seen as replicating rather than challenging or bypassing colonial relations, and this was his reply: "Personally I'm not interested in what people think about whether colonial perceptions about us whitey English boys have been even more cemented by the fact I was the leader of the Drum Ork etc, etc. . . . It tells me more about them than it does about what's actually really happening. . . . One of the drummers Nana Tsiboe had a much more privileged education and up-bringing than myself, for instance. His mother was a politician in Ghana, his father owned a newspaper there, and he was sent to England for a good education. I was brought up in a Northern working class town in the 40s & 50s and left school at 15 after a bad education" (personal correspondence, 2003). Watts sharply identifies class privilege and opportunity—and their lack—working against any simple racial reading.

11 I recognize that there are other issues here having to do with the problematic of folk nostalgia and rural tradition, which has often been identified as idealizing a Merrie England of white folk on green fields, counter to the contemporary reality in Britain's urban centers. Dave Harker too has pointed to the dangers for the political project of the second folk revival inherent in the "chauvinism, mysticism, racialism, and fundamental conservatism" of Cecil Sharp and the earlier folk revival (Harker 1980, 149).

12 The authentic and purist insistence of "Ewan MacColl" of course rides curiously alongside some of the facts of his own life, such as that he was born Jimmy Miller, in Salford, England. Other reinventions were less successful. The jazz trumpeter and broadcaster Humphrey Lyttelton recalls the "Ballad and Blues" radio series of the 1950s, for which his band supplied jazz music and "accompaniments for the folk-singers who took part—Ewan MacColl, A. L. Lloyd, Isla Cameron, Alan Lomax and others. The programmes were not a success. . . . The music we produced was an unhappy mongrel of incompatible parentage" (Lyttelton 1958, 49).

13 Other forms of mass transmission of popular music were available earlier. Shipton describes the black musician James P. Johnson's piano roll of *Steeplechase Rag* (1917) as featuring "a more accomplished composition, a more complex structure, and a more dramatically executed performance than anything the ODJB managed to produce over the next five years" (2002, 105).

14 Sudhalter traces the shifting signification of a key term from the 1920s on:

"Dixieland" and "Dixie" were used freely to identify bands of both races playing any music even distantly reminiscent of a southern Arcadia. Hence the "Dixie Daisies" (white), "Dixie Four" (black), "Dixie Instrumental Four" (white), "Dixie Stompers" (black). . . . "Dixieland," meanwhile, began to take on connotative meanings quite beyond its original, southern, association. Perhaps it had to do with the lasting and vivid impression made by the Original Dixieland Jazz Band; perhaps it stemmed in part from the tendency of white musicians to celebrate the past in a way their black colleagues did not; perhaps it was to some degree racial—white associating with white, black with black. Or even a matter of repertoire choices. Whatever the specific cause, by the mid-1930s the word "Dixieland" was being applied freely to certain circles of white musicians. (Sudhalter 1999, 276, 279)

15 As an imperial center still, London could further internationalize the music's appeal and inspiration. Bruce Johnson mentions the impact of the ODJB's performances in London on the development of jazz in Australia: "In the twentieth century overseas military service introduced Australians to jazz performance, including two airmen who heard the Original Dixieland Jazz Band in London and teamed up as Leslie and Dare to assemble the Syncopas Jazz Band in Sydney in 1920" (2000, 8). The first jazz records available on an Australian label, Zonophone, were ODJB recordings, *pressed in London* for the Antipodean market (Johnson 2000, 9).

16 See Feather 1986, 90–94, 116–26, for an outsider's view of anti-black racism in the United States. He makes an interesting suggestion which illuminates the effort to understand the transatlantic—United States, Europe, North Africa—racial politics of the 1930s: "It struck me as more than coincidental that so many of these [white racist] incidents involved Italian-Americans: Venuti, Prima, Rollini, La Rocca. In the light of Italy's rape of Abyssinia, the evidence at that time seemed even more compelling; but I was wrong" (Feather 1986, 116).

17 LaRocca was still at it in 1936: "Our music is strictly a white man's music. We patterned our earlier efforts after military marches, which we heard at park concerts in New Orleans in our youth. Many writers have attributed this rhythm that we introduced as something coming from the African jungles, and crediting the Negro race with it. My contention is that the Negroes learned to play this rhythm and music from the whites" (quoted in Sudhalter 1999, 753 n. 30).

18 There is a fascinating exception just visible here. In Birmingham, England, one teenager in the 1920s practiced his clarinet playing because it offered the one possibility that he permitted himself of bridging musics and cultures, old and new worlds. According to Jonathan Rutherford, "His love of the clarinet offered him the only glimpse of a life other than one of strenuous scholasticism. . . . The clarinet was an instrument of the disciplined and formal structures of classical music, but for [Enoch] Powell it also featured in band music, suggestive of more anarchic, emotional rhythms" (1997, 115). Going to university, Powell gave up music entirely, and "never looked at a sheet of music since" (Powell, quoted in Rutherford 1997, 115). In Rutherford's view, "There were to be no more illicit fantasies of band music. Powell's nascent exuberance was firmly suppressed" (1997, 115). It is probably too naïve to follow Rutherford's wistful implication that had he only stuck with learning to swing and jam through dance band and jazz musics, Powell might not later, in April 1968, have been the Conservative MP speechifying infamously and influentially (all carefully framed in quotation marks) of the "rivers of blood" that would flow as a result of black migration to Britain, of the view that "in fifteen or twenty years time the black man will have his whip hand over the white man," or of the "charming, wide-grinning piccaninnies . . . [who] cannot speak English, but one word they know. 'Racialist,' they chant" (quoted in Rutherford 1997, 129, 131, 134). Powell's speech remains an influential early invocation of what Vron Ware, writing of white English racist politics in the 1990s, calls "the spectre of a

wider, national community of long-suffering, angry whites, seething with resentment at what they saw as the iniquities of multiculturalism" (1997, 284).

19   It is possible to identify elements of a white scare regarding jazz and blackness in Britain during these early years. In June 1920 the pianist and bandleader Dan Kildare murdered his wife and her sister, and killed himself (Rye 1990, 46). The same year Sydney Bechet's sojourn in Britain was cut short with an appearance before Bow Street magistrates on a charge of attempted rape—he was acquitted, but deported (Godbolt 1984, 17). Is it possible that these assumed primary moments of (black) *jazz madness* set a template for the subsequent exoticizing of black music by white Britain, or its association with criminality or sexual violence, or simply the fear of and fascination with it? Howard Rye notes of the Kildare case, sensationally reported in the *News of the World*, that "already the serious jazz musician was regarded with a mixture of awe and incomprehension as a wayward untutored genius" (1990, 46). That black masculinity is what was perceived as the threat is confirmed by the earlier scare around the victorious black boxer Jack Johnson.

20   Gayle Ward traces the extraordinary intertextual trajectory of Mezzrow's autobiography, *Really The Blues* (1946), showing that it directly influenced Mailer's "The White Negro" (1957), but also, through related writing by Mezzrow's ghost writer Bernard Wolfe, Fanon's *Black Skin, White Masks* (1952) (Wald 2000, 59–60).

21   Gilroy reminds us that as with many so-called race riots, "the rioting crowds were, in fact, 'multi-ethnic' " (2002, xxi). Bill Schwarz has made a different point—the Clash appearing in this chapter again—writing of "The *white riots* in Nottingham and Notting Hill in September 1958" (Schwarz 1996, 199; my emphasis).

22   Remember Gilroy on diaspora: "utopian—technically placeless" (quoted in Rice 2003, 19).

23   I am not suggesting that this kind of black route to the comprehension of white positionality was exclusive to jazz music. Other international black musical figures have spoken progressively to white Britain. Gilroy cites as an example the Jamaican reggae star Bob Marley: "In his egalitarianism, Ethiopianism and anti-imperialism, his critique of law and of the types of work which were on offer, these young [white] people found meanings with which to make sense of their lives in post-imperial Britain" (Gilroy 1987, 227). Bill Schwarz reminds us that "for a particular generation, especially but not exclusively for those active in the labour movement, a perception of [Paul] Robeson commonly provided a potent means by which—for white English men and women—the possibilities of the modern world came to be internally recognised, known, judged and felt. Even today, individual memories remain extraordinarily sharp: *Othello* at Stratford; the CND rally in Trafalgar Square; 'Joe Hill' at Harry Pollitt's funeral. English memories of becoming modern, and of first becoming aware of race, can still work through the figure of Robeson" (Schwarz 1996, 187).

24   I recognize that viewing colorblindness as a route to racial tolerance is problematic. In recent years it has been advocated in the United States as a means of combating the "reverse discrimination" of affirmative action, for instance (Wellman 1997, 313). Even "the metaphor of 'blindness' . . . implies that race is inherently seeable . . . knowable through the 'evidence' of the body" (Wald 2000, 186). At the same time, colorblind-

ness is a long-standing claim of jazz history, is part of its allure. What was it that Louis Armstrong was *supposed to have said* to Jack Teagarden in the 1940s? "You an ofay, I'm a Spade—let's blow!" (quoted in Sudhalter 1999, xx). Viewing color in order to reject it, as Armstrong does, is colorblindness in action, in performance.

25 Frank Kofsky is among those unconvinced, as well as suspicious of Feather's dual roles as jazz critic and promoter: "Leonard Feather, by his constant harping on the role of the white musician in jazz, serves to redirect our gaze from the essential to the ephemeral. In this way he uses his influence to insure that the subject of greatest gravity—the control of black music and musicians by white-owned corporations, with all that situation entails—goes unexamined, undebated, and, therefore, unchallenged" (Kofsky 1998, 86).

26 It is true that the effect of Pink Floyd's light shows, as Barry Miles recalls of the Spontaneous Underground happenings that they shared with AMM, could also be obscuring: "It was hard to make out any of the band because of the continuously moving, changing lights, which rendered them effectively anonymous; an element of the Pink Floyd's show that stayed with them" (Miles 2002, 103).

27 It is important not to overstate the position, though. Postwar, white pleasures as well as anxieties in this area were partly, and swiftly, transferred to new Caribbean migrants in Britain. Val Wilmer traces some of the shifting constructions of whiteness in relation to the black presence in British jazz, and it is interesting that Wilmer relates this shifting attitude to the increasingly confident technique of white British instrumentalists:

> When the music ceased to be such a mystery and local musicians began to develop voices of their own, attitudes changed towards the people who gave them something to play in the first place. . . . The reaction of Whites to the postwar wave of Caribbean migration was not unconnected, of course. Once Black people became more vocal and challenging by their presence, the fantasy atmosphere created by the music's liberal chroniclers began to sour. . . . Indeed the music itself threatens notions of white supremacy and Black subservience. Increasingly in the Britain of the 1960s white men found Black settlers and their visiting heroes echoing each other in condemnation of the racist attitudes that existed on our own doorstep. Such resistance was intrusive on the faraway world of New Orleans and Chicago legend, and as British musicians developed a new self-confidence, so the idolatry began to vanish, the atmosphere becoming overly racist at times. (1989, 45)

28 It is worth noting that jazz musicians may have had a special early position in the British anti-apartheid movement (they were later supplanted by higher-profile pop stars, such as Peter Gabriel and Jerry Dammers, in the 1980s). This status was facilitated by Father (later Archbishop) Trevor Huddleston. The story goes that during the early 1950s as a voluntary priest at St Peter's school for black children in Johannesburg, Huddleston bought for Hugh Masekela, then a fourteen-year-old pupil at the school, his first trumpet, and arranged his first lessons with a black Salvation Army trumpeter. Robin Denselow continues: "The other boys at St Peter's then wanted instruments as well, and the Huddleston Jazz Band was formed. Along with Masekela, it

featured Jonas Gwangwa on trombone. They wore black trousers, grey silk shirts with white braid, and played American, not African music. In such ways is great political pop born" (Denselow 1990, 47). Back in Britain a few years later, Huddleston became president of the British Anti-Apartheid Movement; in the United States in 1956, he arranged for Louis Armstrong to send one of his trumpets to Masekela, who was then still in South Africa (Denselow 1990, 49). Huddleston had long been convinced that artists and other cultural workers could play an important role in challenging apartheid, and jazz musicians in Britain like Dankworth and Laine, Lyttelton, and George Melly were inspired to become involved. (See chapter 3 for an extended discussion of anti-apartheid campaigning and South African jazz.)

29   When Rutherford identifies "the wider political failure of white liberalism to develop a language of self-reflection on the meaning and dynamics of whiteness" (1997, 156), this is a gendered observation. The feminist movement from the 1970s on could be highly sensitive to questions of color and power, seeking to understand the residual imperial traces in British liberatory politics and related cultures. See the comment of Laka Daisical of the feminist jazz and world group the Guest Stars: "It is hard, as privileged white Western women, to get the balance right; to acknowledge the musical debt we owe to Black people, to acknowledge our privileges as white people, and at the same time, to insist that we do have something to say" (quoted in Lock 1985, 41).

CHAPTER 3: THE BLACK ATLANTIC AND THE COMMONWEALTH

1   This is so even though, of course, South Africa formally withdrew from the Commonwealth in 1961, after events like the Sharpeville shootings of 1960 and Prime Minister Harold Macmillan's "winds of change" speech in 1958 in Cape Town about African decolonization (Worden 1995, 107).

2   Among discussions of the UNIA's anti-jazz bias, the extent of Garvey's real interest in jazz and blues music, as opposed to his strategic use of it for political purposes, remains open to debate. Even Vincent acknowledges that "his schooling in Jamaica had been in the stuffy elitist British mode so far as culture was concerned. It appears that, despite a preference for 'serious' music, he was forced to support the black music revolution in America because his followers were part of it, and because to refuse to support the musical culture, which came out of 'the black nation,' would be failing to be true to his nationalist 'race first' philosophy" (1995, 112).

3   Imruh Bakari notes of this: "Godbolt's dismissive and cynical account lacks any awareness that jazz is a component of a global African diasporic experience, and that Britain and the British experience are both implicated in and influenced by its process. His attitude is part of a pervasive response that not only devalues and erases the Black presence from British soil, but seeks to place it firmly beyond the orbit of Britishness" (1999, 100).

4   Green adds South African to his list of the nationalities of musicians in this band, but Val Wilmer has pointed out to me that subsequent research has disproven this (personal correspondence, 2004).

5   There are other interesting cross-cultural relations in early jazz music which illustrate

the complexity of transatlantic circulations, and also problematize simplistic notions of form and genre. As we have seen, for example, the early musical education of the African American bandleader Will Marion Cook, who first came to Britain with his Southern Syncopated Orchestra in 1919, is emblematic: in 1892 he had attended the Conservatory in Berlin and been taught by Antonin Dvořák (Goddard 1979, 32).

6   Other black musics too contributed to political debate during this period. As noted elsewhere, the most famous example was of course provided by Paul Robeson, while smaller events signal the continuing project. "In 1933," notes Chris Stapleton, for instance, "a group of African and Afro-American artists gave a benefit concert at London's Phoenix Theatre in aid of the Scottsboro Boys, who had been imprisoned in Alabama" (1990, 91).

7   There is evidence that jazz played a creative role in what would later become reggae, too. Paul Gilroy describes the early practice of Jamaican sound system DJs and musicians. Significantly in transatlantic terms, Gilroy locates the narrative in the experience of a Jamaican settler in London, the record importer Daddy Peckings: "He has described the gradual transformation of American musical forms, particularly jazz and jump blues, and their junction with traditional Jamaican music. This cross-fertilization would eventually lead to modern reggae.... According to Peckings, the sound-systems playing in the dance-halls of Kingston in the late 1940s and early 1950s . . . offered a mixture of bebop and swing . . . reworked by local musicians" (1987, 216).

8   Hutchinson's preference for black signifiers in band names and images did not extend to his own nickname, "Jiver." According to Val Wilmer, "he was [initially] forced to adopt this nomenclature because of confusion with the better-established 'Hutch' (also Leslie Hutchinson). However, he hated the name. He considered it demeaning and racist and made several attempts to drop it" (personal correspondence, 2004).

9   This partly explains the popularity of clubs as venues for black communities in London. Gilroy notes that "there were up to fifty black-owned and managed basement clubs in South London alone" in the early postwar years (1987, 215). Most had an exclusively black clientele.

10 I think it is worth noting that some of the historical material I employ here, by Richard Noblett (2002) and Andrew Simons (2001), for example, is taken from the copious liner notes to newly released CDs of recordings by black musicians in Britain from the 1930s to the 1950s: the social history is uncovered alongside the cultural manifestations, the cultural legacy insistently explained in relation to the social context of production and consumption. I want here to acknowledge also the pivotal role played by Val Wilmer in these histories: we have all relied on her.

11 Preston later married a West Indian woman and, "apart from his commitment to jazz, he had a special fondness for Jamaican music" (Robertson 2003, 33).

12 Note though Jeffrey Green's cautionary tone about the swift construction of a new cultural hierarchy involving classical performances by black musicians: "Once the numbers of black people in Britain reached level, from the 1950s, where African descent was no longer a novelty, the white audiences for concert presentations seemed to have disappeared. . . . *There was no room in Britain for a black concert hall performer in the 1950s*" (Green 1990, 42; my emphasis).

13 Cowley's reminder, in a brief discussion of this song, that "most be bop performers recorded for US Savoy, with whom Melodisc had a leasing arrangement" in Britain, does suggest an alternative motivation for these lyrics (1990, 69). More intriguingly, did the word "Afro-beat" pre-exist the final line of the lyric here? Did Fela Anikulapo-Kuti, studying and playing in London a few years later, hear it there first, to claim it as his own in 1968 back in Nigeria, where the term was employed "as a reaction to the slavish relationship many other Nigerian bandleaders then had with black American music" (Stapleton and May 1987, 67)?

14 I asked Bruce Johnson if the Australian union's actions were connected to the debates among British musicians at the time:

> My understanding is that the Australian position was parochial, in the sense that there seems to have been little knowledge of or interest in what was happening in the UK/US dynamic. I think that the attitude in the 1920s represented the convergence of three forces: i/ A deep strain of xenophobia and racism in mainstream Australian culture—traceable I think to the sense of insecurity of white Anglo-Saxon identity in a society so remote from Europe, and with Asia in the geographical middle of that gap. These were particularly triggered by African-American revue *The Coloured Idea*, 1928. ii/ In a basically conservative music industry, dominated by musicians brought up in Anglo-European traditions, the impact of US jazz was as inflammatory as the later arrival of rock: morally and aesthetically repugnant. iii/ These combined to exacerbate indignation against the lucrative returns on jazz performance, and especially the runaway success of the visiting [Americans], to what was seen as the detriment of employment opportunities for "straight" local dance musicians. (Personal correspondence, 2003)

> In his history of Australian jazz, *Black Roots, White Flowers*, Andrew Bissett maps the stark ideological use of national music in the contestation of imperial identity: "The dominant classes wanted everyone to listen to British music in the hope that they would act in a British, or conventional, way. If they listened to jazz, it was feared they might not. An editorial in the [Melbourne newspaper the] *Argus* said that British music expressed 'essentially British qualities and British ideals. It is for the most part, sane and wholesome. . . .' The *Argus* hoped that if more people came to like English folk songs, that might 'yet redeem a popular taste perverted by an imported vogue of sheer barbarism, with inspiration no loftier than the savagery of the African Negro' " (Bissett 1987, 42).

15 In a BBC radio feature on what became of Atwell's "other piano," it transpired that "she had copies of it made. This was to enable her to perform at venues miles apart when she was doing a series of one-night stands. Bob Rust from Essex told *Making History* that he had worked for a haulage contractor that specialised in carrying pianos for a London piano-maker, Challen's. He himself had delivered one 'other' piano to Manchester and a second to Glasgow and knew of the existence of at least half a dozen. Unlike the original they did not have initials carved on them but were specially distressed to make them look battered" (*Making History* 2004).

16 Though Val Wilmer pictures a different welcome from white bandleaders and opera-

tors for such musicians during this time: "Any individual who resisted when called on to play 'minstrel' roles earned a 'troublemaker' reputation and suffered unemployment as a result. The status of Caribbean musicians was anyway relatively low in jazz circles, a common belief being that most of them were less than accomplished when it came to improvising, a damaging attitude that would prevail for many years" (Wilmer 1989, 50). It is Wilmer's view that "Jamaican musicians and other Caribbeans only came to Britain because immigration restrictions prevented them from going to the United States, the overwhelming first-choice" (personal correspondence, 2004).

17 Though note Goode's comment about the importance of the classical tradition for such an approach: "He often used to draw analogies with painting. . . . Those of us who had had a bit of classical training could see what he had in mind. Shake Keane, Pat Smythe and myself had had experience of classical music and we could understand that idea of using music impressionistically and creating some kind of overall texture of sound in which each instrument is just a component" (Goode and Cotterrell 2002, 136).

18 The notes are a slightly edited version of an article written by Harriott in 1963 for the British magazine *Jazz News*. The complete original article is reprinted as Harriott 1997.

19 The tenor tyro Tubby Hayes: "If that's fucking jazz, give me trad!" (quoted in Robertson 2003, 105).

20 Coleridge Goode is less certain about the importance of the project to Harriott, though: "Using someone else's musical conception, as in Indo-jazz, must have been no substitute for being able to pursue his own personal vision" (Goode and Cotterrell 2002, 179).

21 There were efforts to exploit this innovation more fully, as in directly imitative projects such as the feebly titled *Curried Jazz* album of 1969 by a group called the Indo-British Ensemble. The composer Victor Graham explained: "I didn't want this record to assume an air of doomy pretentiousness . . . I just wanted everyone to blow some happy exotic music" (quoted in Barnes 1969).

22 Even his gravestone displays the epitaph, his own words: "Parker? There's them over *here* can play a few aces too . . ."

23 The point betrays the continuing reliance on critical evaluation from the United States, of course, and the impact of Harriott's five-star achievement is still remembered— but it is worth noting that it would only be in the following year that the British singer Cleo Laine's album *Shakespeare and All That Jazz* would itself be five-starred (see Laine 1994, 209). While Laine is herself half-Jamaican, more interestingly her album presents a *themed Britishness* in its negotiation and combination of national cultures, of new American culture (jazz) with English iconicity (Shakespeare).

24 Bakari argues that there was also a specific Caribbean impulse to this: "Harriott importantly epitomised a wider cultural movement among African-Caribbean writers and artists in Britain that aimed to establish an independent and assertive global presence. The Caribbean Artists Movement (1966–72) was established by major writers and artists . . . [who] recognised the need to establish an African-Caribbean identity that was not read through the prism of the African-American experience, but in terms of its specific British colonial and post-colonial experience" (Bakari 1999, 102). Harriott's trumpeter Shake Keane was active in the CAM.

25 By contrast, in his book *Improvisations* (1992) the guitarist Derek Bailey allots space to British developments from jazz to free jazz to free improvisation, including material on his own group from the mid-1960s, Joseph Holbrooke—which never released records—while Harriott's catalogue, surely absolutely central to the topic, is ignored.

26 To restate only the most obvious evidence of Harriott's neglect by the very historians whose projects aimed to champion or explore the music's achievements. The following studies or histories of British jazz and improvised music could—*should*—for reasons of chronology or specified music form all contain significant material on Harriott: Carr 1973, Cotterrell 1976, Godbolt 1989, Couldry 1995. None does. It would take Chris Blackford's excellent small publication *Rubberneck* to produce a collection of writings on Harriott, the first in any detail, almost a quarter of a century after his death. Thanks to the sterling effort of a few, Harriott's legacy now seems assured: many of the experimental recordings have now been re-released, Goode's autobiography *Bass Lines*, written with Roger Cotterrell, also redresses the balance somewhat (2002), while Alan Robertson's biography, published in 2003, tells the musical life.

27 His trumpeter Shake Keane described their conversations about philosophy and music as efforts to "unscrew the inscrutable" (quoted in Robertson 2003, 58).

28 Mark Sinker references this in a feature on Loose Tubes in the *Wire* in 1986, in which he writes of "the 'racist and sexist' tag that's been dogging them. There's a relatively tiny percentage of women and of black musicians working in the relevant areas: Loose Tubes, notoriously, have only picked up one from the second category . . . and none from the first. . . . OK, it's a social problem, and they have a duty to consider it. But really it's hard to set out exactly how unfair the charges are, all told. They represent precisely that collective democracy in action that some of their critics only dream of" (Sinker 1986–87, 27).

29 Nor would they be the last: the extraordinary duration of apartheid saw many other musicians, black and white, subsequently take this route, I think inspired and often practically aided by the surviving Blue Notes. For example, 1970 saw the guitarist Lucky Ranku and the bassist Ernest Mothle settle in Britain, followed in 1975 by the percussionist Brian Abrahams and the trumpeter Claude Deppa. Each was to make a contribution to British jazz, and to play his share of fund-raising concerts for the anti-apartheid movement. One of Abrahams's bands was called District Six, after the historic multiracial area of Cape Town, which had been declared a whites-only zone in 1966 and effectively razed over the next few years, with the forcible removal of its sixty thousand inhabitants. See Muff Andersson's "Band on the Run" (1981) for a list of South African exile musicians.

30 The empire would not always approve, no matter where the black presences came from: reviewing a concert by the black American Hampton Singers at Westminster Abbey in 1930, the Johannesburg *Sunday Times* remarked waspishly, "One gets rather nauseated with the manner in which London loses its heart to anything black" (quoted in Oliver 1990a, 13).

31 Kenny Graham's Afro-Cubists was a band in the Dizzy Gillespie Cuban rhythms and bop fusion mode, formed originally in 1950 and re-formed periodically in later years. The tenor saxophonist Graham had played previously in big bands led by Leslie "Jiver" Hutchinson, and the Afro-Cubists' lineup was heavily oriented toward percussion, in-

cluding maracas, congas, and bongos. They played an early modernist music, which included the leader's own compositions and arrangements, with exoticizing titles such as "Mango Walk," "Cuban Canon," and, best, "Afrocadabra" (Godbolt 1989, 113). Joe Harriott played on at least one recording of the band in 1954. Graham frequently employed African drummers such as Billy Olu Sholanke and Guy Warren (Stapleton 1990, 93, 94).

32 During the early 1970s the Afro-rock band Osibisa had significant commercial success in Europe and the United States, which was possible in part because of the West Indian and African musical and social identities that I explore in this chapter. The saxophonist and leader Teddy Osei, who studied music in London in the 1960s on a scholarship from the Ghanaian government (a small part of Kwame Nkrumah's post-independence cultural-national project), explained the bridging of tensions within the band: "We combined the West African and the West Indian elements. Before that there was a barrier, the West Indians thinking the Africans were bush people; the Africans looking down on the West Indians as slaves" (quoted in Stapleton 1990, 99). Interestingly, such cross-black dialogues are almost embodied in one of the award-winning younger voices of the newest generation of black British jazz. The saxophonist Soweto Kinch was born in 1978, named by his Barbadian and Jamaican-British parents after the South Western Townships near Johannesburg that had seen repressed student uprisings in 1976.

33 In a black Atlanticist sweep, now aimed more directly at American jazz, Fanon goes on to critically identify those "white jazz specialists" who reject the new musics of jazz, in his case bebop; for them, "jazz should only be the despairing, broken-down nostalgia of an old Negro who is trapped between five glasses of whisky, the curse of his race, and the racial hatred of the white men" (Fanon 1965, 195).

34 There is in this a certain, perhaps inevitable colonial irony. McGregor himself was from a Scottish missionary family firmly enough established in the cape to have had a village named after it: "McGregor." This casual manifestation of white colonial power would be neatly answered by his exile family's practice of holding an annual weekend-long party or festival around the farmhouse in France, beginning in 1985, called the *Bama-gwedza* — "ba" meaning "family or tribe of," and "Magwedza" being the Africanization of McGregor, much used by Dudu Pukwana (McGregor 1995, 201).

35 *Love* mattered to McGregor; he understood its utopian power, and sought to harness, cherish this in his music. He also aimed to perform it in the music: one terrific manifestation was that he would direct different sections of the Brotherhood big band by blowing kisses on the beat (McGregor 1995, 129).

36 The cultural boycott would finally be adopted as policy by the United Nations a quarter of a century later. See Denselow 1990, 186–202, for detail on pop activism against apartheid in the 1980s, including the international row over Paul Simon's boycott-busting album *Graceland* and Hugh Masekela's intervention in this row.

37 She reminds us of the irony that the Transcription Centre was funded by American "philanthropic" organizations as part of the informal cultural cold war, with the aim of reducing communist influence in the newly forming independent African nations (McGregor 1995, 87).

38 Though of South African origin, D'Oliveira was qualified to play for England and had

already done so. He was not picked for the South Africa tour at first, but only later when the socialist bowler Tom Cartwright withdrew from the squad. Because it practiced a strict sporting apartheid, the South African government made its opposition known, and the tour was canceled. As a result of much grassroots activism in Britain, all official touring links between the two cricketing nations were severed for decades. The sports boycott had already been very successful internationally—as powerfully witnessed by the exclusion of South Africa from the Olympic Games in the 1960s—but the cricket boycott had a strong impact in Britain because of cricket's imperial, white traditions.

39 Others did not use their music as their campaigning medium. As an illustration of the kinds of pressures of exile, Manfred Mann told me: "I did do an Anti-Apartheid Movement gig at the Festival Hall in London in '65, but I stopped associating with the campaign for one simple, compelling reason: I didn't want to be banned from returning to South Africa. I never went to play there, but I *did* want to be able to go back to see my grandmother, father, mother. This was terribly important to me" (personal interview, 2003).

40 Let us acknowledge that their contribution was not even always recognized by those who should have known better. For example, the marathon pop concert held at Wembley Stadium in June 1988 to commemorate the seventieth birthday of the imprisoned Nelson Mandela, and to promote and raise funds for the anti-apartheid cause, found no place for even a short set by the surviving exile South African jazz musicians in Britain, but did manage to include surprise guest Eric Clapton—he of the racist remarks in 1976 that had been partly responsible for the founding of Rock Against Racism (Denselow 1990, 279). After all, as recently as 1985 there had been a series of benefit concerts in response to recent atrocities by the authorities in South Africa: the Action on South Africa Now festival featured Max Roach, Hugh Masekela, and Thomas Mapfumo, as well as some of the British- and European-based South African bands such as Jabula, Dudu Pukwana's Zila, and Johnny Dyani's Witchdoctor's Son.

41 It is worth pointing out that one of the African National Congress's specific conditions for entering negotiations with the remaining South Africa apartheid regime in the period up to 1990 was "the unconditional return of all exiles" (Nixon 1994, 115). The ANC had in mind those who had fought or escaped apartheid and found themselves in neighboring African countries, rather than the cultural exiles who, in Rob Nixon's phrase, had "headed for those venerable magnets of the bohemian diaspora—London, Paris, New York, Chicago and Berlin" (Nixon 1994, 118).

42 Joe Boyd, the band's manager for a period, as well as the producer of what were effectively the first Blue Notes album in 1968 and the first Brotherhood of Breath album in 1971, described the process of reception: at first "they were exotic and interesting and they were going to go home. And when they didn't go home they became a threat. I felt there was a certain amount of racism involved. Visiting black musicians are OK because they are going to go home, but when they stay and they nick your girlfriends, that's a different thing" (quoted in McGregor 1995, 96). The familiar white masculine fear of miscegenation rapidly shifts the context from music to the social in Boyd's observation.

43 The inclusion of sailors' music making is a significant one: it permits us to recognize, as Alan Rice has pointed out, that "the improvisational nature of the [sea] shanty and its changing forms"—as well as its central structuring collective device of call and response—is a significant early instance of at least partial mixing of black music and folk music: "Originating in the Caribbean, in the American Southern states and at sea on the wild Atlantic, shanties are the prototype of a mobile, sea-chopped, African diasporic music" (Rice 2003, 19, 20).

44 They in turn would begin to appear at alternative spaces such as the Implosion festival at the Roundhouse in London, and at occasional rock festivals like Bickershaw, Lancashire, in 1972, alongside the Grateful Dead and Captain Beefheart. At the Roundhouse McGregor felt his view of the music's joyful accessibility validated: the band "started our set backstage and tumbled onto the stage like crazies! By the third bar, everyone [in the audience] was on their feet, shouting! . . . Now, for someone who's thinking in clichés of what pop music's about and what avant-garde jazz is about and have got everything neatly pigeonholed, that's a complete turnabout!" (quoted in McGregor 1995, 124–25, 146).

45 It is important to acknowledge these financial subsidies and grants: even where small, they signal the other side of the narrative, challenging the musicians' familiar and frequent lament about lack of state support for their art.

46 For a different musical perspective I asked Manfred Mann about this. As a white would-be jazzer, he had left South Africa in 1961 with his old school friend and fellow band member Harry Miller, on the same boat for London, to escape apartheid. Now in what he terms the "grandfatherly" stage of his pop and rock career, Mann was reluctant to accept such a simplistic biographical correspondence between exile and short life. Indeed, he identified for me the nomadic career of the international professional musician as one potentially more rather than less comfortable with a personal experience of displacement (personal interview, 2003).

47 Not all Africanizations of jazz in Britain would be as successful. The Ghanaian percussionist Guy Warren had lived in the United States for many years, knew the modernists there, and "according to Max Roach, re-introduced black Americans to their rich heritage of African rhythms. Guy Warren thus had a profound influence on the re-Africanisation which permeated free jazz in the sixties and beyond" (Wickes 1999, 20). When Warren joined the Rendell-Carr Quintet in Britain for a short period in 1969, "he played everything from talking drums to maracas, cowbells, Indian bells, gourd, bamboo flute, harmonica and tambourine—but more than his music, his attitude to music, his dress, his uninhibited manner seemed to epitomise a completely and refreshingly opposite approach to jazz" to Carr's own. "His whole performance was a kick in the teeth for the traditional and hip idea of the cool improvising genius. Under this sort of assault, the reserve, the Britishness of the group, had to crumble and either shatter into embarrassing fragments or with luck metamorphose into something else" (Carr 1973, 123, 124). It is fascinating that all parties on the stage seemed to be conscious of what was effectively the performance of exoticization, with the added dimension that it led to the destruction of a carefully crafted British jazz identity.

1   Charles Jencks proposed the term "adhocism" in 1968—see the early postmodern book of the same name about improvisational cultures, or "mongrel creativity": "Popular music presents such dazzling examples of adhocism that one could scarcely recount them all" (Jencks and Silver 1973, 105, 135 n. 29). Curiously, jazz is not even mentioned. I prefer the term adhockery: it makes no claims to the scientific or theoretical rigor of an -ism, and it rhymes with mockery.

2   Not everyone approved of what could be seen as Eicher's retro approach rooted in a cool aesthetic of the 1950s, by which it could be argued that a certain nostalgia was inscribed in this contemporary music. The German critic—and, it should be noted, rival label producer—Joachim Berendt accused Eicher of presenting a "new jazz fascism" of "pretty sounds," which led a number of musicians to sign advertisements in the music press distancing themselves from Berendt's comments (quoted in Wickes 1999, 138).

3   While the later free musicians are learning their trade in Germany, other British musicians are too: having developed from skiffle roots to building a small but devoted following at clubs like the Cavern in Liverpool, the Beatles moved temporarily to Hamburg in 1960, undertaking a two-month tour of the city, honing their act, music, image, technique, stamina, and lineup. Within a few years the Beatles would lead the extraordinary "British invasion" of American pop, in scale and success a chauvinistic and international narrative through music quite different from the one I am delineating here.

4   See Eddie Prévost's comments on AMM's use of silence in performance: "The silences just happened, and they could be incredibly intense. I had never even *heard* of John Cage at this time, we weren't exploring his ideas, we didn't even know them!" (personal interview, 2002).

5   It is worth noting that there was a musical and political tradition in the Cardew family. Cornelius's uncle, Phil Cardew, was a bandleader and communist, involved in the People's Convention of 1940. The turn in a single generation from popular to avant-garde music was apparently not welcomed by the Communist Party's musical arbiters. According to Hanlon and Waite, "Perhaps these family connections help explain the particular resentment which was directed against Cardew when his [early] art was not in line with communist preferences. He was the composer targeted in a document which the CP Music Group prepared in 1962 as a supplement to the *British Road to Socialism* programme. Considering 'modern trends in composition,' they decided that 'the latest fashion—indeterminism—in particular is a policy of despair, an admission that life has become too much for us, and that we are incapable of controlling it, something no communist can agree to' " (Hanlon and Waite 1998, 82).

6   Along with the saxophonist Evan Parker and the percussionist Tony Oxley, Bailey established the independent record label Incus with what Parker has called "an obsessive non-business approach" to the commercial side of things (quoted in Ansell 1985, 43). When asked in London in 1972 for a definition of the music that crossed or blurred jazz, classical, and rock, Carla Bley ended up with: "Call it non-profit music" (quoted in Fordham 1996, 32).

7   Does the free improvisation scene (continue to) self-marginalize? There is a perhaps slightly waspish passing comment in the *Review of Jazz in England*, published in 1995 by the Arts Council of England: "to many of those playing free improvisation, the fact that there is no formal relationship with the structures of jazz means that this music should not be included under a jazz 'umbrella' " (ACE 1995, 16). It pointedly notes that "self-help organisations include The London Musicians' Collective, one of the longest-surviving organisations, which does not, however, consider itself a jazz-based organisation" (ACE 1995, 20)—perhaps this rare moment of strategic reflexivity and consultation with the improvising community on the part of the major arts funder in the country was not the best time to be overly dogmatic.

8   Debates about the importance of instrumental technique have long played a part in the development of the jazz aesthetic. It is interesting to compare some of the second-generation free British musicians with that early starting point of jazz in Britain, the Original Dixieland Jazz Band. Nick La Rocca and his band proclaimed themselves "musical anarchists" and were dismissive of the importance of technique, flaunting their inability to read music. For the debates on technique in British free music see Couldry 1995, 11–13; Atton 1988, 13–15.

9   For instance, jazz and poetry as a collaborative project *had been positively embraced* by British musicians for a decade by this date (see Robson 1969; Robertson 2003, ch. 7). Michael Garrick and Jeremy Robson organized the first formal poetry and jazz event at the Royal Festival Hall in 1961, attracting an audience of three thousand (Carr 1973, 4). This followed collaborations by the poet Christopher Logue with the Tony Kinsey quintet, and Pete Brown's and Michael Horowitz's New Departures Poetry with Stan Tracey and Bobby Wellins. Joe Harriott was a frequent contributor. This cross-cultural collaboration can be partly explained by the perceived congruity between the two cultures: the masculinity of jazz as well as of most of the poets involved, the importance of the solo stylist, the "purity" of the forms, the vocal and transient aspects of performance, the relative marginality of both to the cultural mainstream, and so on.

10   The counterculture's impact continued to be felt in later decades, perhaps especially so in the provinces, and jazz was understood by the alternative constituency to be part of that project. As late as 1984, for instance, Leeds Jazz was established, the impulse for its existence coming from firmly within the countercultural community. Barry Cooper recalls: "Those were the days of a thriving alternative scene—Leeds Other Paper, the Leeds Trades Club . . . Red Ladder Theatre Company . . . , myriad alternative political and grass-roots community and cultural groups—and it suddenly seemed a short step to the formation of 'Leeds Jazz Promotions' as it was first dreamed up" (Cooper 2002).

11   For Welfare State International's influence on later community music projects see Moser and McKay 2005.

12   The composer, bassist, and jazz author Graham Collier has expressed a more sardonic view of doing political benefit gigs: "In view of this generally bad economic situation [for jazz musicians in Britain], it always affords me a slight chuckle when I hear of jazz groups doing benefits for such as the striking miners . . . Try as I may, I can't imagine the miners' union saying 'Well lads, jazz boys are in a mess in't London. Shall we give today's pay to help them out?' " (Collier 1973, 125).

13 Since punk did not valorize instrumental technique, perhaps the punk years were an appropriate cultural period in which a skilled drummer could relearn his instrument with a drastically curtailed physicality.

14 Despite the musically exclusionary name of the best-known and perhaps most influential of these, RAR, its slogan was "Reggae, Soul, Rock 'n' Roll, Jazz, Funk and Punk: Our Music," while David Widgery articulates his version of the organization's politico-cultural antecedents: "In my dream of [RAR's] christening party Billie Holiday dueted with Paul Robeson, Archie Shepp jammed with Django Reinhardt and Max Roach, James Baldwin swapped jokes with Dorothy Parker, and Colin MacInnes served behind the bar" (1986, 53).

15 Kate Westbrook recalls the importance of the Westbrook Brass Band repertoire at political events, and identifies a limitation in the new Cornelius Cardew politico-aesthetic: "We were involved in a lot of left-wing events with the Brass Band. The big Grunwick demonstration [about a lengthy industrial dispute from 1976 to 1978 involving British Asian women], we were on that. I remember Cornelius Cardew and Keith Rowe and others were all on the back of a wagon, handing out lyric sheets, singing tunes in support of the striking workers, singing perhaps rather banal tunes for such sophisticated avant-garde musicians. [But t]he Brass Band was marching along, playing numbers by Jelly Roll Morton, an Elizabethan piece arranged by Paul Rutherford, 'Hot jamboree' (a Welfare State tune)" (personal interview, 2003).

16 See Waite 1995 for a different perspective on the British Communist Party's and the Young Communist League's sometimes difficult relations with youth culture in the context of popular music more generally, rather than jazz and improvised music alone.

17 One small example from the organizations of 1968 here. Ian Carr describes how "The Jazz Centre Society was set up . . . to find places for regular weekly sessions, and to receive financial aid from the Arts Council. A group of musicians involved in the more extreme forms of radical experimentation[,] believing that the Jazz Centre Society was discriminating against them and their music, broke away and formed the Musicians' Co-operative" (1973, 85).

18 How surprising is this? I am struck severally by my own comparisons in this section of traditional jazz and free music — but why? Apart from their common emphasis on collective improvisation, they are forms of music profoundly *different* from each other, after all. The connection does have something to do with the feeling among exponents of each genre that they are strongly marginalized and unsupported by the cultural establishment, even more so than those working in other jazzes — "despised," to use the shocking word of Eddie Prévost (once a trad drummer). The rationale for lack of support may go thus: trad is dismissed as a retrogressive amateur form, free jazz as a tiny minority interest that hovers uneasily between avant-garde and amateur. One is viewed as too popular with uncritical audiences, the other as too unpopular, and playing only to critics and other musicians.

19 In terms also of a sometimes contumacious anti-music position? I noted earlier the resonance of some LMC rhetoric with the Original Dixieland Jazz Band; with punk there was another intriguing explosion of "musical anarchism," in the ODJB leader La Rocca's phrase (see Savage 1991; Nehring 1993; Marcus 1989; McKay 1996, ch. 3).

20   Southern white Presidents contributed to this: Jimmy Carter holding a jazz concert party on the South Lawn of the White House in 1978, Bill Clinton *playing* tenor sax in the 1990s.

21   Though note the point made by Keith Tippett, who does work with both classical and jazz students in colleges (though "I'm not a teacher, by the way"). As Tippett recognizes, "Of course, the danger is that students can be all taught to sound the same, and you just can't apply the same criteria to jazz as to western classical music. But I always say to [jazz] students: 'Would your mother recognize you on the radio?' " (personal interview, 2003).

22   When I was unemployed in 1985, I managed to get a job with an offshoot project in East Anglia, Community Music East. I spent half my week for two or three years working through Stevens's techniques with my colleagues, and then taking them into the community. Musically, it meant that I learned how to play first in front of and then second with other musicians, and to listen, count, keep all sorts of time signatures together, and have a freer technique on my instrument. On the down side, typical of the musical autodidact, I was never much of a reader, and that didn't change. Socially, I learned a bit about teaching, addressing and working with a group, identifying and solving problems, how to be calm, meeting kinds of people from outside my normal social circle. Politically, well, all the previous, and the experience confirmed what I thought about the importance of culture in social relations, though I appreciate that this sounds a bit feeble. Played some *great* gigs too, with musicians and non-musicians alike.

23   Community music more generally has probably overtaken community theater as the most successful, or most generously funded, community arts form in Britain. See McKay 2005 for that shift.

CHAPTER 5: "MALE MUSIC" TO FEMINIST IMPROVISING

1   According to Leonard Feather, the Musicians' Union persisted for years with the term "sideman" rather than "musician" on its band contracts (1986, 163).

2   See Bayton 1998, 26, for a graphic breakdown of "typical gender distribution of social roles in the popular music world."

3   The avant-garde saxophonist Evan Parker once articulated such a gendered drive toward creativity, but defined it in opposition to more socially acceptable or mundane masculinities: "I don't know whether I should feel: 'Now's the time for me to be a man and support my wife and children,' but I don't feel like that . . . *I really feel that what I'm doing is important enough for me not to behave like a "man" in that sense of the word*" (quoted in Carr 1973, 89; my emphasis).

4   It may be possible to read such constructions of masculinity within a framework of national identity. Bruce Johnson confirms what the critic Jim Godbolt called the "Antipodean cockiness" of Graeme Bell's Australian Jazz Band in London when trad flourished in the late 1940s (quoted in Johnson 2000, 158), extending this as a claim that the music "reflects something of the Australian mythology of 'mateship' " (2000, 162). There was a perception among some of the more sedate British jazzers of a masculine

threat from one of the New Worlds. In Johnson's analysis, the "aggressive egalitarianism of the Australians was frequently interpreted as ockerism and ratbaggery, and their style as brashness in social conduct and music. . . . Strengthened by the virile success of Australian sportsmen, such characterisations were generalised to become part of the 'national character' " (2000, 163).

5 It should be acknowledged, with or without irony, that musicians' experiences in the military forces may help to explain the contributions of jazz to the peace and antinuclear movements.

6 And that, in John Dankworth's words, led to London bebop: "Club Eleven was an indirect result of Ronnie and me and the rest of us coming off the boats full of this music and wanting to try it out on someone" (quoted in Grime and Wilmer 1979, 46).

7 Although, gay or straight, bender or breeder, there could remain an appeal to a crudely controlling normative masculinity in the sexual arena of the period, forcefully illustrated by Colin MacInnes, novelist and critic of the new scenes and sounds of urban black and white Britain: "What you must do, son, is become a fucker, and not become a fucked. It's simple as that. Boys or girls, up the pussy or the arse, whichever you prefer, but you've got to remember there's a cock between your legs and you're a *man*" (quoted in Segal 1997, 18; emphasis in original).

8 Maintaining masculinist positions, when Ken Colyer met him on a reunion tour two decades later, he completely ignored Laurie, stating "*He* cleared off to India to stand on his fucking head leaving *me* to hold the fort" (quoted in Godbolt 1989, 84; emphasis in original).

9 For example, in 1952 there were 654 convictions for "acts of indecency with males" (Montagu 2000, 120). See also Knitting Circle 2002.

10 I mean "minor" in comparison with, say, Edward Montagu's imprisonment in the 1950s, or indeed with the murderous bombing of a gay pub in London in 1999 by a neo-Nazi.

11 The name of a short-lived all-woman big band in London in the early 1980s; a parodic critical response to the predominantly masculine practice of Chris McGregor's various big bands that went under the name of the Brotherhood of Breath. The trombonist Annie Whitehead played in both the Brotherhood and the Sisterhood. As the Sisterhood guitarist Deirdre Cartwright recalls, the name was "a nod to the Brotherhood of Breath big band that had long been active, obviously, but there was also a reference to punk in it: it was 1981 or so, and there was a sense we picked up from punk of 'Yes, we can get up and just do it.' The punk thing was more in terms of its ideals than any musical aesthetic. The Sisterhood came out of the women's movement directly: the Dutch saxophonist Angèle Veltmeijer, who was also in the Feminist Improvising Group, was running a saxophone class at the Women's Arts Alliance, I had run a guitar class there for a short while. The sax class came together with some friends and other musicians to form the big band" (personal interview, 2004).

12 Actually libidinal pleasure has not been the sole preserve of women through improvisation. Clive Bell of the London Musicians' Collective has recalled: "[There was] one musician *warning me* that after a John Stevens workshop he had observed that most of the male participants had erections" (1999; my emphasis).

13 These were important venues for music, and in fact one plays a minor role in the trans-atlantic development of jazz. It was at the Lyons' Corner House on Shaftesbury Avenue that the young John Hammond claimed first to have heard jazz, in the form of an offshoot of the American Paul Specht's band, the Georgians, which played a reper-toire in the style of ODJB. So Hammond, writes Jim Godbolt, "the man with such a distinguished history in supporting black jazz[,] commenced his involvement when only a thirteen-year-old listening to a white group in a London restaurant in 1923" (1984, 53).

14 Cf. Lucy Green: "All-women punk and post-punk bands like the Slits and the Rain-coats grew up, presumably unwittingly, in the wake of their Victorian and Edwardian foremothers" (1997, 76).

15 The date may explain why Benson was receiving national press coverage relatively late in her career: with some irony, the Sex Discrimination Act of 1975 forced a change of name on the band. "Ladies" or "girls" were no longer legal, as this would be discrimi-natory against male musicians, so in Britain the group became Ivy Benson and Her Showband.

16 Sophie Fuller has also argued that "a certain lack of acceptance by the [classical music] establishment has led to women being particularly involved in breaking down some of the boundaries between different kinds of music," providing as an example the trajectory of the bassoonist Lindsay Cooper, who was classically trained at the Royal Academy of Music, worked with the rock group Henry Cow and the Feminist Impro-vising Group, and was also a composer (Fuller 1995, 33).

17 The contents page of this edition of *Musics* shows that this was the only piece in it written by women.

18 Perhaps in an echo of FIG's performative gender critique, the Guest Stars originally planned to give away a free tea towel with each copy of their second album.

19 With the re-forming of the Guest Stars two decades after the band's success, Cart-wright found herself reviewing their political assumptions and achievements, in jazz as well as more widely. "When we folded the band in 1987–88, we did have a feeling that the Guest Stars had done its job: it had allowed us women the opportunity to get valuable new experience in music making. We all then went off to work with other musicians, male and female. I suppose we felt that there were by then lots of women musicians, so there wasn't the same need for a separate project. Getting together again in 2004, we've noticed that actually not that much in the jazz world has changed. The lifestyle of hanging around, the ad hoc nature of things, the lack of rehearsal and band continuity, the word-of-mouth way you get gigs—women still really lose out in that kind of situation" (personal interview, 2004).

20 In *Madame Jazz*, Leslie Gourse mentions in passing that some American musicians have refused to play in "all-women's groups or all-women's festivals out of an unwill-ingness to be ghettoised. . . . [They] have taken a firm anti-women's group stand" (1995, 14).

21 This seemed not to be an issue at all in the Ivy Benson bands. If anything, the oppo-site: Benson regularly complained that she needed to replace a band member because she had left to get married, frequently, it seems, to American GIs met when the band

played at military bases. It is plausible that one of the side attractions of being with Benson was the opportunity for working-class English women to meet a greater variety of men.

CONCLUSION

1 These are some of the legendary moments of British jazz for its enthusiasts. They hold together the fabric of the local scene. They are both narratives of cultural escape, repeated with the envy and admiration that success breeds, and affirmation of the absolute primacy of the United States in jazz culture. Escape from what, though? When Ian Carr's Nucleus returned from the United States in 1970, where the band had appeared at the Newport Jazz Festival and played a set at the Village Gate in New York, Carr described the feeling as "like returning from a forest full of wild beasts where one could never be certain who was the hunter or who or what was being hunted, to a small landscape garden with some plaster gnomes in it" (1973, 144).

BIBLIOGRAPHY

INTERVIEWS AND CORRESPONDENCE

The interviews were variously undertaken person-to-person, by telephone, and in writing concerning agreed-on questions. During personal and telephone interviews I took handwritten notes, which I then edited and transcribed, and offered to send back to the interviewee for correction or amendment. This offer was usually taken up. With each interviewee's permission, I have made the transcripts and most of the correspondence available, interspersed with images, at www.uclan.ac.uk/amatas

Gwen Ansell: e-mail, through 2003
Colin Barker: e-mail, 23 April 2002
Steve Beresford: telephone, 28 November 2002
Alan Bonney (trust secretary, Ken Colyer Trust): in person, 19 January 2002,
     St Albans, Herts.
Colin Bowden: telephone, 10 April 2002
Deirdre Cartwright: telephone, 6 April 2004
Graham Collier: telephone, 13 February 2004; amended by e-mail, 8 March 2004
Gary Crosby: telephone, 2 December 2002
Ben Crow: e-mail, 16 October 2002
John Fox: telephone, June 2004
Brian Harvey (jazz journalist, member, Ken Colyer Trust): in person, 19 January
     2002, St Albans, Herts.
Tony Haynes: telephone, 15 December 2002
Ken Hayton: in writing, 23 December 2003
Eric Hobsbawm: e-mail, 4 May 2004
Captain Peter Hunter (committee member, Ken Colyer Trust): in person, 19 January
     2002, St Albans, Herts.

Bruce Johnson: e-mail, 8 April 2003

Dave Laing: telephone, 2002

Steve Lane: in writing, 16 January 2001; telephone, 11 January 2002

Chris Macdonald: in writing, 9 January 2001

Manfred Mann: telephone, 11 July 2003; revised, December 2003

George Melly: in person, 25 February 2002, London

John Minnion: in person, 12 December 2001, Newport, Gwent

Lord Montagu of Beaulieu: telephone, 1999, 26 March 2004

Keith Nicholls: telephone, 6 December 2003

Maggie Nicols: telephone, 23 November 2002; written amendments, 5 February
2003

Jeff Nuttall: in person, 13 December 2001, Abergavenny

Eddie Prévost: e-mail, 1 November 2002; telephone, 15 November 2002

Keith Tippett: telephone, 29 January 2003

Trevor Watts: e-mail, 12 December 2002, January 2003

Kate Westbrook: telephone, 9 January 2003; written amendments, 16 January 2003

Mike Westbrook: in writing, 16 January 2003

Val Wilmer: in person, 24 January 2002, London; in writing, 20 April 2004, 11 May
2004

Jen Wilson: in person, 11 December 2001, Swansea

OTHER SOURCES

Aaronovitch, Sam. 1951. "The American Threat to British Culture." Sam Aaronovitch
et al., *The American Threat to British Culture*. London: Arena, Fore. 3–22.

ACE [Arts Council of England]. 1995. *Review of Jazz in England: Consultative Green Paper*.
London: Arts Council of England.

Adam, Kenneth, Eric Maschwitz, Gladys H. Davies, and George Mitchell. N.d. *The Black
and White Minstrel Show*. London: BBC Publications.

Adorno, Theodor W. 1941. "On popular music." Simon Frith and Andrew Goodwin, eds.
1990. *On Record: Rock, Pop and the Written Word*. London: Routledge. 301–14.

———. 1967. "Perennial Fashion: Jazz." Theodor W. Adorno. 1981. *Prisms*. Trans. Samuel
and Shierry Weber. Cambridge: MIT Press. 119–32.

AFN [American Forces Network] radio. 2002. www.afneurope.army.mil/. Accessed
4 November 2002.

Anderson, Ian. 2001. "The Cultural Boycott." Editorial in *Folk Roots*, May. http://www
.frootsmag.com/shop/boycott/. Accessed February 2004.

Andersson, Muff. 1981. "Band on the Run." *Music in the Mix: The Story of South African
Popular Music*. Johannesburg: Ravan. 119–22.

Ansell, Kenneth. 1985. "Incus: For the Record." *Wire* 15, May, 42–43.

Ansermet, Ernest. 1919. "Sur un orchestre nègre." Trans. Walter E. Schaap. Robert
Walser, ed. 1999. *Keeping Time: Readings in Jazz History*. Oxford: Oxford University
Press. 9–11.

Atkins, E. Taylor. 2001. *Blue Nippon: Authenticating Jazz in Japan*. Durham: Duke
University Press.

Atticus. 1975 [?] "The Girls in the Band." *Sunday Times*. Posted on Ravenhill 2004.

Atton, Christopher F. 1988. "Improvised Music: Some Answers to Some Questions." *Contact*. 13–17.

Back, Les. 2001. "Syncopated Synergy: Dance, Embodiment, and the Call of the Jitterbug." Vron Ware and Les Back. *Out of Whiteness: Colour, Politics and Culture.* Chicago: University of Chicago Press. 169–95.

Bailey, Derek. 1992 [1980]. *Improvisation: Its Nature and Practice in Music.* Rev. ed. New York: Da Capo.

Bakari, Imruh. 1999. "Exploding Silence: African-Caribbean and African-American Music in British Culture towards 2000." Andrew Blake, ed. *Living through Pop.* London: Routledge. 98–111.

Baker, Paul. 2002. *Polari: The Lost Language of Gay Men.* London: Routledge.

Baldwin, James. 1979. "Of the Sorrow Song: The Cross of Redemption." James Campbell, ed. 1995. *The Picador Book of Blues and Jazz.* London: Picador. 324–31.

Barnes, Ken. 1969. Liner notes, Indo-British Ensemble, *Curried Jazz.* Music for Pleasure MFP 1307.

Baudrillard, Jean. 1986. *America.* Trans. Chris Turner. London: Verso, 1989.

Bayton, Mavis. 1998. *Frock Rock: Women Performing Popular Music.* Oxford: Oxford University Press.

Beaulieu Film Archive. 1961. Movietone newsreel, newsreel compilation tape no. 7. Beaulieu Motor Museum Archive, Hampshire.

Beaulieu Jazz Festival. Press cuttings files, Beaulieu Motor Museum Archive, Hampshire.

Beck, Earl R. 1985. "The Anti-Nazi 'Swing Youth,' 1942–1945." *Journal of Popular Culture* 19, no. 3:45–53.

Belair, Felix. 1955. "United States Has Secret Sonic Weapon: Jazz." Robert Walser, ed. 1999. *Keeping Time: Readings in Jazz History.* Oxford: Oxford University Press. 240–41.

Bell, Clive. 1999. "A Brief History of the L[ondon] M[usicians'] C[ollective]." www.l-m-c.org.uk/archive/history.html. Accessed 28 October 2002.

Berendt, Joachim. 1976. *The Jazz Book.* London: Paladin. Eng. ed. of 1973 rev. ed.

Berg, Ivan, and Ian Yeomans. 1962. *Trad: An A to Z Who's Who of the Traditional British Jazz Scene.* London: Foulsham.

Bissett, Andrew. 1987 [1979]. *Black Roots, White Flowers: A History of Jazz in Australia.* Rev. ed. Sydney: Australian Broadcasting Corporation.

Blackford, Chris. 1997. "In Search of Joe Harriott." Chris Blackford, ed. *Joe Harriott: Forgotten Father of European Free Jazz. Rubberneck* 25:17–27.

Blair, John G. 1997. "Blackface Minstrels as Cultural Export: England, Australia, South Africa." George McKay, ed. *Yankee Go Home (& Take Me with U): Americanisation and Popular Culture.* Sheffield: Sheffield Academic Press. 53–66.

Blake, Andrew. 1997. *The Land without Music: Music, Culture and Society in Twentieth Century Britain.* Manchester: Manchester University Press.

———, ed. 1999. *Living through Pop.* London: Routledge.

Booker, Christopher. 1969. *The Neophiliacs: A Study of the Revolution in English Life in the Fifties and Sixties.* London: Collins.

Borshuk, Michael. 2001. "An Intelligence of the Body: Disruptive Parody through Dance in the Early Performances of Josephine Baker." Dorothea Fischer-Hornung and

Alison D. Goeller, eds. *EmBODYing Liberation: The Black Body in American Dance*. Forum for European Contributions to African American Studies, vol. 4. Hamburg: Lit. 41–57.

Boulton, David. 1958. *Jazz in Britain*. London: W. H. Allen.

Boyd, Joe. 1993. "May 68 remembered." *Wire* 111, May, 31.

Boyes, Georgina. 1993. *The Imagined Village: Culture, Ideology and the English Folk Revival*. Manchester: Manchester University Press.

Bradbury, Malcolm. 1982. *All Dressed Up and Nowhere to Go*. London: Pavilion.

Brunn, Harry O. 1961. *The Story of the Original Dixieland Jazz Band*. London: Sidgwick and Jackson.

Brunner, John. 1983. "Music on the march." John Minnion and Philip Bolsover, eds. *The CND Story: The First 25 Years of CND in the Words of the People Involved*. London: Allison and Busby. 45–47.

Buckman, Peter. 1970. *The Limits of Protest*. 2d ed. London: Panther.

Campbell, Duncan. 1984. *The Unsinkable Aircraft Carrier: American Military Power in Britain*. London: Michael Joseph.

Campbell, Ian. 1983. "Music against the Bomb." John Minnion and Philip Bolsover, eds. *The CND Story: The First 25 Years of CND in the Words of the People Involved*. London: Allison and Busby. 115–17.

Campbell, James. 1995. Introduction. James Campbell, ed. *The Picador Book of Blues and Jazz*. London: Picador.1–8.

Campbell, Neil, Jude Davies, and George McKay, eds. 2004. *Issues in Americanisation and Culture*. Edinburgh: Edinburgh University Press.

Cardew, Cornelius, ed. 1972. *Scratch Music*. London: Latimer.

———. 1974. *Stockhausen Serves Imperialism*. London: Latimer.

Carr, Ian. 1973. *Music Outside: Contemporary Jazz in Britain*. London: Latimer.

Carter, Wyn. 1953. "The Life and Career of Winifred Atwell." *Souvenir Album of Winifred Atwell*. London: Francis and Day.

Chambers, Iain. 1985. *Urban Rhythms: Pop Music and Popular Culture*. London: Macmillan.

———. 1986. *Popular Culture: The Metropolitan Experience*. London: Routledge.

Chilton, John. 1997. *Who's Who of British Jazz*. London: Cassell.

Clarke, Michael. 1982. *The Politics of Pop Festivals*. London: Junction.

Clash. 1978. "(White Man) in Hammersmith Palais" / "The prisoner." CBS Records. CBS 6383.

Cobbold, Chrissie Lytton. 1986. *Knebworth Rock Festivals*. London: Omnibus.

Cohen, Phil. 1997. "Laboring under Whiteness." Ruth Frankenberg, ed. *Displacing Whiteness: Essays in Social and Cultural Criticism*. Durham: Duke University Press. 244–82.

Colin, Sid. 1977. *And the Bands Played On*. London: Elm Tree.

Collier, Graham. 1973. *Inside Jazz*. London: Quartet.

———. 1976. *Cleo and John: A Biography of the Dankworths*. London: Quartet.

———. 1985. "Brave new world?" *Wire* 15, May, 5.

———. 2000. "Song for Europe." Conversation with Janne Murto. www.jazzcontinuum.com/jc_rtcl2.html. Accessed February 2004.

Collin, Dorothy W. 1991. "Sidgwick and Jackson Limited." Jonathan Rose and Patricia J. Anderson, eds. *British Literary Publishing Houses 1881–1965*. Dictionary of Literary Biography, vol. 112. London: Gale. 307–15.

Colyer, Ken. 1989. *When Dreams Are in the Dust: The Path of a Jazz Man*. Ken Colyer Trust.

———. 1992 [1970]. *New Orleans and Back*. 2d ed. Ken Colyer Trust.

Cook, Richard. 1987–88. "The Main Man: Courtney Pine." *Wire* 46–47, December–January, 40–49.

———. 1992. "Major Barbara: Saxophonist and Bandleader Barbara Thompson Reflects on a Life at the Top of British Jazz." *Wire* 97, March, 16–18.

Cooke, Jack. 1997. "Transcending the Ordinary: Memories of Joe Harriott." Chris Blackford, ed. *Joe Harriott: Forgotten Father of European Free Jazz. Rubberneck* 25:28–29.

Cooper, Barry. 2002. "Jazz to the People!" www.leeds.ac.uk/music/LJA/frm/about.html. Accessed February 2004.

Cornwell, Jane. 2002. "Making It Happen: The Increasing Role of Women in Jazz." *Jazzwise* 59, November, 28–29.

Cotterrell, Roger. 1997. "A Joe Harriott Memorial." Chris Blackford, ed. *Joe Harriott: Forgotten Father of European Free Jazz. Rubberneck* 25:4–12.

———, ed. 1976. *Jazz Now: The Jazz Centre Society Guide*. London: Quartet.

Couldry, Nick. 1995. "Turning the Musical Table: Improvisation in Britain, 1965–1990." *Rubberneck* 19.

Coult, Tony. 1999. "One Foot on the Ground, One Foot Moving: An Introduction to the Work of Welfare State International." Tony Coult and Baz Kershaw, eds. *Engineers of the Imagination: The Welfare State Handbook*. Rev. ed. London: Methuen. 1–15.

Coult, Tony, and Baz Kershaw, eds. 1999. *Engineers of the Imagination: The Welfare State Handbook*. Rev. ed. London: Methuen.

Cowley, John. 1990. "London Is the Place: Caribbean Music in the Context of Empire, 1900–60." Paul Oliver, ed. *Black Music in Britain: Essays on the Afro-Asian Contribution to Popular Music*. Milton Keynes: Open University Press. 58–76.

Cowley, Julian. 2002. "People Have the Power.' *Wire* 220, June, 42–47.

Crawford, Helen. 1921. "The Jazz Period." *Communist*, 8 October. www.sites.scran.ac.uk/redclyde/redclyde/rc173.htm. Accessed April 2004.

Croft, Andy. 1998. Introduction. Andy Croft, ed. *A Weapon in the Struggle: The Cultural History of the Communist Party in Britain*. London: Pluto. 1–6.

Dahl, Linda. 1984. *Stormy Weather: The Music and Lives of a Century of Jazzwomen*. London: Quartet.

Davis, Angela Y. 1998. *Blues Legacies and Black Feminism: Gertrude "Ma" Rainey, Bessie Smith, and Billie Holiday*. New York: Vintage.

Dean, Roger. 1992. *New Structures in Jazz and Improvised Music since 1960*. Milton Keynes: Open University Press.

DeNora, Tia. 2000. *Music in Everyday Life*. Cambridge: Cambridge University Press.

Denselow, Robin. 1990. *When the Music's Over: The Story of Political Pop*. Rev. ed. London: Faber and Faber.

Devlin, Joyce. 1993. "Siren Theatre Company: Politics in Performance." Lynda Hart and

Peggy Phelan, eds. *Acting Out: Feminist Performances*. Ann Arbor: University of Michigan Press. 181–200.

Dibben, Nicola. 2002. "Gender Identity and Music." Raymond A. R. Macdonald, David J. Hargreaves, and Dorothy Miell, eds. *Musical Identities*. Oxford: Oxford University Press. 117–33.

Duff, Peggy. 1971. *Left, Left, Left: A Personal Account of Six Protest Campaigns, 1945–65*. London: Allison and Busby.

Durant, Alan. 1984. "Improvisation: Arguments after the Fact." AIM [Association of Improvising Musicians]. *Improvisation: History, Directions, Practice*. London: AIM. 5–10.

Dutch Swing College Band. 2003. www.dscband.nl. Accessed November 2002.

Dworkin, Dennis. 1997. *Cultural Marxism in Postwar Britain: History, the New Left, and the Origins of Cultural Studies*. Durham: Duke University Press.

Dyer, Geoff. 1991. *But Beautiful: A Book about Jazz*. Rev. ed. London: Abacus.

Eley, Rod. 1974. "A History of the Scratch Orchestra." Cornelius Cardew, ed. *Stockhausen Serves Imperialism*. London: Latimer. 11–32.

Eliot, T. S. 1954. *Selected Poems*. London: Faber and Faber.

Elstob, Lynne, and Anne Howes. 1987. *The Glastonbury Festivals*. Glastonbury: Gothic Image.

Eyerman, Ron, and Andrew Jamison. 1998. *Music and Social Movements: Mobilizing Traditions in the Twentieth Century*. Cambridge: Cambridge University Press.

Fanon, Frantz. 1965. *The Wretched of the Earth*. Trans. Constance Farrington. New York: Grove.

Farren, Mick, and Edward Barker. 1972. *Watch Out Kids*. London: Open Gate.

Feather, Leonard. 1946. "The Blindfold Test: Mary Lou Williams." www.leonardfeather.com/feather_blindfold.html. Accessed August 2003.

———. 1974. "Jazz: Goodwill Ambassador Overseas; Fighter against Jim Crow in the U.S." Robert Walser, ed. 1999. *Keeping Time: Readings in Jazz History*. Oxford: Oxford University Press. 302–5.

———. 1986. *The Jazz Years: Earwitness to an Era*. London: Quartet.

Feigin, Leo. 1985. "Notes of a Record Producer." Leo Feigin, ed. *Russian Jazz: New Identity*. London: Quartet. 172–207.

FIG [Feminist Improvising Group]. 1978 [?]. "Feminist Improvising Group: A Discussion about the Music/Context Festival Which Led On to More General Points about our Work." *Musics* [?], 9–11.

Finkelstein, Sidney. 1948. *Jazz: A People's Music*. New York: Citadel.

Fishkin, Shelley Fisher. 1996. "Interrogating 'Whiteness,' Complicating 'Blackness': Remapping American Culture." Henry B. Wonham, ed. *Criticism and the Color Line: Desegregating American Literary Studies*. New Brunswick: Rutgers University Press. 251–90.

Fordham, John. 1986. *Let's Join Hands and Contact the Living: Ronnie Scott and His Club*. London: Elm Tree.

———. 1996. *Shooting from the Hip: Changing Tunes in Jazz*. London: Kyle Cathie.

Forgacs, David. 1993. "Americanisation: The Italian Case, 1938–1954." *Borderlines: Studies in American Culture* 1, no. 2, December, 157–69.

Fox, John. 1999. "Commissions and Audiences: How Welfare State's Events Are Commissioned, Conceived and Carried Out." Tony Coult and Baz Kershaw, eds. *Engineers of the Imagination: The Welfare State Handbook*. Rev. ed. London: Methuen. 16–30.

Frankenberg, Ruth. 1997. "Introduction: Local Whitenesses, Localizing Whiteness." Ruth Frankenberg, ed. *Displacing Whiteness: Essays in Social and Cultural Criticism*. London: Duke University Press. 1–33.

Frith, Simon. 1988. "Playing with Real Feeling: Jazz and Suburbia." *Music for Pleasure: Essays in the Sociology of Pop*. Cambridge: Polity. 45–63.

Fuller, Sophie. 1995. "Dead White Men in Wigs: Women and Classical Music." Sarah Cooper, ed. *Girls! Girls! Girls! Essays on Women and Music*. London: Cassell. 22–36.

Gendron, Bernard. 1995. " 'Moldy Figs' and Modernists: Jazz at War (1942–1946)." Krin Gabbard, ed. *Jazz among the Discourses*. Durham: Duke University Press. 31–56.

Giddins, Gary. 1994. "Leonard Feather Obituary." *Village Voice*. www.leonardfeather .com/feather_obituary.html. Accessed July 2003.

Gill, John. 1995. *Queer Noises: Male and Female Homosexuality in Twentieth-Century Music*. London: Cassell.

Gilroy, Paul. 1987. *There Ain't No Black in the Union Jack: The Cultural Politics of Race and Nation*. Rev. ed. London: Hutchinson.

———. 1993. *The Black Atlantic: Modernity and Double Consciousness*. London: Verso.

———. 2002. "Introduction: Race Is Ordinary." *There Ain't No Black in the Union Jack: The Cultural Politics of Race and Nation*. Rev. ed. London: Routledge. xi–xxxix.

Godbolt, Jim. 1984. *A History of Jazz in Britain: 1919–1950*. London: Quartet.

———. 1989. *A History of Jazz in Britain: 1950–1970*. London: Quartet.

Goddard, Chris. 1979. *Jazz Away from Home*. London: Paddington.

Gold, Harry. 2000. *Gold, Doubloons and Pieces of Eight*. Ed. Roger Cotterrell. London: Northway.

Goode, Coleridge, and Roger Cotterrell. 2002. *Bass Lines: A Life in Jazz*. London: Northway.

Gourse, Leslie. 1995. *Madame Jazz: Contemporary Women Instrumentalists*. Oxford: Oxford University Press.

Green, Jeffrey. 1990. "Afro-American Symphony: Popular Black Concert Hall Performers, 1900–40." Paul Oliver, ed. *Black Music in Britain: Essays on the Afro-Asian Contribution to Popular Music*. Milton Keynes: Open University Press. 34–44.

Green, Lucy. 1997. *Music, Gender, Education*. Cambridge: Cambridge University Press.

Grime, Kitty, and Val Wilmer. 1979. *Jazz at Ronnie Scott's*. London: Robert Hale.

Gubar, Susan. 1997. *Racechanges: White Skin, Black Face in American Culture*. Oxford: Oxford University Press.

Hall, Stuart, and Paddy Whannel. 1964. *The Popular Arts*. London: Hutchinson.

Hanlon, Richard, and Mike Waite. 1998. "Notes from the Left: Communism and British Classical Music." Andy Croft, ed. *A Weapon in the Struggle: The Cultural History of the Communist Party in Britain*. London: Pluto. 68–88.

Harker, Dave. 1980. *One for the Money: Politics and Popular Song*. London: Hutchinson.

Harriott, Joe. 1961. *Free Form*. Liner notes. Polygram CD reissue 538184-2, 1998.

———. 1963. *Abstract*. Liner notes. Polygram CD reissue 538183-2, 1998.

———. 1973. *Memorial 1973*. One-Up: OU 2011.

———. 1997. "The Truth about Free Form Jazz." Chris Blackford, ed. *Joe Harriott: Forgotten Father of European Free Jazz*. *Rubberneck* 25:30–31.

Hart, Lynda. 1993. Introduction. Lynda Hart and Peggy Phelan, eds. *Acting Out: Feminist Performances*. Ann Arbor: University of Michigan Press. 1–12.

Hebdige, Dick. 1988. "Towards a Cartography of Taste, 1935–1962." *Hiding in the Light: On Images and Things*. London: Comedia. 45–76.

Heble, Ajay. 2000. *Landing on the Wrong Note: Jazz, Dissonance and Critical Practice*. London: Routledge.

Heckstall-Smith, Dick. 1989. *The Safest Place in the World: A Personal History of Rhythm and Blues*. London: Quartet.

Hemmings, Susan, and Norma Pitfield. 1977. "Feminist Improvising Group: Review." *Musics* 15, December, 20.

Herbert, Trevor. 2000. "Nineteenth-Century Bands: Making a Movement." Trevor Herbert, ed. *The British Brass Band: A Musical and Social History*. Oxford: Oxford University Press. 10–67.

Hershey, Burnet. 1922. "Jazz Latitude." Robert Walser, ed. 1999. *Keeping Time: Readings in Jazz History*. Oxford: Oxford University Press. 25–31.

Hewison, Robert. 1981. *In Anger: Culture in the Cold War, 1945–1960*. London: Weidenfeld and Nicolson.

Hibberd, Dave. 2000. *My Kind of Town: Recollections of Jazz in Bristol*. Bristol: Fiducia.

Hinton, Brian. 1995. *Message to Love: The Isle of Wight Festivals, 1968–70*. Chessington, Surrey: Castle Communications.

Hinton, James. 1989. *Protests and Visions: Peace Politics in Twentieth-Century Britain*. London: Hutchinson Radius.

Hobsbawm, Eric. 1998. *Uncommon People: Resistance, Rebellion and Jazz*. London: Weidenfeld and Nicolson.

Hobsbawm, Eric, and Terence Ranger, eds. 1983. *The Invention of Tradition*. Cambridge: Cambridge University Press.

Houghton, Jayne. 1986. "Stroppy Cow: Women at Work." *Wire* 26, April, 7.

Hutnyk, John. 2000. *Critique of Exotica: Music, Politics and the Culture Industry*. London: Pluto.

Huxley, Ros, and Sue English. 1998. *Women and Jazz*. Exeter/Chard, Somerset: South West Jazz / Chard Festival of Women in Music.

Jencks, Charles, and Nathan Silver. 1973. *Adhocism: The Case for Improvisation*. New York: Anchor.

Johnson, Bruce. 2000. *The Inaudible Music: Jazz, Gender and Australian Modernity*. Sydney: Currency.

Kamalu, Chukwunyere. 1996. "The Forgotten Ones: Amancio D'Silva." *Jazz Journal International* 49, no. 8, August, 19.

Kater, Michael H. 1992. *Different Drummers: Jazz in the Culture of Nazi Germany*. Oxford: Oxford University Press.

Kent, Greta. 1983. *A View from the Bandstand*. Comp. Carole Spedding. London: Sheba Feminist Publishers.

Kerouac, Jack. 1957. *On the Road*. New York: Viking.

Kershaw, Baz. 1992. *The Politics of Performance: Radical Theatre as Cultural Intervention*. London: Routledge.

King, Clive. 1963. *Stig of the Dump*. London: Puffin.

King, Michael. 1994. *Wrong Movements: A Robert Wyatt History*. London: SAF.

Kitchener, Lord [pseud. of Aldwyn Roberts]. 1951. "Kitch's Bebop Calypso." *London Is the Place for Me: Trinidadian Calypso in London, 1950–56*. Honest Jon's Records HJRCD2.

———. 1953. "If You're Not White You're Black." *London Is the Place for Me: Trinidadian Calypso in London, 1950–56*. Honest Jon's Records HJRCD2.

Knitting Circle. 2002. "The 1950s Great Purge." www.southbank-university.ac.uk/ ~stafflag/purge1950s.html. Accessed 25 June 2002.

Kofsky, Frank. 1998. *Black Music, White Business: Illuminating the History and Political Economy of Jazz*. New York: Pathfinder.

Kroes, Rob. 1993. "Americanisation: What Are We Talking about?" R. Kroes, R. W. Rydell, and D. F. J. Bosscher, eds. *Cultural Transmissions and Receptions: American Mass Culture in Europe*. Amsterdam: VU University Press. 302–18.

Laine, Cleo. 1994. *Cleo*. New York: Simon and Schuster.

Lambert, Constant. 1934. *Music Ho! A Study of Music in Decline*. London: Faber and Faber.

Lang, Iain. 1942 [?]. *Background of the Blues*. London: Workers' Music Association.

———. 1957. *Jazz in Perspective: The Background of the Blues*. London: Hutchinson.

Larkin, Philip. 1985. *All What Jazz: A Record Diary, 1961–71*. London: Faber and Faber. Orig. pubd. 1970 as *All What Jazz: A Record Diary, 1961–68*.

Lhamon, W. T. 1998. *Raising Cain: Blackface Performance from Jim Crow to Hip Hop*. Cambridge: Harvard University Press.

Lock, Graham. 1985. "Paying Guests." *Wire* 22, December, 38–41.

Lyttelton, Humphrey. 1958. *Second Chorus: Drawings by the Author*. London: MacGibbon and Kee.

Maher, James T. 1987. Foreword. Marian McPartland. *All in Good Time*. Oxford: Oxford University Press. vii–xv.

Mairants, Ivor. 1980. *My Fifty Fretting Years: A Personal History of the Twentieth Century Guitar Explosion*. Gateshead: Ashley Mark.

Making History. 2004. "What Happened to Winifred Atwell's 'Other' Piano?" www.bbc.co.uk/education/beyond/factsheets/makhist/makhist8_prog8a.shtml. Accessed 31 March 2004.

March to Aldermaston. 1958. Produced and directed by the Film and Television Committee for Nuclear Disarmament.

Marcus, Greil. 1989. *Lipstick Traces: A Secret History of the Twentieth Century*. Cambridge: Harvard University Press.

Martin, Denis-Constant. 1995. Introduction. Maxine McGregor. *Chris McGregor and the Brotherhood of Breath: My Life with a South African Jazz Pioneer*. Flint, Mich.: Bamberger. i–v.

Martin, T. E. 1997. "Joe Harriott." Chris Blackford, ed. *Joe Harriott: Forgotten Father of European Free Jazz*. *Rubberneck* 25:13–16.

Massey, Doreen. 2000. "The Geography of Power." *Red Pepper*, July. www.redpepper .org.uk. Accessed April 2003.

Matthew, Brian. 1962. *Trad Mad*. London: Consul.

McClary, Susan. 1991. *Feminine Endings: Music, Gender, and Sexuality*. Minneapolis: University of Minnesota Press.

McDevitt, Chas. 1997. *Skiffle: The Definitive Inside Story*. London: Robson.

McGregor, Maxine. 1995. *Chris McGregor and the Brotherhood of Breath: My Life with a South African Jazz Pioneer*. Flint, Mich.: Bamberger.

McKay, George. 1996. *Senseless Acts of Beauty: Cultures of Resistance since the Sixties*. London: Verso.

———. 1997. "Introduction: Americanization and popular culture." George McKay, ed. *Yankee Go Home (& Take Me with U): Americanisation and Popular Culture*. Sheffield: Sheffield Academic Press. 11–52.

———. 1998. "This Filthy Product of Modernity . . ." *Index on Censorship* 27, no. 6. Special ed., *The Book of Banned Music*. 170–73.

———. 2000a. *Glastonbury: A Very English Fair*. London: Gollancz.

———. 2000b. "Anti-Americanism, Youth and Popular Music, and the Campaign for Nuclear Disarmament in Britain." Sylvie Mathé, ed. *Anti-Americanism at Home and Abroad*. Aix-Marseille: Publications de l'Université de Provence. 185–206.

———. 2003. "Just a Closer Walk with Thee: New Orleans–Style Jazz and the Campaign for Nuclear Disarmament in 1950s Britain." *Popular Music* 22, no. 3, autumn, 261–81.

———. 2004. " 'Unsafe Things like Youth and Jazz': Beaulieu Jazz Festivals (1956–61) and the Origins of Pop Festival Culture in Britain." Andy Bennett, ed. *Remembering Woodstock*. Aldershot: Ashgate. 90–110.

———. 2005. "Improvisation and the Development of Community Music in Britain; Followed by the Case of More Music in Morecambe." Pete Moser and George McKay, eds. *Community Music: A Handbook*. Lyme Regis, Dorset: Russell House. 61–76.

———, ed. 1998. *DIY Culture: Party and Protest in Nineties Britain*. London: Verso.

McKibbin, Ross. 1998. *Classes and Cultures: England, 1918–1951*. Oxford: Oxford University Press.

McPartland, Marian. 1987. *All in Good Time*. Oxford: Oxford University Press.

Melly, George. 1965. *Owning-Up*. London: Weidenfeld and Nicolson.

———. 1970. *Revolt into Style: The Pop Arts in Britain*. London: Allen Lane.

Meltzer, David, ed. 1993. *Reading Jazz*. San Francisco: Mercury House.

Mendl, R. W. S. 1927. *The Appeal of Jazz*. London: Philip Allan.

Menter, Will. 1981. *The Making of Jazz and Improvised Music: Four Musicians' Collectives in England and the USA*. PhD diss., University of Bristol.

Mercer, Kobena, and Isaac Julien. 1988. "Race, Sexual Politics and Black Masculinity: A Dossier." Rowena Chapman and Jonathan Rutherford, eds. *Male Order: Unwrapping Masculinity*. London: Lawrence and Wishart. 97–164.

Miles, Barry. 2002. *In the Sixties*. London: Jonathan Cape.

Mingus, Charles. 1971. *Beneath the Underdog: His World as Composed by Mingus*. New York: Alfred A. Knopf.

Minnion, John, and Philip Bolsover. 1983. Introduction. John Minnion and Philip Bolsover, eds. *The CND Story: The First 25 Years of CND in the Words of the People Involved*. London: Allison and Busby. 9–41.

Mishalle, Luk, Boris Howarth, and Peter Moser. 1999. "Street and Outdoor Performance and Music: (ii) Music." Tony Coult and Baz Kershaw, eds. *Engineers of the Imagination: The Welfare State Handbook*. Rev. ed. London: Methuen. 41–57.

Montagu, Edward. 1973. *The Gilt and the Gingerbread*. London: Michael Joseph.

———. 2000. *Wheels within Wheels: An Unconventional Life*. London: Weidenfeld and Nicolson.

Morden, Karen. 2004. *The Odd Boy: Sixties Crossovers and Cultural Explorations in the Work of Vivian Stanshall*. DPhil thesis, University of Sussex.

Morgan, Kevin. 1998. "King Street Blues: Jazz and the Left in Britain in the 1930s–1940s." Andy Croft, ed. *A Weapon in the Struggle: The Cultural History of the Communist Party in Britain*. London: Pluto. 123–41.

Morton, Brian. 1984. "Black Masks, White Masks." *Wire* 10, December, 42–43.

———. 1985. "Heavy Weather: Second Storm." *Wire* 17, July, 5.

Morton, Jelly Roll. 1949. "The 'Inventor of Jazz.'" Robert Walser, ed. 1999. *Keeping Time: Readings in Jazz History*. Oxford: Oxford University Press. 16–22.

Moser, Pete, and George McKay, eds. 2005. *Community Music: A Handbook*. Lyme Regis, Dorset: Russell House.

Myers, Margaret. 2000. "Searching for Data about European Ladies' Orchestras, 1870–1950." Pirkko Moisala and Beverley Diamond, eds. *Music and Gender*. Urbana: University of Illinois Press. 189–213.

Nehring, Neil. 1993. *Flowers in the Dustbin: Culture, Anarchy, and Postwar England*. Ann Arbor: University of Michigan Press.

Nelson, Elizabeth. 1989. *The British Counter-Culture, 1966–73: A Study of the Underground Press*. London: Macmillan.

News from Nowhere, eds. 2003. *We Are Everywhere: The Irresistible Rise of Global Anticapitalism*. London: Verso.

Newton, Francis [pseud. of Eric Hobsbawm]. 1959. *The Jazz Scene*. Rev. ed. Harmondsworth: Penguin, 1961.

NIAS. 1993. "Questions of Cultural Exchange: The NIAS [Theme Group on the European Reception of American Mass Culture at the Netherlands Institute for Advanced Study in the Humanities and Social Sciences] statement on the European reception of American mass culture." R. Kroes, R. W. Rydell, and D. F. J. Bosscher, eds. *Cultural Transmissions and Receptions: American Mass Culture in Europe*. Amsterdam: VU University Press. 321–33.

Nicholls, Brian. 1957. "The British Jazz Scene: The Modernists." Sinclair Traill, ed. *Concerning Jazz*. London: Faber and Faber. 148–60.

Nicholson, Stuart. 1986. "Young Turks: Courtney Pine." *Wire* 25, March, 31–32.

———. 1998. *Jazz Rock: A History*. Edinburgh: Canongate.

Nixon, Rob. 1994. "Refugees and Homecomings: Bessie Head and the End of Exile." George Robertson et al., eds. *Travellers' Tales: Narratives of Home and Displacement*. London: Routledge. 114–28.

Noblett, Richard. 2002. Liner notes to CD *London Is the Place for Me: Trinidadian Calypso in London, 1950–56*. Honest Jon's Records HJRCD2.

Norton-Taylor, Richard. 2003. "Saddam Aims to Drag Allies into a New Stalingrad, Says British Forces' Chief.' *Guardian*, 11 March 2003, 3.

Nuttall, Jeff. 1968. *Bomb Culture*. London: MacGibbon and Kee.

————. 1979. *Performance Art*, vol. 2, *Scripts*. London: John Calder.

O'Brien, Lucy. 1993. "Ivy League Days." *Wire* 114, August, 32–34.

————. 1995. "Sisters of Swing: Stardom, Segregation and 1940s/1950s Pop." Sarah Cooper, ed. *Girls! Girls! Girls! Essays on Women and Music*. London: Cassell. 70–83.

Olewnick, Brian. 2003. "Peacemongering Pianist." *Wire* 230, April, 12.

Oliver, Paul. 1990a. Introduction to part 1. Paul Oliver, ed. *Black Music in Britain: Essays on the Afro-Asian Contribution to Popular Music*. Milton Keynes: Open University Press. 3–15.

————. 1990b. Introduction to part 2. Paul Oliver, ed. *Black Music in Britain: Essays on the Afro-Asian Contribution to Popular Music*. Milton Keynes: Open University Press. 79–86.

O'Meally, Robert G., ed. 1998. *The Jazz Cadence of American Culture*. New York: Columbia University Press.

Osborne, John. 1957a. *Look Back in Anger*. London: Faber and Faber.

————. 1957b. "Sex and Failure." Gene Feldman and Max Gartenberg, eds. *Protest*. London: Panther. 269–71.

Ostrovsky, Sergei. 1993. "Americanisation of Culture in Russia: From Jazz 'on the Bones' to Coca-Cola on the Chest." *Borderlines: Studies in American Culture* 1, no. 1, September, 71–84.

Palmer, Richard, and John White, eds. 1999. *Reference Back: Philip Larkin's Uncollected Jazz Writings, 1940–1984*. Hull: University of Hull Press.

Paul, Kathleen. 1997. *Whitewashing Britain: Race and Citizenship in the Post-War Era*. Ithaca: Cornell University Press.

————. 2001. "Communities of Britishness: Migration in the Last Gasp of Empire." Stuart Ward, ed. *British Culture and the End of Empire*. Manchester: Manchester University Press. 180–99.

Pells, Richard. 1993. "American Culture Abroad: The European Experience since 1945." R. Kroes, R. W. Rydell, and D. F. J. Bosscher, eds. *Cultural Transmissions and Receptions: American Mass Culture in Europe*. Amsterdam: VU University Press. 67–83.

Phillips, Mike, and Trevor Phillips. 1998. *Windrush: The Irresistible Rise of Multi-racial Britain*. London: Harper Collins.

Pleasants, Henry. 1961. *Death of a Music? The Decline of the European Tradition and the Rise of Jazz*. London: Gollancz.

Pound, Ezra. 1975. *Selected Poems*. London: Faber and Faber.

Prévost, Edwin. 1984. "Commentary on the Proceedings." AIM [Association of Improvising Musicians]. *Improvisation: History, Directions, Practice*. London: AIM. 11–13.

————. 1995. *No Sound Is Innocent: AMM and the Practice of Self-Invention: Meta-Musical Narratives: Essays*. Harlow: Copula.

Ramamurthy, Anandi. 2003. *Imperial Persuaders: Images of Africa and Asia in British Advertising*. Manchester: Manchester University Press.

Ravenhill, Brian. 2004. Ivy Benson memorial website, www.ivybenson-online.com. Accessed March–April 2004.

Rebellato, Dan. 2001. "Look Back at Empire: British Theatre and Imperial Decline." Stuart Ward, ed. *British Culture and the End of Empire*. Manchester: Manchester University Press. 73–90.

Reinelt, Janelle. 1993. "Resisting Thatcherism: The Monstrous Regiment and the School of Hard Knox." Lynda Hart and Peggy Phelan, eds. *Acting Out: Feminist Performances*. Ann Arbor: University of Michigan Press. 161–80.

Rice, Alan. 2003. *Radical Narratives of the Black Atlantic*. London: Continuum.

Richardson, Michael. 1996. *Refusal of the Shadow: Surrealism and the Caribbean*. Trans. Michael Richardson and Krzysztof Fijalkowski. London: Verso.

Roach, Joseph. 1996. *Cities of the Dead: Circum-Atlantic Performance*. New York: Columbia University Press.

Roberts, John Storm. 1999. *Latin Jazz: The First of the Fusions, 1880s to Today*. New York: Schirmer.

Robertson, Alan. 2003. *Joe Harriott: Fire in his Soul*. London: Northway.

Robson, Jeremy, ed. 1969. *Poems from Poetry and Jazz in Concert*. London: Panther.

Roy, Arundhati. 2002. "Not Again." *Guardian*, 27 September 2002, § G2, pp. 2–3.

Royal Academy. 1926. *Council Minutes*. Vol. 25. London: Royal Academy.

———. 1958. *Annual Report*. London: Royal Academy.

Russell, Dave. 2000. " 'What's Wrong with Brass Bands?' Cultural Change and the Band Movement, 1918-*c*.1964." Trevor Herbert, ed. *The British Brass Band: A Musical and Social History*. Oxford: Oxford University Press. 68–121.

Rutherford, Jonathan. 1988. "Who's That Man?" Rowena Chapman and Jonathan Rutherford, eds. *Male Order: Unwrapping Masculinity*. London: Lawrence and Wishart. 21–67.

———. 1997. *Forever England: Reflections on Masculinity and Empire*. London: Lawrence and Wishart.

Rye, Howard. 1990. "Fearsome Means of Discord: Early Encounters with Black Jazz." Paul Oliver, ed. *Black Music in Britain: Essays on the Afro-Asian Contribution to Popular Music*. Milton Keynes: Open University Press. 45–57.

Sabin, Roger. 1999. "I Won't Let That Dago By: Rethinking Punk and Racism." Roger Sabin, ed. *Punk Rock: So What? The Cultural Legacy of Punk*. London: Routledge. 199–218.

Sandford, Jeremy, and Ron Reid. 1974. *Tomorrow's People*. London: Jerome.

Savage, Jon. 1991. *England's Dreaming: Sex Pistols and Punk Rock*. London: Faber and Faber.

Schafer, William J. 1977. *Brass Bands and New Orleans Jazz*. Baton Rouge: Louisiana State University Press.

Schwarz, Bill. 1996. "Black Metropolis, White England." Mica Nava and Alan O'Shea, eds. *Modern Times: Reflections on a Century of English Modernity*. London: Routledge. 176–207.

Scott, Richard. 1991. "Call Me Mr Drums." *Wire* 85, March, 34–37, 64.

Seamen, Phil. 1973. *Phil Seamen Story*. Decibel Records, BSN 103.

Segal, Lynne. 1997. *Slow Motion: Changing Masculinities, Changing Men*. Rev. ed. London: Virago.

Shapiro, Harry. 1988. *Waiting for the Man: The Story of Drugs and Popular Music*. London: Quartet.

Shipton, Alyn. 2001. *A New History of Jazz*. London: Continuum.

Simons, Andrew. 2001. Liner notes to CD *Black British Swing: The African Diaspora's*

Contribution to England's Own Jazz of the 1930s and 1940s. Topic Records TSCD781. 7–35.

Sinfield, Alan. 1989. *Literature, Politics and Culture in Postwar Britain*. Oxford: Basil Blackwell.

Sinker, Mark. 1986–87. "Loose Tubes on Tour." *Wire* 34–35, December–January, 24–27.

———. 1987. "Bheki Mseleku: Spirit in the Sky." *Wire* 42, August, 30–33.

———. 1990. "Life during Wartime: Jazz Warriors." *Wire* 76, June, 34–37.

———. 1992–93. "Pining for the Future." *Wire* 106–7, December–January, 48–52.

Small, Christopher. 1984. "No Meanings without Rules." AIM [Association of Improvising Musicians]. *Improvisation: History, Directions, Practice*. London: AIM. 1–5.

———. 1985. Foreword. John Stevens, Julia Doyle, and Ollie Crooke. *Search and Reflect*. London: Community Music. iv–v.

Smith, Julie Dawn. 2004. "Playing like a Girl: The Queer Laughter of the Feminist Improvising Group." Daniel Fischlin and Ajay Heble, eds. *The Other Side of Nowhere: Jazz, Improvisation, and Communities in Dialogue*. Middletown, Conn.: Wesleyan University Press. 224–43.

Smith, Mike. 1977. *The Underground and Education: A Guide to the Alternative Press*. London: Methuen.

Stapleton, Chris. 1990. "African Connections: London's Hidden Music Scene." Paul Oliver, ed. *Black Music in Britain: Essays on the Afro-Asian Contribution to Popular Music*. Milton Keynes: Open University Press. 87–101.

Stapleton, Chris, and Chris May. 1987. *African All-Stars: The Pop Music of a Continent*. London: Paladin.

Starr, S. Frederick. 1983. *Red and Hot: The Fate of Jazz in the Soviet Union*. Oxford: Oxford University Press.

Stevens, Reg. 2004. "Winifred Atwell's Singles." www.45-rpm.org.uk/dirw/winifreda .htm. Accessed 31 March 2004.

Steyn, Melissa. 1999. "White Identity in Context: A Personal Narrative." Thomas K. Nakayama and Judith N. Martin, eds. *Whiteness: The Communication of Social Identity*. London: Sage. 264–78.

Storey, John. 1993. *An Introductory Guide to Cultural Theory and Popular Culture*. Athens: University of Georgia Press.

Stovall, Tyler. 1996. *Paris Noir: African Americans in the City of Light*. New York: Mariner.

Sudhalter, Richard. 1999. *Lost Chords: White Musicians and Their Contribution to Jazz, 1915–1945*. Oxford: Oxford University Press.

Taylor, Helen. 2001. *Circling Dixie: Contemporary Southern Culture through a Transatlantic Lens*. New Brunswick: Rutgers University Press.

Taylor, Peter. 1999. *Modernities: A Geohistorical Interpretation*. Cambridge: Polity.

Taylor, Richard. 1988. *Against the Bomb: The British Peace Movement, 1958–1965*. Oxford: Clarendon.

Tenaille, Frank. 2002. *Music Is the Weapon of the Future: Fifty Years of African Popular Music*. Trans. Stephen Toussaint and Hope Sandrine. Chicago: Lawrence Hill.

Thomas, Lorenzo. 1995. "Ascension: Music and the Black Arts Movement." Krin Gabbard, ed. *Jazz among the Discourses*. Durham: Duke University Press. 256–74.

Thompson, E. P. 1951. "William Morris and the Moral Issues To-day." Sam Aaronovitch et al. *The American Threat to British Culture*. London: Arena, Fore. 25–30.

Thompson, John. 1999. *Globalization and Culture*. Cambridge: Polity.

Thompson, Leslie. 1985. *Leslie Thompson: An Autobiography*. Crawley: Rabbit.

Trinh, Minh-ha. 1994. "Other Than Myself / My Other Self." George Robertson et al., eds. *Travellers' Tales: Narratives of Home and Displacement*. London: Routledge. 9–26.

Turner, Bruce. 1984. *Hot Air, Cool Music*. London: Quartet.

Van Elteren, Mel. 1994. *Imagining America: Dutch Youth and Its Sense of Place*. Tilburg: Tilburg University Press.

Veldman, Meredith. 1994. *Fantasy, the Bomb, and the Greening of Britain: Romantic Protest, 1945–1980*. Cambridge: Cambridge University Press.

Vincent, Ted. 1995. *Keep Cool: The Black Activists Who Built the Jazz Age*. London: Pluto.

Vogel, Eric. 1961. "Jazz in a Nazi Concentration Camp." James Campbell, ed. 1995. *The Picador Book of Blues and Jazz*. London: Picador. 211–23.

Waite, Mike. 1995. "Sex 'n' Drugs 'n' Rock 'n' Roll (and Communism) in the 1960s." Geoff Andrew, Nina Fishman and Kevin Morgan, eds. *Opening the Books: Essays on the Social and Cultural History of the British Communist Party*. London: Pluto. 210–24.

Wald, Gayle. 2000. *Crossing the Line: Racial Passing in Twentieth-Century U.S. Literature and Culture*. Durham: Duke University Press.

Wallis, Bob. 1987 [?]. *Revivalism to Commercialism: A Study of Influences on the Developing Styles of Ken Colyer and Acker Bilk*. Undergraduate diss. Held at National Jazz Archive, Loughton, Essex.

Walser, Robert, ed. 1999. *Keeping Time: Readings in Jazz History*. Oxford: Oxford University Press.

Ward, Brian. 1998. *Just My Soul Responding: Rhythm and Blues, Black Consciousness and Race Relations*. London: UCL Press.

Ward, Stuart. 2001. Introduction. Stuart Ward, ed. *British Culture and the End of Empire*. Manchester: Manchester University Press. 1–20.

Ware, Vron. 1997. "Island Racism: Gender, Place, and White Power." Ruth Frankenberg, ed. *Displacing Whiteness: Essays in Social and Cultural Criticism*. Durham: Duke University Press. 283–310.

Waters, Chris. 1990. *British Socialists and the Politics of Popular Culture, 1884–1914*. Manchester: Manchester University Press.

Webster, Duncan. 1988. *Looka Yonder! The Imaginary America of Populist Culture*. London: Comedia.

———. 1989. "Coca-Colonization and National Cultures." *Over Here: Reviews in American Studies* 9, no. 2, winter, 64–75.

Wellman, David. 1997. "Minstrel Shows, Affirmative Action Talk, and Angry White Men: Marking Racial Otherness in the 1990s." Ruth Frankenberg, ed. *Displacing Whiteness: Essays in Social and Cultural Criticism*. Durham: Duke University Press. 311–31.

Whitehead, Kevin. 1998. *New Dutch Swing*. New York: Billboard.

Whitehead, Stephen M. 2002. *Men and Masculinities: Key Themes and New Directions*. Cambridge: Polity.

Whitney, Jennifer. 2003. "Infernal Noise: The Soundtrack to Insurrection." News From Nowhere, eds. *We Are Everywhere: The Irresistible Rise of Global Anticapitalism*. London: Verso. 216–27.

Wickes, John. 1999. *Innovations in British Jazz*, vol. 1, *1960–1980*. London: Soundworld.

Widgery, David. 1976. "Don't You Hear the H-bomb's Thunder?" David Widgery, ed. *The Left in Britain, 1956–68*. Harmondsworth: Penguin. 100–114.

———. 1986. *Beating Time: Riot 'n' Race 'n' Rock 'n' Roll*. London: Chatto and Windus.

Wilford, Hugh. 1994. " 'Winning Hearts and Minds': American Cultural Strategies in the Cold War." *Borderlines: Studies in American Culture* 1, no. 4, June, 315–26.

Williams, Richard. 2003. "The Dedication Orchestra: Music Illuminated by the African Sun." Programme for Contemporary Music Network tour, March, 8–13.

Wilmer, Val. 1977. *As Serious as Your Life: The Story of the New Jazz*. London: Quartet.

———. 1989. *Mama Said There'd Be Days like This: My Life in the Jazz World*. London: Women's Press.

Women in Jazz. 2004. www.jazzsite.co.uk/wja. Accessed 2003.

Women in Music. 2004. "Programming Survey: How Many Women Composers Were Included." www.womeninmusic.org.uk/framed/jennysresearch.htm. Accessed 23 March 2004.

Worden, Nigel. 1995. *The Making of Modern South Africa: Conquest, Segregation and Apartheid*. Oxford: Basil Blackwell.

Worsfold, Sally-Ann. 1983. "That Hywl Feeling!" *Jazz Journal International* 36, no. 3, March, 8–9.

Worthington, Andy. 2004. *Stonehenge: Celebration and Subversion*. Loughborough: Alternative Albion.

Young, John. 2004. *Trapped inside a Jukebox: The Journalistic and Critical Reception of American Popular Music on Film, 1956–1960*. PhD diss., University of Nottingham.

Zwerin, Mike. 1985. *La Tristesse de Saint Louis: Swing under the Nazis*. London: Quartet.

INDEX

Page numbers in italics refer to illustrations.

326 n. 5, 328 n. 15; efforts to overcome, 73, 142, 270; middle, 23, 50, 113, 151, 228; upper, 23, 58, 81, 271, 312 n. 20; working, xiii, 20–21, 23, 68, 76, 99, 149, 164, 246, 270, 273, 281, 313 n. 10, 327 n. 12

McGregor, Chris, 7–8, *180*, 181–83, 186–87, 195, 302, 325 n. 44; whiteness and, 133, 166, 171–74, 183, 185, 323 n. 34

McGregor, Maxine, 174–75

McPartland, Marian, 274, 298

Melly, George, 15, 48–49, 58, 75, 85, 114, 143, 269, 270–71, 307 n. 14

Meltzer, David, 9, 108

Military, *217*, 291, 330 n. 5; homosexuality in, 269; jazz and, 24, 31, 120–21, 132, 260–61, 263, 266, 301; British, 198, 234–35, 262–63, 272; U.S., 38–41, 56, 136, 159. *See also* American Forces Network; Peace movement

Mingus, Charles, 22, 92, 199

Minnion, John, 32–33, 57, 60

Minstrelsy, 109–13, 131, 140, 320 n. 16

Miscegenation, 9, 106–8, 324 n. 42

Mixed media, 205, 212, 233, 292; jazz and visual culture, 153–54, 204, 321 n. 17; music theater, 194, 200–202, 213–14, 289–91, 299; poetry and jazz, 194, 204, 327 n. 9. *See also* Counterculture

Modernism, 14, 15–18, 72–73, 306 n. 6

Modern jazz, 66, 114, 127; free music vs., 156, 321 n. 19; trad vs., 55, 75, 77, 229, 309 n. 2, 312 n. 18

Moholo, Louis, 171–72, 179, 181, 183, 185, 187, 244, 300

Montagu, Edward (Lord), 69–70, 72–73, 76, 80–82, 269–72, 312 nn. 14–16. *See also* Beaulieu Jazz Festival; Homosexuality

Morgan, Kevin, 50–51, 55, 73, 116, 228, 265

Multiculturalism, 13, 201–2, 214

Music education, 106, 213, 329 n. 21; gender and, 247–48, 284–85, 287; in jazz, 164, 183, 233–34, 272; radical, 218, 226, 234–38, 259, 330 n. 12. *See also* Community Music

Music for Socialism, 209, 221, 223, 227, 288, 289

Music hall, 101, 102, 113, 268, 282, 289

Musicians' Union (Britain), 43, 53, 143, 175, 177, 224, 227–28, 281, 289; American Federation of Musicians ban and, 25–27, 29, 30, 39, 122, 146–47, 276, 320 n. 14

Music press: *Down Beat*, 117, 159, 222, 272; *Jazz Journal*, 220; *Melody Maker*, 72, 97, 107, 122, 123, 152, 159, 166; *Metronome*, 117; *Musics*, 289; small magazines, 53, 60, 229, 265; *Wire*, 165, 240

Narcotics, 81, 258

National identity, 268, 307 n. 8; jazz and American, 19, 307 nn. 9–10; jazz and British, ix–xi, 14, 17, 33–34, 43–44, 68, 72, 84, 99, 114, 126–28, 134–35, 195–96, 298–99, 303, 306 n. 3, 321 n. 23; masculinity and, 329 n. 4; postnational identity, 36, 318 n. 3. *See also* Americanization; Commonwealth; Empire

National Jazz Federation, 153, 227

National Youth Jazz Orchestra, 33, 234

Nehring, Neil, 30, 50

Netherlands, 24, 196, 200

New Left, x, 29, 36, 44, 85–86, 127, 135, 170, 178, 302

New Orleans, 5, 26, 59, 63, 70, 132, 147, 261, 306 n. 4

New Orleans jazz, in Britain, 16, 20, 47–55, 56, 93, 101, 113, 228–29, 302; brass bands, 54, 59, 213, 218, 227, 291, 310 n. 5; free music vs., 309 n. 2, 328 n. 18; "moldy figs," 229, 310–11 n. 7, 312 n. 18. *See also* Colyer, Ken; Dixieland jazz; Omega Brass Band; Revivalist jazz; Traditional jazz

Newton, Francis (pseud. of Eric Hobsbawm), xiii, 9, 11, 23, 25, 30, 46, 50, 54, 72, 83, 124, 245, 275, 309 n. 1

Nicols, Maggie, 100, 179, 180–81, 183, 237–38, 246–47, 267, 276–77, 288–89, 290, 300; revolutionary politics of, 225–26, 241; as lesbian, 252–53, 293–94

Ware, Vron, *8*, 315 n. 18

Warren, Guy, 189, 325 n. 47

Watts, Trevor, 198, 200, 234–35, 236, 238, 262; Moiré Drum Orchestra, 313 n. 10

Webb, George, x, 52–53, 58, 104, 228–29

Webster, Duncan, 27, 32, 38–39

Welfare State International, 214–18, 328 n. 15

Westbrook, Kate, *197*, 200–201, 277, 328 n. 15

Westbrook, Mike, 20, 153–54, 183, 194, 196, *197*, 214–15, 217–18

Westbrook Brass Band, 66, 217–18, 223–24, 277, 328 n. 15

Whannell, Paddy, 30, 37

Whiteness, 7, 48, 119, 133–34, 208, 286, 307 n. 14, 313 n. 9, 320 n. 14, 323 n. 38; blackness of jazz erased by, 10, 92, 104–5, 114, 116–17, 148, 315 n. 17, 318 n. 3; class and, 313 n. 10; as invisible ethnicity, 89, 94–95, 98, 100, 318 n. 29; jazz vs. white supremacism, 89, 96, 114–28, 171; negrophilia, 108, 115–16, 167; white appropriations of black jazz, 22, 113, 323 n. 33; white fear of blackness, 9, 105–8, 120, 263–64, 316 n. 19, 317 n. 27, 319 n. 12, 322 n. 30, 324 n. 42; white jazz, 90–93, 99–101, 103–5,

163–64, 268, 314 n. 14, 317 n. 25, 322 n. 28; "whitewashing," 134–35. *See also* Blackness; Dixieland; Race

Widgery, David, 57–58, 328 n. 14

Wilson, Jen, 34, 253

Wilmer, Val, *8*, 63, 84–85, 99; on gender and sexuality, 264, 276, 291, 293–94; on race in music, 186, 319 n. 8, 317 n. 27, 320 n. 16

Women in jazz, 118, 150, 203, 285–86, 296, 331 n. 16; archive of, 34, 253; extra-musical roles of, 254–55; lesbians, 252, 288, 292, 293–96; scarcity of, 29, 208–9, 245, 247–54, 256, 274–77, 281–82, 322 n. 28; in women-only ensembles and events, 20, 246, 251, 277, 280, 283–84, 286–87, 293, 330 n. 11, 331 n. 14, 331 n. 20. *See also* Benson, Ivy; Dance; Feminist Improvising Group; Guest Stars; Ladies' Orchestras

Wyatt, Robert, 222, 225

Youth subcultures, x, 14, 24–25, 32, 47, 53–54, 57, 60, 65, 68, 70–71, 75–76, 80–82, 85, 90, 239, 293, 328 n. 16

Zwerin, Mike, 10, 40, 257

ILLUSTRATION CREDITS

Figure 28. Reproduced by kind permission of *Resonance* magazine and the London Musicians' Collective. Thanks to Ed Baxter.

Figure 29. Reproduced by kind permission of Women in Jazz. Thanks to Jen Wilson: www.jazzsite.co.uk/wja.

Figure 32. Photographer: Derek Woodall. Reproduced by kind permission. Thanks also to Neil Woodall: www.neilwoodall.com/jazz/.

Figure 36. Reproduced by kind permission. © Cog Design. Thanks to Anne Parry and Claire Turner.